CONTRACT LAW AND CONTRACT PRACTICE

An oft-repeated assertion within contract law scholarship and cases is that a good contract law (or a good commercial contract law) will meet the needs and expectations of commercial contractors. Despite the prevalence of this statement, relatively little attention has been paid to why this should be the aim of contract law, how these 'commercial expectations' are identified and given substance, and what precise legal techniques might be adopted by courts to support the practices and expectations of business people. This book explores these neglected issues within contract law. It examines the idea of commercial expectation, identifying what expectations commercial contractors may have about the law and their business relationships (using empirical studies of contracting behaviour), and assesses the extent to which current contract law reflects these expectations. It considers whether supporting commercial expectations is a justifiable aim of the law according to three well-established theoretical approaches to contractual obligations: rights-based explanations, efficiency-based (or economic) explanations and the relational contract critique of the classical law. It explores the specific challenges presented to contract law by modern commercial relationships and the ways in which the general rules of contract law could be designed and applied in order to meet these challenges. Ultimately the book seeks to move contract law beyond a simple dichotomy between contextualist and formalist legal reasoning, to a more nuanced and responsive legal approach to the regulation of commercial agreements.

Contract Law and Contract Practice

Bridging the Gap between Legal Reasoning and Commercial Expectation

Catherine Mitchell

•HART•
PUBLISHING
OXFORD AND PORTLAND, OREGON
2013

Published in the United Kingdom by Hart Publishing Ltd
16C Worcester Place, Oxford, OX1 2JW
Telephone: +44 (0)1865 517530
Fax: +44 (0)1865 510710
E-mail: mail@hartpub.co.uk
Website: http://www.hartpub.co.uk

Published in North America (US and Canada)
by Hart Publishing
c/o International Specialized Book Services
920 NE 58th Avenue, Suite 300
Portland, OR 97213-3786
USA
Tel: +1 503 287 3093 or toll-free: (1) 800 944 6190
Fax: +1 503 280 8832
E-mail: orders@isbs.com
Website: http://www.isbs.com

British Library Cataloguing in Publication Data
Data Available

ISBN: 978-1-84946-121-4

Typeset by Compuscript Ltd, Shannon
Printed and bound in Great Britain by
TJ International Ltd, Padstow, Cornwall

For Alex and Tom

Preface

The claim that the main function of commercial contract law is to facilitate commercial activity and uphold commercial purposes and expectations is often found in contract law scholarship, contract case law and extrajudicial writings about contract. Yet empirical studies of contracting behaviour undertaken by legal scholars and scholars working within other academic disciplines (organisations, management and business studies) reveal grounds for scepticism over whether law makes a significant contribution to the practice of commercial contracting, either at the project planning stage or if a dispute arises. These studies reveal stark divergences between the simplistic picture of the contracting process presented by the law and the complexity of modern organisations and their methods of forming and performing agreements. Legal expectations concerning certainty, comprehensiveness and completeness in the contract documentation, as well as the legal assumption of self-interested and adversarial contracting parties, contrasts sharply with the existence of significant uncertainty in commercial projects and the reality of partnerships, collaboration and co-operation in business dealings. Of course the fact that there may be a gap between legal assumptions and the experiences of contracting parties does not mean the law does not support contracting parties' expectations about the law, and such parties might pay little regard to the law however it was designed. But in the light of these divergences—usually expressed in the idea of two mutually exclusive worlds regulating the process of economic exchange: a real, social world inhabited by the parties and an artificial legal world created and inhabited by commercial lawyers—it seems pertinent to ask whether the claim that a good commercial contract law will fit the 'commercial expectations' of the business community can be taken seriously. And even to ask what the claim means. In addition, while much scholarly debate has been generated around the question of what design of contract law best facilitates commerce, this debate appears to have had very little sustained impact on contract law itself, although it is evident that courts are well aware of the sometimes sizeable gap between law and commercial expectations. This lack of engagement raises a series of issues concerning the commitment of contract law to supporting commercial expectations: why should contract law be concerned with protecting commercial expectations? How are these commercial expectations identified and given substance? How well does current law support these expectations? What barriers lie in the way to developing a contract law that is more sensitive to commercial practices?

What reforms can be made to contract law and legal reasoning to bring law more into line with commercial expectations?

This book investigates these questions by examining a range of sources: analysis of contract case law, current scholarship in this area and theoretical debates that impinge on our understanding of contracts and contract law. It is not a comprehensive assessment of all aspects of either commercial law or contract law, rather it attempts to engage with some of the debates that permeate the issue of the relationship between contract law and commercial activity. In essence the book examines the claim that a good law of contract will fit 'commercial expectations'. The book will take the view that this is not something that can simply be assumed. Before we can decide what a good contract law looks like we need a clearer idea of the limitations of current contract law in supporting commercial expectations and a better understanding of the commercial behaviour that contract law seeks to govern. It will only be by undertaking these sorts of enquiries that we can identify what an appeal to 'commercial expectations' means, and whether and how the law can support these expectations through a scheme of general rules. This investigation is in turn necessary if we are to reform and develop the doctrines of contract law so they remain relevant and responsive to the needs of commercial contracting parties.

I hope the book will be of interest to a broad readership, including students on advanced courses on contract law, scholars working in the contract law field (and related disciplines) and legal practitioners with an interest in the current debates and themes surrounding modern contract and commercial law. Many people have helped me indirectly in realising this project. More direct assistance has come from Rick Canavan, John Gava and Christian Twigg-Flesner. I owe a great debt of gratitude to the 200 or so students at the Law School, University of Hull, who, as part of their final year on the undergraduate law degree, have opted onto a contract course I have taught there over the last few years—Modern Perspectives on Contractual Obligations. The classes have been fun, challenging and inspiring in equal measure, and have been of enormous influence in shaping some of the thoughts presented here.

April 2013.

Contents

Table of Cases

Table of Legislation

United Kingdom

International

1

Introduction: The Relationship between Contract Law and Commercial Expectations

A RECURRING THEME within some branches of socio-legal and relational contract scholarship has been the divergence between the practice of making and performing commercial agreements and the law of contract that may notionally apply to those agreements. It may be accepted that contracting is an important part of commercial activity, but the precise role of legally enforceable contracts and contract law in this activity is often hard to identify. At its simplest level of expression, the core of the socio-legal critique of contract law is that there is often a significant gap between the 'paper deal', that is, the formal written expression of the parties' contractual obligations, and the 'real deal', which is that diffuse collection of informal norms, implicit understandings[1] and flexible commitments that surround a contractual agreement and will impinge upon how the parties view their obligations.[2] Given contract law's undoubted preference for determining obligations according to the paper statement of express terms, this misalignment may be problematic. In short, commercial contract law does not match commercial expectations. Empirical studies of contracting behaviour, emanating from a wide range of disciplines and sources, have alerted contract law scholars to the limited emphasis placed on legally enforceable agreements by contracting parties and the richness of the normative and institutional structures, such as trust, reasonable expectations and informal sanctioning, that support contract making and

[1] J Wightman provides a useful definition of the elusive notion of 'implicit understandings' in contracts: 'the knowledge, practices and or norms pertaining to contracting in general (or an individual transaction) of which the parties to a particular contract are actually aware, (or can in the circumstances, reasonably be expected to be aware) but which are not typically rendered express in their contracting activity': 'Beyond Custom: Contract, Contexts, and the Recognition of Implicit Understandings' in D Campbell, H Collins and J Wightman (eds), *Implicit Dimensions of Contract* (Oxford, Hart Publishing, 2003) 143, 147.

[2] S Macaulay, 'The Real and the Paper Deal: Empirical Pictures of Relationships, Complexity and the Urge for Transparent Simple Rules' in Campbell, Collins and Wightman (eds), above n 1, 51.

performance.[3] In the face of this evidence, contract law has been criticised as failing to comprehend the parties' agreement as they understand it, seeking instead to impose on the parties a legal structure based on an acontextual and highly abstract model of contracting behaviour. This perceived dissonance between the experiences of commercial contractors and the legal world is in turn taken to be the principal indicator of the law's failure to accord with commercial expectations. Given this, contract law, or at least the classical version of it expounded in textbooks and doctrinal scholarly articles, has often been dismissed as largely irrelevant to commercial transactors, since it rarely impinges on their day-to-day experience of managing their productive and exchange activity. The law only becomes relevant when the business relationship is in trouble.[4]

This critique of contract law is not universally accepted however. Other strands of contract scholarship have accepted that all contracts are socially embedded but have questioned the implications of this for the rules of contract law as applied by judges resolving contract disputes in courts. There is plenty of scepticism that 'what business people do', while arguably of some relevance, should carry determinative weight in the legal regulation of commercial activity.[5] Disagreement centres over whether norms constituting the 'real deal' exist, how they are to be identified, what justifies their use and the circumstances in which legal recognition and enforcement of these is appropriate.[6] Some argue that the complex reality of business dealing vindicates a formal and classical style of contract law where close alignment between law and 'immanent business norms'[7] should be rejected. Instead, the 'neoformalist' argues against the incorporation of the standards and expectations of business people into an agreement in favour of bright-line rules of enforcement, plain-meaning interpretation, legally sanctioned

[3] See, eg, S Macaulay, 'Non-Contractual Relations in Business: A Preliminary Study' (1963) 28 *American Sociological Review* 55; H Beale and T Dugdale, 'Contracts Between Businessmen: Planning and the Use of Contractual Remedies' (1975) 2 *British Journal of Law and Society* 45; L Bernstein, 'Merchant Law in a Merchant Court: Rethinking the Code's Search for Immanent Business Norms' (1996) 144 *University of Pennsylvania Law Review* 1765; L Bernstein, 'The Questionable Empirical Basis of Article 2's Incorporation Strategy: A Preliminary Study' (1999) 66 *University of Chicago Law Review* 710; L Bernstein, 'Private Commercial Law in the Cotton Industry: Creating Co-operation Through Rules, Norms and Institutions' (2001) 99 *Michigan Law Review* 1724. For a review of these studies, and more recent empirical work on commercial contracting practice, see C Mitchell, 'Contracts and Contract Law: Challenging the Distinction between the "Real" and "Paper" Deal' (2009) 29 *OJLS* 675.

[4] H Collins, *Regulating Contracts* (Oxford, OUP, 1999) 136–37.

[5] '[T]he rules that parties follow when they play among themselves are not those that a court should attempt to apply': D Charny, 'Illusions of Spontaneous Order: "Norms" in Contractual Relationships' (1996) 144 *University of Pennsylvania Law Review* 1841, 1854.

[6] J Gava, 'False Lessons from the Real Deal: Campbell, Collins and Wightman on Implicit Dimensions of Contract—Discrete, Relational, and Network Contracts?' (2005) 21 *Journal of Contract Law* 182.

[7] This terminology is attributable to Bernstein, 'Merchant Law in a Merchant Court' above n 3.

standard terms and gap-filling defaults, and a strict parol evidence rule.[8] The justificatory framework for such an approach is usually efficiency. For this branch of contract scholarship, the design of contracts and contract law should reflect instrumental goals such as wealth maximisation. Such theorists may not see themselves as opposed to the socio-legal and relational contract movement, but rather as working within it. Naturally, this is a matter of some controversy.[9]

From the brief outline given here it is apparent that the argument that commercial contract law should track the expectations and practices of commercial people is both complex and disputed. The claim of misalignment, and its consequences for the law, cannot be assessed without considering larger questions concerning how contract law best facilitates commerce, whether it is possible to identify immanent business norms and, where they do exist, the precise role of such norms in legal reasoning. It is the investigation of these particular issues, and the debates that surround them within contract law, that forms the subject matter of this book. The work explores aspects of the general relationship between contract law and commercial activity and considers whether contract law should proceed on the basis of a more enriched understanding and appreciation of the actual practices, norms and expectations that commercial contractors bring to bear on their business relationships or that are generated within these relationships. These matters will not be examined in isolation however, but within the context of other related debates that surround modern contract law. While the concerns emanating from the socio-legal critique of the classical law may appear isolated and remote from other scholarly endeavours within contract, such as the attempt to impart doctrinal coherence to the law, or to explore its normative foundations, they are related since doubts concerning contract law's coherence and fitness for purpose are manifest throughout contract scholarship. Socio-legal and empirical work on contract has brought into question the relationship between law and commercial dealing, but similar disquiet is also manifest in more traditional

[8] See especially RE Scott, 'The Case for Formalism in Relational Contract' (2000) 94 *Northwestern University Law Review* 847. Also D Charny, 'The New Formalism in Contract' (1999) 66 *University of Chicago Law Review* 842; O Ben-Shahar, 'The Tentative Case Against Flexibility in Commercial Law' (1999) 66 *University of Chicago Law Review* 781; R Epstein, 'Confusion about Custom: Disentangling Informal Customs from Standard Contractual Provisions' (1999) 66 *University of Chicago Law Review* 821; W Woodward, 'Neoformalism in a Real World of Forms' (2001) *Wisconsin Law Review* 971; J Murray, 'Contract Theories and the Rise of Neoformalism' (2002) 71 *Fordham Law Review* 869; H Hunter, 'The Growing Uncertainty about Good Faith in American Contract Law' (2002) 20 *Journal of Contract Law* 31; WC Whitford, 'Relational Contracts and the New Formalism' (2004) *Wisconsin Law Review* 631.

[9] RE Scott, 'The Promise and the Peril of Relational Contract Theory' in J Braucher, J Kidwell and WC Whitford (eds), *Revisiting the Contracts Scholarship of Stewart Macaulay* (Oxford, Hart Publishing, 2013) 105, 106.

doctrinal work that has examined whether commercial law is aligned with the practices and expectations of commercial actors.[10] Further, the claim that the function of (commercial) contract law is to facilitate commercial transactions invites consideration of the fit between this aspiration and the need for a system of general law to display certain normative and institutional commitments. Is alignment between contract law and commercial expectations required by a rights-based theory of contract law, an efficiency theory or some other kind of theory? Or does the function of facilitating commerce, if believed to be important, require surrendering these normative commitments in favour of a pragmatic contract law that is not fully assimilated within any of the current normative explanations? This latter position certainly appears implausible. Whatever the precise role of contract law in commercial dealing, it must involve more than simply arbitrarily bestowing legal validity on whatever actions or decisions the community of commercial contractors take in the pursuit of their business interests. Although some scholars would wish to see a stronger instrumental connection between law and commercial practice, at the expense of any deeper normative commitments within commercial contract law,[11] it cannot be the case that what is commercially expedient is thereby legally permitted. Yet it is also clear that the legal regulation of commercial contractual relationships raises complex problems with which the relatively simplistic formula of agreement making and performance assumed by the classical law seems poorly equipped to deal. The question of the balance to be struck between legality and the fulfilment of commercial expectation is a difficult one that does not admit a simple response. This book seeks to make a modest contribution to answering this question by drawing out and exploring some of the various connections, possibilities, problems and tensions raised by the relationship between contract law and commercial contracting practice.

As well as assessing whether the socio-legal criticisms of contract law are apposite and whether change is both necessary and desirable, there

[10] See, eg, the essays in S Worthington (ed), *Commercial Law and Commercial Practice* (Oxford, Hart Publishing, 2003), especially R Bradgate, 'Contracts, Contract Law and Reasonable Expectations', 651 and AJ Duggan, 'Commercial Law and the Limits of the Black Letter Approach', 595. See also C Twigg-Flesner and G Villalta Puig, 'Introduction: The Boundaries of Commercial Law' in C Twigg-Flesner and G Villalta Puig (eds), *Boundaries of Commercial and Trade Law* (Munich, Sellier, 2011), 1.

[11] '[t]he legal structure should support the commercial structure of civil society and not the other way around ... Commercial law, it follows, should do no more than restate commercial practice': G Villalta Puig, 'The Misalignment of Commercial Law and Commercial Practice' [2012] *Lloyd's Maritime & Commercial Law Quarterly* 317, 319. For Villalta Puig such an approach is justified on economic grounds, ibid, 331–32. Against, see D Lawton, previously Director of Markets, Financial Services Authority: '[I]it is important that market participants and investors have confidence in the fairness of UK markets, because bluntly, no one wants to operate in a market where they cannot trust the other side', 'Four Building Blocks of Efficient Capital Markets', address at the Practising Law Institute on 1 February 2013: http://www.fsa.gov.uk/library/communication/speeches/2013/0201-dl.

are other reasons to examine the relationship between contract law and commercial activity. It was mentioned above that it is a recurring theme in contract scholarship that a good *commercial* contract law will meet the needs and expectations of commercial contractors. There are probably very few scholars who would defend an application of contract rules that proceeded without any reference at all to the expectations, practices, behaviours and norms of the commercial community, at least insofar as the law seeks to retain legitimacy amongst such contractors.[12] Of course whether this claim is supportable depends very much on what reference to 'commercial expectations' is taken to signify. This matters since it is clear that the belief that contract law (or the parts of it that are pertinent to business contracting) should uphold 'commercial expectations' is not confined to contract scholars, but also forms an important part of the self-understandings of the judiciary concerning their role in resolving contract disputes, enforcing agreements and developing commercial contract law. There are many judicial proclamations to the effect that the function of commercial contract law is to uphold commercial purposes, support the expectations of business people[13] and incorporate business practice.[14] Certainly in specific areas of commerce, such as obtaining adequate security, transferring title and ensuring payment, the law has upheld the legality of tools designed chiefly by business people. The retention of title clause, the bill of lading and the documentary credit all provide examples of measures developed within the commercial sphere to facilitate trade, particularly at the international level, and mitigate its risks. However, many of these measures did not originate from within contract law, but were rather circumventions of it. That agreements have the security of legal enforcement may matter to business, but the common law of contract, encumbered with an attachment to doctrines such as privity and consideration, could not easily afford recognition to measures designed to facilitate business dealing, such as negotiability and transferability of financial instruments, or the creation and protection of third-party interests. Instead, other areas of law such as property, tort, restitution and, in particular, equity, have been called upon to mitigate the effects of the rigid structures of contract law.

[12] Although J Gava comes close. See J Gava and J Greene, 'Do We Need a Hybrid Law of Contract? Why Hugh Collins is Wrong and Why it Matters' (2004) 63 *CLJ* 605; J Gava, 'Dixonian Strict Legalism: *Wilson v Darling Island Stevedoring* and Contracting in the Real World' (2010) 30 *OJLS* 519; 'How Should Judges Decide Commercial Contract Cases?' (2013) 30 *Journal of Contract Law* 133.

[13] For examples of this in extra-judicial writings see Lord Devlin, 'The Relation Between Commercial Law and Commercial Practice' (1951) 14 *MLR* 249; Lord Goff, 'Commercial Contracts and the Commercial Court' [1984] *Lloyd's Maritime & Commercial Law Quarterly* 382; Lord Irvine, 'The Law: An Engine for Trade' (2001) 64 *MLR* 333.

[14] Lord Irvine, above n 13, 333.

Given its doctrinal commitments, it is not apparent why any supposed lack of fit with commercial expectation should matter to contract law, although it is clear that it does since congruence with commercial interests, reasonableness and practices is often a reference point for articulating and choosing between alternative outcomes in a contract dispute. In the interpretation of contracts, for example, judges have been counselled by the Supreme Court to uphold commercial purposes and pursue commercially reasonable outcomes over absurd ones when interpreting commercial agreements.[15] Despite this surface engagement with the idea of commercial expectations, it is not clear whether the appeal to commercial considerations here entails a set of determinate and readily identifiable values that can genuinely inform legal reasoning,[16] or is just a rhetorical gloss to obscure an exercise of judicial discretion. Certainly there is nothing to suggest that judges are relying on any socio-legal or 'real deal'-derived appreciation of these expectations and outcomes. Lawyers and judges are not unaware of the wider contract context beyond documents and rules, but there is lacking any real penetration of the socio-legal findings into the law, despite indications that occasionally suggest otherwise.[17] It can be doubted then that judicial edicts concerning the importance of 'commercial expectations' should be understood as motivated by a desire to develop a contract law that better reflects the reality of business relationships. Rather, appeals to commercial concerns in judgments will continue to appear to many as a cloaking device that hides, and not particularly subtly, unwarranted judicial interventions into economically driven bargains on 'fair and reasonable' grounds.[18] Given this, it is worth investigating whether the judicial appeal to commercial expectations could be an invocation of a genuine and meaningful standard, thereby rendering the commitments and values it expresses more transparent. Failure to do this only makes more attractive the sceptical position that such expectations are irrelevant to law, particularly since it lends credence to a common criticism of the incorporationist argument—that judges are politically and institutionally limited in their capacity to engage with the internal norms of the business relationship.

[15] See Lord Clarke in *Rainy Sky S A and others v Kookmin Bank* [2011] UKSC 50; [2011] 1 WLR 2900.

[16] For doubts over this see R Barnes, 'Commerciality and the Construction of Commercial Contracts: Some Observations on the Use of Legal Reasoning' in Twigg-Flesner and Villalta Puig (eds), *Boundaries of Commercial and Trade Law*, above n 10, 179.

[17] Some judicial recognition of the contrast between the real and paper deal appears in *Balmoral Group Ltd v Borealis (UK) Ltd* [2006] EWHC 1900 [339]; and *Total Gas Marketing v Arco British* [1998] 2 Lloyd's Law Rep 209. More recently a reference to 'relational contracts' was made by Leggatt J in *Yam Seng Pte Ltd v International Trade Corporation Ltd* [2013] EWHC 111 (QB), [142].

[18] See, eg, Gava, 'Dixonian Strict Legalism', above n 12; M Hogg, 'Fundamental Issues for the Reform of the Law of Contractual Interpretation' (2011) 15 *Edinburgh Law Review* 406, 419.

Ultimately, this work aims to fill a gap in contract law scholarship and to contribute to understanding the relationship between contract law and commercial contracting practice by exploring a point that appears inadequately covered in the literature concerning the existence of the 'real deal' and its effect in the 'non-use' of contract law. While much attention has been devoted to the question of whether the law should track commercial expectations, rather less attention has been devoted to how it could do so, at least insofar as it is reckoned such expectations must be sourced in part from the implicit norms and dimensions that constitute the parties' real deal. This issue is important since if lack of legal engagement with commercial norms and expectations is made out then a case for reform will be easier to establish, although identifying exactly what reforms are necessary, and implementing them, may not be straightforward. Alternatively if it is demonstrated that there is no mismatch between commercial behaviour and contract law, or that there are good reasons why law should not track the norms and behaviours of contracting parties, then the criticisms made by socio-legal and relational scholars, however important and enlightening in other respects, will have minimal relevance for legal development.[19] Examination of the idea of commercial expectation and its role in contract law may also shed light on what judges are doing when they appeal to 'commercial' factors during the course of their judgments and whether the appeal could be made more meaningful and robust. The remainder of this chapter sets out in more detail some background and context to these debates and the specific lines of enquiry that will be pursued in the book. This will give some indication of the structure of the book and the content of the chapters that follow.

CONTEXTS AND BACKGROUND

The Deficiencies of Classical Contract Law

The questions that surround the relationship between English contract law and commercial activity can be perceived as the manifestation of a more general anxiety concerning the relevance of the domestic common law of contract in a modern global economy. While the significance of contracts and contract law can be perceived in broad strokes, it has been evident for many years that the legal principles, or at least those promulgated by judicial development through case law, have been subjected to a wide variety of pressures.[20] Chief amongst these is the reduced scope of operation for

[19] See the conclusions reached by Beale and Dugdale from their study, above n 3, 59–60.

[20] See generally E McKendrick, 'English Contract Law: A Rich Past, an Uncertain Future?' (1997) 50 *Current Legal Problems* 25.

the common law principles of contract. As is often noted, many contractual relationships (for example, employer and employee, landlord and tenant) are subject to their own specially formulated rules and statute-based regulatory schemes. Most contracts between businesses and consumers are likewise subject to significant legislative intervention and separate regulation.[21] Many of these legislative interventions were required precisely because of the deficiencies of classical contract law in addressing substantive unfairness in contract terms or inequality manifest in the contracting relationship. In championing the virtues of freedom and sanctity of contract, voluntariness and consent, the common law of contract lacked the doctrinal tools to deal effectively with contractual relationships characterised by stark inequality in economic power and potential for abuse. The common law contract rules have been rendered largely irrelevant to these contractual arrangements.

The hiving off of a significant number of contractual relationships into separate spheres of regulation could be regarded as an opportunity for the common law of contract, since what remains for the classical law is that branch of contracting that in many respects represents the natural place for the operation of its principles—commercial agreements. But even here the historical and doctrinal difficulties that classical contract law placed in the way of contractors seeking to pursue certain outcomes or create certain interests through contracts—third-party rights for example—are well known. The adherence to doctrine rendered the common law of contract ineffective at upholding contractual arrangements agreed between parties which were clearly intended to have legal effect. Such measures could only be made effective after some imaginative manipulation of the concepts.[22] While not abolished entirely, many of the classic doctrines of the common law of contract have been undermined by statute (for example, the Contracts (Rights of Third Parties) Act 1999) or by the development of numerous exceptions to classical law precepts. These 'exceptions' have often relied on principles derived from other areas of law such as equity (as with promissory estoppel) and restitution, or other hybrid forms of liability, such as misrepresentation, which lie on the boundary between contract and tort. In the commercial sphere the domestic rules of contract law also appear to have dwindling significance in the face of the burgeoning availability of 'private legal systems'[23] and alternative dispute resolution processes, some of these promulgated within domestic courts.[24] Commercial contractors have

[21] H Collins, *The Law of Contract*, 4th edn (London, LexisNexis, 2003) 37–39; R Brownsword, *Contract Law: Themes for the Twenty-First Century*, 2nd edn (Oxford, OUP, 2006) ch 4.

[22] See, eg, *New Zealand Shipping Co Ltd v AM Satterthwaite & Co Ltd, The Eurymedon* [1975] AC 154, per Lord Wilberforce.

[23] See generally R Canavan, 'English Commercial Law and Private Legal Systems' in Twigg-Flesner and Villalta Puig (eds), *Boundaries of Commercial and Trade Law*, above n 10, 153.

[24] A new mediation scheme was introduced in the Court of Appeal in April 2012 for personal injury and contract claims up to £100,000. The scheme was due to run for a

a choice between various systems within which to frame their agreement and resolve disputes. Suites of terms and conditions and private dispute resolution regimes may be provided either within specific trades[25] or within the international commercial community more generally.[26] These alternatives may seek to cater to a demand for contract governance according to an international scheme that is reflective of the global nature of the trade and its participants, rather than the local law of a particular nation state, even for parties based within a single jurisdiction. Thus the line of modern contracts scholarship that has called into question the assumption that contracts and contract law contribute in any significant way to the process of commercial dealing can be regarded as just a part of a more general attack on the significance and relevance of classical contract law.

Despite these various pressures, some scholars remain sanguine over the judicial capacity to incorporate elements of the real deal into legal reasoning, arguing that contract law contains methods and techniques that are sufficiently adaptable to recognise such norms and in this way stay connected to commercial expectations.[27] Others are less optimistic. David Campbell and Hugh Collins have argued that the classical-law model of economic relationships is built upon a flawed foundation of discrete contracts and self-interested contracting parties that is at variance with the reality of co-operative commercial dealing. For them, isolated departures from the classical rules that attempt to give effect to an agreement's implicit dimensions only serve to compound a lack of coherence in the law.[28] While making inroads into the classical law, the counternorms' status as 'limited exceptions' to the rules have not led to a sustained challenge to that model's central place in the organisation and understanding of contract law. It has

year: www.judiciary.gov.uk/media/media-releases/2012/news-release-mediation-pilot-court-of-appeal. On the social cost of the 'vanishing trial' see generally L Mulcahy, 'The Collective Interest in Private Dispute Resolution' (2013) 33 *OJLS* 59, 59–63.

[25] W Konradi, 'The Role of *Lex Mercatoria* in Supporting Globalized Transactions: An Empirical Insight into the Governance Structure of the Timber Industry' in V Gessner (ed), *Contractual Certainty in International Trade* (Oxford, Hart Publishing, 2009) 49; Bernstein, 'Private Commercial Law in the Cotton Industry', above n 3; L Bernstein, 'Opting Out of the Legal System: Extralegal Contractual Relations in the Diamond Industry' (1992) 21 *Journal of Legal Studies* 115.

[26] Eg, the UNIDROIT Principles of International Commercial Contracts (2010). Dispute resolution procedures are provided by the likes of the International Chamber of Commerce under their own arbitration rules.

[27] Brownsword, above n 21, 139ff. See also R Austen-Baker, who argues that 'much of existing contract jurisprudence copes well with the reality of the contract relation, as seen through the lens of relational contract theory': 'Comprehensive Contract Theory: A Four-norm Model of Contract Relations' (2009) 25 *Journal of Contract Law* 216, 219.

[28] D Campbell and H Collins, 'Discovering the Implicit Dimensions of Contracts' in Campbell, Collins and Wightman (eds), above n 1, 25–27. See also D Campbell, 'The Relational Constitution of the Discrete Contract' in D Campbell and P Vincent-Jones (eds), *Contract and Economic Organisation* (Aldershot, Dartmouth, 1996) 40, 43–45.

simply heralded a system of 'rules + standards' labelled 'neoclassical' law.[29] This manner of organisation and understanding of the law serves to diminish our appreciation that what are presented as exceptions to freedom of contract (illegality or contracts contrary to public policy, duress and misrepresentation) are in fact constitutive of contracts and thus fundamental to any conception of what a contract is. Other socio-legal scholars point to a distinct lack of engagement between the law and socio-legal findings concerning the important role of 'relational norms' in functioning business relationships, and regard this deficiency as setting an important future agenda for contract law development: 'The need to reform contract law doctrine better to reflect and therefore support relational norms [trust, co-operation, reciprocity, flexibility and contractual solidarity] in commercial practice is widely accepted as a central task of contemporary socio-legal scholarship'.[30]

Even when contract law appears to take on board the implicit dimensions of an agreement and commercial expectations—through a flexible, contextual approach to doctrine and contract interpretation for example—this is only in a pseudo-sense, a superficial veneer on an approach which resolutely remains confined within classical and neoclassical traditions. A case in point which can be used to illustrate these distinctions is the legal approach to contract interpretation. A classical-law approach to contract interpretation might privilege a literal or plain meaning method to understanding the words of the contract. This statement of express terms, recorded in a document and containing manifestations of objective consent (usually signatures) *is* the contract. It is the supreme statement of the parties' obligations and assumed to be relatively complete. A literal method of interpretation upholds these parties' intentions and cuts down considerably the scope for a judge to substitute their own view of what the contract means for that assumed to be held by the parties. While it can be doubted that the classical law invariably adopted such an approach towards interpretation, this outline is in keeping with the characteristics of the classical law and its underpinning assumptions concerning freedom of contract, party consent and the *possibility* of positing a complete statement of contractual obligations, at the precise moment of formation, to govern even long-term performance. A neoclassical approach to contract interpretation would differ in that it might permit enquiries outside the documents to decide what the parties meant by the words they have used, although

[29] J Feinman, 'Relational Contract Theory in Context' (2000) 94 *Northwestern University Law Review* 737, 748. See also O Williamson, *The Economic Institutions of Capitalism* (New York, Free Press, 1985) 68–72.

[30] P Vincent-Jones, *The New Public Contracting* (Oxford, OUP, 2006) 8.

this might achieve the same result as literal method.[31] Troublesome words or phrases are read within a wider context of the matrix of fact or other relevant background information available to the reasonable contractor.[32] Congruence with standards such as 'commercial reasonableness' and 'business common sense' may decide what interpretation is to be adopted in the face of plausible alternatives.[33] This contextual interpretation exercise, while arguably an improvement on the plain-meaning method, still manifests its classical commitments by assuming the object to be interpreted is the express terms. A 'real deal' or fully contextual approach to the agreement differs again since it would not begin the interpretative task by attention to the documents at all, but would examine other aspects of the contractual relationship. The use of contextualism in such a method may reveal that the written documents were not that important to the parties at all and may be manifestly unreliable as a statement of their understandings about their agreement. Such a conclusion simply cannot be countenanced within classical and neoclassical contract law, unless one of the exceptional doctrines can be brought into play.

The Wider Debate: A Contextual and Relational Approach to Contracts

If commercial expectations are taken to denote the extra-legal or social sphere of contractual relationships, the issue about dissonance between contract law and commercial expectations is part of a larger debate concerning the limitations of the legal understanding of the social embeddedness of contracting. Sheinman has written that contracts are, first and foremost, 'social norms recognized by law, not legal norms. The legal intervention is designed to support the pre-existing practice, not create a new one'.[34] The argument advanced by some scholars is that the law should develop a better understanding of the 'pre-existing practice' of commercial dealing and utilise it as part of commercial contract law method. At present the classical law generally isolates the express terms of the agreement and places them at the centre of the analysis. For some this approach is incorrect, since the

[31] Eg, consider the different approaches of Lord Mance and Lord Collins in *Belmont Park Investments PTY Limited v BNY Corporate Trustee Services Limited and Lehman Brothers Special Financing Inc* [2011] 3 WLR 521; [2011] UKSC 38, concerning whether there had been an evasion of the anti-deprivation rule of insolvency. For Lord Collins the parties' contractual motive and the overall commercial sense of the provision were important. Lord Mance preferred to base his decision on a close reading of the contract whereby Lehmans were not 'deprived' of any property, thus falling outside the scope of the rule.

[32] Lord Hoffmann, *Investors Compensation Scheme v West Bromwich Building Society* [1998] 1 WLR 896, 912–13.

[33] *Rainy Sky v Kookmin Bank*, above n 15.

[34] H Sheinman, 'Contractual Liability and Voluntary Undertakings' (2000) 20 *OJLS* 205, 219.

express terms can only be understood as a part, and sometimes a relatively insignificant part, of the entire business relationship and the transaction.[35] Ian Macneil is most closely associated with this criticism of the classical law, and the development of an alternative relational theory of contract that attempted to capture the complexity of contract as a social phenomenon. For Macneil the legal construct of 'the contract' is embedded within a wider network of social norms and expectations, which will, to a greater or lesser degree, determine how any formal statements of obligations should be read and understood.[36] While relational theory, at least as envisioned by Macneil, is multifaceted and reflective of the complexity of the contractual relationship itself, it is the importance attached to social context that lies at its heart.[37] Contract law has traditionally sought to ignore this complexity, emphasising the discreteness of the transaction by its assumptions concerning the parties and their agreement—objectivity, arm's-length dealings, party autonomy and self-interestedness, rather than trust, co-operation and interdependence. Of course the parties might choose to downgrade the role of relational factors in their contract, creating an 'as-if-discrete' contract which they expect to be regulated according to formal legal norms.[38] In this way, classical contract law has become synonymous with the impersonal market transaction, enforced through litigation in courts of law. The commercial expectations argument can be understood as part of this debate, and the call for the law to align itself with commercial expectations understood as an appeal to develop a relational contract law in the sense of one that responds to the findings of relational theory and in particular that version advanced by Ian Macneil.

SPECIFIC LINES OF ENQUIRY

Defining and Identifying 'Commercial Expectations'

If the above outlines the contours of the debate and part of its context, what specific lines of enquiry are pursued in this book? First, the concern is with how the notion of 'commercial expectations' should be understood. The appeal for law to reflect 'commercial expectations' or 'the

35 Collins, above n 4, 271.

36 See generally I Macneil, 'Reflections on Relational Contract Theory after a Neo-Classical Seminar' in Campbell, Collins and Wightman (eds), above n 1, 207.

37 Ibid.

38 The discrete norms controlling this choice are 'effectuation of consent' and 'implementation of planning': I Macneil, *The Relational Theory of Contract: Selected Works of Ian Macneil*, D Campbell (ed) (London, Sweet and Maxwell, 2001) 154, 158.

reasonable expectations of honest [commercial] men'[39] is usually advanced as a justificatory argument for contract law to incorporate such matters as shared commercial practices and implicit understandings into contract legal reasoning.[40] Currently these often vital elements in a business relationship have only an attenuated role in legal analysis, the law preferring to confine its attention to the documented agreement wherever possible. Evidently expectations have a substantive element concerning what, exactly, is expected by commercial contractors, both from their contracting partners and the law. Such substantive expectations must be infinitely variable and could be derived from a variety of sources.[41] Here there is a problem of over-inclusiveness since not all, or even any, of these expectations may be intended by the parties to be legally enforceable, nor should they be. The appeal that contract law should be better aligned with commercial expectations must mean something more specific than this, even accepting that commercial expectations is a mutable concept. In a more general sense, and in the context of reaching and performing agreements, commercial expectations generally refers to the collection of beliefs that surround the commercial contracting process, which are derived from outside the parties' legal statement of the express terms and conditions, but may impinge on that legal statement. Assuming for the moment that greater incorporation of these alternative norms is required, then how are these to be identified and why are they compelling? While commercial expectations may be used to refer to the subjective beliefs commercial contractors bring to bear on their agreements and business relationships, the claim that contract law should be better aligned with commercial expectations contains a normative dimension. It is an appeal for contract law to assess its effectiveness by reference not just to coherence with its internal principles and rules, but to an external vantage point that seeks to 'import non-legal values into a legal judgement'.[42] In this sense the commercial expectations concept seeks to add to the judge's arsenal of justificatory arguments that can be drawn upon in decision making. While this might be readily understood as the general idea, teasing out the specifics of what sensitivity to commercial expectations requires in each particular case or from the law more generally is difficult. For example, does it require (i) an incorporationist strategy, that takes account of implicit dimensions of agreements as well as, or instead of,

[39] Lord Steyn, 'Contract Law: Fulfilling the Reasonable Expectations of Honest Men' (1997) 113 *LQR* 433.

[40] Campbell and Collins, 'Discovering the Implicit Dimensions of Contracts', above n 28, 28.

[41] Thus, commercial expectations mirror the idea of 'reasonable expectations', which can also be derived from various sources: see R Brownsword, 'After *Investors*: Interpretation, Expectation and the Implicit Dimension of the "New Contextualism"' in Campbell, Collins and Wightman (eds), above n 1, 103, 105–08; and C Mitchell, 'Leading a Life of its Own? The Roles of Reasonable Expectation in Contract Law' (2003) 23 *OJLS* 639.

[42] Barnes, above n 16, 185.

express and formal contract terms; or (ii) that contract law should become more relationally constituted; or (iii) that contract law should routinely seek to legalise the practices or devices that commercial people use in their contracting activity, or seek inventive ways of overcoming legal barriers (as with, historically, privity of contract); or (iv) that judges become more commercially active, using 'commercial reasonableness' (however this is determined) as a touchstone for reaching decisions in commercial contract cases; or (v) that judges should pay more attention to the effects or consequences of their rulings for the commercial community? It might be thought that any or all of these could be countenanced and pursued within a contract law that is attuned with commercial expectations, but they are not necessarily compatible and they may encounter different levels of resistance. The claim that contract law should be better aligned with commercial practice and expectations could be interpreted as a more general appeal to the law to recognise the social values and behavioural norms that almost *all* commercial contractors, to a greater or lesser degree, bring to bear on their trading relationships. This entails a much wider brief for law than simply enforcing a norm, practice or custom on the isolated basis that it reflects the internal understanding of participants about the way things are invariably done in a particular industry. The law frequently implies 'trade customs' into contracts in particular cases, usually without controversy, but the notion that law must recognise that certain values such as trust and co-operation inform a contractual relationship, and to reorient its reasoning processes appropriately across all contract cases (including identifying the situations in which such norms should *not* be applied), may encounter considerable resistance. The difficulties of explanation and identification are considered further in Chapter 2.

Descriptive Accuracy of the Mismatch Claim

The suggestion that contract law should be better aligned with commercial expectations is often followed by the different claim that the present law, or some aspect of it, does not support these expectations or commercial practices. This issue concerns the accuracy of descriptive claims about the existence and extent of discrepancies between contract law and commercial expectations. What evidence is there to suggest that there is some mismatch between law and commercial expectations? This question in itself could lead to several sub-enquiries, such as what substantive expectations contractors may have, and the organising criteria or theoretical framework by which lack of fit between law and commercial expectations is established. This enquiry could demonstrate that English contract law already does an adequate job of meeting such expectations. In other words, the claim about a mismatch may be descriptively false. The English classical law of contract is often perceived as highly formal, both in what it requires from commercial contracting parties (relatively complete contractual documents) and in its rules and doctrines.[43] Yet it is clear to anyone with more than a cursory appreciation of the law that the rigid classical model of contract law has been undermined in many different ways and that contract law is not completely isolated from commercial expectations and practices. Some statutory reforms within contract law have specifically sought to address commercial concerns over the rigidity of doctrine[44] and judges frequently assert that the aim of commercial contract law is to facilitate commerce, or that law and legal concepts are the servants of commerce not the master.[45] It is clear that courts do not simply apply express terms at face value, but take context into account when interpreting agreements, implying terms or policing one party's exercise of contractual rights, such as termination,[46] as well as displaying a willingness to look behind contractual labels to the reality of the parties agreement.[47] That contract law can respond adequately to the expectations created by different commercial contracting contexts is supported by some scholars. Roger Brownsword has written that commercial contract law has long exhibited a tension between the ideologies of static and dynamic market-individualism. Static market-individualism broadly reflects the concerns of classical contract law—the imposition of bright-line ground rules for trading that are generally known by the participants and that effectively constitute the market. Dynamic market-individualism, on the other hand, is displayed by a law more reliant on norms and expectations created by the parties and their situation. These norms might arise from the parties' economic and social relationship, from within the industry in which their trading takes place, or from moral requirements of fair dealing. The latter norms may often qualify the operation of the classical ground rules, even if they do not fully substitute for them, and even if they can only be rendered effective through some other branch of the law. There may be a more open engagement with values such as fairness, justice and reasonableness in contract outcomes when such an approach is adopted.

[43] Lord Steyn, 'Does Legal Formalism Hold Sway in England?' (1996) 49 *Current Legal Problems* 43, 58; C Sunstein and A Vermeule, 'Interpretation and Institutions' (2003) 101 *Michigan Law Review* 885, 924–25; AW Katz, 'The Relative Costs of Incorporating Trade Usage into Domestic versus International Sales Contracts' (2004) 5 *Chicago Journal of International Law* 181, 187.

[44] The Contracts (Rights of Third Parties) Act 1999 is perhaps the most obvious recent example. The Law Commission highlighted the difficulties caused to commerce by the third-party rule in their proposals for reform: Law Commission, *Privity of Contract: Contracts for the Benefit of Third Parties* (Law Com no 242, Cm 3329) (London, HMSO, 1996), paras 3.9–3.27.

[45] Goff LJ in *Clough Mill v Martin* [1984] 3 All ER 982, 987.

[46] *Schuler AG v Wickman Machine Tool Sales Ltd* [1974] AC 235; *Rice v Great Yarmouth Borough Council* [2000] All ER (D) 902.

[47] Eg, *Schuler (L) AG v Wickman Machine Tool Sales Ltd* [1974] AC 235; *Re Spectrum Plus Ltd* [2005] UKHL 41; [2005] 2 AC 680.

Thus Brownsword argues that contract law is already partly constituted by norms that limit the operation of untrammelled self-interest characteristic of the classical-law approach.[48] On this basis, there may not be much more for the law to do to align itself with expectations. The issue of descriptive accuracy is assessed in Chapters 3 and 4.

Theoretical Difficulties Posed by the Commercial Expectations Argument

(i) Efficiency and Rights-based Theories

Problems of definition and identification encountered in aligning contract law with commercial expectations are matched by the theoretical difficulties. Neither efficiency- nor rights-based theories of contract law immediately suggest themselves as the underpinning foundation from which the claim that contract law should better support commercial practices and expectations can straightforwardly be derived. In part this is because the claim that the law does not support such expectations is advanced on empirical rather than theoretical grounds. In addition, the argument about the role of commercial norms and expectations in contract law engages the debate about the relative merits of intersystemic and extrasystemic factors in legal reasoning, or the legitimacy of policy-based and principle-based arguments in the law. Some of the difficulty here relates to the lack of precision in the claim that a good commercial contract law will meet the expectations of the contracting parties. As has been seen, this could be a specific entreaty for the courts to uphold particular commercial practices or a more general appeal for the law to engage more fully with relational norms of flexibility and co-operation in commercial dealing. Justification for such a position could be based on grounds either of efficiency (legal incorporation of norms or certain contextual interpretative methods might cheapen the contracting process for the parties); or upholding contracting parties' rights (upholding the rights and obligations of the agreement, whether based on formal terms or informal norms, is to enforce the agreement created and intended by the parties). Here it is important to keep separate the justification for contracting, that is, for the parties to seek to create a relatively comprehensive, legally enforceable contract, and the justification for contract law that is applicable to that agreement. The parties may enter into contracts to maximise wealth and may write a complete contract for reasons of efficiency, but this does not mean the law applied to that contract must track these values, although many efficiency theorists would subscribe to the view that contract law does or should commit to efficiency (wealth maximisation)

[48] Brownsword, above n 21, 139ff.

as a social goal. In the contract literature, the efficiency position usually manifests as a preference for an anti-incorporationist and formalist reasoning strategy in contract law, although there is no immediate reason to think an incorporationist strategy could not be shown to be efficient or wealth maximising for the parties, or superior in some other way.[49] Locating the commercial expectations argument within a specific normative framework underpinning contract is difficult, although some of these difficulties are largely the result of problems emanating from within the normative positions themselves. For example, in relation to the efficiency of incorporating business norms, do we assess the efficiency of the individual transaction before the courts, which might demand an expansive enquiry into contractual context to determine the optimal outcome for these parties? Or do we assess efficiency of the resulting ruling for the general body of commercial contractors to whom the ruling may be applicable? A decision that promotes individual wealth maximisation between the parties may not be optimal for other contracting parties. Further, the process costs of an expansive approach to contract interpretation may also create inefficiencies in itself, as would litigating the problem. These inefficiencies may largely undercut whatever benefits might be derived from seeking the optimal outcome in the individual case. Similarly the parties may rely on norms of trust in their business dealings, but it may not be appropriate for the law to enforce such arrangements in all circumstances. These issues concerning the normative foundation for a commercial expectations argument are considered further in Chapter 5.

(ii) Relational Contract Theory

It could be argued that the claim about misalignment between contract law and commercial expectations is a response to a social, rather than philosophical, component of contracts. In essence, then, the claim that contract law reflects commercial expectations may be fundamentally different to one concerning the efficiency of contract law or its commitment to upholding the rights and autonomy of contracting parties, although arguments on such grounds could undoubtedly be built. Thus it may be relational theory that provides the prime justification for addressing the misalignment between commercial contract law and commercial expectations.[50] Relational theory and Ian Macneil's work seeks to bring to the fore the complexity of

[49] Ian Macneil argues that a relational approach to contracts that tracks the internal norms of the business relationship is likely to be more efficient than classical contract law: 'Reflections on Relational Contract Theory after a Neo-classical Seminar' in Campbell, Collins and Wightman (eds), above n 1, 207, 208. These claims are difficult to establish however: see further Ch 5.

[50] See generally Macneil, above n 38.

contracting behaviour in the real world, including the self-understandings of the parties about their contractual relationship, and social norms and institutions (apart from law) that impinge on and direct the conduct of their exchange activity. Of course a law that reflects and incorporates these understandings may be justified by an appeal to party autonomy, but this higher theoretical justification may not be of much importance to the broad thrust of the relational project, which rests on a combination of authenticity and legitimacy in the law's approach to the parties' agreement. But here again the retort may be that while contracts may be relational, contract law is not,[51] and thus relational theory can yield no particular insight that can inform the development of the common law of contract. Macneil's relational theory is considered further in Chapter 6.

The Capacity of Contract Law

It has already been mentioned that the impetus for the claim about misalignment between contract law and commercial practice and expectations derives not from traditional contracts jurisprudence but from empirical studies demonstrating the attitudes of business people towards contracts and contract law. Early empirical studies found that the law was marginal, although not entirely irrelevant, to the conduct of commercial dealing. Other studies emanating from a wide range of sources and with an increasingly wide array of agendas, such as to defend formalism,[52] or to examine the law's role in economic development, or the place of legally enforceable contracts in functioning business relationships,[53] have added to the knowledge gained from these early studies. If one concentrates on the findings themselves, rather than the normative conclusions that the scholar may attempt to draw from the findings, then the studies are relatively consistent in demonstrating that commercial contracting activity is varied, complex and underpinned by a wide variety of normative structures. The legal framework for the agreement, associated with express terms and legally enforceable agreements, insofar as it exists at all, may play a more or less enhanced role in this scheme. Although the academic literature generated by these studies has been rich and detailed, on the whole contract law has appeared to be relatively immune to the issues revealed by these empirical studies and the ensuing scholarly debate. Given the evidence, some of which is explored in greater depth in Chapter 3, it might be wondered why the findings of empirical studies and broadly relational theory appear to have had such little impact on the law, beyond occasional recognition amongst

51 RE Scott, above n 8, 852.
52 In this context see the studies conducted by Lisa Bernstein, above n 3.
53 For an overview of some of this literature see Mitchell, above n 3.

the judiciary that a contract may have relational features, or that the paperwork does not provide the whole story about a contractual agreement.[54] The reasons for this seeming lack of engagement are complex, but two particular factors may have been significant.

(i) The Character and Limits of Legal Regulation

The first limitation relates to the capacity of law itself. Collins has described the classical law of contract as having two particular characteristics—self-reference and closure.[55] Law presents itself as formal in the sense of being neutral, autonomous and external to the phenomena it seeks to regulate, facilitate or control. Law is a certain kind of technique, backed by a particular institutional framework and distinct methodology.[56] Within the common law, this is reflected partly in a set of institutional constraints operating on judges. New rulings have to be brought within an existing body of law or its justifying principles and this is not always readily achieved without either distorting the legal categories or excessive abstraction in isolating the relevant facts.[57] Justification for those principles is usually sought within broadly normative criteria, rather than pragmatic considerations concerning their congruence with what commercial parties expect or demand—although these considerations are certainly not ignored. In contrast with the tenacity of classical contract law, with its relatively simple model of the single seller and buyer involved in a discrete exchange, business practice, in particular the way that commercial entities organise themselves and their productive activities, is increasingly complex. In addition, contracts have lost none of their resonance, both as a matter of practical importance in the facilitation of trade, as a mechanism by which voluntary obligations can be assumed and given substance, and as a repository of normative value and symbolism.[58] The stability of law in the face of great change and developments in economic activity, commercial practices and commercial contracting could be regarded as one of its prime virtues, reflective of commercial contract law's character as *common law* and one of the hallmarks of specifically the *legal* regulation of commerce.[59] On this

[54] A recent notable example is Leggatt J's comments on relational agreements in the High Court in *Yam Seng Pte Ltd v International Trade Corporation Ltd* [2013] EWHC 111.

[55] Collins, above n 4, 37.

[56] E Weinrib, *The Idea of Private Law* (Cambridge MA, Harvard University Press, 1995) 4–5.

[57] Ibid 38.

[58] T Roxenhall and P Ghauri, 'Use of the Written Contract in Long-Lasting Business Relationships' (2004) 33 *Industrial Marketing Management* 261, 267; Lord Devlin, above n 13, 266.

[59] Gava, 'Dixonian Strict Legalism', above n 12, 521–24. See also 'How Should Judges Decide Commercial Contract Cases?', above n 12.

basis contract law is a scheme of *general rules* that cannot be expected to function as descriptions of commercial behaviour.

A related difficulty is that a commercial contract law informed by relational factors or commercial expectations and practices may be associated with a degree of commercial activism that would not sit well with the traditional approach of contract law to the commercial agreement. It might be doubted whether in practical terms generalist judges have the expertise and experience within a litigation setting to make accurate and workable judgments about commercial practice and commercial expectations.[60] The empirical studies reveal a range of implicit social norms and behaviours that govern a relationship, not all of which can even be apprehended by the law, still less given the badge of legal enforceability. The commercial settings generating such norms are likely to be heterogeneous and too fragmented to form the basis of a coherent law. Law by its nature may not be able to reflect commercial practices and expectations without fundamentally transforming them in significant and possibly unpredictable ways, rendering the legal understanding of them quite different to the parties' understanding.[61] It may therefore be entirely right that there are elements of commercial dealing that should be left to the self-regulation of the parties through social and informal norms. These are cogent arguments, but while the general scepticism concerning whether evidence of actual business behaviour yields any insights for legal reasoning about contracts is understandable, it will nevertheless be misplaced if strong justificatory arguments can be raised in support of developing a more relational contract law. These issues concerning the capacity of contract law to reflect commercial expectations are considered further in Chapter 7.

(ii) The Limits of the Socio-legal and Empirical Scholarship

The second reason for the lack of impact of socio-legal work has been the lack of attention to this issue amongst socio-legal scholars themselves.[62] Some socio-legal and relational studies emanating mostly from the US have concentrated on critiquing the classical and neoclassical law, arguing that classical contract law is not fit for purpose in regulating complex commercial agreements. Socio-legal scholars themselves have not been forthcoming over whether they are simply pointing out an under-appreciated element of contracting behaviour or seeking to reform and develop contract law in the

[60] Gava and Greene, above n 12, 616ff.

[61] R Cranston, 'What Do Courts Do?' (1986) 5 *Civil Justice Quarterly* 123, 130–32.

[62] Although see Feinman, above n 29, 737. Other theorists have considered the move to a more substantive and contextual version of contract law as either appropriate, or already existing. See especially, M Eisenberg, 'The Emergence of Dynamic Contract Law' (2000) 88 *California Law Review* 1743. In the UK noteworthy contributions to this question about contract law design are Collins, above n 4; Brownsword, above n 21; Campbell, Collins and Wightman (eds), above n 1.

light of the 'real' behaviour they have identified. If the latter, then it is not always made clear whether and how contract law can be reformed in the light of the empirical findings.[63] The crux of the debate between formalists and contextualists/relationalists is whether commercial contract law should be expanded to encompass the internally generated norms of the business relationship or reduced to a set of predictable formal rules, whose justification arises externally to any specific contractual agreement to which they might be applied.[64] This debate might be thought to be highly relevant to the issue of the design of contract law, yet it has remained frustratingly theoretical and abstract in nature. Questions concerning whether these two alternatives exhaust the possibilities for legal reasoning about contracts, what each approach precisely requires and how a judge chooses between these approaches in an individual case have not had satisfactory answers. While this polarised theoretical debate appears destined to continue indefinitely, it offers scant guidance to lawmakers, particularly within the English legal system, on how contract law might be designed to overcome the limitations identified. This will be examined further in Chapters 6 and 7. More specifically, the lack of a fully worked-out version of what might be called relational legal reasoning has arguably impeded the reception of relational theory into the law. Ian Macneil's 'essential contract theory', for example, did not include a comprehensive account of legal reasoning about contracts under dispute, although his work includes many relevant insights and suggestions concerning how a relational contract law might be modelled and the commitments that it would display. While Macneil's particular contribution is examined in Chapter 6, the issue of what a broadly relational legal reasoning method may look like, and why this is better attuned with commercial expectations, is addressed in the final chapter.

COMMERCIAL AGREEMENTS, CONTRACTS AND CONTRACT LAW

Before leaving these introductory matters, a few remarks about the confines of the book. The book is not intended to be a complete exposition of the

[63] Some general guidance is provided by RE Speidel, 'The Characteristics and Challenges of Relational Theory' (2000) 94 *Northwestern University Law Review* 823. Some scholars doubt that findings from social theory and empiricism can simply be absorbed into legal theory, rather they must be reconstructed in legal terms: G Teubner, 'Coincidentia Oppositorum: Hybrid Networks Beyond Contract and Organisation' in M Amstutz and G Teubner (eds), *Networks: Legal Issues of Multilateral Co-operation* (Oxford, Hart Publishing, 2009) 3, 9–10.

[64] For general outlines of the positions see Macaulay, above n 2; and the works cited above n 8. For a sceptical view about whether contract law can better facilitate market transactions by incorporating commercial practice, see J Gava, 'Can Contract Law Be Justified on Economic Grounds?' [2006] *University of Queensland Law Journal* 253 and 'False Lessons from the Real Deal', above n 6.

rules of classical contract law that have particular relevance to commercial contracting, nor is it concerned with commercial law in its entirety, nor even particular aspects of it. Rather it is concerned with contract law's general approach towards commercial contracting and its own role within it. Given its specific focus, it concentrates on the various debates that surround the relationship between the common law of contract and the commercial community whose dealings it seeks to facilitate and regulate. But even in relation to contract law, the work's engagement with specific doctrines will be minimal. The work may appear frustratingly limited to some readers, particularly in its concentration on the domestic law of contract, and in particular the judicially created rules. But there is a long-standing debate here, which impinges on how contract law should at least be perceived and understood, and which may also have implications for its future direction and reform. Thus further attention to these issues seems warranted.

The book is concerned with the general law of contract as it is applied to commercial dealings. To explain this in a little more detail, commercial agreements are taken to be those where participants do not act as consumers, but in the course of a business.[65] To confine examination to contracts made as part of business activities is hardly to impose a radically limiting criterion, given that 'commercial contracting' covers a wide variety of agreements made by different types of contractor operating within vastly different contexts, generating their own expectations and understandings. The sheer breadth of contracting behaviour caught by such a criterion is a major source of difficulty for this work, since it might be thought that there is little to be gained by examining the issue of commercial expectations and their connection to contract law in a general and abstract sense, particularly since this book is necessarily selective over the areas of contract law examined, and the aspects of commercial expectation and practice that it explores. So, one limitation is that it is not part of this work to make any extended comment on the legal controls that should apply to agreements which, while notionally made between commercial contractors, occur within business relationships characterised by stark inequalities in bargaining power. The relative lack of attention to this issue here might be regarded as a serious omission, since one important commercial expectation may be that a weaker commercial party will be given some protection by the law from an economically stronger party.[66] One reason for the omission is that some protection already exists for commercial contracting parties

[65] This is intended as a general definition here, rather than any specifically legal one as, eg, the definition of consumer under the Unfair Contract Terms Act 1977, s 12, or acting in the 'course of a business' under the Sale of Goods Act 1979.

[66] The problem of inequality of bargaining power between businesses was recognised in the Law Commission's 2005 report *Unfair Terms in Contracts* (Law Com No 292, Cm 6464). They recommended extending further protection to businesses with fewer than nine employees: see generally Part 5 of the report.

through doctrines such as economic duress, misrepresentation and certain provisions of the Unfair Contract Terms Act 1977.[67] These measures may be criticised as wanting in various respects, but the focus of this work is narrower. It has less to say about the general expectations of fairness that contractors might have and more about the norms of practice and behaviour that may operate within commercial contracting relationships and the relevance of these for contract law and legal development. Contract law has long grappled with considerations of fairness in contractual bargains, and while contractors may have certain expectations of the law in this respect, the primary analysis here concerns expectations that might arise out of business relationships and contractual contexts, rather than moral considerations attaching to contractual obligations more generally. While much evidence is available of the mismatch between law and commercial dealing, it appears an underdeveloped area within scholarship to tease out the implications of this for the common law of contract. Issues about fairness and inequality cannot be entirely ignored however, since they impinge upon matters which are relevant to this work, such as the role of good faith in business relationships, and how the balance of power between the parties may be an important part of contractual context which explains, at least in part, the choice of contractual arrangements. Neither is this work an exposition of the areas of contract law that have special relevance to commercial dealing. It might be thought that abstraction is a weakness here, but if the argument is that the law must tap into the context of all contractual relationships of whatever type, then what this requires can be considered in general, as well as specific, terms.

By the general law of contract is meant that set of rules developed and applied by courts to voluntarily assumed obligations, as well as relevant legislative provisions of contract law that have general scope and are not confined to any particular trade or industry. Given the increasing complexity of business dealing, it not certain that the non-use-of-contract claim can be maintained without qualification. Contracts and the law may be largely invisible in functioning commercial dealings, but this does not mean they are entirely irrelevant, as the early empirical studies themselves demonstrate. The rules promulgated by judges and legislators continue to set the conditions of legal enforceability for contracts, vitiating factors, remedies for breach and so on, providing guidance to other contractors on these issues, irrespective of whether the legal requirements are essential or only marginal to the individual contracting arrangements. Whatever the level of scepticism that may exist, commercial contractors continue to bring their claims before the courts. This suggests that contract law still matters and

[67] Most notably under parts of ss 3, 6 and 7. These allow the courts to assess the reasonableness of some types of excluding and limiting terms in commercial contracts.

that there is more to say concerning the role of contract law in regulating commercial activity, not least how the institution of contract law can appear at once both central and peripheral to the practice of commercial contracting.[68]

While it might be relatively easy to identify what commercial contract law looks like, deciding what is meant by 'a contract' is not straightforward. Legal identification of the contract with the documented agreement is common but has been questioned.[69] Insights gained from a socio-legal appreciation of contractual obligations suggest that whilst the legal framework to the contract is important, the extent of its importance—particularly to the contracting parties, as opposed to their lawyers—should not be overemphasised. In *Regulating Contracts* for example, Collins takes a sceptical view about the relevance of the legal contract and contract law rules to the agreement the parties make. In his view, the legal rules and decisions in cases frequently undermine the reasonable expectations of the parties which, in the commercial context, are based on 'considerations of the long term business relation, the customs of the trade, and the success of the deal'[70] rather than the contractual planning documents. It is this social framework, or context, of agreements that gives rise to most of the contracting parties' intentions and expectations, not the legal regulation. Some judges are aware of the limitations of the written contract in this regard, often revealing anecdotally that contracting parties seem to care little about the legal documents.[71]

The issue of how one understands 'the contract' is an important one to the socio-legal critique, since one strategy for upholding commercial expectations (but also possibly undermining them) is for the law to attempt to incorporate more of these social and relational norms into an agreement. Faced with the criticism that the law is simply irrelevant to most transactions, it seems the effectiveness of contract law can no longer be measured by its certainty in promulgating and enforcing a strict body of doctrinal rules, but by its success in supporting and upholding the more elusive 'reasonable expectations of the parties'.[72] The view of many notionally 'commercial contractors' may be that legal contracts and contract law get in the way of doing business.[73] The increasing sensitivity to the issue of whether the documents really capture all the parties' understandings about their agreement is one aspect of the question of whether contract law reflects and upholds 'commercial expectations'. It may be that the genuine agreement

[68] Collins, above n 4, 5.

[69] P Linzer, 'The Comfort of Certainty: Plain Meaning and the Parol Evidence Rule' (2002) 71 *Fordham Law Review* 799, 822; Macaulay, above n 2, 53–56; Collins, above n 4, ch 6.

[70] Collins, above n 4, 271.

[71] Lord Devlin, above n 13, 252.

[72] Lord Steyn, above n 39.

[73] Lord Devlin, above n 13, 252; Beale and Dugdale, above n 3, 47–48.

cannot be yielded from the documents at all, although contracting parties may be compelled to draft express terms in order to give legal certainty to their agreements. In identifying 'the contract' it is possible to rely on the definition that would appeal to the law, which is simply an agreement that the law will enforce. This could be interpreted as agreements that meet strict legal requirements for enforceability—coincidence of offer and acceptance, consideration and intention to create legal obligations. It is well known that in practice these requirements are malleable and the courts will attempt to enforce agreements when it is tolerably clear that the parties both intended to be legally bound and there is some identifiable content to the obligation.[74] In part though, this study is precisely concerned with what 'contracts' and 'contractual obligations' are taken to be more generally, and particularly within the commercial contracting community. Some participants within such a community may have a legalistic view of what a contract is, others a more flexible view of what a 'contractual commitment' to a contracting partner entails. The latter may not make much of a distinction between legal obligations and obligations of a more nebulous or moral kind. Since this is one of the concerns of this book, there is little more to be said about this within the introduction. Suffice to say that it should be clear when a distinction is made between contract law and contracts, and in relation to the latter, when the legal meaning is relied upon or some other more flexible understanding.

Finally, some cautionary words. It is very far from straightforward to reach determinate conclusions about the relationship between contract law and commercial activity, still less about how contract law could display relational concerns and commitments within its scheme of rules and dispute resolution processes. At best this work will make only a modest contribution to these issues. Most of its conclusions are tentative. The claim that contract law should track or uphold commercial expectations cannot be assumed to be self-evident, but neither is it the case that the debates in this area can be defined out of existence by maintaining that contract law is only concerned with formal and legally enforceable commitments. The findings from empirical studies are arguably inconclusive about the role of law in commerce, and they certainly do not suggest the law plays no role in regulating and facilitating commercial dealing.[75] If anything, the studies tend to suggest that the law has a greater role to play in certain kinds of commercial relationship. But these empirical findings do give rise to more

[74] A recent example is provided by the Supreme Court decision in *RTS Flexible Systems Ltd v Molkerei Alois Müller GmbH & Co KG (UK Productions)* [2010] UKSC 14; [2010] 1 WLR 753.

[75] D Campbell, eg, once referred to the 'devastating empirical finding of non-use' of contract law in business relationships: 'Reflexivity and Welfarism in the Modern Law of Contract' (2000) 20 *OJLS* 477, 480.

basic issues about the rules of contract law that appear only obliquely addressed by unpacking the normative commitments of contract law or by tracing the analytical contours of a contractual obligation. These are important endeavours, but they arguably have little impact on the practical reality of many commercial agreements. The reverse is also true of the socio-legal critique of contract law. Evidence about the practical reality of contracting appears to have had remarkably little impact on contract law, at least insofar as the identification of its main doctrines goes. In short then, this book attempts to pick up the story where other accounts end. These other accounts and judicial views assert that serving commercial expectations, purposes and so on is an end point in the analysis of what contract law is for and how its success is to be judged. Here, the attempt is made to understand better what this claim might mean, whether and how it should be pursued and what reforms to contract law might be necessary to render these claims more than merely rhetorical. The work attempts to provide an overview of the issues, problems and potential for developing greater alignment between commercial expectations and contract law through the broad understandings that are presented by relational theory. Relational scholars may regard the application of the theory to law as immaterial or going beyond their concerns or even impossible, but if so, they can then hardly be surprised or disappointed if a lawyer (or even a business person) greets their claims with a sceptical 'So what?'.[76] Since so many claims of relational theory are critical of the classical law it is hard to believe such theories have, or should have, no reforming aims whatsoever. Similarly, if the law relating to commercial contracts must be based on some assumptions about the contracting parties, it is necessary to ask what justifies its current set of assumptions and whether an alternative set of assumptions based on different criteria, including the real behaviour of contractors, might not be preferable.

[76] Campbell remarks that Macneil evinced disappointment with the reception of his work: 'Ian Macneil and the Relational Theory of Contract' in Macneil, above n 38, 5.

2

Understanding Commercial Expectations

THIS CHAPTER ATTEMPTS to get a better grasp of the idea of 'commercial expectations' and why they are important in commercial contract law. The immediate problem with any appeal to 'expectations' in a legal setting is that the basis for these expectations, and hence *what* is expected, will vary. Nevertheless, there ought to be a readily understandable idea behind the appeal to commercial expectation more generally, particularly if contract law is thought deficient in some respects in failing to accord with these expectations. If 'commercial expectations' is merely an umbrella term that covers a loose and heterogeneous group of concerns whose only shared feature is that they may be held by business contractors, it is quite obvious that contract law could never hope to achieve any kind of correspondence with such an amorphous range of understandings. In the light of these difficulties, this chapter seeks to scrutinise the ideas that may lie behind the appeal to commercial expectation and in doing so reach some preliminary conclusions over what the claim of misalignment between contract law and commercial expectations might mean. In particular it addresses two related issues. First, how the idea of commercial expectation should be understood and how it might be distinguished from other similar ideas that are found in contract law. Second, whether a prima facie case can be established for why commercial expectation *generally* (rather than any specific expectations) are relevant in the application and development of commercial contract law. This part in particular utilises the idea of the internal point of view to build an argument as to why the understandings of the participants in the practice of commercial dealing should matter to contract law. In addition, the chapter considers the values that lie behind commercial law generally that might help to support closer alignment between law and commercial expectation. It also considers how changes in commercial contracting practice have led to a need for contract law to be more sensitive to considerations of context in resolving disputes. Chapter 3 then considers further the question of identification by examining some possible sources of these commercial expectations.

WHAT DOES AN APPEAL TO COMMERCIAL EXPECTATIONS MEAN?

Broadly speaking, an expectation (a belief that something will or ought to be the case) might be based on one of three broad foundations: it might be grounded in one's experience (empirically based), it might be grounded on some normative commitment thought valuable, or it may be derived from or protected by some social institution.[1] If an empirically based understanding is relied upon, then there are a range of outcomes to be justified on the basis of their accordance with commercial expectations, depending on the type of transaction and the social norms operating in that particular contracting context or wider business community. If a normative standard is advanced as the basis for the expectation, then there is a filtering process whereby the range of possible outcomes may be more limited and evince a concern with moulding the behaviour of contractors, as far as possible, to reflect some ideal-type, rather than necessarily seeking to reflect or uphold contractors' real behaviour and actual practices. This ideal may be derived from more general normative grounds, such as justice, fairness or some other moral imperative, whether or not it is recognised by the participants or protected by the law.[2] In addition, an expectation could be derived from institutional grounds, such as where an expectation is protected by way of a legal rule, or more indirectly, by way of an obligation stated in a set of express terms which will be upheld as enforceable by the law of contract.[3] A slightly weaker institutional ground might be if particular expectations concerning commercial conduct in particular industries or markets are promulgated by trade associations. The point here is that commercial expectations are multilayered. They can be derived from different starting points and it is possible for the basis for the expectation to veer between these alternative grounds, rendering the boundaries between them opaque. This raises the problem that the concept appears radically indeterminate and substantially meaningless. If commercial expectation has no understandable idea behind it, then the misalignment claim is emptied of much of its sense and force. However, while indeterminacy cannot be completely eradicated, it is possible to move towards a more fixed understanding of commercial expectation since some starting points for understanding the idea are more illuminating than others.

[1] See generally C Mitchell, 'Leading a Life of its Own? The Roles of Reasonable Expectation in Contract Law' (2003) 23 *OJLS* 639; R Brownsword, 'After *Investors*: Interpretation, Expectation and the Implicit Dimension of the "New Contextualism"' in D Campbell, H Collins and J Wightman (eds), *Implicit Dimensions of Contract* (Oxford, Hart Publishing, 2003) 103, 105.

[2] See Brownsword, above n 1.

[3] Mitchell, above n 1, 647–54.

The possibility of an institutional basis for expectations could easily be turned to support various formalistic arguments along the lines that a contractor's expectations can only be derived from contract law or from the contract's express terms.[4] Since it is precisely this sort of understanding of expectations that has generated the misalignment criticism, this does not seem to be the most helpful way of understanding commercial expectation in this context. Certainly the law and contract terms can raise expectations about entitlements but there is no need to rely on an expectations argument to support their being enforced; one could justify an outcome by reference to a contractor's legal entitlement and leave it at that (although of course it could be a separate expectation that those strict legal rights will be applied over any more flexible understandings). One can make the same argument in relation to the normative basis for expectations. Once the normative principles underlying the expectation are identified, the appeal to expectation becomes redundant in favour of the moral argument used to support it, although one still might refer to the thing believed as the expectation, as distinguished from the normative grounds on which the belief rests. So, for example, a contract law system may evince a general commitment to good faith as a normative underpinning, which may give rise to certain more specific commercial expectations on the part of contractors, such as that a contracting partner will share relevant information over the course of performance.

In view of the problem of redundancy, it appears appropriate to accord 'commercial expectation' a meaning that reflects the concerns of those who regard the dissonance between law and expectations as problematic. Thus a better interpretation of 'commercial expectation', and indeed other forms of commercial criteria (commercial practices, purposes, reasonableness and so on), is as a non-legally derived view of how commercial contractors conduct business. Thus reference to commercial expectation gives expression to a viewpoint operating outwith the contract terms and contract law doctrine. Granted, such a broad interpretation is still likely to capture a wide range of informal understandings, practices, behaviours and norms that operate within the commercial community, as well as the belief that these sorts of standard *should* inform contract legal reasoning. But to say that an appeal to commercial expectations refers to these kinds of factors is not to say that all of these should be legally recognised, nor that such expectations may not embrace formalism, insofar as a contractor expects the formal legal-contractual scheme will govern the relationship and will be the basis for resolving disputes. Such a belief would only be correctly labelled an expectation in the sense adopted here to the extent it was derived from

[4] Examples of where such a legalistic interpretation (a contractor cannot reasonably expect what the contract terms do not offer) was rejected include *Timeload Ltd v British Telecommunications plc* [1995] EMLR 459 and *Zockoll Group Ltd v Mercury Communications Ltd (No 2)* [1999] EMLR 385.

the context surrounding the agreement, rather than derived wholly from the existence of a set of express contract terms. Reference to commercial expectations then should be understood as appealing to factors external to the operation of the legal imperatives, but internal to the parties and their contracting context.

Expectations are not the only external referent that may be appealed to in contract law. Another of these sorts of standard is a commercial practice. Commercial practice is more easily explained than commercial expectation. It usually refers to a manner of conducting dealings which has hardened into a recurring pattern of behaviour, either between two contracting parties, or within an industry. Given this pattern of regularity, commercial expectations could be derived in an empirical sense from commercial practices. Repeated practices may become norms or conventions followed by participants who internally accept that the norm represents the way in which things should be done.[5] Systems of commercial practice can develop and maintain such a level of institutional complexity, normative richness and acceptance amongst participants that they effectively oust the operation of the national system of contract law. Assessing the conditions under which this occurs is not straightforward. Specific factors such as cultural homogeneity, history, locality—what Badawi has termed 'insularity'[6]—and control over access to the industry play important roles.[7] While there are some business relationships that may display such normative richness that they can essentially do without the law, although recourse to law can never be ruled out,[8] all effective and functioning contractual relationships will rely on extra-legal practices and norms to some degree, whether these arise from the specific industry in which the contractors find themselves, their previous dealings, or more general and diffuse moral standards that operate amongst commercial contractors or the social community more generally. Thus every contractual relationship has the capacity to be informed by commercial expectations and experience in this external sense.

WHY DO COMMERCIAL EXPECTATIONS MATTER?

Relational and contextual contract law scholars may point to the existence of behaviours, norms and expectations that lie beyond the legally significant

[5] R Cooter, 'Decentralised Law for a Complex Economy: The Structural Approach to Adjudicating the New Law Merchant' (1996) 144 *University of Pennsylvania Law Review* 1643, 1665.

[6] AB Badawi, 'Interpretative Preferences and the Limits of the New Formalism' (2009) 6 *Berkeley Business Law Journal* 1, 12.

[7] See, eg, L Bernstein, 'Opting Out of the Legal System: Extralegal Contractual Relations in the Diamond Industry' (1992) 21 *Journal of Legal Studies* 115.

[8] As in *Baird Textile Holdings Ltd v Marks and Spencer plc* [2001] EWCA Civ 274.

statement of obligations, but it must be asked why such expectations are thought relevant to the determination of legal disputes about contract? What business people may expect regarding their entitlements, how their dispute is resolved and how their relationship with a contracting partner will be conducted may be reckoned to carry little weight in the face of express contract terms and legal rules. Why should it be grounds for criticism of the law that it has only an attenuated grasp of the expectations, normative frameworks and implicit dimensions that arise externally to its operation?

A More Accurate Picture of the Parties' Agreement

It is undoubtedly the case that classical contract law relies on generalisations and abstractions concerning the contracting parties and the contracting process. While this might be thought necessary for the operation of a set of general rules, as more empirical evidence of business behaviour becomes available to the legal scholar it is clear that there are few generalisations that can reliably be made about the process of commercial contracting. Macaulay has argued that greater attention to law and contracts in action, is important because:

> if legislatures, courts or law students were to pay any attention to contracts scholarship, our reliance on inadequate navigational charts might cause some serious damage. For example, we may advocate particular contract rules because of what we think their likely consequences would be. The law in action or the living law might doom our proposed legal solution to having little or no impact, or our proposals might provoke unexpected and unwanted consequences if enacted or adopted.[9]

Macaulay points out that reliance on a handful of higher-court judgments as providing a map of an entire field of activity is likely to lead to dangerous distortions concerning the activity being regulated. Similarly Weintraub has written, 'Laws opposed to practice are unlikely to change practice, but will, when haphazardly and occasionally applied, condemn what should be encouraged'.[10] It would be easy to assert here that if law has such a limited effect on practice and commercial conduct, then there is no particular need to be concerned about misalignment—the lack of engagement between law and commerce is likely to remain whatever the design of the rules, except perhaps in those rarefied areas of commerce where expectations are more likely to be moulded and informed by the legal framework. Of course this

[9] S Macaulay, 'Contracts, New Legal Realism, and Improving the Navigation of The Yellow Submarine' (2006) 80 *Tulane Law Review* 1161, 1162.

[10] R Weintraub, 'A Survey of Contract Practice and Policy' (1992) *Wisconsin Law Review* 1, 5.

argument can be made to support change as much as it can be made to support the status quo. But in any case the assertion seems mistaken, since however difficult it may be to decide on the precise nature of the relationship between law and business, it surely cannot be the case that the legal rules have no effect on the conduct of commercial activity generally.

There are various reasons why it may be important to gain a more accurate picture of a field of activity and for saying that this is relevant to the development of the activity. As Macaulay notes, while investigation into contract practice may reveal when law reform might be necessary, it may also demonstrate that what appears to be a legal problem may not be so in practice due to the operation of social norms developed between the parties that mitigate what are taken to be the deleterious effects of the legal rules. An example of potential distortion is provided by Lewis's study of tendering practices in the construction industry.[11] Lewis examined the problem of subcontractors ('subs') withdrawing firm price bids (or offers which stipulated that they would remain open for a specified time) submitted to main contractors ('generals') after the generals had used the price bid in preparing and submitting a successful tender for the main contract. Under the classical law, subs were free to do this notwithstanding that the specified time limit had not expired, since the generals had not strictly 'accepted' the offer under the precepts of classical contract law, nor was there any separate consideration to keep the bid open for the specified period. The Law Commission had put forward proposals to reform the law to make a sub's bid binding if it was used by the general in preparing what turned out to be the successful tender. Following his own survey of subs and generals in the Cardiff area, Lewis found that generals did not regard the subs' capacity to withdraw a 'firm offer' as presenting a difficulty[12] and that generals placed greater emphasis on previous dealings with subs, from which they could judge reliability and suitability, than on simply choosing the lowest bid.[13] Generals rarely took steps to protect themselves from withdrawn bids (by requesting 'bid bonds' or creating option contracts) and subs usually felt at least ethically bound to their bids once the general had been awarded the main contract, and this expectation was shared by the generals.[14] Generals considered that non-legal sanctions for withdrawing offers, such as bringing pressure to bear on the sub or not allowing him to submit tenders for future work, were effective in reducing the extent of the problem. Thus while the Law Commission found that a legal problem existed which was

[11] R Lewis, 'Contracts Between Businessmen: Reform of the Law of Firm Offers and an Empirical Study of Tendering Practices in the Building Industry' (1982) 9 *Journal of Law and Society* 153.

[12] Ibid, 161.

[13] Ibid, 161.

[14] Ibid, 163.

assumed to cause hardship, adopting the legal point of view tended to overstate the extent to which a problem existed, and overlooked that informal and social sanctions, as well as cultural norms of feeling 'obliged' to honour a firm offer, reduced the impact of the problem considerably.[15] The thicker context that Lewis was able to provide on the business relationship between generals and subs, and its internal mechanisms for regulating behaviour, rendered legal reform redundant as well as manifesting the possibly unwelcome effects of legal interference.

Accordance with the Self-understandings of Participants in the Practice

JH Baker, in answering the question of why reasonable expectations should be enforced, writes, 'the justification which most readily suggests itself ... is that they may mean more to the parties than the finer points of classical contractual theory'.[16] The dissonance between law and commercial expectations could be considered as a problem of the law lacking meaning for the parties because it fails to reflect the internal point of view of business people concerning how commercial relationships and contracting activity are conducted. It has been noted that the commercial-expectations argument, if it is to be accorded a sensible meaning, must refer to the norms, standards and behaviours that arise externally to the law, but internally to the parties and their relationship (although this internal understanding could be informed by a range of external factors). This internal point of view will differ from the understandings of contracting practice held by lawyers or judges and promoted through the legal machinery of contracts and contract law. While the differences between these points of view may not be problematic—they are partly a reflection of the difference between the social practices of 'commerce' and 'law', and there may be very good reasons why the law does not reflect the self-understandings of those involved in the practice of commercial contracting—it is important to at least draw out these differences and to address their possible implications. The idea of the internal point of view is associated in English jurisprudence with HLA Hart. Hart criticised a wholly external, sanctions-based understanding of why citizens may generally obey legal rules (such as fear of punishment) in favour of a view that citizens often manifested an internal acceptance of rules as providing reasons for action, grounds for criticism of rule breakers and as capable

[15] Ibid, 169. S Wheeler's empirical study on the operation of reservation of title clauses confirms the lack of connection between the legal regime for recognition of such clauses and the conduct of insolvency practitioners which undermined such clauses in practice: *Reservation of Title Clauses* (Oxford, OUP, 1991) 68–75.

[16] JH Baker, 'From Sanctity of Contract to Reasonable Expectation' (1979) 32 *Current Legal Problems* 17, 23.

of giving rise to obligations.[17] Expressed in this way, the existence of an internal point of view may appear to have little resonance when discussing commercial contractors' attitudes towards the rules of contract law. Those to whom the rules are addressed (the commercial contracting community) are likely to differ significantly in relation to how much the law matters to them, how much they refer to the law in constructing their deal and their overall view of the role of law in regulating and facilitating productive exchange. Nevertheless, the idea of the internal point of view is helpful in understanding and supporting the misalignment claim.

First, contract law regulates a pre-existing practice of productive exchange, it does not wholly create the practice. Admittedly contract law is itself a practice that in part shapes and is in part shaped by the practice of making and performing agreements, but as a matter of social fact there will be a set of expectations, understandings and experiences of the participants which they will bring to bear, in different combinations and in different contexts, to their contracting activity. Of course, parties may be fully accepting of express terms and contract law as giving rise to obligations, but this may either be in conjunction with the other norms and practices they bring to bear on their agreement, or itself be a manifestation of their own internal point of view. In the latter case the parties' internal acceptance may well be directed towards the formal contract terms and contract law, although this too is likely to be the result of contextual understandings (a further layer of internal points of view) which operate in a particular industry or business relationship which accepts formalism as the way things are done. To the extent that these other norms and practices impinge on the parties' internal understanding of their obligations, then they will be relevant to the obligations the parties believe they have assumed towards each other. In short, attention to the internal point of view identifies and connects to what the parties regard as binding obligations and acceptable modes of behaviour. Insofar as rules of contract law are understood, even if only in part, as power conferring and facilitative, the law must surely be mindful of the existence of the internal point of view of participants. This is not to say that attention to the internal point of view will provide evidence about the concrete expectations that exist in a relationship, nor is it to suggest that these will be shared—it is the concept of the internal point of view that is relevant, rather than any individual internal point of view. In simple terms, recognising the existence of the internal point of view forces acknowledgment that the understandings of those who participate in the practice are important to identifying norms that might be regarded as obligation imposing.

[17] HLA Hart, *The Concept of Law*, 2nd edn (Oxford, OUP, 1994) 89–91.

Second, the idea of the internal point of view brings into sharper focus the existence of the external point of view. It appears in many cases, although not all, that contractors 'accept' the rules of contract law only as external standards. Parties often recognise the importance of legal enforceability for their agreements and attempt to achieve it, but fail[18] or else pay little heed to the doctrinal rules that might impinge upon how performance proceeds.[19] Alternatively, the parties may attempt to contract for outcomes and obligations within the legal framework, but which are not possible under the law for a variety of reasons. Contracting for flexible duties such as to negotiate in good faith, for example, may be void for uncertainty under the present law,[20] or otherwise be rendered ineffective by the law.[21] These instances demonstrate that parties are not using the rules of contract law as guides to conduct—otherwise it might be assumed they would follow them more conscientiously—but rather act in ignorance of them, or indeed attempt to subvert them. Thus while businesses may 'use' contract law in the sense that they may attempt to create legally enforceable agreements, this demonstrates only that the parties may have an internal acceptance of the broad idea that legal enforceability may be beneficial, not an internal acceptance of the rules themselves. This suggests that for some contracting parties the contract law rules and the express contract terms constitute *a* practice—contract law—but not *the* practice of commercial dealing that the participants are engaged in. Arguably this in itself *creates the need* amongst commercial parties for a separate legal framework. Although it may be important that their agreements are legally enforceable, this may be regarded as a safeguard to deal with future and unhoped-for contingencies rather than because conducting relationships in accordance with the legal rules is regarded as desirable in itself. This lack of congruence with the internal point of view poses problems for law's legitimacy since the law fails even to uphold its own purposes of contributing to the facilitation of commerce, except for that body of contractors who accept contract law's precepts as representing the way in which things should be done in their particular industry. Parties may well be aware of the legal norms, and may accept them as positing the requirements for legality, but do not necessarily accept them as directing how the business relationship should be run or managed. The law then ceases to be an authoritative guide to the way in which things should be done by the participants.

[18] Eg, *RTS Flexible Systems Ltd v Molkerei Alois Müller* [2010] UKSC 14; [2010] 1 WLR 753.

[19] *Williams v Roffey Bros* [1991] 1 QB 1.

[20] Discussed further in Ch 4 below.

[21] For a very recent example see *Mid Essex Hospital Services NHS Trust v Compass Group UK and Ireland Ltd (t/a Medirest)* [2013] EWCA Civ 200.

Empirical studies of contracting behaviour tend to demonstrate that the internal point of view of 'norm acceptance' in commercial relationships does not revolve around the legal rules, but the internal norms generated by the parties' relationships and the trade in which they operate. To the extent that the law does not accept such norms and practices it is itself taking an external point of view of the business relationship, and regulating it according to that view. Contract law may aspire to engage this internal aspect on the part of the participants. For example, it often seeks to encourage and impose its view of how contracting should be conducted.[22] But this seems to proceed without appreciation of what can and cannot be achieved within a legal framework. Without this appreciation, law can only ever remain external to the practice of business contracting and many participants will therefore not achieve legal 'contracts', only approximations of them as against the legal ideal. Indeed the legal position may be regarded as upholding a mode of behaviour that might be criticised or sanctionable among the commercial contracting community.[23] This line of argument also suggests that the application of the classical law is most appropriate where the legal framework is accepted internally and externally by participants.[24] Such contractors are participants in the legal-contractual world, not external observers of the 'legal world' in operation, attempting to meet its requirements.[25]

The Role of Co-operation in Business Dealings

The above argument might be criticised on the basis that the internally generated norms of the business relationship will simply reflect the multiplicity of internal points of view of the practice of commercial contracting. While recognition of the internal point of view may assist in identifying the substance of commercial expectations, to pick one such set of expectations as the standard which informs contract law development or informs the rules

[22] See, eg, Lord Clarke's injunction in *RTS v Müller* that the 'moral of the story is to agree first and to start work later': above n 18, at [1].

[23] As with upholding no legal duty to disclose information despite the norms of the insolvency workout procedure in *National Westminster Bank plc v Rabobank Nederland* [2007] EWHC 1056 QBD. On the normative framework for workouts see J Armour and S Deakin, 'Norms in Private Insolvency: The "London Approach" to the Resolution of Financial Distress' (2001) 1 *Journal of Corporate Law Studies* 21, 37–49.

[24] Eg, *Scandinavian Trading Tanker Co AB v Flota Petrolera Ecuatoriana (The Scaptrade)* [1983] 1 QB 529 (CA). Relief against forfeiture was not available to a charterer when the shipowner sought to withdraw the ship for non-payment in order to take advantage of a rising market, notwithstanding that the shipowner had previously accepted late payments of hire. Robert Goff LJ observed that '[t]he possibility that shipowners may snatch at the opportunity to withdraw ships from the service of time charterers for non-payment of hire must be very well known in the world of shipping': 540. The ruling was affirmed by the House of Lords at [1983] 2 AC 694.

[25] Cooter, above n 5, 1643.

would be arbitrary and subjective. Given the lack of ability to generalise about immanent business norms across contracting contexts, general rules are unable to reflect detailed substantive commercial expectations since these are unlikely to be shared by all contractors and may just reflect a contractor's preferences. Under this line of argument, the point of law is to provide the meta-normative scheme that is *precisely required* because of the discrepancies and inconsistencies between these internal points of view, even if this means applying an entirely different set of standards. Thus the internal point of view of participants in commercial contracting is not one, but a multiplicity of points of view of the practice. Choice of any particular substantive internal point of view to inform the rules, for example, that business relationships are underpinned by trust and loyalty, would need to advance a non-contingent argument explaining why it is superior.

There are two particular responses that could be made here. The first is to say that the argument is not that the law should choose one of these points of view to inform its ideas of substantive commercial expectations, or that one of these should be taken as manifesting the expectations that should be supported, but that the law is simply required to recognise that this internal point of view, in all it manifestations, exists and that participants do not share the same view of the contracting process as the law. Initially then, this reliance on the internal point of view serves as a methodological and procedural justification for taking immanent business norms into account rather than a normative one. Under such a view, a problem only occurs for the law if it believes it must single out one internal perspective from which to develop its rules. It could be argued that the classical law did exactly this by building its rules around a model of contractors and the contracting process as self-interested and adversarial. It is not clear why law must take this step rather than embrace what appears the most appropriate approach within the context of the parties' agreement. There is no reason why a set of immanent norms cannot be understood in an objective sense—if reliable evidence of them exists and they are shared by the parties, or they are promulgated by trade associations and the like. The identification of such norms may be context dependent, but that does not mean the identification and application of them is completely arbitrary.

A second response involves grasping this particular nettle and arguing that a commercial-expectations approach requires the law to move beyond the methodological understanding of the internal point of view towards the normative position of isolating a single internal point of view as representing a superior understanding and reflection of the participants' practices and expectations. This line of argument requires a choice to be made by the law in identifying a particular internal point of view of the participants in the practice and ensuring that the law's defaults uphold the underpinning values suggested by this preferred internal point of view. Such an approach need not mean the law compromises its capacity for pluralism in upholding commercial expectations, since it could set its defaults according to some standard (real or ideal) which represents how commercial contracting is undertaken, while also embracing pragmatism in allowing the parties to contract around the default, either expressly or impliedly. One possibility is that the law should support and reflect the internal point of view of participants where the contract is regarded as a co-operative endeavour, simply because co-operation is necessary as a precursor to all contracting activity—co-operation and consent mark the distinction to be drawn between taking and trading. This understanding of co-operation does not so much stress a normative commitment of contract as accept the practical point that all contractors must display co-operative behaviour with contracting partners to some degree. However, while co-operative dealing would be manifest in most instances of commercial dealing, this says nothing about what motivates co-operation in any given agreement, whether a moral imperative or a form of enlightened self-interest. It simply recognises that the underpinning value of contract law could be sociologically derived from the fact that some minimum co-operation is necessary for contracting to take place at all.[26]

It is of course possible to go further and recognise that the methodology of isolating an internal point of view can be applied to co-operation itself to tease out the different motivations that a contractor may have for being co-operative and flexible. From here one may reach a conclusion that contract law should adopt a default model of the ideal co-operative contractor as the basis for its rules. This is naturally very controversial. Brownsword has developed an argument along these lines. He maintains that the 'essence of co-operative dealing lies in the subordination of self-interest to a contractual community of interest'.[27] In terms of what behaviour is required by the co-operative ideal there are two possibilities: one could refer to the norms and practices of other commercial contractors in the relevant field, or a more general, morally informed conception of co-operation. Brownsword's preference is for the latter, noting correctly that if co-operation is to do useful work as an alternative underpinning foundation for contract law, then this must be based on rejecting a self-interested or prudential conception of co-operation which is readily assimilated within the existing classical model.[28] In addition, the multiple-commercial-norms approach is subject to the ebb and flow of commercial opinion on these matters. Thus the contract law default could be readily justified by reference to this model of moral

[26] See D Campbell, 'Ian Macneil and the Relational Theory of Contract' in I Macneil, *The Relational Theory of Contract: Selected Works of Ian Macneil*, D Campbell (ed) (London, Sweet & Maxwell, 2001) 9–11.

[27] R Brownsword, 'From Co-operative Contracting to a Contract of Co-operation' in D Campbell and P Vincent-Jones (eds), *Contract and Economic Organisation* (Aldershot, Dartmouth, 1996) 14, 16–17.

[28] Ibid, 23.

co-operation, but with an allowance for the parties to contract around it and provide for themselves a different set of ground rules which they would have to provide in their contract. The surrounding context could also support the view that the contractors intended a governing norm of self-interest to apply. The idea that commercial expectations could have a normative dimension will be examined further below, but for now it should only be observed that it might be expected that a contract law aligned with commercial expectations would recognise, first, that contractors have internal understandings of the practice and, second, that these may have an important bearing on how the contractors comprehend their 'legal' obligations.

The Perceived Values of Commercial Law

Commercial lawyers often point out that certain values underpin the pursuit of commercial activity and the legal regulation of it. Goode writes that there are eight principles that make up the philosophy of commercial law: party autonomy; predictability; flexibility; good faith; the encouragement of self-help; the facilitation of security interests; the protection of vested interests; and the protection of innocent third parties.[29] It is immediately evident that contract law as it currently stands may uphold these particular values to a greater or lesser extent. The law of contract has been criticised for its rigidity, and this is often taken to be an important indicator of its dissonance with commercial needs and expectations.[30] Protection of third parties under the common law of contract has had a very chequered history, and there is no general duty of good faith. Of course the perceived values of commercial law are not necessarily those that inform commercial practice for the participants, but there is reason to think that the values Goode identifies are broadly consistent with expectations that commercial contractors may have of commercial contract law. Some empirical evidence to support this is provided by a survey conducted by Stefan Vogenauer and Stephen Weatherill.[31] The survey examined business attitudes towards harmonisation of European contract law. Respondents were asked to identify the characteristics that influenced their choice of contract law to govern their agreements: 'most answered that a suitable contract law had to enable trade, and be predictable and fair. A smaller number thought that it was

[29] R Goode, 'The Codification of Commercial Law' (1988) 14 *Monash University Law Review* 135, 148.

[30] R Goode, *Commercial Law in the Next Millennium* (Hamlyn Lecture Series, London, Sweet & Maxwell, 1998) 32–33.

[31] S Vogenauer and S Weatherill, 'The European Community's Competence to Pursue the Harmonisation of Contract Law—An Empirical Contribution to the Debate' in S Vogenauer and S Weatherill (eds), *The Harmonisation of European Contract Law* (Oxford, Hart Publishing, 2006) 105.

important that the governing contract law be flexible, short and concise, or prescriptive'.[32] While these expectations may be castigated as inconsistent (flexibility or predictability?), the diversity in requirements is hardly surprising, given the diversity of contractors themselves and the conditions under which commercial dealing takes place. Diversity of itself does not excuse contract law from assessing the extent to which it is in keeping with such values and expectations.

To the extent that the values identified by Goode may be taken to underpin commercial expectations, an examination of one of these principles—good faith—will demonstrate contract law's limitations in upholding these values. Most contracting parties feel they have duties to one another beyond those stipulated by the express terms, or that certain standards of behaviour can be expected from a contracting partner. Expectations that parties have about such standards in partners are often crucial in determining whether parties will enter into an agreement at all. Contracting parties would usually expect to display some level of trust in one another, and behave co-operatively or flexibly towards each other for the sake of the business relationship and success of the project.[33] However, whether legal duties to act in good faith in negotiation or performance are rightly imposed on contractors, as they are by some legal regimes,[34] is disputed. Partly this is due to the equivocation of the concept itself. The ideas lying behind good faith are often expressed in binary and overlapping terms. Good faith can be understood as requiring contractors to manifest certain types of behaviour (inclusive good faith) or simply requiring a party to avoid various forms of unfair treatment and bad-faith behaviour towards a contracting partner (exclusive good faith).[35] Good faith can also be understood as involving either substantive content or procedural duties, or both.[36] The law may

[32] Ibid, 122. The actual figures are 'Enable trade: 87%, predictable: 79%, fair: 78%, flexible: 66%, short and concise: 61%, prescriptive 39%, other: 12%': ibid, fn 51.

[33] An obligation of good faith has recently been implied into an agreement by Leggatt J in *Yam Seng Pte Ltd v International Trade Corporation Ltd* [2013] EWHC 111. The particular characteristics of the contract—a distributorship agreement—appear to have been material in the implication.

[34] See, eg, the European Commission's proposed Regulation on a Common European Sales Law. Art 2(b) states 'good faith and fair dealing means a standard of conduct characterised by honesty, openness and consideration for the interests of the other party to the transaction or relationship in question'. This duty cannot be excluded by contract terms.

[35] R Summers, '"Good Faith" in General Contract Law and the Sales Provisions of the Uniform Commercial Code' (1968) 54 *Virginia Law Review* 195, 196. In *Philips Electronique Grand Public SA v British Sky Broadcasting Ltd* [1995] EMLR 472, the Court of Appeal hinted that there might be an implied duty of good faith in performance of the contract, but since the trial judge had found that the defendant had not acted in bad faith, according to the limits prescribed by the adversarial model, such a duty was not material: per Bingham LJ, 483. See also R Brownsword, *Contract Law: Themes for the Twenty-first Century*, 2nd edn (Oxford, OUP, 2006) 129–30.

[36] For an example of duties of good faith expressed in substantive terms, see the proposed Regulation on a Common European Sales Law, above n 34. For a procedural understanding

recognise such duties of good faith in some contexts, but this might be regarded as stipulating an exception to the classical model of self-interested dealing, leaving that model substantially intact. Alternatively, recognition could be regarded as setting the legal default position whereby parties are expected to act in good faith towards one another, but are able to bargain for more attenuated duties.[37] There is no developed concept of good faith in general English contract law, although certain contracts (for example, insurance) and jural relationships (involving fiduciaries) have good faith duties attached. To the extent that good faith is recognised within general English contract law, this tends to be in exceptional, exclusive and procedural terms. In terms of contract negotiations, that English law recognised any duty to negotiate in good faith and reach agreement was roundly rejected by Lord Justice Ackner in *Walford v Miles*.[38] In other commercial contexts, however, parties may owe duties to one another that are broadly consistent with an idea of good faith—to make a party aware of onerous or unusual terms, for example—in order for these terms to be incorporated into the agreement.[39] English law does impose other duties during the negotiating process enforced through the law relating to deceit, misrepresentation and estoppel. However, these are general duties not to commit fraud, act dishonestly or mislead. To act in good faith usually requires something more than just the absence of fraud or dishonesty.[40] What this 'something more' is remains a matter of debate. In substantive terms it usually requires one party to take some account of the legitimate interests of the other party. A more rigorous interpretation may be that it involves duties of loyalty, at least to the contract purpose. English law may not impose default duties of good faith in performance, but may achieve such outcomes indirectly through contractual routes, such as implied terms.[41] Similarly contextual interpretation methods may prevent a party relying on a contract's literal meaning if that would defeat the contract purpose or extend its ambit in ways not intended,[42] or a reasonable person would understand that the contract communicated something different to its strict literal meaning.[43]

see Brightman LJ in *Interfoto Picture Library v Stiletto Visual Programmes Ltd* [1989] QB 433, 439: 'its effect is perhaps most aptly conveyed by such metaphorical colloquialisms as "playing fair", "coming clean" or "putting one's cards face upwards on the table". It is in essence a principle of fair and open dealing'.

[37] R Brownsword, 'Two Concepts of Good Faith' (1994) 7 *Journal of Contract Law* 197, 199–200.

[38] *Walford v Miles* [1992] 2 AC 128, 138.

[39] *Interfoto v Stiletto*, above n 36.

[40] See Bingham LJ in ibid, 439.

[41] See, eg, the different approaches between the majority (implied term) and minority (bad faith) in the Court of Appeal decision in *Bournemouth and Boscombe AFC Ltd v Manchester United FC Ltd* [1980] *The Times*, May 22. See also Brownsword, above n 37, 204.

[42] *Lloyds TSB Foundation for Scotland v Lloyds Banking Group plc* [2013] UKSC 3, per Lord Mance, [23].

[43] *Mannai Investment Co Ltd v Eagle Star Life Assurance Co Ltd* [1997] AC 749.

These instances may be regarded as examples of good faith in substance. The argument in support of this fragmented approach may be that specific doctrines allow for greater certainty and integrity in the legal rules. The response is that working out the precise sphere of operation of each of these doctrines and their requirements depends on drawing fine distinctions which are easier in theory than in practice and that ultimately they raise indistinguishable issues of principle. Lord Steyn, writing extra-judicially, supports the ideas that lie behind the concept, although in line with many judges he is not convinced that such a general provision is necessary in the law.[44] English law's approach has been heavily criticised, however, on the basis that judging contracting parties' behaviour through the filters imposed by existing doctrine tends to obscure and distort the genuine problem with which the law must wrestle.[45] Thus implied-terms doctrine presents the issue as whether a contract contains a gap that the law should fill. It is an extension of the process of interpreting the contract.[46] A more accurate articulation of the issue at the heart of a case may be to ask whether the defendant has behaved reasonably.

The reluctance of the law to embrace an overriding concept of good faith could be regarded as a necessary corollary of its general approach to contracts—that they are the product of individualism, consent and autonomy, and it is not the law's role to police contractor behaviour except within narrow limits prescribed by the law. One of the results of this commitment is that outcomes are sought to be mediated through contractual routes, that is, justification for imposition of duties that do not expressly appear in the contract are nevertheless sought to be derived from the parties' agreement, however oblique the connection. This is illustrated in relation to the controls on the exercise of discretionary powers in a contract. Such powers should not be exercised arbitrarily or capriciously[47] but genuinely and rationally, in light of the aims of the agreement, the common interests of the parties and the likely behaviour of reasonable counterparts to the actual parties.[48] This is regarded as giving effect to the intended agreement rather than imposing a wholly external standard. While the idea that English

[44] Lord Steyn, 'Contract Law: Fulfilling the Reasonable Expectations of Honest Men' (1997) 113 *LQR* 433, 438–39.

[45] Brownsword, above n 35, 123–24.

[46] *Attorney General of Belize v Belize Telecom Ltd* [2009] UKPC 10; [2009] Bus LR 1316.

[47] *Paragon Finance plc v Staunton and Nash* [2002] 1 WLR 685; *GAN Insurance v Tai Ping Insurance (No 2)* [2002] EWCA Civ 248, [2002] All ER (D) 10.

[48] *Horkulak v Cantor Fitzgerald* [2004] IRLR 942. In that case it was held that even what appear to be unlimited contract discretionary powers were subject to an implied term that they must be exercised 'genuinely and rationally'. See also *Abu Dhabi National Tanker Company v Product Star Shipping Ltd (The 'Product Star')* [1993] 1 Lloyds Rep 397, per Leggatt J, at 404.

law rejects a notion of good faith is overstated,[49] it is accurate to say that what is rejected is a freestanding version of good faith that operates independently of the contract, the contracting community and market context, or some other external referent that both explains why its application is appropriate and gives the duty some content.[50] The difficulty then is not that English law does not recognise broad duties of good faith, but that the conceptualisation of it is disjointed. Filtering the operation of good-faith concerns through doctrines or contract terms tends to obscure its precise role in the law, and also renders more difficult any attempt to make the good-faith duty a standard that underpins the conduct of the entire business relationship. This latter issue will be illustrated in Chapter 4.

Similar issues are raised over the interaction between commercial law and equity. Equity in particular, perhaps by its mandate to pursue a more individualised and context-specific form of justice, has played a more direct role in lending effectiveness to the merchant-created tools of commerce, such as reservation of title clauses.[51] Equity has also furnished general concepts, such as promissory estoppel, that have mitigated some of the rigidity of contract law. As with good faith though, these are treated as exceptional interventions into the classical law. There is a marked reluctance to let general equitable considerations play any consistent role in commercial contract law, perhaps because of equity's emphasis on good conscience as a standard, which appears opposed to the self-interested economic rationality that is often thought to characterise the model of the contractor underlying classical contract law.[52] So equity will not assist in overturning freely agreed transactions, even in the face of what appear to be minor infractions of the contract terms.[53] This is thought necessary for certainty in trading and to take speedy action at short notice without concern about the possibility of unwarranted, unpredictable and potentially vexatious legal intervention. The parties may manifest a degree of trust in one another, but as far as the law is concerned, the basis of the relationship is not fiduciary but bargain.[54] A corollary to this is that there are some relationships between the parties

[49] See the remarkable recent judgment by Leggatt J where he was willing to imply an obligation to act in good faith on the parties to a distributorship agreement: *Yam Seng Pte Ltd v International Trade Corp Ltd*, above n 33, [142].

[50] V Sims, 'Good Faith in Contract Law: Of Triggers and Concentric Circles' (2005) 16 *Kings College Law Journal* 293, 295.

[51] *Aluminium Industrie Vaassen BV v Romalpa Aluminium Ltd* [1976] 1 WLR 676.

[52] TT Arvind, 'Contract Transactions and Equity' in LA DiMatteo, Q Zhou, S Saintier and K Rowley (eds), *Commercial Contract Law: Transatlantic Perspectives* (Cambridge, CUP, 2013) 146, 166.

[53] See *The Scaptrade*, above n 24; *Union Eagle v Golden Achievement* [1997] AC 514. Relief against forfeiture was denied in both cases, consistent with the idea that commercial contracting parties are not fiduciaries.

[54] Sir J Mummery, 'Commercial Notions and Equitable Potions' in S Worthington (ed), *Commercial Law and Commercial Practice* (Oxford, Hart Publishing, 2003) 29, 42–43.

that can be regarded as 'exclusively commercial'[55] and with this comes the understanding that only the attenuated duties stipulated by the contract and contract law are owed between the parties. Given that law entertains the possibility that such 'arm's-length' trades exist, it is easy to regard notions of good faith or equitable considerations as antithetical to the underpinning foundation of commercial contract law. This may be again due to the impersonal and abstract nature of the express terms that the law often takes as constituting the basis upon which business proceeds. The irony is that judges appear to be acutely aware that this model does not reflect reality in all but a few contracting contexts. Lord Justice Millett put this well when he wrote,

> there has never been a greater need to impose on those who engage in commerce the high standards of conduct which equity demands. The common law insists on honesty, diligence and the due performance of contractual obligations. But equity insists on nobler and subtler qualities: loyalty, fidelity, integrity, respect for confidentiality, and the disinterested discharge of obligations of trust and confidence.[56]

Context plays an important role here, suggestive of the circumstances, in particular the expectations of participants in the market, in which courts may be prepared to be more flexible.[57] All this suggests that while there are conditions under which attention to self-interest would be warranted as opposed to any other regarding behaviour, this should not be taken to be the governing and underpinning norm that either fully explains, or should explain, exchange behaviour. Thus it does not seem too much to say that such duties may form an important part of the expectations of commercial contractors.

This brief discussion of good faith and equity raises a more general point concerning the extent to which general normative criteria could be regarded as a source of commercial expectations. Courts appear reluctant to admit any default role for co-operative norms in the contractual relationship (unless filtered through express or implied contract terms) lest it oust the competitive model of the contractor. Yet there appears to be no concession that the courts often prevent the untrammelled consequences of this competitive model from taking effect, usually by appealing to commercial reasonableness, and that this constitutes in itself an implicit appeal to certain values and standards. It has been noted that Brownsword supports the contention that contract law adopt a default position of co-operative dealing. Co-operation is not a moral theory in itself though, but rather may be the conclusion or result that follows from the application of a moral theory

[55] PJ Millett, 'Equity's Place in the Law of Commerce' (1998) 114 *LQR* 214.
[56] Ibid, 216.
[57] See Leggatt J in *Yam Seng v International Trade Corporation Ltd*, above n 33.

to the rules of contract law.[58] Could a commercial-expectations argument be constructed on such a normative basis?

NORMATIVE DERIVATION OF COMMERCIAL EXPECTATIONS

Two different possible assertions should be distinguished here. The first is that a contractor might advance a normative argument concerning why a particular expectation of theirs should be enforced. Here the expectation itself may not be based on a general normative ground, but the reason for the law to enforce it is. So, to give an example, a business contractor may have a certain expectation concerning the extent of his liability for breach of contract based on his experience of trade practice. Whether a court should enforce this expectation may depend on normative grounds of general fairness that contract law (or fringe doctrines, such as estoppel) often support, such as one party's reliance on the other's assurance that the expectation would be honoured. Under English contract law though, it is more likely that enforcement of the expectation is sought through incorporating it into the contract. Even here though, it is often apparent that fairness considerations may be working in the background, strengthening the justification for the incorporation. In *The Achilleas*, for example, Lord Hoffmann was not prepared to hold that a ship's charterer accepted liability for the shipowner's wider consequential losses on the late redelivery of a ship just because the possible loss could be foreseen.[59] It was necessary to demonstrate that the charterer had *assumed responsibility* for the loss. In this case no such responsibility had been assumed because of the industry understanding that the charterer was only liable for losses arising from the period of the delay, not beyond. This appears as a straightforward recognition of practice-based commercial expectations. But considerations of commercial prudence (no reasonable business person would accept liability for an unquantifiable loss) and fairness (the extent of liability should be proportionate to the degree of fault) also played a role.

The second assertion is that the expectation itself should be supported because it is a reflection of a moral commitment that the law ought to enforce, whether it constitutes a matter of commercial practice or not. The idea that substantive commercial expectations could be normatively derived is quite controversial, particularly if the norms appealed to encompass general moral

[58] Thus Brownsword derives his support for a default of co-operative dealing for contract law from the application of Alan Gewirth's moral theory and 'Principle of Generic Consistency': Brownsword, above n 27, 27–30.

[59] *Transfield Shipping Inc v Mercator Shipping Inc (The Achilleas)* [2008] UKHL 48; [2009] 1 AC 61.

standards and not just the locally operating practices in isolated industries or geographical areas, or in specific contractual relationships. On the other hand one could argue that the whole of contract is ultimately underpinned by a normative expectation—that a contractor will keep their word and do what they said they would do. There is some empirical support for the idea that the majority of commercial contractors have such an expectation of their contracting partners.[60] Beyond this rather basic moral feature, however, the extent to which contractors are required to act morally or ethically towards one another, and whether this is a justified expectation amongst commercial contractors, is uncertain.

It might be argued that contracts and contract law are precisely required to assist non-trusting and impersonal contractors to make agreements with each other. In other words the point of contract law is to facilitate the arm's-length deal between relative strangers.[61] In such a conception, the law's role is fairly limited and certainly it cannot shield people from all instances of immoral behaviour. The courts have consistently denied that they have explicit power to impose autonomous requirements to act reasonably on commercial contractors, or that contracts themselves have to be reasonable, although there can be no doubt that there is some implicit support for this standard, exercised through doctrines such as interpretation and implied terms. Another problem is that it may be difficult to distinguish between when a commercial contractor is acting out of true moral consideration for a contracting partner, which must fundamentally be other-regarding, and when he is merely undertaking an act of enlightened self-interest. This might be thought to be a minor point, however, since first, separating out the other-regarding and self-regarding motivations for action is difficult, and second, if commercial contractors display certain normative commitments in their behaviour towards one another, their motivation for doing so is immaterial. What matters is what their outward conduct may lead the other to believe. Contract law has always taken the view that actions and the reasonable beliefs that may be raised in others are more important than any inner intentions. Of course it is in the traditional character of commercial contract law that it appears largely unconcerned with matters of personal ethics and equity between the parties. What may appear unethical by the standards of a reasonable person may nevertheless be permissible according to the law. This can been seen in the courts' attempts to police a boundary between unacceptable, dishonest or unconscionable behaviour

[60] Macaulay in his seminal 1963 study identified one widely accepted norm in business: 'Commitments are to be honoured in almost all situations; one does not welsh on a deal'. See 'Non-Contractual Relations in Business: A Preliminary Study' (1963) 28 *American Sociological Review* 55, 63.

[61] D Kimel, *From Promise to Contract* (Oxford, Hart Publishing, 2005) 78–80 and 'The Choice of Paradigm for Theory of Contract: Reflections on the Relational Model' (2007) 27 *OJLS* 233, 247.

and acceptable negotiating tactics or the legitimate pursuit, and pressing home, of a market advantage.[62] The lines between acceptable and unacceptable forms of behaviour retain a reassuring fuzziness however.

While positing universal standards of ethical business behaviour which the law will uphold would seem to be problematic,[63] there appears to be no reason to think that a lack of normative or ethical commitments is characteristic of commercial dealing generally. As will be seen in the following chapter, expectations of loyalty, trust, flexibility, co-operation, honesty and information sharing may be seen in many contractual contexts. Courts are increasingly recognising the importance and role of these values and norms in commercial contracting. Consider this very recent statement from Leggatt J in *Yam Seng Pte Ltd v International Trade Corporation Ltd*:

> [T]he relevant background against which contracts are made includes not only matters of fact known to the parties but also shared values and norms of behaviour. Some of these are norms that command general social acceptance; others may be specific to a particular trade or commercial activity; others may be more specific still, arising from features of the particular contractual relationship. Many such norms are naturally taken for granted by the parties when making any contract without being spelt out in the document recording their agreement.
>
> A paradigm example of a general norm which underlies almost all contractual relationships is an expectation of honesty. That expectation is essential to commerce, which depends critically on trust. Yet it is seldom, if ever, made the subject of an express contractual obligation. Indeed if a party in negotiating the terms of a contract were to seek to include a provision which expressly required the other party to act honestly, the very fact of doing so might well damage the parties' relationship by the lack of trust which this would signify.[64]

It might be argued here that the mere existence of such norms is not in itself an argument for the legalisation of them, and that there may be good reasons why such broad normative commitments or standards of flexibility, co-operation and loyalty to a contracting partner remain outwith the legal sphere. Alternatively though, it is possible to build arguments that support the legal enforceability of the normative commitments that may be apparent in business dealing. The reason why general normative values might be thought important to contract practice and hence commercial expectations is simply because of an often overlooked fact that was noted in relation to co-operation: that contracting will not take place at all without some bare level of commitment to these values, particularly trust. While there seems to be some scepticism on the part of judges and contractors themselves

[62] *George Wimpey UK Ltd v V I Construction Ltd* [2005] EWCA Civ 77 [60]; also *CTN Cash and Carry Ltd v Gallagher Ltd* [1994] 4 All ER 714.

[63] Although supported by some, eg B Mescher, 'Business Ethics and the Law of Contract' (2009) 8 *Journal of Law and Financial Management* 8.

[64] Above n 33 [134–35].

that the law can create a commitment to such values by mandating that contractors display them, undoubtedly law can play an important role in encouraging and supporting the development of such values between the parties themselves.

While freedom of contract may be regarded as the mantra of English contract law, this should not be taken to mean the law adopts or supports an amoral attitude towards commercial contracting, such that it perceives its role as ascribing legal validity to whatever actions a contractor takes in furtherance of their commercial interests. Far from it. Although it may be difficult to discern if there exist any absolute and universal standards of commercial behaviour as opposed to practice-based ones, clearly any 'expectation' that contractors might have that they could behave completely in their own self-interest are not supported by law. Thus a contract whose performance has become unprofitable for one of the parties will still be legally enforceable if there are no legally mandated avenues of escape.[65] Change of circumstances does not generally allow parties to depart from the agreed terms, since one important function of contract law is to provide security for transactions. So, while contract law is important to facilitating commercial transactions, this is not its only function and it has a regulatory role in commercial dealing that extends beyond merely curbing the very worst excesses of self-interested behaviour.

It must also be remembered that contract law is the *generally applicable law* on contractual obligations and part of a larger set of rules of private law. Stephen Smith writes that private law presents itself in normative language: the language of 'duties', 'rights', 'wrongs' and, as a normative institution, it 'tells citizens how they ought to behave'.[66] Hence one talks not just of contracts, but contractual *obligations*. This normativity is important if people are to perceive that the law provides reasons for obedience and action that are not solely instrumental or concerned with avoiding unpleasant sanctions. Certainly the rules of contract law may be regarded as more power conferring than duty imposing,[67] but nevertheless this normative basis is not absent since 'welfare-enhancing exchange necessarily rests on a moral framework institutionalized in law'.[68] Under this view, contract law cannot be concerned solely with interpreting commercial contract behaviour, but directing and guiding it according to this moral framework. The precise point of many, although not all, rules of law is to articulate this normativity in more concrete terms. As has been seen the courts have implied

[65] Eg, *Durham Tees Valley Airport v BMIBaby Ltd* [2010] EWCA Civ 485; [2011] 1 All ER (Comm) 731.

[66] SA Smith, 'The Normativity of Private Law' (2011) 31 *OJLS* 215, 215 and 221.

[67] Hart, above n 17, 27–28.

[68] D Campbell, 'The Incompleteness of Our Understanding of the Law and Economics of Relational Contract' (2004) *Wisconsin Law Review* 645, 673.

terms into agreements which require a contractor to undertake some act according to a standard of reasonableness, to avoid arbitrary and capricious decision making, or not to act so as to damage a relationship of trust and confidence between the parties.[69] While these terms were applied in specific and largely non-commercial contexts, they are all instances where a court has recognised that something more than simple performance in accordance with the express terms was required. While it may be difficult to posit universally accepted norms of business ethics, contract context may suggest that a normatively richer background informs trading beyond the bare legal minimum and there is no compelling reason to think that commercial relationships will never display this quality, nor that the law cannot respond to it.

CHANGES IN CONTRACTING PRACTICE

If the classical law of contract is built upon a representative ideal of a single buyer and seller meeting in a market place, haggling over terms, reaching agreement on all issues and then performing, it is abundantly clear that few agreements match this model. Of course it could be argued that the model is necessarily simplistic and has never been intended as a description of reality. Rather it a necessary feature of the law's generalising nature, which tends towards abstraction in analysing the transaction or individual bargain as a separate entity from anything else that may occur between the parties. Although commercial transactors manage their productive and exchange relationships through a variety of complex methods, the law assumes most of this complexity can be reduced to a set of terms or a series of transactions. This form of simplification has been reinforced by the approach of institutional economics, which has considered how far it is specific transactional features that give rise to distinctive types of contract governance. In very simple organisational terms, contracting is usually associated with the market transaction between relatively independent organisations relying on impersonal third-party enforcement according to a set of rules. At the other end of the organisational spectrum are firms, where productive activity and exchange are organised internally within a hierarchical structure. Governance within firms is according to internal management directives, administrative processes and company law rather than the law of contract. Of course there are other methods of managing exchange between independent economic actors along this spectrum, such as by reference to informal norms and reputational sanctions, or through relatively formal private

[69] *Malik and Mahmud v Bank of Credit and Commerce International SA (in liq)* [1997] 3 WLR 95.

clubs or trade associations.[70] Institutional (or transaction cost) economics has been very influential in strengthening the association between contract law and the impersonal market transaction. This line of scholarship is considered further below, along with two developments that have served to undermine the findings of institutional economics: the phenomenon of contract networks and umbrella agreements. These new forms of governing agreements have implications for contract law, since the latter's forms and assumptions may conflict with the conditions and constraints under which these new forms of governance have emerged, leading to dissonance between contract law and commercial expectation.

The Influence of Transaction Cost Economics

Perhaps the most influential institutional economist, Oliver Williamson, considered the factors giving rise to contract governance regimes and in particular the motivation behind 'make or buy' decisions by firms with respective 'hierarchy or market' governance mechanisms. Williamson identified the transaction costs associated with each form of governance as largely determinative of the choice between these methods. He pointed to three specific transactional features that influenced the decision over whether transactions are integrated within firms or pursued through contracts: level of asset specificity (or sunk investments) involved in the relationship, level of uncertainty and frequency of the transactions.[71] Thus high levels of these variables give rise to a greater likelihood of a transaction or exchange occurring within a firm, or the product or process being absorbed within the firm. Williamson also sought to associate these characteristics with Ian Macneil's typology of contract law schemes, distinguishing in particular the circumstances where the classical law-grounded agreement, as opposed to the relational contract, would be more appropriate. Market governance, enforced and defined through the rules of classical contract law is appropriate for standardised, non-specific transactions, where identity of parties is unimportant (asset specificity, frequency of exchange and levels of uncertainty are low).[72] This corresponds with Macneil's idea of discreteness in contracts and enforcement by litigation. Specialised and relational governance structures are appropriate for recurrent transactions (high frequency) with mixed

[70] See especially the work of Lisa Bernstein, discussed in Chs 1 and 3.

[71] O Williamson, *The Economic Institutions of Capitalism* (New York, Free Press, 1985) 72. See also EB Rock and MLWachter, 'Islands of Conscious Power: Law, Norms, and the Self-Governing Corporation' (2001) 149 *University of Pennsylvania Law Review* 1619, 1631–32; and A Ogus, *Costs and Cautionary Tales* (Oxford, Hart Publishing, 2006) 47–56, distinguishing market contracting, relational contracting and various forms of business integration, substantially following Williamson.

[72] Williamson, above n 71, 74.

or highly specific investments where the transaction cannot be standardised. Increasing degrees of asset specificity give rise to an increased likelihood of integration, whereupon the transaction moves out of the market to be subject to hierarchical (management) governance within the firm.[73] Contract law has little role to play in regulating these internal arrangements.

Williamson's classification has been criticised as too tidy in its distinctions and insufficiently attentive to the complexity and amorphism that occurs within exchange forms, each with its own unique social and economic context.[74] Thomas Palay's study of rail freight contracting bears out this criticism in some respects.[75] For example, transportation of fungible goods requiring no special accommodation might be thought appropriate for market governance through impersonal contracts. Yet Palay found such agreements were found to require little contract planning or co-ordination, and enforcement mechanisms relied on the very credible threat to switch to alternative sources of supply.[76] Even in the case of the 'discrete agreement' it was still hoped that a relationship of repeat trading would develop and this motivated performance more than any legal mechanisms. As soon as specific investments were required, for example, as the goods transported became less standardised (finished automobiles, hazardous chemicals), requiring modifications or special accommodations, then there was a shift to more relational forms of contracting.[77] Parties often undertook what might be regarded as uncommercial behaviour (for example, undertaking actions to accommodate customers which offered no immediate benefit to the railroad) to maintain a business relationship.[78] However, Palay also found that idiosyncratic transactions (involving specific investments) were more likely to engage in exchanges of information for structural planning (for example, the development of rules or procedures for dealing with unforeseen contingencies and long-term problems). The findings show that a mixture of relational and 'classical' formal norms operate in all kinds of agreement. Spot contracts involving fungible goods are partly enforced by the desire for repeat trades, and not just contract law. Transactions

[73] Ibid, 78.

[74] WW Powell, 'Neither Market Nor Hierarchy: Network Forms of Organisation' (1990) 12 *Research in Organizational Behaviour* 295, 299.

[75] TM Palay, 'Comparative Institutional Economics: The Governance of Rail Freight Contracting' (1984) 13 *Journal of Legal Studies* 265. See also PL Joskow, 'Contract Duration and Relationship-Specific Investment: Empirical Evidence from Coal Markets' (1987) 77 *The American Economic Review* 168; and JP Esser, 'Institutionalizing Industry: The Changing Forms of Contract' (1996) 21 *Law and Social Enquiry* 593, 598.

[76] Palay, above n 75, 268.

[77] See also Joskow, above n 75: agreements involving relationship-specific investments rely less on repeat bargaining and more upon long-term contracting (which at the time could be assimilable with relational contracts). That is, parties will try and set the terms from the start for a longer duration of expected repeat trades. They will not keep negotiating specific transactions.

[78] Palay, above n 75, 277.

involving uncertainty and specific investments, while showing a high degree of relationality, also show a level of information exchange and planning, although ensuring this planning was legally binding was not of paramount concern. Idiosyncratic investments may be a strong motivator to develop relational bonds in order to deal with trouble informally, but planning was also thought to be important. Thus in both a discrete and a more idiosyncratic exchange, relational norms of co-operation may be relevant. Idiosyncratic investments may be a strong motivator to develop relational bonds in order to deal with trouble informally to avoid wasted sunk costs, but planning and information sharing may also be important and neither of these things (bond of trust and planning) guarantee there will be no recourse to courts to enforce rights. Even in the classically discrete 'spot trades', a desire for repeat custom may be an important norm which has the potential to affect how the relationship is conducted.

Although Williamson's analysis may be a little too precise, isolating the features of relationships and transactions in this way is valuable in identifying some of the factors that might dictate preferences for certain forms of governance. In ascertaining the likely users of legally enforceable agreements, it suggests who the 'audience' for contract law rules might be. However, it has less to say about the design of the rules themselves. The law is simply the set of rules that organises the market exchange, and most of its content will be taken as a given. Despite this, Williamson's work has led others to consider what transactional features will lead to a preference for a specific type of *contract* regime and contract interpretation method. Badawi has considered how different kinds of contractual arrangements and interpretative regimes in the US (general commercial arbitration, industry-specific arbitration, formal methods under the common law of contract and the more contextual methods used by the Uniform Commercial Code) correspond with particular features of transactions. Understandably he focuses on the costs involved in *ex ante* gap-filling (that is, trying to write complete contracts) as the most important factor governing this choice. Thus it is not possible to choose between either formalist or contextualist interpretative method as superior in abstract terms since this must depend on the merits of the transaction.[79] Legal rules may constitute the market, especially for those diffuse and heterogeneous contractors that cannot rely on kinship networks, reputational sanctions and private legal systems to provide low-cost security for trading, but one cannot conclude from this that agreements between heterogeneous contractors will always proceed along formalist lines. Badawi argues formalism of common law methods is likely to be preferred where 'transactions are frequent and certain because

[79] D Charny, 'Nonlegal Sanctions in Commercial Relationships' (1990) 104 *Harvard Law Review* 373, 466–67 arguing neither formalism nor contextualism has a priori dominance since the decision to rely on legal or non-legal sanctions is transaction dependent.

those situations present optimal conditions for drafting nearly complete contracts, which parties would want enforced by the agreement's express terms'.[80] In these circumstances there is a reduced need for extrinsic evidence to interpret the agreement. Infrequent, complex transactions, where there is significant predictive or linguistic uncertainty, impose higher transaction costs on contractors, which leaves them less likely to draft a complete contract. Such agreements may be better served by more contextual interpretative standards such as those adopted by the Uniform Commercial Code. Contract measures may be dispensed with entirely if the 'insularity' of a group is likely to make it more reliant on reputational and social sanctioning. Insular groups have less incentive to develop formal legal contracts and institutional enforcement processes, although when a group becomes more heterogeneous or geographically dispersed, reliance on social and reputational sanctions becomes less effective, and more formal rule systems and dispute resolution processes may be developed. This Badawi finds borne out by Bernstein's empirical studies across various commodity markets in the US, which he characterises as high frequency, low uncertainty and, in some instances at least, high insularity.[81] These features give rise to use of formal contracts and formal interpretation methods applied by formal dispute resolution procedures, but governed by trade associations rather than the public legal system. Parties that rely on a high degree of trust or that display cultural homogeneity will be very unlikely to litigate their disputes before courts.[82]

The findings of the work of Williamson and Badawi may be assumed to vindicate the design of classical contract law since they show that there are parties contracting in certain contexts who may display a strong preference for relatively formal enforcement. Transactions involving low risk (low uncertainty), low frequency and low asset specificity may be particularly suitable for governance by contract and contract law. At the other end of the scale, high levels of each of these variables may lead to increasingly tailored contract regimes, including more relational contract methods and possible greater reliance on trust and informal norms to govern the agreement. Such arrangements may fall outwith the scope of contract law (at the parties' choice) and into the territory of arbitral or industry-specific dispute resolution. However, while undoubtedly illuminating in some respects, there is a danger of over-simplification. Courts do not select the disputes that come before them on the basis of fit with transaction cost economics' methods and assumptions. Rather the law must resolve any and all kinds of dispute brought before it. Many if not most exchanges are unlikely to fall neatly into either wholly formal or wholly relational camps, but will

[80] Badawi, above n 6, 5.
[81] Ibid, 21.
[82] See, eg, Bernstein, above n 7.

lie somewhere in between. For example consider an agreement between relative strangers on a long-term project involving high risk, high uncertainty, high asset specificity, but little chance of repeat trading. This kind of arrangement appears to have no obvious 'contract governance' corollary in the above scheme. Such a project may be highly reliant on co-operation, information sharing and flexibility over performance, yet the high-risk and uncertain nature of the project, combined with lack of trading history between the parties, may also lead to a preference for a comprehensive written contract to govern the arrangement. As far as a written agreement is achievable at all, this may be in only very open-ended terms with many gaps. These gaps are not easily filled by 'custom or usage', because there is none, and contextual understandings are not derived from repeat trading or any developed sense of trust. Such parties may need to rely to some extent on the law or formal contracts to govern their agreement, but an application of the classical law, with its emphasis on certainty and formality, appears highly inappropriate. This matters since it is apparent that such agreements are not exceptional or isolated phenomena, but represent an increasingly prevalent norm.

Networks

An analogue to the above sort of market arrangement in the business studies, management and social science literature is the hybrid or network. These are relationships facilitating inter-firm trades that are not fully assimilated with the market exchange (between completely separate or economically autonomous entities) nor hierarchy (within firms). Such looser structures embody 'relations of mutual dependence between organisations which retain their separate identity as legal and/or economic entities'.[83] These relations 'exemplify a distinct form of economic coordination which is 'neither market nor hierarchy'.[84] Networks display no obvious and exclusive overriding commitment to any of the traditional forms of exchange governance. They have been described as characterised by 'reciprocal patterns of communication and exchange' and as such fall within a space between markets and hierarchies, giving rise to a third, 'middle' form of exchange.[85] It may be disputed whether networks fall between market or hierarchy on the basis that this suggests networks are something like *both* market and

[83] A Arrighetti, R Bachmann and S Deakin, 'Contract Law, Social Norms and Inter-firm Co-operation' (1997) 21 *Cambridge Journal of Economics* 171, 172.
[84] Ibid.
[85] Powell, above n 74, 295. Powell gives publishing and construction as two examples of industries based on network organisation.

hierarchy, when arguably they are an entirely different concept,[86] but it is a helpful way of conceptualising networks for the issue that is of concern here, namely contract law's capacity to deal with different ways of organising exchange. Factors such as complexity, vertical disintegration and the need for innovation in rapidly changing environments has led to more collaboration between independent firms.[87] Powell writes that the three critical components of networks are the demand for speed, know-how and trust.[88] These imperatives have given rise to specialised, long-term and relatively co-operative contracting regimes where continuity of relationships is valued between the independent firms. While the idea of collaboration suggests co-operation is key, there is still the need for this to be managed, particularly if a fully trusting relationship has not yet developed. This collaboration may be more or less contractual and may demonstrate repeat patterns of contracting. This need to manage the relationship may manifest itself in some degree of planning, but this is fairly open ended, often specifying collaborative processes rather than outcomes,[89] since 'the precise goal and manner of achieving [the outcome] only become clear in the course of the parties' collaboration'.[90] Change is anticipated throughout the life of the project and is expected to be dealt with flexibly.

These kinds of agreement display many features that, on the face of it at least, would make contract law a poor choice for their regulation. Lorenz, for example, examined the phenomenon of 'disintegration' amongst firms (hiving off activities previously undertaken 'in-house' to subcontractor firms in an effort to lower costs) thus signalling a return to market transactions over hierarchical forms of governance. However, the expectations about how these market transactions would be conducted was very different. Expectations were not of arm's-length contracts, conducted anonymously or atomistically, but with reference to 'partnership' loyalty, a 'moral contract' and mutual trust.[91] The expectations that go along with partnership include a guaranteed level of orders in return for quality work, full information on pricing, adaptations responding to genuine changed circumstances only and not opportunistic ones.[92] Thus in such long-term, ongoing relations, trust is essential, since it reduces the need for comprehensive and costly planning,

[86] Ibid, 299.

[87] RJ Gilson, CF Sabel and RE Scott, 'Braiding: The Interaction of Formal and Informal Contracting in Theory, Practice and Doctrine' (2010) 110 *Columbia Law Review* 1377, 1382.

[88] Powell, above n 74, 324.

[89] Gilson, Sabel and Scott, above n 87, 1404.

[90] Ibid, 1385.

[91] EH Lorenz, 'Neither Friends Nor Strangers: Informal Networks of Subcontracting in French Industry' in D Gambetta (ed), *Trust: Making and Breaking Cooperative Relations* (Oxford, Basil Blackwell, 1988) 194, 195–96.

[92] Ibid, 206.

and any planning undertaken is necessarily imperfect.[93] Even if there is a set of contractual documents these may serve as a comprehensive 'constitution' for governing the relationship, specifying procedures for monitoring performance, reporting progress and stipulating incentives, rather than legal obligations to achieve certain outcomes.[94] Given the incompleteness involved, the role of courts in this type of arrangement is ambiguous.[95] Even though these agreements are planned, the focus of the planning may be different and less amenable to regulation by classical contract law, which assumes relatively fixed and certain planning tailored to the legal obligations assumed by the parties, according to which disputes will be resolved. Contract law enforcement appears less suitable to relationships where the contract documents perform more diffuse functions.

The extent to which networks fall to be regulated or facilitated by contract law might be regarded as a matter of debate, at least insofar as faithfulness to the network concept involves something more than breaking the diffuse relationships down into their constituent contractual parts and dealing with each as a separate contractual event, requiring an isolated and individual response. Contracting may be associated with low commitment between independent actors in a climate of suspicion, whereas a network is based on relational means of communication with a high level of commitment and trust between interdependent actors in a climate of open-ended information exchange.[96] If falling within neither contracts nor organisations, networks might be thought more suitable to regulation through the law of tort rather than contracts, or else some special rules for 'contract clusters' or network contracts, sensitive to contract purpose, should be developed.[97] Alternatively it may be thought that networks are simply too nebulous, diffuse and indeterminate to be subject to legal regulation at all.[98] Law must work networks through its own conceptual machinery, such that what emerges from the other side of this legalising process will be transformed from what it was.[99] Collins describes contractual networks as consisting

> of a number of independent firms that enter a pattern of interrelated contracts, which are designed to confer on the parties many of the benefits of co-ordination

[93] Ibid, 202.

[94] P Vincent-Jones, 'Contractual Governance: Institutional and Organizational Analysis' (2000) 20 *OJLS* 317, 327–28. See also M Suchman, 'The Contract as Social Artifact' (2003) 37 *Law and Society Review* 91, 99–100 and 107; and C Bridgeman, 'Contracts as Plans' (2009) *University of Illinois Law Review* 341.

[95] Lorenz, above n 91, 199.

[96] Powell, above n 74, 300.

[97] R Brownsword, 'Network Contracts Revisited' in M Amstutz and G Teubner (eds), *Networks: Legal Issues of Multilateral Co-operation* (Oxford, Hart Publishing, 2009) 31, 32.

[98] RM Buxbaum, 'Is "Network" a Legal Concept?' (1993) 149 *Journal of Institutional and Theoretical Economics* 698.

[99] M Amstutz, V Karavas and G Teubner, 'Preface: What is Legal Analysis of Contractual Networks?' in Amstutz and Teubner (eds), above n 97, ix.

> achieved through vertical integration in a single firm, without in fact ever creating a single integrated business entity such as a corporation or a partnership.[100]

Collins regards the network concept as neither covered by business-organisations law nor the law of contract, and a new legal concept is required[101] that can reflect the dynamic of the network which commits itself to competition and co-operation at different times.[102] Certainly a multi-party network would face difficulty in contract law. The law tends to regard such arrangements as a linear chain where obligations are owed only to the next party in the chain, and the extent of liability and obligation is prescribed by the doctrine of privity of contract.[103]

Whatever doubts are harboured about the applicability of contract law to these new forms of agreement, there are lessons for contract law in the academic debate surrounding networks, since the issue of what to do about networks relates in part to the characteristic features of these phenomena (insofar as these can be identified) which are not necessarily confined to multiparty or multilateral relationships, but affect bilateral relationships also. Thus there may be many bilateral arrangements which, while not fitting Collins's definition of 'network', either display network features or demonstrate the constraints that make network forms of contracting attractive: uncertainty, the need for innovation and adaptability to respond to rapid change, and information sharing. These network features would make an alternative approach to formalistic legal reasoning appealing even in a two-party context. Perhaps the greatest contribution that 'network' thinking can make to contract law development is to manifest the need for and role of complexity in economically productive relationships, the need to manage complex projects and the particular attitude that this produces in the participants. Powell, for example associates the rise of networks with particular constraints and risks on business actors—notably bounded rationality, the risk of opportunism, underlying economic volatility and uncertainty—which give rise to particular requirements on the participants—the need for quick adaptation to changing conditions or technological innovation, reliable information flows and trust. He associates networks less with 'multilateralism' and more with the qualities that such constraints produce in participants:

> In network modes of resource allocation, transactions occur neither through discrete exchanges nor by administrative fiat, but through networks of individuals engaged in reciprocal, preferential, mutually supportive actions ... In essence the

[100] H Collins, 'Introduction to Networks as Connected Contracts' in G Teubner, *Networks as Connected Contracts* (Hugh Collins (ed), trans M Everson) (Oxford, Hart Publishing, 2011) 1.

[101] Ibid, 21.

[102] Ibid, 22–24.

[103] Brownsword, above n 97, 35–36.

parties to a network agree to forgo the right to pursue their own interests at the expense of others.[104]

Thus the law must be alive to the possibility that agreements will display network features or will combine in various ways both formal and informal norms. Chiefly this would involve protecting the commitment to collaborate, through awards of reliance damages for example, but not necessarily its hoped-for outcome.[105]

Certainly the rigid application of the classical law of the discrete exchange to networks appears inappropriate and perhaps even impossible, yet the law is already called upon to deal with contractual arrangements that display network, hybrid or relational features, or are themselves networks. These are either long-term commitments between multiple parties or embody elements of relationalism in the context of an agreement between relative strangers. Thus one interpretation to be placed on provisions such as good faith clauses, or obligations to undertake reasonable and best endeavours, is to harness the benefits of advance planning concerning processes and expectations, without incurring the high costs and risks of attempting to specify outcomes with lawyerly precision. If contracting parties choose to contract in these forms then it is incumbent on the law to adapt. Senior judges have remarked that the law should be slow to regard commercial practices as conceptually impossible, absent any argument of policy otherwise[106] and commentators have suggested that if there is a conflict between legal doctrine and commercial practice then the former must yield to the latter.[107] However, the legal approach to such network forms may be found wanting in several respects. This is illustrated by the Court of Appeal decision in *Tekdata Interconnections Ltd v Amphenol Ltd.*[108] The case involved a supply chain comprising business relationships lasting for 20 years. When a dispute arose between two parties in the chain the law predictably interpreted the network as a series of transactions taking place on express terms that could be analysed separately and in isolation.[109] Yet this overlooked the connections between all the participants in the chain and the largely unacknowledged role of one of them in orchestrating important aspects of the others' relationships. The trial judge took a holistic approach to the arrangements, appreciating the overall function of the network, including the ultimate destination of the final product (aero

[104] Powell, above n 74, 303.

[105] Gilson, Sabel and Scott, above n 87, 1403.

[106] Per Lord Hoffmann, in *Re Bank of Credit and Commerce International SA (No 8)* [1998] AC 214, 228.

[107] See R Bradgate, 'Contracts, Contract Law and Reasonable Expectations' in Worthington (ed), above n 54, 651, 687.

[108] *Tekdata Interconnections Ltd v Amphenol Ltd* [2009] EWCA Civ 1209; [2010] 1 Lloyd's Rep 357.

[109] Collins, above n 100, 13.

engines). This attention to whole contract purpose is important in deciding network obligations: 'The central idea of the theory of connected contracts is that the quasi-organisational qualities of networks make it possible to envision that the entity as a whole has a purpose or aim'.[110] This demands of the participants a duty to consider the interests of the network as whole, rather than their own individual self-interest, although there may be no requirement to completely subjugate one participant's interests to those of another.[111] For a court it requires 'subtle tweaks to the interpretation of the parties' obligations in the light of the purpose of the network'.[112] More concretely, given that parties are seeking to create a long-term co-operative relationship, courts should 'interpret the contract in such a way as to imply more diffuse obligations of co-operation and loyalty than would be appropriate in a discrete transaction conducted at arm's length'.[113] Under this conception the stark error displayed in a case like *Tekdata* is to impose the discrete contract model on the network and regard an isolated instance of transacting as the prime focus for the legal analysis, ignoring the other aspects of the relationship and its 20-year history and the expectations amongst participants to which this would give rise.

Umbrella Agreements

While there might be scepticism over whether networks or other collaborative arrangements are best managed through contracts and contract law, there are legal decisions that demonstrate the considerable risk of not having such contractual arrangements in place.[114] Thus while networks and 'hybrid contracting' may challenge the contractual model, there is a simultaneous need to rely on legal enforceability to some extent to mitigate risk. It has already been noted that networks, to the extent that they are planned, may evince a concern with processes rather than outcomes. If networks, hybrids, braiding, the importance of trust and the inevitability of uncertainty have a role in explaining certain features of contracting practice then it might be expected that, to the extent such features are thought manageable through formality, contracts themselves will increasingly demonstrate hybrid tendencies. It can be noted that contracts themselves often display the simultaneous commitment to both competition and co-operation that contractors

[110] Ibid, 41.
[111] Ibid, 48.
[112] Ibid, 51.
[113] Ibid, 41.
[114] Perhaps the most notorious decision in this respect is *Baird Textile Holdings v Marks and Spencer plc* [2001] EWCA Civ 274. S Mouzas and D Ford, 'Managing Relationships in Showery Weather: The Role of Umbrella Agreements' (2006) 59 *Journal of Business Research* 1248.

themselves are required to manage in their productive relationships. Contract law is already familiar with this phenomenon to some extent. Contracting parties often seek to control the legal 'grey area' between negotiations and the 'final contract' with letters of agreements, heads of agreement and so on. This appears to be an attempt to reconcile the conflicting pressures involved in project planning, maintaining flexibility and ensuring security. The legal significance and effect of these kinds of measures is uncertain and seems to vary with the circumstances.[115] Certainly there are legal risks involved in using such measures, despite their efficacy for the parties. A series of letters of intent rather than a final contract may appear to the law to signal the short-term nature of the relationship, or the parties' aspirations for their agreement, rather than strict entitlements.[116] Of course it may be said that the entire point of letters of intent is that they have no legal effect, but the lack of legal formality may be more a reflection of the parties' oversight than anything else, prompted by their desire to engage in contract performance rather than extensive legal planning.

These more flexible contractual arrangements provide a way to marry the requirement for flexibility with the need for risk management. Use of such 'informal' measures may therefore be a manifestation of the parties consciously pursuing a contracting strategy that concurrently embraces both formal planning, to the extent to which this is possible, and relational elements. Thus the parties' paperwork may increasingly reflect the dynamic nature of the relationship, and arguably dealing with such arrangements requires a more dynamic and individualised contract law to match. In this respect the concept of umbrella agreements is helpful. Umbrella or framework agreements 'are not concerned with immediate contractual decisions. Instead, umbrella agreements provide an explicit framework of norms within which contractual decisions can be made'.[117] In this way they differ from other 'advance' contractual measures such as letters of intent. The latter are designed to guide contract performance during an extended negotiating process so the parties can begin performance with some safeguards in place, particularly as to payment. In contrast with umbrella agreements, the letter of intent is not intended to govern the entire relationship, although it may occasionally fulfil this role. A formal contract is usually anticipated and worked on during this performance and negotiation stage.

Umbrella agreements, on the other hand, are often designed to operationalise the informal norms that underpin the parties' relationship and can

[115] M Furmston and GJ Tolhurst remark: 'Perhaps the only general rule is that there is no general rule, that is one cannot say in advance that a Letter of Intent has or has not legal effect and if it does what the effect would be': *Contract Formation: Law and Practice* (Oxford, OUP, 2010) 197.

[116] See, eg, *Emcor Drake and Scull Ltd v Sir Robert McAlpine Ltd* [2004] EWCA Civ 1733.

[117] Mouzas and Ford, above n 114, 1249.

be useful not only to record but also to mould expectations.[118] They are frameworks for managing the relationship, rather than a specific project with measurable outcomes.[119] Thus they may stipulate for such matters as information exchanges and regular interactions, project review milestones renegotiation, *force majeure*, payment procedures, intellectual property rights and so on. These obligations provide the overarching framework within which repeated transactions or interactions will take place. Mouzas and Furmston regard umbrella agreements as covering the 'area where there are obligations and understandings but not yet a fully completed contract'.[120] Such agreements may be quite formal, but still manifest a concern with providing a constitution for governing the conduct of the deal or deals (if not the individual deals themselves), to save negotiating or renegotiating each individual contract.[121] Understood in this way, such agreements are about reassurance and encouragement of co-operation, and hence may be more aspirational of obligations rather than certain stipulations of them. This characteristic makes the legal status of such agreements uncertain. Such contracts are not amenable to analysis by traditional doctrinal approaches, such as those involving offer and acceptance.[122] It could be said that these new contract forms are motivated by a desire among the commercial community to make contractual agreements better reflect and deal with the actual difficulties contractors face. This is discussed further in Chapter 4, but for now it should be noted that these changes in contracting practice, precipitated by the need to manage complexity, risk and uncertainty, may demand a different and more flexible approach from the law.

CONCLUSION

If a contract law in touch with commercial expectations looks to external factors to determine outcomes, some justification for doing this can be derived from the internal understandings of the contractors themselves. Since contractual processes among such participants are changing, it is incumbent upon the law to change too, particularly since the law cannot rule out regulating these more flexible and hybrid agreements. It would also require greater enforceability of flexible commitments and sensitivity to overall project purposes. It is evident that the existence of such obligations, and their increasing prevalence, is indicative of a wider trend towards

[118] Ibid, 1250.

[119] Ibid, 1251.

[120] S Mouzas and M Furmston, 'From Contract to Umbrella Agreement' (2008) 67 *CLJ* 37, 37.

[121] Ibid, 39.

[122] Per Steyn LJ, *G Percy Trentham Ltd v Archital Luxfer Ltd* [1993] 1 Lloyd's Rep 25, 27.

different kinds of transacting models that have various features, chiefly a concern with contract processes rather than outcomes and an attempt to combine formalism with relational norms and understandings. These hybrid forms of contracting are a way of managing the risk of project failure.

It is of course tempting to argue that agreements that display a high reliance on informal norms and sanctions are outwith the scope and purview of contract law. The difficulty here is that a neat dividing line between formal and informal agreements cannot be drawn, given the complexity of what is being analysed. It is rare for a litigated transaction, series of transactions or relationship to fit neatly into a typology of transaction-governance 'models' from which straightforward conclusions can be derived regarding the appropriateness of contract law regulation and the design of the rules. The reasoning process appears to be that agreements and transactions can be analysed as belonging to a particular type, which then 'plugs into' a specific governance technique or particular design of rules. While undoubtedly helpful, the analysis should not be pressed too far. Classical contract law has been taken to apply to market transactions or discrete transactions, but it is not clear that any such pure form of transaction has ever really existed. The law does not reflect the discreteness of real transactions, but rather has constructed this model and tends to impose it on all forms of exchange behaviour. The law's knowledge and understanding of the business relationship is gained through the choice of relevant facts which fit within its own framework of discrete analysis and filtering these through various doctrines which posit specific criteria of relevance and significance. Most complex transactions will display elements of both relationality and formalism regarding the business relationship and the contract itself. Given this, it is not particularly helpful for some theorists to vindicate the design of the classical law by seeking to show how it is appropriate to, or derives from, transactions displaying a set of relatively constant features. It appears more accurate to say that the law has posited the discrete model of the 'transaction' as the basis for the contract law rules and then theorists have sought to identify, and treat as ripe for separate analysis, the 'market transaction' features of real relationships, the conclusion then following that the application of the discrete model is appropriate, even necessary, to transactions that display enough of the features. The symmetry between the reality of some transactions, the theory and the law that is suggested by the model is constructed and apparent, rather than genuine. The starting point has been the law, not the transactions themselves and the inevitable wider relationships within which such transactions occur. All these factors taken together appear to build at the very least an initially plausible argument for greater alignment between contract law and the reality of commercial practice and expectations.

3

The Contours and Sources of Commercial Expectations

THE PREVIOUS CHAPTER examined how the idea of commercial expectation might be understood and suggested at least a prima facie case for contract law to consider its degree of alignment with the norms, practices and implicit dimensions that lie outside the express contract terms and also outside the rules and principles of contract law. Many questions arise from this claim, but perhaps the primary one is how these commercial expectations are identified and given substance. Attempting even a broad identification of what commercial contractors may expect from their contracts, the law and each other presents great challenges. Nevertheless it is important to get some grasp on this, however tenuous, since it is necessarily the prior step to deciding that dissonance exists between commercial expectations and contract law. Identification is also important to making out the case why expectations are relevant, even compelling, in contracts dispute resolution.

Evident difficulties arise in identifying substantive commercial expectations: expectations have multiple bases, business relationships are infinitely varied and the commercial contracting community is not a homogeneous group sharing the same level of interest in the detail of contract law. The position is complicated by the realisation that in many cases commercial expectations about contract entitlements or outcomes may be strongly connected to the institutional framework. A very sharp division between expectations and strict legal entitlements under classical contract law may be difficult to sustain, particularly in some industries. Nevertheless, while it is open to judges to conclude that in a particular case party expectations are to be institutionally derived, it is important to recognise that under a commercial-expectations approach this can only result from an assessment of the context and circumstances that arise externally to the operation of the law or express terms, so that a judgment is taken as saying, *in this context*, the terms mean what they say and the parties are bound by them.[1] An additional

[1] J Wightman, 'Beyond Custom: Contract, Contexts, and the Recognition of Implicit Understandings' in D Campbell, H Collins and J Wightman (eds), *Implicit Dimensions of Contract* (Oxford, Hart Publishing, 2003) 158.

difficulty is that a court may believe good reasons exist to take the dispute before it as representative of other potential disputes, leading to a decision made by reference to the likely effect of the judgment on the wider commercial community, and not just the individual parties that have raised the dispute. On this basis a court may seek to justify a decision according to the expectations and concerns of the commercial actors identified as the audience for the outcome, even if it defeats the individual parties' expectations.

Despite these difficulties, there are various ways in which the broad shape of these norms and expectations could be made out. First, it is possible to get some direction on this by considering empirical evidence of contracting behaviour. This evidence suggests the ways in which contract law may be misaligned with the practice of commercial exchange and thus may assist obliquely in helping to identifying what contractors expect. Second, it is possible to identify many *sources* of commercial expectations—trade customs, practices and so on—and assess the relative benefits and drawbacks of relying on these norms in contract dispute resolution. There is considerable debate surrounding the extent to which contract law should incorporate such standards, and this impinges on the strength of the misalignment claim. Third, if our attention is directed to the beliefs, understandings and norms generated outside the formal contract scheme then the literature on the connection between trust and contract may help to illuminate the relationship between formal and informal norms in a contractual arrangement, since 'trust' is often taken to be the informal and social analogue of formal contracts in business dealings. This chapter considers these points in turn. The overall objective is to identify the general scope and source of expectations, as well as exploring some of the problems that arise from the claim that courts should seek to incorporate these understandings into contract legal reasoning processes. There is no particular concern here with expectations that have their source in general social structures, and which operate as foundational tacit assumptions, such as shared language or currency. Attention is rather on those factors which are more specific to the relationship or contract context, and might be thought to inform or even completely constitute the parties' understandings concerning their agreement. How the law has responded to the idea of commercial expectation and practices, and the specific expectations that might arise, will be explored further in Chapter 4.

EMPIRICAL STUDIES OF COMMERCIAL CONTRACTING BEHAVIOUR

Preliminaries

One important source of evidence fuelling the misalignment claim is empirical evidence concerning how contracts are made and performed in society.

Since empirical studies suggest a lack of fit between contract law and the practices and expectations of the business community then these studies could be a useful source of general evidence about what these commercial expectations are. Empirical studies of contracting behaviour amongst firms present something of a paradox for commercial contract law. Insofar as empirical studies tend to *describe* the contracting process, they are not themselves evaluative or justificatory, although they may be used to support a researcher's broader hypothesis concerning various aspects of the contracting process and the law's role in this. As Korobkin notes, the conclusions drawn about the incorporation (or not) of commercial norms into law does not necessarily follow from the empirical data (whatever that data shows), but is contestable.[2] On the one hand the studies provide very good evidence of what the expectations of commercial contract parties may be, particularly concerning how the business relationship will be conducted and the role that contracts may have in this. The findings are thus invaluable to the development of a contract law that facilitates commerce insofar as this is taken to mean a contract law that tracks and reflects actual commercial norms and behaviours. On the other hand, the evidence shows that while there certainly are informal norms, practices and behaviours that have an important role to play in commercial dealing, law and legally enforceable contracts are often thought not that important, or even positively unhelpful, to the process of productive exchange. One result of this is that the findings from the studies have been used to support claims about contract law design emanating from neoformalist contract commentators working within efficiency-based justificatory frameworks.[3] These scholars have constructed a critique of the contextual or incorporationist legal-reasoning approach, arguing that the empirical evidence shows a preference amongst contractors for bright-line rules of legal enforcement which supplement a range of non-legal norms and sanctions, rather than open-textured standards which would seek to allow the incorporation of internal and informal norms into legal reasoning.[4] Thus empirical studies have been used to support two opposing lines of argument concerning the design of contract law rules.

Irrespective of the side one takes in these deeper arguments concerning the relevance of the empirical findings for contract legal reasoning, there is immense value in empirical studies for those interested in the connection between contract law and commercial contracting. While the empirical studies may not be a complete guide to the substance of what contractors

[2] R Korobkin, 'Empirical Scholarship in Contract Law: Possibilities and Pitfalls' (2002) *University of Illinois Law Review* 1033, 1057.

[3] See Ch 1.

[4] See especially RE Scott, 'The Case for Formalism in Relational Contract' (2000) 94 *Northwestern University Law Review* 847. Contra, see Collins, *Regulating Contracts* (Oxford, OUP, 1999) 143–48.

expect, they are important because they provide a relatively unmediated account of how contracts work in successful projects and they provide a window into the experiences of those who may be reckoned by the law to be the prime audience for its contract rules. They shed light on why legally enforceable contracts and contract law may be used, and for what purposes, but also the circumstances when commitment to such legal forms may be weaker. Empirical studies of business practices may therefore be an important indicator of the law's role and success in supporting commercial activity. They may also provide evidence of whether reform is necessary, how it should be undertaken, and indeed the effect of any reform or legal development.[5] As an example of the possible significance of the empirical material, consider the Macaulay finding that modifications to contracts during the life of the business relationship were usually agreed without dispute and without heed to the legal formality of fresh consideration required to make such adjustments legally binding.[6] If this is found to be a fairly standard commercial practice, should this empirical evidence of what parties do influence the law relating to consideration? The blanket lack of legal enforceability for modifications in the absence of consideration would appear to defeat a commercial expectation that freely negotiated modifications should be binding. To be sure, it could also be assumed to be a commercial expectation that changes procured by duress would not be upheld by law, but the point here is that the locus for the business expectation is the need for flexibility and modification in the wake of altered circumstances and not the legal doctrine. It is well known that in *Williams v Roffey Bros*,[7] the Court of Appeal took a flexible approach to the requirement of consideration, allowing that practical benefits to a contractor, judged in accordance with the wider agreement context, could constitute good consideration for a modification to the original agreement. However, it should be noted that although the legal outcome may be said to accord with commercial expectations it was only achieved by an expansive reading of what constitutes good consideration. There was no direct engagement with the commercial-expectations argument itself as justifying a relaxation of the consideration doctrine. While the outcome may be lauded for its realism, the method for achieving it—keeping a classical law doctrine substantially intact—is still open to criticism. This is not to suggest the legal doctrine is irrelevant or without function, but the law lacks transparency in failing to clearly articulate the range of concerns and policy considerations that

[5] See, eg, S Wheeler, *Reservation of Title Clauses* (Oxford, OUP, 1991); R Lewis, 'Contracts Between Businessmen: Reform of the Law of Firm Offers and an Empirical Study of Tendering Practices in the Building Industry' (1982) 9 *Journal of Law and Society* 153.

[6] S Macaulay, 'Non-Contractual Relations in Business: A Preliminary Study' (1963) 28 *American Sociological Review* 55, 60–61.

[7] *Williams v Roffey Bros* [1991] 1 QB 1.

determine whether an agreed modification should be upheld. Instead, these factors are obscured and mediated through a technical legal requirement.[8]

Despite the undoubted value of empirical study in providing evidence of the operation of contracts and contract law in the real world, some care is required in handling the empirical material. As has been alluded to above, it may be difficult to draw direct conclusions about the design and development of contract law from the studies. In addition, some of the most well-known studies within law are now quite old. Korobkin, while accepting that empirical scholarship is important, warns of three particular problems: (i) the difficulty of generalising from the findings—empirical studies tend by their nature to be limited in scope, either in terms of the industrial sector studied, geographically, or in the number of relationships examined; (ii) the empirical evidence may not wholly support the thesis the author is attempting to advance; (iii) the empirical findings are inconclusive.[9] With regard to (ii), it should be pointed out that the extent to which scholars articulate an explicit reforming agenda in the light of their empirical findings, or engage directly with the normative question of what contract law doctrine should look like, varies.[10] Some are more interested in exposing the gap between the rules and assumptions of contract law and the practical management of business exchange.[11] The authors of such studies may have no further ambition beyond reporting what they find simply as a matter of interest and a supplement to theoretical and doctrinal explanations of contract law.[12] Others may be interested in the effects the rules have, if any, on those to whom they notionally apply.[13] In relation to (iii) it is the case that the empirical findings may not allow hard and fast conclusions to be drawn about the contracting regime that would be favoured by most contractors and the conditions under which they would prefer it, but this does not mean any conclusions drawn are completely unreliable. The empirical findings add another layer to what is an already complex and controversial issue concerning the relationship between contract law and commercial practice. The conclusions to be drawn from empirical studies concerning the role of contracts and law in business dealings may appear plausible but contingent,

[8] See Collins, above n 4, 148.

[9] Korobkin, above n 2, 1034. See also S Macaulay, 'Contracts, New Legal Realism, and Improving the Navigation of the Yellow Submarine' (2006) 80 *Tulane Law Review* 1161: 'We must be careful to read a study so that we rely on what was found and not on the researcher's discussion that may go far beyond the researcher's results': 1186.

[10] Korobkin, above n 2, 1048.

[11] See S Wheeler, 'Contracts and Corporations' in P Cane and HM Kritzer (eds), *The Oxford Handbook of Empirical Research in Law* (Oxford, OUP, 2010) 125, 133.

[12] See, eg, H Beale and T Dugdale, 'Contracts Between Businessmen: Planning and the Use of Contractual Remedies' (1975) 2 *British Journal of Law and Society* 45, 59–60.

[13] Korobkin, above n 2, 1045. He identifies Macaulay's 1963 study as an example of this kind of work and also D Keating, 'Measuring Sales Law Against Sales Practice: A Reality Check' (1997) 17 *Journal of Law and Commerce* 99.

rather than fully determined and absolute, but it is arguable that this affects only the force with which a reforming agenda can be advanced on the basis of empirical evidence, rather than rendering such evidence entirely irrelevant to contract law.

A further criticism of early empirical studies is made by Wheeler. She notes that the assumptions and starting points of the studies are derived from within a classical contract law framework.[14] For example, the Macaulay finding concerning the modification of agreements during their lifetime appears to start from the legalistic premise that agreements are fixed at a point in time and may therefore require some change as the relationship proceeds. This premise may be criticised on the basis that the parties are unlikely to view their agreement as 'final' at a particular point at the beginning of a project. Rather, the parties' whole conception of agreement may have a fluidity that is alien to the relatively fixed understanding of the law. The studies therefore do not offer a fully internal point of view on business relationships and how contracts may operate within these. In some of the studies, the point is to detect the role played by formal legal contracts and contract law in business dealings, to see how far the 'real deal' reflects, or not, the classical law paradigm. The studies do not theorise over or examine why some exchanges may be more formal whereas others can effectively rely on informal norms and sanctions.[15] Business behaviour is organised and examined through contract law doctrines which provide the framework for understanding the relationship. It may be that there is little that can be done about this, since the theorist who has tasked themselves with enquiring about the role of law (or express terms) in a business relationship is bound to take law (or legal contract) as their starting point and the 'thing' that is sought to be explained. They will thus formulate hypotheses that appear to put law at the centre simply because of the focus of their research questions and their disciplinary emphasis. This concern with the primacy accorded to the legal framework abates when one looks beyond the material produced by contract law scholars, since studies from outwith the legal literature engage more directly with the motivations of contractors in favouring an informal governance regime over a formal legal one. These studies do not take as their starting point the role of contract law in business relationships. The classical legal regime is usually taken as a background fact, not the major focus of the enquiry. Bearing in mind these caveats, empirical studies will be examined to discover what they reveal about commercial practices, norms and expectations in contracts. It will also be considered whether it is possible to make any generalisations from the findings concerning the design of contract law rules and legal reform.

[14] Wheeler, above n 11, 126–27.
[15] Ibid, 133.

The Use of Legally Enforceable Contracts

Perhaps the main revelation of empirical studies is the diversity and complexity of methods of organising productive exchange. No business relationship relies on a singular method of facilitating its trading activity. As a result, there is a very nuanced interrelationship between legal and non-legal norms and sanctions in business transacting. While the empirical studies may show a myriad of individual expectations on the part of contractors from which it may be difficult to generalise, they do demonstrate the circumstances in which contracts are used or when legal enforcement is thought to be particularly beneficial or important. Contrary to how it may often be understood, the subtlety of the relationship between legal and non-legal regimes in business arrangements was borne out even by early empirical studies of contracting behaviour. The findings of the empirical studies of Macaulay[16] and Beale and Dugdale[17] are well known for their suggestion that the law's role in planning, facilitating and enforcing agreements between firms was marginal, and that the significance of written contracts and classical contract law in trading activity tended to be overstated by lawyers and legal scholars. These early studies were important in establishing the dissonance between legal assumptions about contractors and actual business practice. Nevertheless, neither study found that legal measures and legally enforceable agreements were of *no relevance* to the way in which business was conducted. These studies largely confirmed that the choice between legal and non-legal measures in regulating transactions and enforcing obligations depended on a delicate interplay between various factors: the qualities of the contracting partner, the type of contract, the level of risk undertaken and the staff involved.[18] A greater degree of advanced planning was manifest in high-risk, high-value or non-routine ventures or when the other contracting party was an unknown quantity.[19] Both studies found that contractual documents were often exchanged and signed, with some attempt to reach agreement on terms in some cases, even if the resulting contract was only filed away and rarely referred to in resolving day-to-day performance issues.[20]

While written contracts appeared to be unimportant, the studies also demonstrated that steps were occasionally taken to 'boilerplate' the deal

[16] Macaulay, above n 6.

[17] Beale and Dugdale, above n 12.

[18] Considered from an economic perspective by D Charny, 'Nonlegal Sanctions in Commercial Relationships' (1990) 104 *Harvard Law Review* 375; L Kaplow, 'Rules versus Standards: An Economic Analysis' (1992) 42 *Duke Law Journal* 557; AW Katz, 'The Economics of Form and Substance in Contract Interpretation' (2004) 104 *Columbia Law Review* 496.

[19] Macaulay, above n 6, 57; Beale and Dugdale, above n 12, 47.

[20] Macaulay, above n 6, 57–59; Beale and Dugdale, above n 12, 48–51.

by exchanging standard terms, although this attempt at legal planning was often ineffective due to 'battle of the forms' problems where lack of a complete match between offer and acceptance may lead to legal doubts either about the terms of the agreement[21] or whether an enforceable agreement is achieved at all.[22] This lack of legal enforceability was not necessarily appreciated by participants, and even if it was appreciated, the parties were generally unconcerned.[23] A set of express terms may do useful work even if their enforceability is doubtful. Commercial contractors often use standard terms to mould the expectations of their contracting partners in a quite subtle form of manipulation that is entirely unrelated to the issue of their legal enforceability.[24] Similarly, formalisation of obligations and sanctions may change perceptions of the censured behaviour, making it seem more, rather than less, socially acceptable (provided of course that one is willing to pay the price for defection[25]). Yates conducted a small-scale study of business attitudes towards the use of liquidated damages clauses and terms which excluded and limited liability for losses arising on breach. Such clauses are controlled by statute[26] and common law, although courts display a higher degree of tolerance towards such clauses in commercial contracts, where they may be accepted as reflecting a reasonable allocation of risk between economically matched participants in the trade. Yates found that while these clauses were inserted to obviate what were taken to be unacceptable commercial risks (for consequential damages, for example), it was also recognised by contractors that they served important psychological functions unrelated to their risk-allocation function.[27]

Both the Beale and Dugdale and Macaulay studies showed that business people were generally aware of contract law requirements and the possibility of litigation if problems arose. Litigation was rarely pursued however, although it was more likely to be utilised in cases where either the procedure was fairly quick, cheap and formal (for example, debt recovery) or the relationship was effectively at an end and there was nothing to lose by taking the other party to court.[28] Interestingly, the Beale and Dugdale

[21] *Tekdata Interconnections Ltd v Amphenol Ltd* [2009] EWCA Civ 1209; [2010] 1 Lloyd's Rep 357.

[22] *British Steel Corporation v Cleveland Bridge Engineering Co Ltd* [1984] 1 All ER 504.

[23] Macaulay, above n 6, 60; Beale and Dugdale, above n 12, 50.

[24] See D Yates, *Exclusion Clauses in Contracts*, 2nd edn (London, Sweet & Maxwell, 1982) 19, 30. See also T Wilkinson-Ryan, 'Do Liquidated Damages Encourage Breach? A Psychological Experiment' (2010) 108 *Michigan Law Review* 633.

[25] U Gneezy and A Rustichini, 'A Fine is a Price' (2000) 29 *Journal of Legal Studies* 1.

[26] Chiefly the Unfair Contract Terms Act 1977 in the case of exclusions and limitations of liability.

[27] Yates, above n 24, 19, 30.

[28] Macaulay, above n 6, 65–66; Beale and Dugdale above n 12, 51. The anti-litigation stance of small businesses in particular was confirmed recently by the Federation of Small Businesses, who reported their members avoided litigation 'like the plague': Lord Justice Jackson, *Review of Litigation Costs: Final Report* (London, TSO, 2010), 258.

study did report 'signs of a gradual change in attitude towards tightening up procedures and creating legally enforceable agreements'.[29] Some of their interviewees put this down to greater professionalism amongst younger managers, many of whom had knowledge of contract law. Similarly, Macaulay found that 'legal sanctions, while not an everyday affair, are not unknown in business'.[30] Macaulay also suggested that the level of antipathy towards formal contracts tended to vary with staff roles. Legal and finance departments preferred a greater degree of advance planning, often for internal processes and to keep sales staff in line, while sales teams regarded contract negotiations and formalities as an impediment to making sales and a nuisance.[31] This illustrated the then little-known and -appreciated phenomenon of written contracts as an internal management and organisation tool. In this way, formal contracts were of benefit in addressing various agency and record-keeping problems within the firm.

Despite the findings that the law had some role in commercial activity, these early studies are more famous for alerting lawyers to the greater importance of informal and internal norms and sanctions—maintaining good business relationships, preserving a good reputation, keeping open the possibility of future dealings with partners and taking a flexible approach to contingencies as they arise. The Beale and Dugdale study found that factors such as low risk, mutually accepted norms and customs, self-help and non-contractual devices all combined to require infrequent recourse to legal mechanisms, and that there was some degree of resistance to writing informal and customary norms into contract standard terms and conditions.[32] Macaulay similarly found that respondents regarded excessive planning as counter to developing a good business relationship. Legal planning was felt to undermine trust and create inflexibility. When terms are reduced to writing it was felt that 'one gets performance only to the letter of the contract'.[33] Vagueness in stipulations was regarded as preferable so that parties could negotiate solutions to problems as they arose during performance. The relative completeness of contractual documents may also be a feature of specific trades. Trusted trade associations may bear the costs of providing such documentation which can be used on a repeat basis by contractors.[34]

[29] Beale and Dugdale, above n 12, 51.
[30] Macaulay, above n 6, 62.
[31] Ibid, 66.
[32] Beale and Dugdale, above n 12, 59.
[33] Macaulay, above n 6, 64.
[34] See generally, W Konradi, 'The Role of *Lex Mercatoria* in Supporting Globalized Transactions: An Empirical Insight into the Governance Structure of the Timber Industry' in V Gessner (ed), *Contractual Certainty in International Trade* (Oxford, Hart Publishing, 2009) 49.

The degree of indifference towards legal enforceability revealed by early empirical studies seems partly rooted in distrust of the law and lawyers. The law is often perceived as inflexible and its rules appear remote from the everyday concerns of business people. Thus the rules of offer and acceptance may lead to *legal* problems concerning contract formation for firms, but insofar as such firms do not engage with these legal processes, these problems do not hinder the firm's productive efforts. Meeting the legal conditions for enforceability often creates a fresh set of problems for the parties, problems that they may be none too concerned to address. Nevertheless, the firm may regard the lack of legal enforceability of their preferred terms as exposing them to an unwelcome degree of risk, even if the risks are thought unlikely to materialise. Contractors also face trade-offs between contract value and costs of negotiating and recording a legally enforceable agreement. With low-value and relatively low-risk contracts it is unlikely to be thought worth the time and cost to develop a certain and complete (or as complete as possible) contract. The findings from the early studies therefore reveal firms to be largely ambivalent about legal enforceability except in relatively well-defined circumstances. An approximation to legal enforceability, almost mimicking the conditions of legal enforceability by attention to the trappings and symbols of contracts and contract law (documents, signatures), and not the substance, seemed to serve their purposes just as well.

One clear finding from these early empirical studies is that even if the parties do go to the time, expense and trouble of planning their relationship, the planning is rarely regarded as exhaustive of their obligations towards one another. This is not just a matter of the transaction costs involved in developing a comprehensive set of express obligations, processes and so on, nor the impossibility of writing a complete contract, but simply reflects the expectation that while performance includes things agreed on, it also includes actions outside the letter of the agreement that benefit a contracting partner. A firm's evaluation of a contracting partner's performance is not necessarily tied to the paper record of obligations, or even informal agreements of what the parties said they would do: 'To move a relationship to the next level, firms need to go beyond the terms of the contract. It is favorable performance in the extracontractual venue that influences and redefines the other party's expectations over time'.[35] Similarly Lisa Bernstein's cotton industry paper points to two particular expectations that contractors will have: first, a contractor should not breach and pay—contractors expect performance not payment for non-performance (breach and performance

[35] D Narayandas and VK Rangan, 'Building and Sustaining Buyer-Seller Relationships in Mature Industrial Markets (2004) 68 *Journal of Marketing* 63, 70.

were not regarded as good substitutes)—and second, contractors would sometimes take a loss to protect a trading relationship.[36]

The Use of Private Legal Systems

Some of the empirical work on contract has examined the use of what are in effect private legal systems in commercial dispute resolution. If disputes cannot be resolved between the parties it is likely that they will rely on informal dispute resolution mechanisms and procedures promulgated by their own trade associations, where available, rather than the courts. The existence of private legal systems has many implications for national contract law, chiefly that the resolution of disputes by these alternative methods will not add to the stock of contract law rules. This may diminish the law's capacity to develop rules that can respond appropriately to the diversity of commercial contract problems, simply because the reach of the law is limited to a particular kind of contractor and dispute. The general implications of the availability of different methods of dispute resolution in commercial contracting, and the effect that this has on contract law development, is addressed further in Chapter 7. Here, the phenomenon of the private legal system is examined to see what light it sheds on the question of whether commercial contractors display a preference for particular styles of dispute resolution.

Lisa Bernstein has undertaken empirical work on the use of private legal systems in various commodity markets in the US, notably diamonds, grain and feed, and textiles.[37] The organisations running these industries vary from the equivalent of a private club characterised by a high degree of insularity and cultural homogeneity (Jewish diamond merchants[38]) to geographically and culturally diverse traders operating on a global scale, yet still forming information-sharing networks via social events, newsletters and the like (cotton merchants). Despite the differences in detail, all business relationships examined in these studies relied to a greater extent on non-legal sanctions and mechanisms such as reputation networks and cultural, symbolic or informal norms, in order to keep them working effectively. Yet while

[36] L Bernstein, 'Private Commercial Law in the Cotton Industry: Creating Co-operation Through Rules, Norms and Institutions' (2001) 99 *Michigan Law Review* 1724, 1755–56.

[37] L Bernstein, 'Opting Out of the Legal System: Extralegal Contractual Relations in the Diamond Industry' (1992) 21 *Journal of Legal Studies* 115; 'Merchant Law in a Merchant Court: Rethinking the Code's Search for Immanent Business Norms' (1996) 144 *University of Pennsylvania Law Review* 1765; 'The Questionable Empirical Basis of Article 2's Incorporation Strategy: A Preliminary Study' (1999) 66 *University of Chicago Law Review* 710; 'Private Commercial Law in the Cotton Industry: Creating Co-operation Through Rules, Norms and Institutions', above n 36, 1724.

[38] See also BD Richman, 'Ethnic Networks, Extra-legal Certainty and Globalisation: Peering into the Diamond Industry' in Gessner (ed), above n 34, 31.

long-term trading relationships are characteristic within such industries, many of the individual transactions are standardised and repeat in a spot market. There is an incentive to use formal contracts to govern such trades since trade associations have largely borne the cost of developing standard terms. In grain and feed markets, for example, Bernstein notes that sources of difficulty are known in advance, so it is possible to create detailed rules to deal with what are relatively complete contracts.[39] Bernstein provides evidence of trading carried on without state institutions of enforcement and she details the private, often relatively formalistic arrangements within the various industries for settling intra-industry disputes, usually administered by the local or national trade association, rather than state institutions. In Bernstein's grain and feed study she considers the procedures and rules applied by the arbitrators to resolve disputes. Bernstein found that dispute resolution did not rely on 'open textured' standards, such as good faith or reasonableness, nor trade customs, but formalistic trade rules applied with a minimum of discretion by industry insiders and enforced through possible expulsion from the trade association for non-compliance.[40] She argues that the bright-line rules 'reduce the cost of entering into an agreement by providing a comprehensive set of well-tailored default rules that reduce the negotiation costs, specification costs, information costs, and relational costs of contracting, as well as the risk of transaction breakdown.'[41] Bernstein's studies also suggest that contracting parties who opt for litigation to resolve disputes are a self-selecting group who have resorted to law because non-legal sanctions have failed, or they are seeking an exit from the relationship.

Other scholars have cast doubt on whether alternative dispute resolution procedures always display formalist tendencies. As a counter to the evidence supporting formalism offered by Bernstein, Drahozel examined international commercial arbitration, which is more akin to national litigation than the industry-specific dispute resolution procedures administered by trade associations that formed the subject of Bernstein's analysis. He argues that arbitral tribunals rely more on the flexible Uniform Commercial Code-type approach, and duties of good faith, and not formalistic rules.[42] He notes though that greater reliance may be placed on 'trade usage' and practice, rather than course of dealing, prior dealings or course of performance between the parties themselves.[43] This suggests some level of

[39] This may also be true for contractors involved in long trading relationships who are able to predict and deal with problems in contract terms: see R Epstein, 'Confusion About Custom: Disentangling Informal Customs from Standard Contractual Provisions (1999) 66 *University of Chicago Law Review* 821, 828.

[40] Bernstein, 'Private Commercial Law in the Cotton Industry', above n 37.

[41] Ibid, 1741–42.

[42] CR Drahozel, 'Commercial Norms, Commercial Codes and International Commercial Arbitration' (2000) 33 *Vanderbilt Journal of Transnational Law* 79, 83.

[43] Ibid, 84.

generality in the practice is required before arbitrators take notice of it. Thus assessments of both good faith and reasonable expectations take commercial norms, in the sense of industry practices, as a reference and baseline. He argues that since general arbitration is a competitive system—general arbitration systems will not survive if they use rules that do not make commercial parties better off *ex ante*—then they are good examples of systems that have responded and adapted to the requirements of commercial parties, and thus provide good evidence that the benefits of a flexible approach are thought to outweigh the costs,[44] although he admits that given the secrecy of arbitrations, and consequently the lack of available detail, his arguments are impressionistic. The reliance on informal norms is not just down to an individual preference of the arbitrator. He finds that arbitral rules often require arbitrators to consider trade usage.[45] However, he also finds that arbitrators will rely on the terms of the contract, if the terms are clear, although there is 'some indication' that express terms may give way to trade usage.[46]

One conclusion to draw from these empirical studies is that there may be industry-specific factors that tend to support expectations for both a certain kind of dispute resolution procedure and disposal of the dispute according to the established rules. For example, a series of long-term, repeated and fairly homogeneous trades in an industry with strong trade associations providing standard forms will tend to proceed on a formal contract basis. While there will still be non-contractual expectations working in the background, this environment may be likely to reproduce a set of standard expectations in the participants that may well embrace formalism, simply because this is the environment within which the parties become used to working. Of course it might be a controversial matter to determine whether the rules closely tracked the commercial practices of the participants at their inception or whether they were imposed by the trade association. After a number of years, however, it may be impossible to tell. The contractors' expectations are likely to be moulded to fit the institutional structures. In turn, these structures are a combination of imposition by the trade associations and organic growth from practices established between participants through repeated dealing. These processes are likely to be mutually reinforcing. The important point is that the expectation must be that everyone abides by these rules and processes, at least as long as they want to participate in the trade. This model of contracting behaviour and preference for formalism will not suit all contracting parties. Contractors engaged on a risky joint venture, developing or exploiting new technology with considerable uncertainty or

44 Ibid, 93.

45 Ibid, 111, citing ICC Rules of Arbitration 1998, Art 17(2) as an example (referring to provisions of the contract and relevant trade usages).

46 Drahozel, above n 42, 123.

attempting to develop a working relationship, appear unlikely to display such a preference for formalism in dispute resolution. Given this, it is difficult to extrapolate from Bernstein's findings to a conclusion concerning what a system of general national law charged with resolving a wide range of agreement disputes should look like.

This brief examination of some of the findings of empirical studies draws out the importance of informal norms and sanctions in business relationships, but it is difficult to reach definitive conclusions concerning the relationship between these informal understandings and the law. Certainly if law is assumed to be the realm of the formal and impersonal contractual obligation, then it is easier to attempt to draw a rigid dividing line between the legal and social world of business contracting. Such a reaction to the studies would seem to be premature however. The precise role of informal norms and expectations in each case, and the relationship with the legal framework where it exists, is a matter of the specifics of the relationship, and is not something over which one can reach robust general conclusions applicable to the entire commercial contracting community. Thus expectations may arise that are moulded by the legal framework, the informal norms or some combination of these. The precise interconnections to be made between these phenomena cannot be decided except by a close examination of contract context.

At this point it may be helpful to examine more closely the idea that there are 'immanent business norms' that exist in a commercial relationship, and that can be drawn out and utilised by contract law. This examination is necessary since business norms would evidently be an important potential source of information about what contractors expect, insofar as these norms could be understood and given meaningful content.

NORMS OF THE BUSINESS RELATIONSHIP

The idea that there are a set of 'immanent business norms', whether derived from the parties' specific relationship, trade customs or the industry in which the parties participate, has been very influential in the debates surrounding commercial contract law development. Usages of trade are often regarded as a source of obligations in various international contract conventions and harmonising rules.[47] Under English law a term will

[47] Eg, Art 9 of the United Nations Convention on the International Sale of Goods states, '(1) The parties are bound by any usage to which they have agreed and by any practices, which they have established between themselves. (2) The parties are considered, unless otherwise agreed, to have impliedly made applicable to their contract or its formation a usage of which the parties knew or ought to have known and which in international trade is widely known to, and regularly observed by, parties to contracts of the type involved in the particular trade concerned'. See also the proposed Regulation on a Common European Sales Law at Arts 5, 59

be implied on the basis of custom if the usage is 'invariable, certain and general' or 'notorious, certain and reasonable' and not contradicted by express terms.[48] Customs and business practices may be relevant as the background context according to which an agreement could be interpreted or in relation to judging standards of reasonableness or 'onerousness' in particular terms.[49] A recent example of legal receptiveness to commercial practices is provided by *The Achilleas*.[50] Here, the contractors' understandings that an implied limitation on liability for consequential loss operated in charter markets was sufficient for two members of the House of Lords to conclude that the default rule of *Hadley v Baxendale*[51] had been effectively ousted by the market convention. No judgment is made concerning the normative appropriateness or appeal of this convention, it is simply recognised as an element of practice, although Lord Hoffmann evidently regarded this convention as independently reflecting the expectations of a reasonable or prudent commercial contractor. This demonstrates some sensitivity to the idea that the rules of law should be read in the light of industry practice, even if this means modifying or abandoning them in certain instances. In *The Achilleas* itself, however, it is not clear if the expectations were those of contractors themselves or their lawyers, although to the extent that expectations of participants in the shipping industry are formally derived, these may be one and the same.

This attitude towards custom and practice also manifests itself in a general view that contract law, at least insofar as understood as part of commercial law more generally, ought to be supportive of commerce and not operate as an impediment. Goode has written that 'commercial law evolves from the usages of business ... Commercial law is about problem-solving, about fashioning the contract structures and other legal tools by which the legitimate needs of the market can be met'.[52] The belief that law should reflect business practices owes a lot to the continuing influence of the idea

and 67. Under these Articles reasonableness is assessed with regard to 'usages and practices of the trade', interpretation may also have regard to these standards, and they can be a source of contract terms and thus binding between the parties. Usage is also a feature of many contract codes and model laws. Art 9:101 of the Draft Common Frame of Reference, for example, allows that contract terms may be established by practices and usage.

48 See the authorities summarised in *Exxonmobil Sales and Supply Group v Texaco (The Helene Knutsen)* [2003] EWHC 1964 (Comm); [2003] 2 Lloyd's Rep 686; *Goshawk v Tyser* [2006] EWCA Civ 54, [47–50]; *British Crane Hire v Ipswich Plant Hire* [1975] 1 QB 303.

49 In *Interfoto v Stiletto* [1989] QB 433, for example, the Court of Appeal considered evidence of practice amongst libraries for judging what would be an appropriate level of fine imposed by a library for the return of overdue phototransparencies.

50 *Transfield Shipping Inc v Mercator Shipping Inc (The Achilleas)* [2008] UKHL 48; [2009] 1 AC 61.

51 *Hadley v Baxendale* (1854) 9 Exch 341.

52 R Goode, *Commercial Law in the Next Millennium* (Hamlyn Lecture Series, London, Sweet & Maxwell, 1998) 4.

of the law merchant. Although difficult to fully explain since definitions tend to vary with the exponent, the law merchant (*lex mercatoria*) is the generic term for 'mercantile customs and practices ... eventually recognised and absorbed by the common law (or continental codifications)'.[53] Some accounts emphasise the law merchant as a separate international system from the common law, with its own merchant-courts and merchant-judges, utilising norms used by merchants and motivated by the merchants' need for prompt local dispute resolution, a flexible approach to evidence and procedure, and recognition of measures of practical importance such as negotiable instruments[54] and transferability of debts.[55] It is claimed that the law merchant often conflicted with the common law, at least until the latter began developing its own commercial character during the course of the seventeenth and early eighteenth centuries. The chief architect of this development was Lord Mansfield. One of his objectives was 'to make the law more serviceable to the commercial community'[56] and incorporation of the methods and customs used by the commercial community were of central importance to this endeavour.[57] Lord Devlin remarked on how the law merchant became part of the common law and that consequently 'commercial law ought to be a reflection of the constantly changing ideas of conduct which merchants may have'.[58] Yet Lord Devlin goes so far as to blame the written contract for killing the customs of merchants as a source of law, rendering custom neutral in this respect.[59] The idea that the law merchant was absorbed into common law has been challenged. It has been said that the common law took direct evidence of commercial custom rather than absorbing it through the law merchant and thus independently developed its own way of facilitating commercial dealing, with occasionally unfortunate results, such as the commitment to *caveat emptor* and privity of contract.[60] Yet despite the seeming incompatibility between elements of contract law and the conduct of commerce, the idea that the law in this area

[53] C Twigg-Flesner and G Villalta Puig, 'Introduction: The Boundaries of Commercial Law' in C Twigg-Flesner and G Villalta Puig (eds), *Boundaries of Commercial and Trade Law* (Munich, Sellier, 2011) 4.

[54] PS Atiyah, *The Rise and Fall of Freedom of Contract* (Oxford, OUP, 1979) 135ff. The thesis that the common law incorporated the law merchant is challenged by some on the basis that the common law was attentive to the needs of commerce even before the incorporation of the law merchant: see JS Rogers, *The Early History of the Law of Bills and Notes* (Cambridge, CUP, 1995) 17ff, 54–68.

[55] See generally E McKendrick, *Goode on Commercial Law*, 4th edn (London, Penguin, 2010) 3–8.

[56] Atiyah, above n 54, 122.

[57] Ibid, 121ff.

[58] Lord Devlin, 'The Relation Between Commercial Law and Commercial Practice' (1951) 14 *MLR* 249, 250.

[59] Ibid, 251.

[60] Atiyah, above n 54, 137; McKendrick, above n 55, 6.

should reflect commercial practice has filtered down through judicial minds over the following centuries.

Although the acceptance of trade customs and practice appears a good way for contract law to stay in touch with commercial expectations,[61] the idea that industry practices, customs or immanent business norms can be sources of law has been challenged on various grounds. Clearly for customs and commercial norms to be regarded as a source of expectations in commercial dealing they must be identifiable.[62] The genesis of trade customs may be unclear and it can be difficult to decide what separates a custom or course of dealing from habitual practices to which nobody objects.[63] Something beyond a mere trading or market practice is usually required,[64] in favour of some belief that the parties, or one of them, has a 'legally binding right to demand [the usage]'.[65] As Goode notes, this is a rather strange way of according legal significance to the custom, since it suggests legal effectiveness results from the view accorded to the custom that it is already legally binding, not the result of any independent merit attaching to the custom itself.[66] The existence of a custom which is over and above 'the way in which that particular [contractor] has become habituated to doing business' is notoriously difficult, although not impossible, to prove.[67] A custom may be deemed contrary to law irrespective of the fact that it is invariable or has been followed without complaint for a number of years.[68] The reverse is also true however, and commercial practices may change while trade customs, at least in legal hands, may retain a degree of semi-permanence. The result is that a custom may become as entrenched as a rule, so that if a current commercial practice conflicts with an 'established custom', the custom prevails.[69]

The main difficulty here is the inconsistency between the dynamic nature of commerce and the relatively static nature of law. The liability of commercial practice and usage to change may make it less amenable to reception within a common law system that prizes certainty, predictability and

[61] Eg, Lord Lloyd once remarked, 'in the field of Commercial Law ... the custom of merchants has always been a fruitful source of law': *Kleinwort Benson Ltd v Lincoln City Council* [1998] 4 All ER 513, 549.

[62] See general discussion in J Gava and J Greene, 'Do We Need a Hybrid Law of Contract? Why Hugh Collins is Wrong and Why it Matters' (2004) 63 *CLJ* 605, 621–26.

[63] *London Export Corporation v Jubilee Coffee Roasting Ltd* [1958] 2 All ER 411. See also *Crema v Cenkos Securities plc* [2010] EWCA Civ 10, [6]; *Goshawk Dedicated Ltd v Tyser & Co Ltd* [2006] EWCA Civ 54, [47–50].

[64] *Sucre Export SA v Northern Shipping Ltd* [1994] 2 Lloyd's Rep 266.

[65] Per Slade LJ in *General Reinsurance Corp v Forsakringsaktibolaget Fennia Patria* [1983] 1 QB 856, 874. See also R Goode, 'Usage and its Reception in Transnational Commercial Law' (1997) 46 *ICLQ* 1, 8.

[66] Ibid, 9–10.

[67] Lord Devlin, above n 58, 251.

[68] *London Export Corp Ltd v Jubilee Coffee Roasting Co Ltd* [1958] 1 Lloyd's Rep 367.

[69] *Workers Trust & Merchant Bank Ltd v Dojap Investments Ltd* [1993] AC 573.

stability as virtues reckoned to be important to the commercial contracting community. In this way legal recognition of the custom may not be without consequence, since it does not just support the custom, but effectively creates a new rule. Similarly, practice and custom may conflict with the express terms of an agreement, although it is settled English law that in such a situation the terms will prevail.[70] These difficulties may lead to a degree of scepticism that the common law is amenable to direct enforcement of commercial practice and 'usage'. Baker remarks that 'Shifting usages can hardly be treated as common law. They can explain contracts, but cannot create obligations'.[71] This can be seen in the way that English contract law does not simply make such customs directly enforceable through law—they are not without more regarded as a source of law for the parties—rather it seeks to impart legality by filtering them through doctrinal tools that effectively sever the link between the custom and the practices of the commercial community from which it developed. Thus trade customs may be the source of commercial expectations, but these are accorded legal validity only by linking the custom to core contract notions of individual consent and agreement, usually through the mechanism of implied terms. The legal force of custom and usage must derive from incorporation into the contract, or else they operate as interpretative criteria. They are not independent sources of obligation.

Trade associations may play a more important role than the law in formalising customs by developing standard forms in particular industries that incorporate commercial practice to a greater or lesser degree. Alternatively such forms may be developed by industry bodies to impose terms in the wake of various competing and inconsistent 'customary' understandings that may militate against trading. An example is the development of Universal Customs and Practice on Documentary Credits created under the auspices of the International Chamber of Commerce.[72] Here it is traders themselves, rather than lawyers, that have created bodies of functioning rules in order to facilitate trade and resolve problems of co-ordination, security and certainty. These commercial practices have arisen externally to the legal framework of rights and obligations represented by the contract, often

[70] Eg, *Total Gas Marketing v Arco British* [1998] 2 Lloyd's Law Rep 209; *Les Affréteurs Réunis SA v Leopold Walford (London) Ltd* [1919] AC 801. Compare the European Commission's proposed Regulation for a Common European Sales Law. Under CESL, usages will be binding provided they do not contradict individually negotiated express terms or the mandatory rules of the instrument. This suggests that usages or practices established between the parties may override standard terms that have not been negotiated: see Art 67(1) and (2).

[71] JH Baker, 'The Law Merchant and the Common Law before 1700' (1979) 38 *CLJ* 295, 298.

[72] J Ulph, 'The UCP 600: Documentary Credits in the 21st Century' [2007] *Journal of Business Law* 355; M Bridge, 'Documents and Contractual Congruence in International Trade' in S Worthington (ed), *Commercial Law and Commercial Practice* (Oxford, Hart Publishing, 2003) 213.

effectively bypassing the way in which these legal rights and obligations are usually created, or providing a commercially developed practical solution to a problem where contract law, due to its doctrinal strictures, is unable to assist. Although in resolving commercial disputes the common law may take some direction from the systems set up by international organisations to facilitate global trading, how the growth of transnational commercial law affects or influences domestic contract law has not garnered much attention, perhaps because of the different functions of international model contract laws, which favour more informal dispute resolution processes, and the national contract law operating in a particular jurisdiction. Benson reiterates the words of Coke, that 'an arbitrator's purpose was ... to find a suitable compromise, while a judge's purpose was to rule on the merits of the case'.[73] It is perhaps easier for arbitrators to fashion their rules according to current and changing usage than judges ruling on the common law in national courts. Thus it could be argued that, if anything, the *lex mercatoria* bears a greater resemblance to, and affinity with, a modern system of international commercial arbitration than the common law of contract enforced through litigation.

Despite the seeming importance of custom and usage to commercial dealing, doubts may remain about how far contract law can really attune itself with commercial behaviour and expectations as sourced from immanent business norms. As a practical matter the law is always likely to lag behind commercial practices, since business people face challenges that demand quick solutions and opportunities that demand immediate responses. They cannot always wait for a determination concerning the strict legality of the contractual techniques they may develop in furtherance of their business interests. Given this, it is difficult to keep law and practice together, and most commentators believe the law should do more to align itself with commercial expectations in this respect.[74] Thus the reception of custom and practice in some circumstances is not wholly indicative of contract law adopting a commercial-expectations approach. Apart from these general difficulties there are three more specific arguments that may be raised about custom: whether customs exist; the possibility of legalisation reducing the value of customs and informal norms—the parties may prefer these to remain outside the scope of legal control;[75] and the costs involved in courts considering custom. These are considered further below.

[73] BL Benson, 'The Spontaneous Evolution of Commercial Law' (1989) 55 *Southern Economic Journal* 644, 653.

[74] Ibid.

[75] Bernstein, 'Questionable Empirical Basis' above n 37, 752.

Do Customs Exist?

Lisa Bernstein has been a particular critic of the idea of both the existence of trade customs and the appropriateness of incorporating what she calls 'immanent business norms' into contract legal reasoning. Her work has generated considerable debate about the role of informal norms in a business relationship. Bernstein's work is in the context of the Uniform Commercial Code, which requires courts to supplement written agreements with commercial usage and practices.[76] So, the Uniform Commercial Code maintains at Article 2-202 (although this incorporationist spirit is repeated elsewhere) that, unless the intention is found to be otherwise, the written agreement can be supplemented 'by course of performance, course of dealing, or usage of trade'. Bernstein's attack is broadly along two fronts: first, that agreement on the content and meaning of trade customs in a uniform, consistent, industry-specific and industry-wide sense, which can be used to supplement the rules and express contract terms, 'is a legal fiction rather than a merchant reality';[77] and second, as has been described above, that many trades opt out of the public legal system and UCC in favour of their own more formal rule systems and dispute resolution procedures. In one article she examines a range of merchant industries and their national associations' attempts at the turn of the last century to codify customs of the trade into rules.[78] She discovered that only very localised, not industry-wide, trade customs existed. With regard to the hay trade, for example, trade association rules were drafted and codified specifically to remedy the situation of varying local customs concerning grading and specification of hay bales, charges, reasonable delivery times and varying local interpretations of contract language.[79] Codification was in many cases an attempt to impose uniform standards on products to pre-empt disputes. These 'customs' were not reflective of any single enduring set of accepted norms but a compromise position only achieved after a lengthy process of negotiation between the different sets of interests in the trade.[80] Codified conventions may therefore not provide good evidence of business usage or what commercial contractors actually want, but represent an attempt to forge a mutually acceptable path between the different interests and norms, reconciling these where possible

[76] Bernstein, 'Merchant Law', above n 37, 1768.

[77] Bernstein, 'Questionable Empirical Basis', above n 37, 717.

[78] Ibid.

[79] Ibid, 722–23.

[80] See also R Goode, above n 65, 3: 'It is in the nature of conventions and codifications that they do not simply reproduce the *status quo*; they change it, and sometimes quite radically'. This kind of reasoning seems implicit in the rejection of a custom in favour of an express term in *Les Affréteurs Réunis SA v Leopold Walford (London) Ltd* [1919] AC 801—if the 'custom' has to be embodied in writing then it cannot be a custom: 807–08.

and imposing a solution where not.[81] This debate concerning whether trade customs, understood as a kind of independent normative standard, can be said to exist mirrors a similar debate over whether the 'law merchant' really exists and the substance of the rules it contains.[82] Even if there is broad agreement that the law merchant exists debate remains as to what its principles are and what kind of rules it promulgates. Bernstein concludes that while trade customs do not consistently exist, nevertheless 'merchants do consider it valuable to have an understanding of the ways transactions are usually done, an understanding gleaned from a rough aggregation of practices in the market as a whole'.[83] This knowledge is useful in the early stages of a contracting relationship, when the parties are trying to assess who will perform and who will default, but becomes less important as the relationship develops and creates its own normative benchmarks. As Bernstein argues, specific norms are likely to develop only within a relationship and will be tailored to that relationship rather than arising from the commercial community as whole, and having universal applicability across all commercial relationships. Given the conditions under which commercial practices may harden into a normative system, it might be argued that an externally operative system of state-backed contract law is required precisely because the conditions for 'spontaneous order' to arise between diffuse and heterogeneous contracting parties do not exist.[84]

These claims about custom are highly controversial however. Critics of Bernstein's position argue that the findings raise 'questions of evidence rather than challenge the entire approach of the UCC'[85] or that 'research into discrete industries, while valuable, is very inconclusive on the desires of business people more generally'[86] or that the time in which the availability of customs is examined (turn of the last century) tells us nothing about the existence of customs here and now.[87] However, her argument is

[81] See Goode, above n 65, 24.

[82] PM Flanagan, 'Dymythologising the Law Merchant: The Impropriety of the Lex Mercatoria as a Choice of Law' (2004) 15 *International Company and Commercial Law Review* 297, 301; RA Epstein, 'Reflections on the Historical Origins of the Law Merchant' (2004) 5 *Chicago Journal of International Law* 1.

[83] Bernstein, 'Questionable Empirical Basis', above n 37, 716–17.

[84] FA Hayek, *Law, Legislation and Liberty* (London, Routledge and Kegan Paul, 1982) 46–54.

[85] S Macaulay, 'Relational Contracts Floating on a Sea of Custom? Thoughts about the Ideas of Ian Macneil and Lisa Bernstein' (2000) 94 *Northwestern University Law Review* 775, 787–88. See also, 'The Real Deal and the Paper Deal: Empirical Pictures of Relationships, Complexity and the Urge for Transparent Simple Rules' in Campbell, Collins and Wightman (eds), above n 1, 51, 65–68.

[86] W Woodward, 'Neoformalism in a Real World of Forms' (2001) *Wisconsin Law Review* 971, 980–81.

[87] JS Kraus and S Walt, 'In Defense of The Incorporation Strategy' in JS Kraus and S Walt (eds), *The Jurisprudential Foundations of Corporate and Commercial Law* (Cambridge, CUP, 2000) 193, 202.

not that trade customs do not exist, but that uniform industry-wide trade customs do not exist, and as such she casts doubt on whether custom can provide any sort of consistent normative framework for deciding disputes across particular industries. For some, that customs might only exist on a local level is enough to justify their incorporation in local disputes.[88] This might cause a problem for courts though, since if local customs are used to resolve a dispute this reduces the case's general precedential value across the industry (which has implications for costs). Alternatively, in another dispute the local custom may mistakenly be given 'industry-wide' relevance by a court. An alternative criticism of the custom issue is that the identification of applicable customs is, in part, an act of interpretation where the 'normative premises' of the judge must play a role.[89] The judge must distinguish and define the precise scope of the custom. This turns the application of customs into a species of 'moral reflection'. The problem here is that there are also other competing sorts of 'moral reflection' such as economic analysis or philosophy.[90] Given the doubt and ambiguity about custom, it is plausible that contracting parties might wish to ensure that trade custom is ousted altogether in solving disputes.[91] On the other hand, however, it could be said that this argument only raises doubts about whether it is possible to believe in the existence of general, industry-wide customs. There is no reason to think that these problems could not be overcome in at least some instances. Parties can present evidence of custom to a court, and even if an industry-wide custom cannot be established, there may be patterns of behaviour between the parties over the course of a trading relationship that can raise expectations between the parties which can be established by evidence.

Legalisation of Immanent Business Norms

Bernstein further asserts that, contrary to UCC methods, parties do not intend nor want these extra-legal standards to be used in interpreting express contract terms. This is an issue about maintaining control over how trading relationships are conducted and risk managed. She maintains that parties do not want to cede power to the courts (nor to the other party) to regulate what is perceived to be a matter of internal and differentiating discretion. The creation of a legal duty, for example requiring consistency in treatment between different contracting partners or flexibility, runs counter to this

[88] Ibid.
[89] R Craswell, 'Do Trade Customs Exist?' in Kraus and Walt (eds), above n 87, 118, 118.
[90] Ibid, 142.
[91] Eg, *Exxonmobil Sales And Supply Corporation v Texaco Ltd (The Helene Knutsen)* [2003] EWHC 1964 (Comm).

since legalising informal and relational norms will prevent parties entering into, and gaining benefits from, extra-legal agreements. Thus to search for the 'bargain in fact' may not be the optimum strategy, but may encourage contractors to be inflexible since they do not want to engage in a pattern of behaviour which may then cause flexibility to be imposed upon them by a court. In other words, parties want to maintain control over flexibility, they do not want it forced upon them.[92] This point is echoed by Woodward, who points out that permissive rules about extrinsic evidence may actually make the parties more strict in relation to their contracts since they will not want to create any 'hostages to fortune' that hamper their future action.[93] It can be appreciated that one party's effort to be co-operative, for example by accepting late or partial delivery or other changes to the contract without taking steps to reserve his legal rights, may be judged, according to the legal framework, to be acquiescence or accepting a variation. A further argument along these lines is that legal enforcement of such norms is inefficient because legalisation would have the effect of reducing the value of the social norms.[94] Many writers have pointed out that legalisation may harm the development of trust between contractors, since 'legalisation' reduces a contractor's ability to manifest trustworthy behaviour towards a contracting partner *outside* of legal-contractual commitments. It is also argued that it will impair the effectiveness of non-legal sanctions, which are often more effective in securing compliance and co-operation, and deterring opportunism, than the formal legal framework of contractual rights.[95] Thus to legalise these norms may harm their development and 'weaken the moral and social institution of non-legal promises'.[96]

There are counter-arguments that can be made to these points concerning the legal 'crowding out' of flexible norms. The crowding-out argument suggests that the law has no role in encouraging contractors to display certain qualities, or observe certain standards of behaviour towards their contracting partners, if those qualities are not already existing in a relationship. This appears to rely on a very impoverished view of law's potential to mould

[92] Bernstein, 'Private Commercial Law in the Cotton Industry', above n 36, 1743, 1776–77; Bernstein, 'Merchant Law in a Merchant Court', above n 37, 808–09; RE Scott, 'The Death of Contract Law' (2004) 54 *University of Toronto Law Journal* 369, 375.

[93] Woodward, above n 86, 982; O Ben-Shahar, 'The Tentative Case Against Flexibility in Commercial Law' (1999) 66 *University of Chicago Law Review* 781, 784.

[94] E Posner, 'The Parol Evidence Rule, the Plain Meaning Rule and the Principles of Contractual Interpretation' (1998) 146 *University of Pennsylvania Law Review* 533, 566; Scott, above n 92, 388.

[95] D Charny, above n 18, 428; RE Scott, above n 4, 852; JS Johnstone, 'Should the Law Ignore Commercial Norms? A Comment on the Bernstein Conjecture and its Relevance for Contract Law Theory and Reform' (2001) 99 *Michigan Law Review* 1791.

[96] A Porat, 'Enforcing Contracts in Dysfunctional Legal Systems: The Close Relationship Between Public and Private Orders: A Reply to McMillan and Woodruff' (2000) 98 *Michigan Law Review* 2459, 2473.

contractors' conduct and their conceptions of acceptable behaviour. It is akin to suggesting it is pointless for the law to legislate for sexual or racial equality if the community does not ultimately believe in equality. Law does not always follow: it can, and sometimes must, lead. The essence of legality is not just in imposing sanctions but in channelling behaviour. In any case, in most instances immanent business norms will not be imposed on the parties, the law will recognise and apply the norms that are already operating in a business relationship. The crowding-out argument assumes that the recognition and enforcement of informal norms is a graft onto the classical law rather than changing the current understandings of the law. On this basis it is easy to perceive that a party might assume that their opposite number acts in a co-operative and flexible manner only because that is what the law demands, and, since the (current) classical law appears predicated on the pursuit of self-interest as the prime incentive for any contractor, any display of reciprocal behaviour encouraged by such a law can only be motivated by self-regarding reasons. This superimposition of a reciprocal norm onto the classical law certainly would crowd out any understanding that a contractor displaying reciprocity is acting in an other-regarding fashion. But if the law supports other-regarding displays of co-operation because they are other regarding, then there is no crowding out—the legal norms would no longer be predicated on an individualistic and self-interested model of the contractor. The law would simply be enforcing the co-operative norms that the parties have brought to bear on their relationship if the parties fail to do so. To suggest otherwise is to maintain that the law can never be responsible for altering behaviour. Certainly the legal enforceability of the gift may empty or reduce the value of personal gift giving between individual contractors. But in the main the concern here is with commercial relationships where the parties will be aware that self-interest is operating at some level. The law may not be able to impose a co-operative attitude where none existed before but it can certainly support the co-operative arrangements that the parties have created between themselves. This is considered further in Chapter 4.

Costs of Enforcement

A further influential argument against incorporation of business norms concerns the costs for courts in deciding cases according to internal norms.[97] One of the arguments in favour of contextualism over formalism is that it has the potential to lower transaction costs, since it relieves the parties of having to reduce all the terms and standards that govern the agreement

[97] Scott, above n 4 at 874; Posner, above n 94, 540–01.

to writing in the final document.[98] Parties can write a simpler document, leaving it to the courts to fill gaps through the process of contextual interpretation or incorporation of business norms. The difficulty is that relying on the court's gap-filling function may reduce the costs of reaching agreement for the parties, but the price is increased enforcement costs if disputes arise.[99] Of course, contracting parties may prefer reduced agreement costs since 'contracting costs are incurred today with certainty while dispute resolution costs are incurred tomorrow and probabilistically'.[100] Litigation may be regarded as a remote contingency, the costs of preparing for which do not appear worth it at the agreement phase. Nevertheless, if litigation results, where substantial gap filling is required, this may add significantly to the costs. This is because the relevant context and business norms have to be established. Expert testimony may have to be adduced, preliminary hearings may be required on matters of evidence and procedure and so on.[101] There is no guarantee that this additional evidence would change the outcome a judge would reach on consideration of a much more limited range of evidence.[102] Higher 'interpretive error costs'[103] are also a risk—in seeking to establish the relevant context, the courts may make mistakes. The greater the amount of contextual material, the greater the possibility for error. Evidently a large part of the argument about costs relates to the likelihood of judicial error in dealing with material and evidence outside the traditional legal forms. These specific arguments concerning judicial error and expertise are considered further in Chapter 7.

In terms of the costs incurred by the parties in deciding the extent to which they engage in formal planning of their agreement, Charny argues that parties are likely to allocate different sanctioning systems to breach of different kinds of norm, depending on the interplay of drafting and enforcement costs.[104] From this inferences may supposedly be drawn about the types of commitments that appear better suited to legal enforceability:

> One type is the commitment that is easily specified—so that litigation is straightforward, with predictable outcomes—and for which there are high stakes relative to litigation costs. A second type is the high stakes commitment that will be subsequently interpreted only with much information, particularly with regard to damages. In contrast, vaguer commitments whose interpretation depends on

[98] Kraus and Walt, above n 87, 200. Collins, above n 4, 177–78.
[99] Charny, above n 18, 405.
[100] A Schwartz and RE Scott, 'Contract Theory and the Limits of Contract Law' (2003) 113 *Yale Law Journal* 541, 585.
[101] E McKendrick, 'The Interpretation of Contracts: Lord Hoffmann's Restatement', in Worthington (ed), above n 72, 139, 147.
[102] A Vermeule, 'Three Strategies of Interpretation' (2005) 42 *San Diego Law Review* 607, 614.
[103] Kraus and Walt, above n 87, 193.
[104] Charny, above n 18, 400.

> 'embedded' norms or expert decisionmaking, and commitments that have low stakes relative to litigation costs, appear better suited for nonlegal sanctions.[105]

The initial plausibility of this argument is striking, but it is addressed to parties themselves rather than courts. Since parties frequently bring 'vaguer commitments' before the courts for interpretation and enforcement, courts cannot escape making determinations on the meaning of these commitments and their enforceability. Of course Charny's argument could be that courts should simply refuse to engage with the question of the legality of these vague commitments, which are better suited to non-legal sanctions. Charny's division is quite precise in its assumptions about what kind of commercial relationship and dispute is better suited to non-legal enforcement. This may be true in a business relationship where legal formalities are simply not relied on at all, but many contracting regimes will display a complex mix of norms governing the relationship, these being difficult to separate into the 'legal' and 'non-legal'. The parties' attempts to contract for flexible obligations and duties of good faith provide an example. Rendering these attempts to formalise flexibility as unenforceable due to uncertainty may not allow the parties to reach an optimum agreement. It also overlooks the social costs that may be incurred in not developing the law to allow parties to use contractual forms to achieve a better fit with their relationship, purposes or project. If parties make an attempt to ensure the contract documents capture the complex reality of their relationship then it is by no means clear that the courts should be encouraging the parties to adopt different and inappropriate forms of contract on the basis of cost.[106] Thus it might be doubted that the costs argument should be compelling, since it is both difficult to verify, and is itself ambiguous and indeterminate.

THE ROLE OF TRUST IN THE BUSINESS RELATIONSHIP

Empirical studies demonstrating co-operation and flexibility in business relationships, and the complex interaction of informal and formal norms, mirror a line of scholarship in the business organisations and management literature about the role of trust in business relationships and its connection to contracting. While early legal empirical studies are famous for demonstrating the selective role of contracts in business relationships, research

[105] Ibid, 409–10.

[106] In another article Charny seems to appreciate these difficulties. He writes, 'Although a set of simple formal rules saves on the costs of administering the legal system, it may do so at the risk of drastically increasing the costs of transacting, by requiring the anticipation of numerous improbable contingencies or forcing parties to avoid altogether transactions that might culminate in punitive forfeitures as a result of mere small misunderstandings': 'The New Formalism in Contract' (1999) 66 *University of Chicago Law Review* 842, 850.

undertaken within other disciplines pursues no particular agenda concerning the use or design of contract law rules. This research is much more equivocal concerning the role of formal contracts in business, bringing into sharper focus the role of trust and informal norms. It is difficult to make direct comparisons across these different literatures because 'contract' usually has a wider meaning in the business studies literature beyond its connotations of legal enforceability. Nevertheless, this problem is itself instructive since it illustrates the difficulty of clearly separating the spheres of trust and contract in the minds of the parties and assigning them distinct and isolated roles in the business relationship. Scholars in business studies and related disciplines became interested in trust for its potential to reduce the uncertainty and risk involved in co-ordinating behaviour and interaction.[107] Trust is one of the mechanisms, but obviously not the only one, that allows social interaction to occur. In the non-simultaneous economic exchange, if one trusts the other participant in the exchange, there may be no need to adopt formal contractual measures to ensure performance. Early work in this vein regarded trust and (legal) contracts as substitute governance mechanisms. When one could rely on interpersonal trust in a business partner, one had no need for legally enforceable contracts.[108] This is consistent with the early empirical studies of law and business behaviour which indicated that insistence on a written contract and contract formalities was often interpreted as manifesting a lack of trust in a business partner, which could be detrimental to the relationship. In these studies, formal contracts and reliance on legal enforcement through contract law were seen as impeding the development of informal trusting norms,[109] leading to a failure to harness the possible benefits of trust and co-operation in business dealings.

The 'substitutes' view of trust and contracts calls into question the extent to which legal regulation is appropriate or necessary to business relationships built upon trust. At an extreme level, one might regard relationships displaying a high level of trust or reliance on social norms as outside the realm of law altogether. Building a relationship on the basis of trust might be regarded as a risk, but as has been seen above, it might also be argued that legalisation and legal enforcement of trusting norms may impair their value, and possibly render them less effective in regulating behaviour. Similarly legal regulation may be thought inappropriate since breach of

[107] B Lyons and J Mehta, 'Private Sector Business Contracts: The Text Between the Lines' in S Deakin and J Michie (eds), *Contracts, Co-operation and Competition* (Oxford, OUP, 1997) 43; B Lyons and J Mehta, 'Contracts, Opportunism and Trust: Self-interest and Social Orientation' (1997) 21 *Cambridge Journal of Economics* 239, 239.

[108] MJ Smitka, 'Contracting without Contracts: How the Japanese Manage Organizational Transactions' in S Sitkin and R Bies (eds), *The Legalistic Organization* (Thousand Oaks, Sage, 1994) 91, 95.

[109] See, eg, Macaulay, above n 6, '[contractual] planning indicates a lack of trust and blunts the demands of friendship, turning a cooperative venture into an antagonistic horse trade' (64).

trust cannot really be compensated in money.[110] After all, the law cannot shield contractors from the consequences of a contracting partner's failure to be trustworthy, as opposed to their failure to perform a contract. Thus it can be argued that contract law and its remedies are fundamentally incompatible with the idea and operation of trust. One might point out here that the problem identified is not so much that trusting and contracting are fundamentally incompatible as that one cannot *contract* for a business partner to be trusting or trustworthy. While this is true, this does not necessarily mean that the law should have no role in policing the business relationship that appears to be based on trust rather than contract. It may be that on closer inspection agreements relying solely on trust are non-existent, although much depends here on how 'trust' is conceptualised. Similarly, trust-based relationships may break down at any point with dire consequences for one of the parties. As far as the law is concerned, the lack of a formal agreement to govern the relationship is likely to lead courts to the conclusion that there was no intention to create legal obligations governing the long-term relationship, even if a string of discrete contracts existed between the parties over many years.[111]

The converse of this issue concerning the appropriateness of law in governing business relationships characterised by a high degree of trust is the question of whether, given their inevitable competitive element, it is ever appropriate to analyse business dealings in terms of trust. For some scholars trust must, at its core, be understood as expressing personal and altruistic values. These values are fundamentally at odds with commercial relationships where it remains doubtful that one party will ever fully subjugate their own interests to benefit a contracting partner.[112] Even if on occasion they do, their behaviour can be attributed to a form of enlightened self interest, not a willingness to make themselves vulnerable to the other party. It has been argued that this extrapolation from individual and interpersonal relationships to the institutional-organisational level is liable to distort understandings about how businesses do and should behave.[113] On this basis 'trust' is an unhelpful and inappropriate concept since it suggests that

[110] According to Stephen Smith even specific performance does not compensate for this kind of harm as it is in the nature of trust that it cannot be forced upon persons. Certainly money cannot compensate for the loss of trust—'it is like trying to buy friendship or love': SA Smith, 'Performance, Punishment and the Nature of Contractual Obligations' (1997) 60 *MLR* 360, 370.

[111] As in *Baird Textile Holdings v Marks and Spencer plc* [2001] EWCA Civ 274.

[112] See O Williamson, 'Calculativeness, Trust and Economic Organization' (1993) 36 *Journal of Law and Economics* 453, 484; B Burchell and F Wilkinson, 'Trust, Business Relationships and the Contractual Environment' (1997) 21 *Cambridge Journal of Economics* 217, 219.

[113] K Blois, 'Is it Commercially Irresponsible to Trust?' (2003) 45 *Journal of Business Ethics* 183, 190; also S Mouzas, S Henneberg and P Naudé, 'Trust and Reliance in Business Relationships' (2007) 41 *European Journal of Marketing* 1016, 1017.

commercial contracting behaviour, which is fundamentally about generating surplus from economic exchange, can be conceptualised as involving benevolent values beyond the necessary minimum required for exchange to actually occur.[114] Contract law itself recognises that there are important limits to the extent to which corporations can be imbued with positive human emotions or feelings.[115] Individuals may act ethically even when it may not be in their interests to do so, but agents acting for corporations by whom they are employed will always have a much narrower scope for altruistic action in this respect. The employers' interests must usually come first. In such contexts it may even be said to be socially and economically irresponsible to trust.[116]

The understanding of trust and contract as substitutes, and the denial of the role of (altruistic) trust in business relationships, has impinged on the debate about contract law and informal norms in two related ways. The first is that an incorporationist contract law might be understood as seeking to impose trusting and altruistic norms of behaviour on contracting parties. The second is that since trust is assumed to displace contracts and contract law, it vindicates a formal contract law design for those contracting parties that cannot rely on trust. Questioning the place of trust in contracting reinforces that trust and contract are separate spheres of a business relationship with largely separate enforcement mechanisms. It reiterates and legitimises the divide between the formal and informal: those who can trust will use trust and those that cannot will use formal contracts and contract law.[117] Following the substitutes line, therefore, it is easy to generate scepticism that contract law and formal contracts have any role to play in business relationships grounded fully on trust (if there are such relationships), or that such trusting norms of behaviour (where found to exist), are relevant to the resolution of a dispute once it reaches litigation. It is also easy to conclude that it is entirely inappropriate for contract law to assume or support the altruistic values or motives that underlie interpersonal trust.[118] To the extent that relational governance is often thought characterised by

[114] D Campbell, 'What Do We Mean By the Non-Use of Contract?' in J Braucher, J Kidwell and WC Whitford (eds), *Revisiting the Contracts Scholarship of Stewart Macaulay* (Oxford, Hart Publishing, 2013) 159, 163–64.

[115] Eg, companies cannot feel disappointment on breach: 'Contract breaking is treated as an incident of commercial life which players in the game are expected to meet with mental fortitude' per Lord Cooke in *Johnson v Gore Wood & Co Ltd* [2001] 2 WLR 72, 108.

[116] Blois, above n 113.

[117] Campbell, above n 114, 164; D Kimel, *From Promise to Contract* (Oxford, Hart Publishing, 2005), 78–80 and 'The Choice of Paradigm for Theory of Contract: Reflections on the Relational Model' (2007) 27 *OJLS* 232, 247.

[118] Mouzas et al argue that reliance is the rational counterpart to interpersonal, emotive trust and is therefore the effective concept with which to analyse institutional behaviour and business relationships. While interpersonal trust may not be manifest in all business relationships and commercial agreements, acts of reliance are almost always evident: above n 113, 1018.

interpersonal trust, thus requiring an enhanced role for the notion of trust in contract law—such as the assumption that all contractual relationships involve duties of trust and confidence—it would likewise be rejected. This would be a misunderstanding of relational theory however, or at least that version of it advanced by Ian Macneil. This will be discussed further in Chapter 6.

This negative and substitutes view of the relationship between law and trust is not accepted by all however, although the precise connection between law and trust in each business relationship depends very much on its own unique context, history and internal dynamic. This might be regarded as partly a pseudo-debate since 'trust' and the sources of trust are not always understood in a uniform way by the theorists using the concepts. When trust is presented as largely a personal, emotional or fundamentally altruistic concept, then this understanding is hard to reconcile with the commercial contracting process. Alternatively trusting may also be regarded as having a rational and self-interested motivation, which makes trust and contract easier to reconcile and easier to perceive as having complementary roles in a business relationship.[119] Thus some theorists point out that while shared cultures, ethnicity and experiences are important to the development of interpersonal trust, trust can also be understood in institutional terms. In the latter sense, social systems such as the legal system, prevailing social norms, industry associations and professional bodies can act as trust-facilitating institutions. Legally enforceable contracts may assist in harnessing and developing the necessary level of co-operation and relationship building for the parties to maximise the gains from trade. In effect contract is perceived as a way of formalising trust, or as a form of institutionalised trust.[120] This might be regarded as further muddying the already murky waters that surround the notion of trust and its relationship to contract.

In terms of complementarity, the relationship between contract and trust may be conceptualised in at least two different ways. First, contract may be *a trust-facilitating* institution. Second, contract may be a *trust-mimicking* institution. These can occur separately or together. In the latter sense, contracts, as supported by legal institutions, may mimic the effect of trust by facilitating exchange without the need to expend time developing interpersonal trust beyond the minimal level whereby the contracting parties satisfy themselves that their opposite is not untrustworthy. In the former sense, the parties may eventually develop a level of interpersonal trust through a series of interactions, such as satisfactory repeated dealings, initially based

[119] FB Cross, 'Law and Trust' (2005) 93 *Georgetown Law Journal* 1457, 1483.

[120] R Bachmann and AC Inkpen, 'Understanding Institutional-based Trust Building Processes in Inter-organizational Relationships' (2011) 32 *Organization Studies* 281, 285 and 288.

on contracts.[121] There is a distinction between an institution which mimics trust in formal terms, that is an institution that provides reliable enforcement mechanisms, provides security and allows trading to take place on certain imposed standards, and an institution that truly complements trust in allowing for the embedding, fostering and growth of trusting relationships akin to those that may be built between persons. The former system may not be designed to facilitate trust, but simply to replicate the practical benefits of it. Thus contract law may be regarded as a way for persons not already in a relationship of trust to effectively gain the benefits of interpersonal trust without the level of personal investment necessary to develop it and while maintaining personal detachment.[122] Arguably a contract law that upholds the alternative position (as a trust facilitator) would support the parties' efforts to build trusting and co-operative relationships when these are perceived as a more effective method than formal contracts to manage productive exchange relationships.

This distinction between the trust-facilitating and trust-mimicking functions of contracts is important since it provides one answer to those who may argue that a commercial-expectations approach to contract legal reasoning or a relational contract law may seek to impose norms of trust or altruism on the parties when it is not appropriate to do so. This is not the case. In seeking to uphold norms of trust and co-operation in some relationships when they are manifestly important (given the contracting context) there is no warrant for the law to assume that all commercial contracting relationships are trusting in an altruistic sense. Neither is this to suggest that only two alternatives are possible and that when legal contracts act as a trust facilitator this is always with the aim of eventually dispensing with contract altogether. Interpersonal trust may or may not eventually replace contracting, and the conditions under which it does so probably cannot be generalised. One empirical study found that even parties who are confident that they can rely on the benefits of personal trust in their dealings still draw up legally enforceable contracts without sensing any apparent conflict.[123] Similarly, Lane and Bachmann in a study of buyer-supplier relations in Britain and Germany distinguished 'process-based trust' or personal trust arising from relationships and 'institutional-based trust' founded on formal structures.[124] While process-based trust as developed in long-term relationships was found to be important, the legal framework, exemplifying institutional-based trust was also reckoned to be important for reassurance

[121] Ibid, 282.

[122] On the idea of contracts as mimicking trust see Kimel, above n 117, 66.

[123] RK Woolthuis, B Hillebrand and B Nooteboom, 'Trust, Contract and Relationship Development' (2005) 26 *Organization Studies* 813, 829–32.

[124] C Lane and R Bachmann, 'The Social Constitution of Trust: Supplier Relations in Britain and Germany' (1996) 17 *Organization Studies* 365.

and often internal, rather than external, planning. Thus one respondent from the UK mining industry said that 'I am firmly in favour of a formal contract which you never have to look at'.[125]

It is not clear that anyone adheres to the view that benevolence- or altruistic-trust should explain or underpin contract law, but such a view can be rejected at least in a commercial setting. Beyond that, however, the matter of the relationship between trust and contracting is complex. It is equally clear that one cannot completely oust the notion of trust from contracting. However intuitively appealing it may be to believe that legal contracts are only necessary because self-interested, socially isolated and atomistic individuals do not act under the social conditions conducive to the development of trusting relationships, it is clear that there must be some basic level of trust and willingness to make oneself vulnerable to another, or at least a significant lack of distrust, if contracting is likely to occur at all. Thus trust and contract do not necessarily operate as substitutes, nor with trust gradually 'replacing' formal contractual measures as the relationship develops. This entails that while both the *benevolence* and *substitutes* view of trust and contract should be rejected, commercial parties may still have expectations not wholly derived from the legal framework, even when a relatively robust legal framework exists—both contracts and a degree of trust are often present and these are not mutually exclusive or easily separable. For the purposes of this work, the point is that expectations may arise from trust, contract and the combination of both these two.

That both trust and contract may inform commercial expectations in various ways is manifest from modern empirical studies that suggest both trust and formal contract documents may be present in a relationship. Burchell and Wilkinson undertook a study of firms in Germany, Britain and Italy. Respondents were asked to say what they thought trust meant. Responses tended to fall into two groups. One group associated trust with substance—honesty, reliability, openness, fairness, co-operativeness—and the other associated trust with the processes by which it was established. Experience of a contracting partner doing what he said he would do was the most important consideration for this latter group.[126] While this might suggest that the contract has a role in the establishment of trust between parties, it was clear that 'contract adherence' was not solely associated with honouring the express terms of a legally enforceable written agreement. It also incorporated 'observing standards *and* the honouring of more informal commitments'.[127] Evidently what the respondents understood by 'contract' when comparing it with trust mattered a great deal, but as alluded to earlier this

[125] Ibid, 385.

[126] Burchell and Wilkinson, above n 112, 224.

[127] Ibid, 233. It is therefore not surprising that A Kalnins and K Mayer argue that the literature on trust and contracts has not reached consistent conclusions: 'Relationships and Hybrid

means that contracting or agreement making as a process is not understood as a purely legal construct. Nevertheless, to the extent that 'contracting' was at least partly understood as a legal concept, contract (reliance on legally enforceable agreements to govern a relationship) may have a role in the establishment of trust between parties.

More specifically directed to the role of written agreements and contract law was the study of Arrighetti, Bachmann and Deakin. They found that 'contract law may play an important role in underpinning long-term relations based on co-operation and trust'.[128] Their study analysed the phenomenon of 'inter-firm co-operation' occurring through the mechanism of 'networks' or 'hybrids' which are ill explained by either theories of market or hierarchy. As was seen in the last chapter, such arrangements take a variety of forms but are usually characterised as long term and where expectations of risk sharing, exchange of information and expertise are the norm. Their study focused on the mining machinery industry and kitchen units manufacturing in the UK, Italy and Germany. Respondents were questioned as to the prevalence of written contracts as a planning and incentive tool. Although a few firms (especially in the UK) reported little use of written contracts, preferring 'gentlemen's agreements' and letters of comfort, this attitude was not common. The authors write that 'the vast majority of firms saw both the use of writing and the attachment of legal force as important means of clarifying the agreement and providing for security in the event of a dispute'.[129] The security of legal enforceability was thought important even though few respondents envisaged litigation as a way of resolving problems. Contrary to Macaulay, who explained lack of court-based procedures and contracts amongst businesses as manifesting a desire not to interfere with trust, Arrighetti et al found that use of formal contracts was compatible with reluctance to use courts.[130] Somewhat counterintuitively, they discovered that use of looser commitments, particularly based on interpersonal relationships, could often be a source of disputes. UK firms that placed less emphasis on strict contract performance often had more direct recourse to courts to enforce payment: 'British respondents in the kitchen furniture sector, who placed the least emphasis on contract from the point of view of planning, were also the most likely to have to

Contracts: An Analysis of Contract Choice in Information Technology' (2004) 20 *Journal of Law, Economics and Organization* 207, 209.

[128] A Arrighetti, R Bachmann and S Deakin, 'Contract Law, Social Norms and Inter-firm Co-operation' (1997) 21 *Cambridge Journal of Economics* 171, 171.

[129] Ibid, 186.

[130] See also Bachmann and Inkpen, above n 120, 289. The authors hypothesise that the common law is a relatively weak institution at fostering trust since it leaves much to the parties to determine through contract terms, which function less as a reassuring device and more as an attempt to work outside the legal precepts. Thus contracts under the common law system are more repositories of power and a symbol of distrust rather than trust: 289–90.

go to court to enforce their agreements.'[131] As with the Beale and Dugdale study, the authors found courts were often used as a first resort, especially in the UK in relation to payment disputes.[132] The authors concluded that it was in fact knowledge of law and legal processes that made recourse to law unnecessary, particularly since institutions, including that of commercial contract law, act as guides to behaviour: 'The importance of the institutional framework lies instead in providing a powerful set of incentives for the maintenance of stable, long-term relations, which serve to enhance quality'.[133] Similarly, Poppo and Zenger[134] also argued that contracts and relational governance functioned as complements, since precise specifications included in written contracts reduce risk which in turn can encourage co-operation. Along similar lines, Scott argues that experience in a trusting commercial relationship increases predictability, which is conducive to greater planning (sources of difficulty are revealed through experience, and thus become 'contractible').[135] On this basis the real progression in transactions and exchanges between complex organisations may be from trust to contractual commitment, rather than the reverse.[136]

There is a wider point to be made here. The difficulty of articulating the precise connection between contract and trust reflects the inherently contradictory nature of contractual relationships. Such relationships appear *simultaneously* co-operative and competitive.[137] Macneil regards this dualism as a reflection of human nature. He writes, 'Man is both an entirely selfish creature and an entirely social creature, in that man puts the interests of his fellows ahead of his own interests *at the same time* that he puts his own interests first'.[138] One of the effects of this is that, as Woolthuis et al have noted, conceptualising commercial relationships according to poles is not possible: such relationships will generally display a multidimensional governance strategy, relying simultaneously on norms of contract

[131] Arrighetti et al, above n 128, 191.

[132] Ibid, 187–88.

[133] Ibid, 189.

[134] L Poppo and TR Zenger, 'Do Formal Contracts and Relational Governance Function as Substitutes or Complements?' (2002) 23 *Strategic Management Journal* 707, 721. Similarly, FB Cross has concluded that law may have a positive effect on trust development by giving legal assurances and remedies for breach of trust in some cases: above n 119. Others have also found, using experimental methodologies, that contracts can support co-operation and that co-operative behaviour was not crowded out by formalisation: SG Lazzarini, GJ Miller and TR Zenger, 'Order with Some Law: Complementarity versus Substitution of Formal and Informal Arrangements' (2004) 20 *Journal of Law, Economics and Organization* 261.

[135] RE Scott, 'The Promise and Peril of Relational Contract Theory' in Braucher, Kidwell and Whitford (eds), above n 114, 105, 132.

[136] Narayandas and Rangan, above n 35, 74: 'Trust between individuals spurs the development of commitment between firms'.

[137] Burchell and Wilkinson, above n 112, 224 (emphasis in original). See also Lane and Bachmann, above n 124, 367–68.

[138] I Macneil, *The Relational Theory of Contract: Selected Works of Ian Macneil*, D Campbell (ed) (London, Sweet & Maxwell, 2001) 153, emphasis in original.

and trust.[139] Whether these two are conflicting or mutually reinforcing, substitutes or complements, is not an issue that can be decided in the abstract, but only upon close examination of each individual commercial relationship. It has been noted that more recent contributions to trust scholarship have asserted the complementary nature of contract and trust, as well as the role of legal institutions in developing and supporting trust between businesses. This line of scholarship is less supportive of the idea of easily severable worlds of business relationships in favour of one, complex, indeterminate world where contract governance structures are infinitely varied. Vlaar has pointed out that polarisation of positions as formalist or not-formalist obscures the complexity of what are in effect co-existing yet contradictory pressures. Managers and contractors have to make a variety of trade-offs and it is too simple to reduce these to a choice between two worlds of 'flexibility' and 'control', or between 'competition' and 'co-operation'.[140] This suggests that a responsive commercial contract law cannot be developed while the belief is retained that there are only two variables—formalism or contextualism; trust or contract—that inform legal reasoning in this area.

The conclusion from this discussion is that complex contracts are not necessarily anomalous in trusting relationships, and that both trust and contract/informal and formal norms matter in many business relationships, particularly when project constraints and complexity demand some degree of formalisation, but when substantial trust and co-operation are also necessary to the successful realisation of the project.[141] It is not always the case therefore that relationships can be predicted as moving through a contract–trust trajectory. It is likely that choosing between these 'complements or substitutes' models of the relationship between contract and trust is both unnecessary and unhelpful, and that the push to generalise across these varying contexts to determinate conclusions has the potential to lead to error. Thus the literature on trust and contract raises questions concerning the capacity of the law to achieve greater understanding of commercial relationships by proceeding on the basis that there are mutually exclusive worlds of (legal) contract and trust, that the parties will have consciously decided to emphasise either one or the other, and that legal reasoning techniques need only identify the correct world within which to situate the deal, whereupon the applicable norms for dispute resolution will become apparent. The more complex reality

[139] Woolthuis et al, above n 123, 835–36.

[140] P Vlaar, F Van Den Bosch and H Volberda, 'Towards a Dialectic Perspective on Formalization in Interorganizational Relationships' (2007) 28 *Organization Studies* 437, 440.

[141] J Zheng, JK Roehrich and MA Lewis, 'The Dynamics of Contractual and Relational Governance: Evidence from Long-term Public-Private Procurement Arrangements' (2008) 14 *Journal of Purchasing and Supply Management* 43, 48.

is that legal reasoning in contract is required to appreciate and make sense of both the competitive and co-operative character of contractual relationships. So, for example, that the parties were in a trusting relationship (the relationship displays elements of personal trust) need not lead to the conclusion that a co-operative attitude towards the agreement was always expected. Rather, the trusting relationship may provide a vital element of context which ought to affect the interpretative strategy placed upon the formal contractual scheme. It is unlikely that 'trusting' parties use a formal contract to determine in absolute terms their legal rights and obligations. Instead, the documents may perform a variety of more nebulous functions designed to harness the trusting relationship and transform it into a productive one, such as by stipulating project milestones, or managing the consequences of staff turnover. By paying attention to this issue of role, a court is more likely to come to a decision that genuinely reflects the 'reasonable expectations of the parties' (understood in a non-legal sense), rather than one which champions the operation of one distinct value over its competitor. This is not to say that contract and trust, where existing together, must always be harmonious. Where an organisation's productive activities undergo transition from trust to contract there may be considerable negative effects on a relationship.[142] The lesson to be learned, however, is not that contracting will always oust the operation of trust, co-operation and informal norms, but that it can help or hinder a business relationship. This must in part relate to how the law itself responds to the contracting arrangements that firms make and the external and internal constraints operating on firms. A close examination of contracting context in each case should make this more apparent to the law.

CONCLUSION

While it might be difficult to detect in advance what a contractor's substantive expectations in any given contract context might be, the discussion above demonstrates the existence of a wide variety of sources for commercial expectations operating outside the contract terms. It would seem therefore that the claim that contract law should be better aligned with commercial expectations is not defeated by an argument that there is no way of knowing what these expectations are. However, empirical and theoretical work on the role of trust and the interconnection between formal and informal norms in business contracting also points to the difficulty of articulating the relationship between contracts and commercial expectations in completely opposed terms. Business contracting in many contexts involves a complex

[142] W Seal and P Vincent-Jones, 'Accounting and Trust in the Enabling of Long-Term Relations' (1997) 10 *Accounting, Auditing & Accountability Journal* 406, 407.

interplay between formal legal-contractual and informal social norms and sanctions. A degree of trust and reliance in a contracting partner and an expectation of flexibility and co-operation between contractors is apparent, even in situations where the contracting parties may engage in some comprehensive planning of the agreement. Parties often display a certain duality in the governance scheme they adopt, and the legal machinery is often well aware of this. The Scottish Law Commission recently remarked in their discussion paper on contract interpretation:

> [E]vidence from the Business Advisory Group suggests that businesses generally place great emphasis and care on the detail of their contracts, and view the content of contractual provisions as an important element in any smooth running commercial enterprise. Entire agreement clauses are favoured as a means of ensuring that the contractual documentation is readily identifiable and can be distinguished from the discarded preceding material. Businesses generally expect contractual provisions to be clear and well articulated but, crucially, recognise in certain circumstances that a flexible approach to interpretation of such provisions will be required.[143]

To the extent that the law ignores these wider contexts for contract planning and performance, and relies upon a model of the contracting process where the parties act self-interestedly and should be encouraged to take care of themselves and their own interests, the law could be said to be deficient. As well as identifying the sources of commercial expectations, this chapter has therefore also provided additional arguments for why these expectations matter to contract legal reasoning—because the legal-contractual relationship cannot be fully understood except by attention to these expectations. The normative richness of these expectations suggests that each contract case requires a careful examination of the facts and consideration of the interaction between the three particular variables that impinge on the issue of the relationship between contracts and informal norms: the parties' relationship; the nature of the project; and the norms themselves. If commercial contractors expect anything from the law it is likely to be that courts will be mindful of the constraints they are under in managing their exchange relationships and productive activity, and will tailor their legal reasoning techniques with some sensitivity to this. The following chapter considers the extent to which aspects of current contract law accord with this ideal.

[143] Scottish Law Commission, *Discussion Paper on Interpretation of Contract* (no 147), (Edinburgh, TSO, 2011) para 6.3.

4

Current Contract Law and Commercial Expectations

ONE RESPONSE TO the claim about misalignment between contract law and commercial expectations is to question its accuracy. It would certainly be a distortion to present current commercial contract law as excessively formal. Parties will not always commit their obligations to paper and even when they do, the use of trade customs, implied terms and interpretative processes all provide avenues for judicial consideration of business practices. Lower courts cannot resolve disputes without undertaking a sometimes very detailed investigation of the facts, including hearing evidence from those directly involved in the events and experts in the particular industry. Nebulous doctrines derived from equity (such as estoppel, rectification, variation and waiver) and restitution also allow the law to implement a more standards-based approach to the commercial agreement which may often have the effect of implementing the parties' 'understandings' over formal contract terms.[1] These approaches are often organised under an umbrella concept of protecting the 'reasonable expectations' of the parties.[2] It might be argued that classical contract law is sufficiently adaptable to absorb, reflect and stay connected to commercial expectations.

This is a cogent argument but as with most debates about the relative formalism of the law, the question is one of degree. For every commercial contract case that displays some appreciation of the informal norms and expectations that surround the legal agreement,[3] there are counter-examples that display a more attenuated commitment to recognising and enforcing the 'real deal'.[4] Of course it could be that a formal approach to a

[1] For a recent example of the use of variation and waiver see *RTS Flexible Systems Ltd v Molkerei Alois Müller Gmbh & Co KG (UK Production)* [2010] UKSC 14; [2010] 1 WLR 753.

[2] Lord Steyn, 'Contract Law: Fulfilling the Reasonable Expectations of Honest Men' (1997) 113 *LQR* 433–42. For comment on this idea see C Mitchell, 'Leading a Life of its Own? The Roles of Reasonable Expectation in Contract Law' (2003) 23 *OJLS* 639.

[3] For cases that show some sensitivity to the 'real deal' see *Williams v Roffey* [1991] 1 QB 1 and *Blackpool and Fylde Aero Club v Blackpool Borough Council* [1990] 1 WLR 1195.

[4] *Baird Textiles Ltd v Marks and Spencer plc* [2001] EWCA Civ 274; *Carlton Communications plc and Granada Media plc v The Football League* [2002] EWHC 1650.

particular contract is fully justifiable by reference to the surrounding context. But if specific contextual factors play a role in compelling a formalist approach to resolving a particular dispute, this is not always detectable on the surface of a judgment. This gives an ad hoc and impressionistic feel to any differentiation between similar cases on the basis of their distinctive contexts.[5] The question of whether the law already takes sufficient account of expectations therefore cannot be taken at face value, but requires some further investigation.

This chapter will explore how well contract law copes with the reality of commercial dealing. Given the range of contract law areas that could be examined to this end, the chapter is necessarily selective, focusing in particular on issues such as the legal commitment to the contractual documents and legal expectations concerning certainty in agreements. It will be seen that in many respects contract law, at least in the hands of judges, does engage with the problems that arise from issues such as the failure to plan deals, and the dissonance between obligations as stated in formal documents and those created by the informal norms of co-operation and flexibility that surround the legal framework. However, while the law often does take account of implicit dimensions and understandings that arise outside the contract terms, the legal approach is neither systematic nor consistent. Given the assumptions upon which its scheme of rules is based and that in the main it appears 'designed for big business',[6] English contract law is often presented with problems that appear anomalous to it. Parties may attempt to contract for flexible commitments, such as duties of good faith and co-operation,[7] or bind themselves to use their 'best endeavours' to achieve some end. Commitments may be left deliberately vague or open ended, or parties may embark upon performance of sometimes very complex agreements without contract formalities in place.[8] It is clear that these 'anomalous' contractual arrangements very often reflect the realities of commercial dealing in uncertain environments, or for innovative projects, and may represent the best that can be achieved by parties attempting some degree of advance planning. While courts may give effect to what they take to be commercial expectations through an assortment of doctrinal techniques and utilising a range of justificatory arguments, this engagement is limited in that it does not appear to lead to any sustained appreciation of, or

[5] Compare, eg, two contrasting decisions on the right to terminate a contract: *Rice v Great Yarmouth Borough Council* [2000] All ER (D) 902 and *Total Gas Marketing v Arco British* [1998] 2 Lloyd's Rep 209.

[6] H Beale, 'The Impact of the Decisions of the European Courts on English Contract Law: The Limits of Voluntary Harmonization' (2010) 3 *European Review of Private Law* 501, 526.

[7] See, eg, *Mid Essex Hospital Services NHS Trust v Compass Group UK and Ireland Ltd (t/a Medirest)* [2013] EWCA Civ 200.

[8] See, eg, *RTS v Müller*, above n 1.

coherent approach to dealing with, the complexities of business contracting and the constraints under which it operates.

TENSIONS BETWEEN LAW AND COMMERCIAL CONTRACTING BEHAVIOUR

That contractors may have expectations about obligations and performance outside of the express contract terms comes as no surprise to the law. Lord Justice Thomas in the 2009 Lord Merlyn-Rees Lecture recognised that the legal framework was premised on the practice of the mercantile community to trust those with whom they do business that they will carry out their bargains,[9] but that the law also had its limitations in this respect:

> [E]veryday business life is conducted on the assumption that you choose carefully the person with whom you do business and enter into business only with a person in whom you believe you can trust. That is so because it is quite impossible to devise a legal regime, whether by the terms of a contract or otherwise, that can in detail supervise the conduct of another party to a bargain ... unless you wish to buy yourself a dispute, you would never contemplate entering into a contract with someone whom you did not trust.[10]

While there can be little doubt that courts appreciate the social embeddedness of commercial contracts, they may doubt the relevance of this for the operation of the rules of contract law. The law recognises that many obligations remain valuable because they are outwith the scope of legal control. Thus one interpretation of the doctrine of consideration is to uphold the value of altruism represented by the gift promise precisely by leaving it within the private sphere.[11] This public–private distinction cannot be pressed too far however, and it is particularly troublesome to maintain in commercial contexts where distinguishing the business equivalent of the 'gift' may be problematic.

This lack of legal engagement with the social side of agreement making and performance is one of the effects of the anti-paternalistic character of classical contract law. The most prevalent understanding of the English law of contract is that it is largely a system of defaults that commercial parties can contract around at will. Thus it perceives its role as setting the outer

[9] Relying on dicta from Bowen LJ in *Sanders v Maclean* (1883) 11 QBD 327.

[10] Lord Justice Thomas, 'The Financial Crisis: The Role of Law and Regulation', University of Glamorgan, 5 March 2009, http://www.judiciary.gov.uk/Resources/JCO/Documents/Speeches/ljt-speech-lord-merlyn-rees-lecture-2009.pdf. See also *Ultraframe (UK) Ltd v Tailored Roofing Systems* [2004] EWCA Civ 585, [2004] 2 All ER (Comm) 692, per Waller LJ, [14].

[11] M Chen-Wishart, *Contract Law*, 3rd edn (Oxford, OUP, 2010) 122–23; H Collins, *The Law of Contract*, 4th edn (London, LexisNexis, 2003) 59.

limits on tolerable commercial behaviour.[12] There is also an influential belief that commercial contractors, particularly those with the resources to employ lawyers and to litigate, neither wish for nor require an activist judicial approach. Such parties can largely take care of themselves.[13] The extent to which parties do contract around the legal rules is a matter for empirical investigation, but irrespective of the results of this enquiry, most of the rules of contract law are reckoned to be excludable.[14] Yet the law does not completely cede control to the parties and the court remains the ultimate arbiter over whether the parties have been successful in contracting out of the general law. Examples can readily be found which demonstrate a court refusing to sanction a commercial practice as legally valid, even if agreed between the parties,[15] or otherwise of long standing.[16] Likewise, decisions taken as a matter of commercial prudence do not thereby become legally acceptable.[17] Although the courts maintain that their role in commercial dealing is to uphold the agreement the parties made, not to make it more fair or reasonable, nor to substitute a different agreement,[18] in setting the requirements for legal enforceability, the courts essentially decide what can and cannot be achieved through the medium of contracting. In doing so, they oversee and control the connection between contract law and commercial behaviour. This can work in a positive fashion, as when courts communicate to contracting parties how certain commercial ends might be effectively achieved through contract mechanisms.[19] But policing this border between law and practice by promulgating rules with general applicability in order to regulate the parties' exercise of freedom of contract also gives rise to considerable tensions within commercial contract law, most notably between the demands that the law makes upon parties seeking legal enforceability for their agreements and actual commercial practices. The sources of some of these tensions are examined below.

[12] Beale, above n 6, 521–23. See also H Collins, 'Lord Hoffmann and the Common Law of Contract' (2009) 5 *European Review of Contract Law* 474, 474–75. See also I Ayres, 'Valuing Modern Contract Scholarship' (2003) 112 *Yale Law Journal* 881, 885–86.

[13] See, eg, Lord Nicholls in *Royal Bank of Scotland v Etridge (No 2)* [2002] 2 AC 773 [88]; and Hobhouse J in *EE Caledonia Ltd v Orbit Valve Co Europe* [1993] 4 All ER 165, 173.

[14] A recent example of contracting around is *Belmont v Lehmans* [2011] UKSC 38 [159].

[15] A recent example of the necessity for a clear intention to contract around the general rules is provided by *Re: Sigma Finance Corp (in administrative receivership)* [2009] UKSC 2; [2010] 1 All ER 571.

[16] *Re: Spectrum Plus Ltd* [2005] UKHL 41; [2005] 2 AC 680.

[17] Per Lord Mance, *Belmont v Lehmans* [2011] UKSC 38 [159].

[18] Eg, *Attorney General of Belize v Belize Telecom Ltd* [2009] UKPC 10; [2009] Bus LR 1316, per Lord Hoffmann [16].

[19] As with the development of 'Himalaya' clauses for example, to afford third-party stevedores the benefit of exclusion clauses in the main carriage contract: *The Eurymedon* [1975] AC 154, now rendered much simpler by the operation of the Contract (Rights of Third) Parties Act 1999, s 1(6).

The Significance of the Documents

While empirical studies demonstrate that many commercial contractors display some equivocation over the need to plan their projects by documenting their commitments in a legally enforceable agreement, in legal contexts the documented agreement is regarded as the definitive statement of legal obligations and as constituting 'the contract'. It is usually the case that the documents will, in large part, be the focus of the legal dispute and its resolution, particularly in complex commercial contexts. Thus the interpretation of the contract within the law does not involve interpreting the *contractual agreement*, but the *contract text*. However, the legal reliance on formal contractual documents has also been a focus for criticism concerning the law's misalignment with commercial expectations. If contract law regards the documents as constituting the agreement, most modern scholars with an appreciation of literature from the social sciences regard the contract as something more elusive—the agreement the parties make, which may or may not be the same thing as expressed in the written terms.[20] Taking the documents as evidence of what was agreed would seem to raise several related problems. Many formal contractual documents are drafted by lawyers, rather than the contracting parties,[21] and while the documents may record fully negotiated and genuinely agreed terms, they may also contain standard or boilerplate provisions whose inclusion is difficult to attribute to the intentions of the parties in any meaningful sense. Express terms may be 'cobbled together' from various different sources and forms,[22] and thus may be less a reflection of the parties' actual agreement and more an attempt to impose an externally derived order upon it. The documents may be an unreliable record of the parties' agreement, may contain significant gaps (either by design or by oversight) and may be signed without being read or understood.[23] The contractual text may not reflect all the parties' understandings about their obligations and their relationship, and may be written in fairly technical 'legal' language.

If one takes the view that contract law is ultimately a pragmatic response to a problem of co-ordinating activities over time, allowing for the possibility of the non-simultaneous exchange, the documents are undoubtedly

[20] Eg, P Linzer, 'The Comfort of Certainty: Plain Meaning and the Parol Evidence Rule' (2002) 71 *Fordham Law Review* 799, 822.

[21] Collins, *Regulating Contracts* (Oxford, OUP, 1999) 153–54, 159.

[22] MJ Radin, 'Boilerplate Today: The Rise of Modularity and the Waning of Consent' in O Ben-Shahar (ed), *Boilerplate: The Foundation of Market Contracts* (Cambridge, CUP, 2007) 189, 191.

[23] Courts frequently recognise this: see, eg, the comments of Mance LJ in *Sinochem International Oil (London) Co Ltd v Mobil Sales and Supply Corporation* [2000] 1 Lloyd's Rep 339, [28].

important in assisting with this formal planning element.[24] For lawyers, documents minimise the possibility for error in recalling what was agreed (in the drafting stage lawyers will be anticipating, and seeking to minimise, the possibility of a dispute). Written, and signed, contracts may still have an important social function of symbolising the seriousness and implications of the undertaking as well as providing manageable evidence of what was decided.[25] The existence of the lawyer-drafted written document may constitute a 'context' in its own right. Thus Smith argues that

> the context of commercial drafting ... is one that asks the reader to ignore the context outside of the physical document. *Why* this is the context is not strictly relevant, but the reason is undoubtedly found in the importance that commercial lawyers place on reducing opportunities for misunderstandings.[26]

One reason for drafting comprehensive documents is to provide a more reliable source of evidence about the agreement than witnesses. Attention to the documents may 'restrict arbitrator discretion and minimize the need for arbitrators both to rely on and assess the credibility of testimony'.[27] This commitment to documents is often defended by reference to the 'will of the parties', but a more plausible explanation is that a strict approach to the documents communicates to commercial contractors generally that the law seeks to maintain the integrity, significance and utility of the formal documented agreement with strictly limited avenues of escape from agreed express terms.[28] This in turn will encourage parties to formalise their obligations in writing, to record their obligations in clear language and to read and review documents carefully to ensure they reflect their intentions and expectations.[29] This will also discourage parties from acting strategically in attempting to displace the express terms of the contract in favour of more nebulous understandings, and also prevent the parties making self-serving statements concerning their intentions during the course of negotiations. English law is also committed to the objective theory of agreement which prioritises the outward expressions and manifest signs of the contract rather than any inner intentions. The legal attachment to documents is reinforced by the operation of the parol evidence rule, which dictates that where a

[24] C Bridgeman, 'Contracts as Plans' (2009) *University of Illinois Law Review* 341.

[25] L Fuller, 'Consideration and Form' (1941) *Columbia Law Review* 799, 800–03.

[26] SA Smith, *Contract Theory* (Oxford, OUP, 2004) 276; Lord Nicholls, 'My Kingdom for a Horse: The Meaning of Words' (2005) 1 *LQR* 577, 585.

[27] L Bernstein, 'Merchant Law in a Merchant Court: Rethinking the Code's Search for Immanent Business Norms' (1996) 144 *University of Pennsylvania Law Review* 1765, 1819. In *Inntrepreneur Pub Company Ltd v East Crown* [2000] All ER (D) 1100, a witness for Inntrepreneur could not recall the details of crucial conversations he held with the defendant. The judge nevertheless described him as an 'impressive witness', at [18].

[28] *Chartbrook Ltd v Persimmon Homes Ltd* [2009] 1 AC 1101; [2009] UKHL 38, [41].

[29] See R Posner, *Law and Literature*, rev'd edn (Cambridge MA, Harvard University Press, 1998) 210.

contract is in writing, it may not be varied by extrinsic evidence of its terms. Like the requirement of consideration, the parol evidence rule is subject to so many exceptions that it rarely causes injustice or practical problems, and its very existence has been questioned,[30] but at least two relatively recent House of Lords decisions demonstrate its continuing influence as part of the underlying fabric of contract law.[31]

One of the effects of this commitment to the written agreement is that the courts are willing to support the parties' attempts, through the medium of the documents, to create a kind of alternative legal reality to the actual reality in which they found themselves, not least by setting out the factual basis for the transaction, irrespective of whether it accords with the actual state of affairs that existed when the agreement was made. Thus contract terms such as 'acknowledgments of non-reliance'[32] and the entire agreement clause[33] act as formal devices to legally prevent a claimant's assertions of alternative obligations arising outwith contract terms. Such clauses operate independently and quite irrespective of the claimant's actual beliefs and acts of reliance.[34] Thus the parties' real understandings about their agreement may not be permitted to encroach upon the contractual statement of 'facts'. This legal attitude towards the terms and the documented agreement is connected to the importance of objectivity, but also reflects an understanding that the basis upon which a party undertakes an obligation may be part of an agreed allocation of risk which is reflected in the price charged for performance. Thus the parties may 'set the facts' in order to put their agreement on a jointly acknowledged footing. This might serve a variety of pragmatic purposes, such as providing assurance that certain things will be taken to be the case, despite the future being uncertain and unknowable. A similar attitude pervades the legal approach to contract interpretation, where the law attaches pre-eminence to the point of view of 'reasonable persons' about what the contract means, rather than the actual

[30] Law Commission Report No 154, *Law of Contract: The Parol Evidence Rule* (London, HMSO, 1986) para 2.7; E McKendrick, *Contract Law: Text, Cases and Materials*, 2nd edn (Oxford, OUP, 2005), 340: Collins, above n 21, 159–60.

[31] See Lord Hobhouse, *Shogun Finance Ltd v Hudson* [2003] UKHL 62; [2003] 3 WLR 1371, 1386. See also Lord Hoffmann in *Chartbrook Ltd v Persimmon Homes Ltd*, above n 28. However, courts recognise that a contract is to be interpreted according to what it meant at the time it is agreed, it does not necessarily govern the entirety of the relationship into the future: *Lloyds TSB Foundation for Scotland v Lloyds Banking Group plc* [2013] UKSC 3.

[32] *Alman v Associated News*, unreported, 20 June 1980, per Browne-Wilkinson J.

[33] Effective for precluding collateral contracts, but not misrepresentation (although much depends on the drafting of the term): *Deepak Fertilisers v Davy McKee (UK) London Ltd* [1999] 1 Lloyd's Rep 387; *Axa Sun Life Services plc v Campbell Martin Ltd* [2011] EWCA Civ 133; [2012] 1 All ER (Comm) 268. See generally C Mitchell, 'Entire Agreement Clauses: Contracting out of Contextualism' (2006) 22 *Journal of Contract Law* 222.

[34] *Peekay Intermark Ltd v Australia and New Zealand Banking Group Ltd* [2006] EWCA 386 [56].

contracting parties.[35] Lord Hoffmann recognised an element of artificiality in interpretation when he wrote, extra-judicially, 'the people whose utterances have to be interpreted by the courts are often to a greater or lesser extent imaginary'.[36] There is also the concern for speedy and effective dispute resolution which demands a difficult balance to be struck between maximising the accuracy of the determination of the case by reference to the minimum amount of reliable evidence. This is not to say that the courts are blind to the social framework that informs the parties' expectations about their business relationship. Courts are well aware of the distinction between the real and paper deal, and the artificiality of the latter.[37] Nevertheless, while there might be good reasons for the law to rely heavily on the documented agreement in working out the content of the agreement, there is the danger that the document becomes a fictional entity almost wholly removed from the relationship and project to which it relates.

This is not to say that contract interpretation is a mechanical exercise leaving no sphere of influence for the parties' more elusive understandings concerning their agreement. The courts often uphold outcomes that appear contrary to express contract wording, motivated seemingly by equitable considerations of fairness and balance.[38] They may also take into account context in deciding the role of the documents and what a contractor can be expected to take note of within those documents. However, consistency is not necessarily evident in this area. Lord Hoffmann in *The Starsin*, for example, readily understood that bankers did not read the reverse of the bills of lading and were therefore not required by the law to do so.[39] While this might be taken as legal appreciation of the constraints under which business people operate when dealing with contractual paperwork, the courts may still impose an expectation that documents are read and understood in other cases.[40] Naturally contract context may play an important role here in distinguishing when there is an operative expectation to read the small print. But if contract context does supply the justification for differentiating between situations this is not transparent, with the result

[35] *Investors Compensation Scheme v West Bromwich Building Society* [1998] 1 WLR 896.

[36] Lord Hoffmann, 'The Intolerable Wrestle with Words and Meanings' (1997) 114 *South African Law Journal* 656, 661.

[37] *Balmoral Group Ltd v Borealis (UK) Ltd* [2006] EWHC 1900, at para [339]. See also Collins, above n 21, 155.

[38] *Bank of Credit and Commerce International SA (in liquidation) v Ali* [2001] UKHL 8 [2001] 2 WLR 735. For judicial criticism see K Gibbons, 'A Conversation with Lord Hoffmann' (2010) 4 *Law and Financial Markets Review* 242, 244–45.

[39] *Homburg Houtimport BV v Agrosin Private Ltd and others (The Starsin)* [2003] UKHL 12; [2004] 1 AC 715, [75–77] and [188].

[40] *Peekay Intermark Ltd v Australia and New Zealand Banking Group Ltd*, above n 34. There is some empirical support for the idea that business people rarely read the back of standard forms: B Lyons and J Mehta, 'Private Sector Business Contracts: The Text Between the Lines' in S Deakin and J Michie (eds), *Contracts, Co-operation and Competition* (Oxford, OUP, 1997) 43, 58.

that no meaningful prediction or assessment can be made of when nebulous 'practices' (for example, not reading the back of form) will be determinative over close attention to express terms.

Apart from these general problems with the commitment to the documented agreement, difficulties arise where incompatible expectations are generated by the legal and social frameworks for an agreement.[41] Even if contract law is amenable to incorporating elements of commercial practice and immanent business norms into legal reasoning, such standards are often rendered 'invisible' to the law. Battle lines in cases may be drawn between the informal expectations derived from outside the legal framework and the statement of express terms and conditions, but the informal expectations may have little impact in the face of what appears to be a comprehensive set of terms. This leads to a very attenuated engagement with the internal norms of the business relationship on the part of the law, since the 'non-legal' understandings are easily dismissed as irrelevant. Two examples follow of this lack of engagement: the first where the parties' agreement appeared governed in part by both legal formalities and implicit understandings, and the second when it appeared the latter only were in play.

(i) Differing Frameworks for an Agreement

The first example, *National Westminster Bank plc v Rabobank Nederland*,[42] concerned the extent of a banker's duty to disclose material information to fellow bankers during a 'workout'. The workout process operates outside formal legal insolvency procedures and is designed to allow creditor banks time to formulate a co-ordinated response to a debtor facing financial problems. The ultimate aim is to restructure a corporate debtor's financing so that a viable business is not put into insolvency. Although no creditor is legally obliged to take part in a workout, it is generally recognised as advantageous to do so since workouts avoid the transaction costs that would be incurred if creditors engaged in a 'race to collect' as soon as a company's financial problems become apparent.[43] During the case, evidence was presented that workouts generate certain expectations of co-operation amongst participants, particularly in relation to unanimity of consent to proposals and sharing of material information concerning the debtor.[44] Rabobank argued NatWest had caused them loss by failing

41 Collins, above n 21, 128–36.

42 *National Westminster Bank plc v Rabobank Nederland* [2007] EWHC 1056 QBD.

43 See J Armour and S Deakin, 'Norms in Private Insolvency: The "London Approach" to the Resolution of Financial Distress' (2001) 1 *Journal of Corporate Law Studies* 21, 24.

44 Armour and Deakin studied the practices of workouts as they operated during the 1990s. On the basis of interviews conducted with participants they found that while workout norms were not legally binding, they were largely self-enforcing and were rarely transgressed: ibid, 37–49.

to disclose all material information they had about the debtor's finances, leading Rabobank to agree to take out NatWest's lending in return for a discount on the lending, which they would not otherwise have done. In legal-doctrinal terms, the question for Colman J was whether NatWest had committed a misrepresentation which induced Rabobank to enter into an agreement with NatWest. Colman J's conclusion was that both parties were aware that, absent an express contractual duty allowing for more extensive duties of disclosure, there was no legal duty to disclose the pertinent information. In sum, the rule of caveat emptor applied and Rabobank had to make their own enquiries and satisfy themselves that they had all the material facts before agreeing to the transfer of NatWest's lending. The co-operative aspects of the workout process were subordinate to the overriding norm of individual due diligence. A fairly clear distinction was drawn between what was owed as a matter of legal obligation (judged by reference to the express terms) and the informal workout practice.[45]

It might be argued here that in refusing to legalise the practice, Colman J recognises that disputes arising from the operation of implicit norms are more appropriately dealt with by non-legal and reputational sanctions.[46] He also recognises that legalising the workout expectations may be incompatible with the practical need for workouts to be organised and conducted at speed. Thus the identification of the norms governing the workout process is not regarded by the judge as solely a matter of fact, but involves a value judgment concerning the areas of social life where the law will not interfere. This reluctance may be on the basis that what the law requires may be much less than what persons of honour would feel bound to do,[47] even if it constitutes a recognised practice in the industry generating its own norms of behaviour which are well known to those involved in the process. In response to this, however, it could be noted that the law does nothing to resolve the tension between these frameworks for behaviour and understanding as much as compound it. One could argue that a weakness lies in perceiving these systems—contract and workout—as essentially separate and incompatible processes that bear no relation to each other. On this basis, Rabobank's expectations concerning disclosure of material information were driven by the norms of the workout process and NatWest's by the legal position that no duty to disclose arose outwith that provided by the express terms of the contract between them. The problem with this analysis is that it assumes that the way the case is presented at trial is an accurate representation of the way the business relationship was actually conducted,

[45] *National Westminster Bank plc v Rabobank Nederland*, above n 42, [101], [113].

[46] D Charny, 'Non-legal Sanctions in Commercial Relationships' (1990) 104 *Harvard Law Review* 375, 408–09.

[47] See Beale, above n 6, 522, quoting Cockburn CJ in *Smith v Hughes* (1870–71) LR 6 QB 597, 603–04.

rather than a reconstruction of it in an adversarial atmosphere, made to fit the contract rules, driven by the ultimate desire to succeed in the litigation. Although it is difficult to be certain, it is more likely that both Rabobank's and NatWest's expectations were driven in part by the legal framework and in part by the norms of the workout process. If this was the case, it is problematic to separate these two into different, entirely self-contained and unconnected 'worlds' governed in one case by legal norms of contract terms (inhabited solely by NatWest) and in the other by the social norms generated in the context of the workout and the parties' dealings with one another (inhabited solely by Rabobank). What is not considered here is that the expectations generated by the workout procedure may have been material in influencing the final contract entered into and also into how that contract was to be understood. It raises the possibility that Rabobank agreed to the express terms precisely because they believed all material facts had been disclosed to them during the workout procedure. The contract was simply intended as a formalisation of that process. In other words, the approach of the law in treating the workout and the express terms as isolated worlds that can be analysed and understood separately may result not just in ignoring the informal norms, but in misunderstanding the role of the legal framework. This does not uphold commercial expectations but subverts them by according pre-eminence to the legal-contractual framework as a free-standing entity existing in isolation from the rest of the relationship. There is little consideration of the wider contextual understandings that might render this approach inappropriate. One point to grasp here is that these are not necessarily *exceptional* circumstances with which the law of contract must deal, but paradigm instances of commercial contractual arrangements. Similar problems arise when the parties fail to put their agreement on a formal footing at all. The lack of formality may lead the law to conclude that it simply has no role to play in the business relationship, as the next example demonstrates.

(ii) Absence of Formalities

Some businesses may avoid legal formalities to govern their long-term exchange relationships. For the operation of contract law this might be regarded as conclusive of an intention not to be subject to law at all. *Baird Textile Holdings v Marks and Spencer plc*[48] is perhaps the most notorious modern example. Retailer M&S had enjoyed a close business relationship with clothing supplier Baird (one of a number of suppliers), adhering to a renowned business model that had served the company well for 30 years. The long-term relationship was not governed by any legally enforceable

[48] *Baird Textile Holdings v Marks and Spencer plc* [2001] EWCA Civ 274.

agreement, although there were a series of short-term order contracts each year. M&S broke off the relationship without warning when a sharp decline in sales and a change in senior management triggered abandonment of the company's 'partnership' philosophy and its practice of maintaining close ties with a limited number of suppliers.[49] Baird took M&S to court arguing that they were entitled to a notice period of three years, either on the basis of an implied contract or promissory estoppel. On a trial of preliminary issues, the Court of Appeal determined that legally there was no case for M&S to answer. There was no contract governing the long-term relationship and M&S, and also Baird for that matter, were free to exit the relationship at will and without obligation. No contract could be implied since the parties manifestly did not intend to create legal obligations and the application of estoppel offended the rule that the doctrine operates as a shield and not a sword.

The formalist may argue that it is not immediately apparent what the precise role of law is in these circumstances. A strong formalistic approach can dispose of the case simply: the parties have no contract in place, there is no intention to create legal obligations but rather a concern to avoid legal enforceability. The finding that the parties acted outwith the law is the natural conclusion. Of course it may well be that the failure to put the long-term relationship on a legal basis reflected a precise choice of the parties to reject legality in favour of informal norms of trust and co-operation, and was thus the product of a conscious decision to effectively remove the relationship from the sphere of legal control. If formalism is to be taken seriously as an attempt to draw accurate conclusions about the parties' intentions, rather than just imposing a legally driven interpretation of the parties' conduct, then it must assume the parties have considered legal enforceability as a method of governing their long-term relationship and rejected it in favour of informal norms and sanctions. This may be a difficult conclusion to reach however, since empirical studies and socio-legal work demonstrate that parties' attitudes towards legality may be much more ambivalent. The conclusion that the parties consciously rejected legality appears more from the legal manipulation of the facts to fit criteria of relevance and significance as presented by the legal framework, than a reflection of the genuine motivations of the parties. The conclusion that there was no intention to create legal obligations should not automatically follow from the absence of formalities. Arguably, it can only be derived from the context surrounding the parties' relationship, not from the application of the legal norms themselves.

[49] Described by one commentator as a 'corporate nervous breakdown': K Blois, 'B2B "Relationships"—A Social Construction of Reality?' (2003) 3 *Marketing Theory* 79, 88.

The formalist might respond that this misunderstands the nature of legal regulation—that the legal implications of the parties' behaviour are to be judged by reference to the parties' outward actions and not their inner intentions. If the parties' outward actions manifest a lack of concern with legal enforcement for the long-term relationship, it is immaterial that the parties may not have consciously considered whether to place their relationship on a formal legal footing. There are two responses that could be made. The first is to point out that the parties did not wholeheartedly reject measures of legal enforceability, and appear to have embraced them where their short term obligations were easier to commit to a legally recognised form (the parties did enter into short-term supply contracts to govern each clothing season). The second, and converse, point is that the parties may have intended that their long-term agreement should give rise to some legal obligations, but, given the nature of the relationship, it was impossible, or too costly, to write these in a legally enforceable document. To this extent the parties may have rejected putting their long-term relationship on a legal footing, but only because the legal commitments could not be formulated with the precision demanded by the law. Of course legal imposition of an implied contract governing the long-term relationship may appear to the classical law as an unwelcome interference with freedom of contract. But freedom of contract is not a principle that explains the whole of contract law. Contract law regulates the process of exchange as well as facilitating it. In addition there is no imposition, the law is simply giving appropriate legal force to obligations the parties created towards one another by their conduct. The sum of these points is that commercial parties are not free to determine that their behaviour has no legal consequences simply because they do not write contracts. It is possible to clothe this in doctrinal terms by reference to flexible doctrines such as implied contract, or even an expanded form of promissory estoppel. This is amply demonstrated by Mulcahy and Andrews, who skilfully use orthodox legal method and doctrine to argue for an entirely different result in the *Baird* case.[50] The formalist may respond that it is impossible to know the parties' actual intentions on this issue of legal enforceability, and this is of course true. But attention to context may make one interpretation of the parties' conduct more plausible than another. Mulcahy and Andrews, along with scholars interested in the case from a management and organisations background, point out the one-sided nature of the relationship, the short-term contracts for each season weighted in M&S's favour and M&S's degree of control over the internal organisation and management of Baird, including directing Baird's financial

[50] L Mulcahy and C Andrews, 'Judgment: Baird Textile Holdings v Marks and Spencer' in R Hunter, C McGlynn and E Rackley (eds), *Feminist Judgments: From Theory to Practice* (Oxford, Hart Publishing, 2010) 189.

and investment decisions.[51] While the parties may not have had a formal contract, many of the features of the relationship are also inconsistent with the idea of trust and sole reliance on informal norms and sanctions. Thus it is difficult to confidently categorise this as a business relationship where norms of trust, rather than contract and power, governed the relationship.[52] In an adversarial litigation process it is even more difficult to establish the importance of norms of co-operation in the relationship and any attempt to recast obligations in terms of legal entitlements when the relationship breaks down may be doomed to fail.[53] Doubtless neither party anticipated the use of law to govern their long-term relationship when all was well, and in these circumstances the courts may regard their role as less to do with achieving justice between these two parties and more with discouraging what may appear as commercially irresponsible behaviour by other commercial contractors. This may be a laudable aim on the part of the law, but one result is that commercial agreements that are neither entirely relationally constituted, where recourse to law may be unnecessary, nor fully arm's length, where we might be more confident that *caveat emptor* was the relevant default, are allowed to fall through a regulatory net. Irrespective of what can be demonstrated concerning the intentions of the parties, the law has a role here as 'standard-setter' in commercial agreements.[54] This is not a role it should readily abdicate.

Contract Interpretation and Commercial Reasonableness

In attempting to demonstrate alignment between contract law and commercial expectations, one could point out that courts frequently refer to standards such as commercial reasonableness, or justify their preferences for particular outcomes and contract interpretations on the basis that the alternatives produce uncommercial results or flout business common

[51] Ibid. See also R Bradgate, 'Contracts, Contract Law and Reasonable Expectations' in S Worthington (ed), *Commercial Law and Commercial Practice* (Oxford, Hart Publishing, 2003) 651, 674–78. This blindness to an element of de facto control that one party may effectively exert over another was also illustrated, although in a very different set of circumstances and context, in *Carlton Communications plc and Granada Media plc v The Football League* [2002] EWHC 1650: see C Mitchell, 'Contract: There's Still Life in the Classical Law' (2003) 62 *CLJ* 26.

[52] Blois, above n 49, characterises the relationship as vertical quasi-integration, manifesting integration in fact without legal form, 86.

[53] This draws implicitly on Bernstein's distinction between relationship-preserving norms and endgame norms in commercial relationships: 'Merchant Law in a Merchant Court: Rethinking the Code's Search for Immanent Business Norms' (1996) 144 *University of Pennsylvania Law Review* 1765.

[54] H Collins, 'Competing Norms of Contractual Behaviour' in D Campbell and P Vincent-Jones (eds), *Contract and Economic Organisation: Socio-Legal Initiatives* (Aldershot, Dartmouth, 1996) 67, 93.

sense. While interpretation does afford judges the opportunity to consider the reasonableness of competing outcomes, it is clear that 'commercial reasonableness' does not express any definitive, consistent idea or uniform value, but varies across both judicial minds and commercial contexts. It is not clear that judges make much effort to establish that their judgments of commercial sense are actually shared by the commercial community. Rather they are expressions of judicial ideas of sensible commercial behaviour built up over years of experience of hearing and resolving commercial contract disputes.[55] Given that the legal context in which this is done is adversarial litigation, judgments of commercial sense and reasonableness may be reflective more of the kinds of cases heard and judicial opinion regarding how problems could be prevented from the outset by legal measures (for example, more careful contract drafting), than judicial appreciation of the day-to-day management of commercial activity.

This is not to say judges are in agreement over whether it is permissible for them to make assessments of commercial reasonableness or expediency during dispute resolution. The Supreme Court and the Court of Appeal differed over precisely this issue in *Rainy Sky SA v Kookmin Bank*.[56] The question in the case was whether a payment refund guarantee supplied by a shipbuilder's bank was triggered by the shipbuilder's insolvency, there being no express mention of this in the wording of the contract. The contract referred to the repayment of sums only in the event of 'termination, cancellation or rescission of the contract or upon a total loss of the vessel'. The majority of the Court of Appeal in the case thought it impermissible for the court to look into the commercial sense behind the agreement:

> In this case (as in most others) the Court is not privy to the negotiations between the parties or to the commercial and other pressures which may have dictated the balance of interests which the contract strikes. Unless the most natural meaning of the words produces a result which is so extreme as to suggest that it was unintended, the Court has no alternative but to give effect to its terms. To do otherwise would be to risk imposing obligations on one or other party which they were never willing to assume and in circumstances which amount to no more than guesswork on the part of the Court ... it is impermissible to speculate on the reasons for omitting repayments in the event of insolvency from the bond ... This is not a case in which the construction contended for would produce an absurd or irrational result in the sense described in the cases I have referred to and merely to say that no credible commercial reason has been advanced for the limited scope of the bond does, in my view, put us

[55] On the general difficulties here see JD Heydon, 'How the Courts Develop Commercial Law by Looking Outside the Trial Record into the External World' [2012] *LMCLQ* 30, 43ff.

[56] *Rainy Sky SA v Kookmin Bank* [2011] UKSC 50; [2011] 1 WLR 2900.

> in real danger of substituting our own judgment of the commerciality of the transaction for that of those who were actually party to it.[57]

For Lord Clarke in the Supreme Court, however, this omission could not be explained for any commercial reason. The insolvency of the shipbuilder was the most obvious eventuality for which the security of the bond to repay was required. This outcome was consistent with the commercial purpose of the bonds. Thus, if a term is capable of bearing two meanings, a commercially sensible result is to be preferred over a commercially 'absurd' one. It is difficult to censure Patten LJ for his cautious approach in refusing to engage with the commercial reasonableness argument, given that other judges have been criticised by higher courts for using their 'commercial experience'[58] in resolving disputes, and commercial parties have themselves been warned by courts that whether deals make commercial sense is a matter for them to determine and not their legal advisers.[59] Similarly, one could argue that the Supreme Court in *Rainy Sky* does not consider whether, in a system that supposedly champions freedom of contract, they should be the arbiters of what is commercially reasonable or absurd.[60] Despite indications to the contrary then, there may be a certain amount of ambivalence amongst the judiciary over the extent to which judges should or can pursue commercially reasonable outcomes in dispute resolution. Clearly some judges will regard their role, at least in part, as to encourage other contractors to adopt sensible contract practices. If so, this may raise some sympathy for the Court of Appeal's approach: parties who want to make their position absolutely clear can choose an appropriate form of words. On the other hand the general difficulties (and costs) the parties face in committing their obligations accurately to paper may render the Supreme Court's 'anti-absurdity' stance more appealing. The point is that there is no warrant to believe that appeals to 'commercial reasonableness' on the part of the judiciary mark a unified and principled attempt to achieve greater alignment between law and commercial expectations. It may also be the case that attention to a greater range of contextual evidence surrounding the agreement may make the parties' intentions much clearer.

If 'commercial reasonableness' cannot be understood as encapsulating a single or universal standard or particular reasoning technique, then this must be because contract context plays a large role in these determinations about commercial reasonableness. Context may tacitly be at work even in

[57] Per Patten LJ in the Court of Appeal [2010] EWCA Civ 582; [2011] 1 Lloyd's Rep 233, [51].

[58] See for example Longmore LJ's criticism of the first-instance judge in *Tekdata Interconnections Ltd v Amphenol Ltd* [2009] EWCA Civ 1209; [2010] 1 Lloyd's Rep 357, [15–21].

[59] *The Football League Ltd v Edge Ellison* (a firm) [2006] EWHC 1462; [2006] All ER (D) 263, [132], [218], [252], [268].

[60] See F Schauer, *Playing by the Rules* (Oxford, OUP, 1991) 214.

the Court of Appeal's reasoning in *Rainy Sky*: reasonable parties with the characteristics of the claimant and defendant do not need (or should not receive) the court's help to get it right. 'Context' is not a certain qualifier with precise ambit however. Rather it suggests a range of considerations may weigh into the balance. Courts evidently differentiate between contracting situations, but the precise basis for drawing material distinctions between one context and another may be opaque. In *Aberdeen City Council v Stewart Milne Group Ltd*,[61] for example, the Supreme Court held that contractual profit-sharing provisions based on a percentage of 'gross sale proceeds' in a land deal between the council and the company should be based on the open market value of the land, notwithstanding that the company had sold the land to an associate company at considerably less than open market value. The contract did not state expressly that 'gross sale proceeds' assumed a sale at arm's length in the open market, but the Supreme Court were prepared to allow that this was what the contract meant.[62] The case has naturally been criticised for allowing a feckless contractor to be rescued from the consequences of their own folly through a spurious reference to 'commercial sense',[63] with the result that the Council get the benefit of a deal they did not make.[64] In a different case a land sale between a commercial concern and a local authority was judged according to important matters of context, including the authority's statutory duty to get the best price it could for the land,[65] and a judicial assessment of 'commercially reasonable' behaviour, that is to say, the unlikelihood that a commercial contract would allow one party to secure an uncovenanted windfall unless expressly agreed.[66] That both these cases involved a local authority is not fully explored as an important element of context justifying the decisions reached. It appears as a shadowy background influence, bringing to bear a range of wider considerations from which the outcomes are ultimately derived, but which are not fully articulated as important reasons driving the conclusion. In other more commercially competitive arenas, the contextual background that influences the parties' understandings about their obligations may be quite different. Barnes draws attention to the very different context of rights to withdraw ships for late hire payments in charterparties, which is treated as more or less an absolute right unlimited in its exercise by any considerations of equity and reasonableness that might be used to

[61] *Aberdeen City Council v Stewart Milne Group Ltd* [2011] UKSC 56; 2012 SCLR 114.

[62] Different strategies were adopted however. Lord Hope reached this conclusion using interpretation and Lord Clarke by using implied terms.

[63] M Hogg, 'Fundamental Issues for Reform of the Law of Contractual Interpretation' (2011) 15 *Edinburgh Law Review* 406, 419.

[64] Ibid, 420.

[65] *Multi-link Leisure Developments Ltd v North Lanarkshire Council* [2010] UKSC 47; [2011] 1 All ER 175, per Lord Hope [22].

[66] Lord Hope, ibid [23]; Lord Rodger, ibid [26].

censure behaviour falling short of 'sharp practice'.[67] An important consideration here must be the general awareness of how things in particular markets are done, an awareness which must be assumed to be shared by all the participants and hence not unexpected by any of them. The position in charter markets contrasts sharply with the position of the local authority entering into a relatively isolated but high-value contract with a developer where no such internally generated norms of acceptable commercial behaviour within *that contracting context* are available. It would certainly to be wrong to extrapolate from the isolated context of shipping, with its own set of background assumptions about how things work in that market, in order to formulate the rules applicable to all other contracts. While the courts appreciate that contracting contexts will vary, they do not do enough to draw out these contextual differences and explain how they impinge on the contract legal reasoning process. An appeal to 'commercial reasonableness' without express attention to matters of context that inform the criterion of reasonableness is much too blunt and over-inclusive to provide either adequate justification or explanation for the deeper considerations that are undoubtedly at work.

This point about context can be expanded to cover the characteristics assumed by the law to be held by commercial contractors. Empirical studies may reveal that contractors very often demonstrate a flexible and co-operative attitude within their business relationships, motivated by a desire to engage in repeat trading and maintain reputation. For the law, however, the characteristics that should be displayed by the reasonable commercial contractor may judged in economic terms, or according to the assumptions upon which the law rests—for example, that large sophisticated commercial concerns will have reliable written records of contracts and internal management policies,[68] that they will write relatively complete documents that deal with the main contingencies of performance before they embark on performance[69] and that they will not act against their own commercial interests. Thus Lord Hoffmann's assessment of commercial prudence in *The Achilleas* was that a party would not assume a risk just by knowledge or foreseeability of it, since it was unquantifiable, and 'Anyone asked to assume a large and unpredictable risk will require some premium in exchange'.[70] Whether or not these statements are descriptively accurate, they may be elevated to the status of distinct virtues of the commercial contractor as far as the law is concerned. Perhaps the most famous statement along these lines occurs in

67 See R Barnes, 'Commerciality and the Construction of Commercial Contracts: Some Observations on the Use of Legal Reasoning' in C Twigg-Flesner and G Villalta Puig (eds), *Boundaries of Commercial and Trade Law* (Munich, Sellier, 2011) 203–04.

68 *Bank of Tokyo-Mitsubishi UFJ Ltd v Baskan Gida Sanayi Ve Pazarlama AS* [2009] EWHC 1696 [304].

69 Per Lord Clarke, *RTS v Müller*, above n 1, [1].

70 *The Achilleas* [2008] UKHL 48; [2009] 1 AC 61 [13].

Walford v Miles,[71] where a picture was painted of the commercial contractor being adversarial, self-interested and bringing a distinct economic rationality to bear on his commercial dealings. Under English law a contractor is entitled to seek to advance their own interests provided they do not cross a nebulous boundary into fraud or dishonesty, and it seems it may even be reasonable for commercial contractors to follow an advantage-seeking course.[72] Certainly there is no legal expectation of general co-operative behaviour beyond that necessary to perform the contract.

In some contractual contexts these assumptions about ideal commercial qualities of the contractor may well be accurate. There is a temptation to regard contracting parties as individual persons, but in many, if not most, contracting situations they will be firms. Individuals acting for these bodies will rarely act on their own account but as representatives and agents for these larger organisations. Even though individuals will be responsible for negotiating and performing the agreement they will be doing so in a particular capacity which itself carries with it a set of expectations, limitations and behaviours which attach to *the role* quite apart from the person who inhabits it. These attitudes may follow through into assessments about how much assistance a commercial actor can expect from the law. The belief that certain characteristics are manifest in commercial contractors as a class is latent, often patent, in many judgments, leading to a degree of entrenchment of the economically rational and adversarial model of the commercial contractor.[73] In relation to consumers it appears the law may be willing to take more account of the rationality constraints that operate on them, for example, in processing and acting upon information contained in contract terms. As the Law Commission has recently recognised, 'consumers are only rational up to a point',[74] and that rational decision making was hampered by 'an undue focus on the present', 'over-confidence' or optimism about the future, and 'loss aversion to sunk costs'.[75] While the cognitive limitations operating on judges expected to process extensive evidence of business relationships have been noted, findings from behavioural economics and psychology have had less of an impact on the development of the legal rules, certainly at the common law level. The limitations imposed by

[71] *Walford v Miles* [1992] 2 AC 128, 138.

[72] Lord Steyn, above n 2, 434.

[73] See, eg, Lord Scarman's comments in *Pao On v Lau Yiu Long* [1980] AC 614, denying any extended role for public policy in relation to 'businessmen ... negotiating at arm's length' who should be held to their bargains, 634. See also *Scullion v Bank of Scotland plc* [2011] EWCA Civ 693: house purchasers in the buy-to-let market are assumed to have some 'commercial astuteness' over a house buyer seeking a home, and as a consequence are 'less deserving of protection by the common law against the risk of negligence [by a valuer]' per Lord Neuberger, [49].

[74] Law Commission and Scottish Law Commission, *Unfair Terms in Consumer Contracts: A New Approach? Issues Paper* (2012), para 3.3.

[75] Ibid, para 3.28.

bounded rationality, and the use of satisficing and heuristics amongst commercial contractors, rather than a hard-headed rational choice analysis, are well noted in the scholarly literature however.[76] Such evidence may assist in identifying the genuine constraints under which business contractors formulate and perform the 'commercial contract' and thus may inform a court as to why certain problems arise and recur in the first place. Without this more nuanced understanding of the limitations on commercial contractors, judicial appeals to 'commercial reasonableness' will appear less as an attempt at genuine engagement with commercial norms, and more as impositions on contractors that reflect legal rather than commercial expectations.

CONTRACTS AND THEIR CONTENTS

The legal expectation is that parties will agree on terms and then perform the obligation in accordance with those terms. Commitment to this model may constitute an important message that courts wish to communicate to contractors about how they should go about organising their contractual affairs.[77] This overlooks that in some contexts problems affecting performance may be difficult to predict in advance and, when problems do arise, will be resolved by the parties themselves during performance. In these circumstances it may be unrealistic to expect the parties to record accurately in advance what will simply *happen* during performance. The legal preference for advanced planning itself creates the likelihood of possible later conflict between contract terms and the actions and understandings of commercial people, particularly if circumstances change and strategic reliance on terms will yield benefits for one party. The other outcome that results from this requirement of advanced planning is a manifest attempt by the parties to create a formal contract and to regulate the process of doing so through a series of quasi-formal measures designed to manage the negotiations leading to a final contract or to control other aspects of 'pre-contract' performance. Commitment to planning in advance also manifests itself in problems related to the battle of the forms. These factors may also lead to dissonance between law and expectations, and are considered in more detail in what follows.

The Battle of the Forms

When deciding if a legally enforceable contract has been created, the court looks for an offer matched by an unequivocal acceptance. The courts have

[76] C Jolls, CR Sunstein and RH Thaler, 'A Behavioral Approach to Law and Economics' (1998) 50 *Stanford Law Review* 1471.

[77] *RTS v Müller*, above n 1, per Lord Clarke, [1].

recognised that the rule structure used to decide if agreement has been reached makes for a poor fit with actual practice.[78] It often occurs in commercial agreements that parties will exchange various letters and their own standard conditions, possibly several times, without finally resolving which terms govern the transaction. This is the famous problem of the 'battle of the forms'. If a legal perspective is taken of the issue then it is easy to discern why battle of the forms problems exist. If a contractor has their own standard set of terms then they can enter into agreements relatively quickly on conditions advantageous to them. If they do not have to engage in protracted negotiations to create a bespoke set of terms to govern every routine transaction, this may encourage them to enter into agreements, particularly with untried and untested partners. The contractor will only get this advantage if they can be sure that their terms govern the agreement. A contractor could attempt to achieve this contractual superiority by negotiation, but this only results in incurring the costs that the use of the standard form were designed to save. Another alternative is to consider the legal rule about whose terms win the battle of the forms and manoeuvre to be in this winning position. The problem is that any rational contracting partner is likely to think and act along similar lines, leading to a possibly protracted process of exchanging of standard terms and conditions.

According to the legal authorities, there are three basic choices in dealing with this problem. First, the contract is treated as a single transaction on one of those sets of terms, the buyer's or the seller's, depending on who submits their terms last and (seemingly) without objection from the other party. This is the 'last shot' rule.[79] Second, the contract is on a set of terms which are a compromise between the competing terms, or a different set of implied terms, judged according to the conduct of the parties.[80] Third, if there is no correspondence between offer and acceptance then there is no contract, and, if work has already been undertaken (which invariably it will have been) the parties will have to rely on another area of law to enforce payment conditions.[81] Thus the conflict here might be said to be between

[78] 'English Law, having committed itself to a rather technical and schematic doctrine of contract, in application takes a practical approach, often at the cost of forcing the facts to fit uneasily into the marked slots of offer, acceptance and consideration', per Lord Wilberforce *New Zealand Shipping Co Ltd v A M Satterthwaite & Co Lt (The Eurymedon)* [1975] AC 154, 167.

[79] Recently reaffirmed in *Tekdata Interconnections Ltd v Amphenol Ltd*, above n 58.

[80] Lord Denning seemed to endorse this approach in *Butler Machine Tool Co Ltd v Ex-Cell-O Corp Ltd* [1979] 1 WLR 401, but ultimately applied the last shot rule in the case. In the first-instance decision in *Trebor Bassett Holdings Ltd v ADT Fire and Security plc* [2011] EWHC 1936 (TCC), the judge drew parallels between Lord Denning's 'holistic' approach in *Butler* and Lord Steyn's approach in *G Percy Trentham Ltd v Archital Luxfer Ltd* [1993] 1 Lloyd's Rep 25, see [153]. The decision was upheld on appeal: [2012] EWCA Civ 1158.

[81] Such as restitution and *quantum meruit*: *British Steel Corporation v Cleveland Bridge Engineering Co Ltd* [1984] 1 All ER 504. One evident problem of course is that it fails to

a contract rule-based approach, a contract context- and conduct-based approach, or it might be conceded that this problem does not concern the law of contract at all since the parties have failed to reach agreement. The 'last shot' rule is very much a product of the classical law. The rule assumes there is a precise moment at which a party assumes legal obligations on certain terms, leading to an interrogation by the courts into the communications between the parties to discover precisely when this has occurred. This method is currently the favoured one for dealing with the battle of the forms.[82] The no-contract/restitution approach appears to have fallen out of favour in commercial cases where there is substantial performance (or part performance) of the main obligations, but the parties have failed to reach an agreement on terms.[83] Courts are rightly reluctant to conclude that such an agreement fails for uncertainty.[84]

One could defend the last shot rule by saying that the rule is designed to encourage the parties to reach a final agreement on the terms governing the transaction and to be certain about their obligations before they embark on performance. In other words, the last shot rule operates as a penalty default.[85] The difficulty with this argument is that it relies on the idea that finality and completeness in planning performance is possible before performance begins. It may also be the case that the restitutionary approach of 'no contract' would act as a better incentive to the parties in this respect. The position is complicated by the fact that courts in many cases enforce agreements as contracts even if the formalities remain incomplete, somewhat undermining the 'penalty default' explanation.[86] In some relationships the requisite degree of advanced planning is possible, because the trades are frequent and not complex. But in many other business relationships the parties will be uncertain about their obligations until they begin performance. The 'penalty default' explanation means there is no attempt on the part of the law to decide the actual basis upon which the parties contracted

protect the parties' expectation interest: see *Yeoman's Row Management Ltd v Cobbe* [2008] UKHL 55; [2008] 4 All ER 713.

[82] *Tekdata v Amphenol*, above n 58.

[83] See, eg, *RTS v Müller*, above n 1; *G Percy Trentham Ltd v Archital Luxfer Ltd* above n 80; *Pagnan SPA v Feed Products Ltd* [1987] 2 Lloyd's Rep 601. The restitutionary basis for recovery in such circumstances was reasserted in *Whittle Movers Ltd v Hollywood Express Ltd* [2009] EWCA Civ 1189. Many contract law codes and optional instruments, such as the Uniform Commercial Code, UNIDROIT principles and Draft Common Frame of Reference, acknowledge that a contract is formed in such circumstances, although may vary as to upon whose terms.

[84] *Hillas & Co v Arcos* Ltd [1932] All ER 494; *Barbudev v Eurocom Cable Management Bulgaria EOOD* [2012] EWCA Civ 548 [32].

[85] See I Ayres and R Gertner, 'Filling Gaps in Incomplete Contracts: An Economic Theory of Default Rules' (1989) 99 *Yale Law Journal* 87.

[86] *RTS v Müller*, above n 1.

or to make reasonable assumptions about this based on the context of the agreement, practices in the industry, behaviour of the parties and so on.

What is often overlooked in relation to the battle of the forms is how the legal rules themselves contribute to the problem, if not create it entirely, by demanding that the parties follow certain patterns of behaviour to ensure legal enforceability. First, the law encourages the parties to write standard terms and conditions. Of course there is a commercial reason for a firm drafting standard terms, not just a legal reason, and it may be that the parties would trade terms and conditions irrespective of the legal rules, but it is difficult to be certain about this. Second, parties that care about legal enforceability will seek to ensure that their terms govern the particular deal by constituting the last word. By emphasising the importance of finality and completion in the contract terms, the law has mandated certain behaviour, failing to recognise that the last shot rule militates against such finality by encouraging the parties (or at least those parties attentive to the legal position) to continually trade terms and conditions until one side effectively gives up or performance occurs without problems.

Aside from these issues concerning how the classical law rules create problems for the parties, the outcome dictated by the application of the last shot rule may run counter to commercial expectations derived from other aspects of the business relationship. This is demonstrated by *Tekdata Interconnections Ltd v Amphenol Ltd.*[87] Here the expectations, practices and behaviours that underpinned a business relationship lasting 20 years were regarded by the Court of Appeal as irrelevant to the issue of whose terms governed a sale contract between two parties in a contractual network. Contractual liability was determined by the Court of Appeal on the basis of the last shot rule (on the seller's terms). This was despite cogent evidence of context that suggested the parties had a different understanding about their agreement produced by the long-term nature of their relationship, the consequences of delivery of defective products to the ultimate purchaser (Rolls Royce) and the role of other network members in orchestrating aspects of the relationships between other participants in the chain. These facts were sidelined by analysing the relationship as a series of transactions between a single seller and buyer, only one of which was relevant to the actual dispute. The trial judge took a different approach, pointing to important elements of contract context, including the ultimate use to which the final product would be put and the behaviour of the parties (the seller did not claim their own terms governed the agreement until well into the legal proceedings), which all suggested that the buyer would not have agreed to the seller's terms and that the behaviour and expectations of the parties were consistent with the finding that the contract was on the buyer's

[87] *Tekdata Interconnections Ltd v Amphenol Ltd*, above n 58.

terms. That the seller had performed certain acts consistent with the idea that the agreement was on the buyer's terms, such as signing a certificate of conformity as required under the buyer's terms, was marginalised by Longmore LJ's sharp distinction between the realm of legal obligation and everything else that passed between the parties: 'parties to contracts often do things in the course of performance which is working well, which they might not strictly be obliged to do'.[88] This conveniently overlooks that the determination of what a party is 'strictly obliged to do' depends upon the prior finding that, on applying the last shot rule, the transaction is on the seller's terms. The conclusion may follow necessarily from the premises, but ignores the possibility that there is a choice to be made over the premises. The assumptions involved in this kind of 'legalising' of the issues and analysis are quite startling. Thus Longmore LJ writes that 'It ... appears that the parties had an opportunity to agree a single set of terms, if they wanted to, but that was something which they conspicuously did not do'.[89] This attributes to the parties an awareness about the legal implications of their arrangements that was most likely lacking, and has the effect that an omission to do something, which in reality could be explained on a variety of grounds, is to be interpreted as conclusive evidence that the parties intended that it *should not be done*.

There may well be justifications for deciding the case on the basis of the last shot rule. Dyson LJ defended the rule in *Tekdata* with the observation that it had 'the great merit of a degree of certainty which is both desirable and necessary in order to promote effective commercial relationships'.[90] This may be a consideration, although it is evidently directed towards lawyers rather than the parties. The last shot rule appeared to make no impression on the parties in *Tekdata*, since the claimant believed that contracts always came into existence on their terms.[91] The law may seek to encourage greater negotiation of terms, to encourage parties to read terms, to improve the quality of standard terms (if one cannot guarantee to win the battle of the forms, a party may try to develop fairer or more balanced terms so one derives efficiency gains from not engaging in the battle or negotiating terms[92]), but if this is the case then these should be drawn out and explored directly and the weight these considerations may carry in different contractual contexts made manifest. As it is, the parties' practical behaviour in response to the legal requirements works against the finality and certainty that the rules are supposed to achieve. It also gives rise to

[88] Ibid, [18].
[89] Ibid, [17].
[90] Ibid, [25]. See also D Keating, 'Exploring the Battle of the Forms in Action' (2000) 98 *Michigan Law Review* 2678, 2696–97, 2703–04.
[91] *Tekdata Interconnections Ltd v Amphenol Ltd*, above n 58, [6]–[7].
[92] Keating, above n 90, 2702.

the possibility of opportunism by one party in relying on the battle of the forms rules, never before thought that important, when that party seeks a particular legal interpretation of his obligations.[93] This militates against the parties' expectations by disregarding wider contextual factors which might suggest exchanging terms and conditions was largely an automatic process, and that the parties' intentions concerning their agreement could be sourced from other parts of their relationship.

Contracting for Flexible Commitments

To the extent to which parties plan performance, particularly in long-term agreements, this may be in contingent rather than absolute terms. Parties may attempt to combine the benefits of some advance planning with the need for flexibility. There are various contractual means open to them to achieve this balance. Parties may deal with the uncertainty of future costs by including price variation clauses that stipulate a formula for determining increases in costs. However, managing even this relatively obvious source of uncertainty requires a degree of foresight, and while there may be some contingencies whose effect on the contract may be relatively straightforward to predict and deal with (as with price variation), other sources of uncertainty may be less amenable to specific control through complicated procedures written into contract terms. One method of dealing with these uncertainties may be to formulate express obligations to adopt general co-operative attitudes towards achieving the outcomes of the agreement during performance, or in dealing with variations in performance throughout the life of the relationship or project.

In legal terms, the contract is often thought of as the thing that creates the relationship and governs performance of the discrete deal. Yet planning may relate to both the substantive deal (project) *or* the relationship itself (process), or indeed elements of both. Parties may concentrate their efforts on processes for governing performance when detailed planning of the project is difficult to achieve. Ian Macneil regards the planning of processes governing the relationship to be one of the hallmarks of the relational over the discrete agreement.[94] This process planning involves stipulating certain behavioural norms that the parties are expected to uphold in their dealings with one another, setting out how the parties will attempt to achieve performance outcomes rather than the outcomes themselves. For example, provisions requiring the use of 'best' or 'reasonable' endeavours to achieve

[93] See D Campbell, 'The Incompleteness of Our Understanding of the Law and Economics of Relational Contract' (2004) *Wisconsin Law Review* 645, 654.

[94] I Macneil, 'Economic Analysis of Contractual Relations: Its Shortfalls and the Need for a Rich Classificatory Apparatus' (1981) 75 *Northwestern University Law Review* 1017, 1044.

some end may be used when the parties want to set out some level of obligation, but the nature of the project, or the conditions under which it is undertaken, or the constraints operating in the industry, mean it is difficult to mandate in absolute terms that a party achieve a specific result in a specified time. Other possibilities are that the parties may include duties to co-operate, negotiate or perform an agreement in good faith. What each of these may precisely require depends upon the circumstances and the duties stipulated. At the very least, such duties would demand a certain attitude to be adopted towards possible modification of the agreement. Most likely they would require suspending the pursuit of one's own self-interest in search of a position that ensures the continuation of the project and the realisation of the expected gains for all the parties. These terms can therefore arise from a need to manage project risk and uncertainty, and deal with co-ordination problems. Alternatively, parties may seek to use such clauses to prevent the court from taking a formalistic, competitive, individualistic approach to the agreement in resolving any disputes.

At first glance express terms contracting for flexible commitments appear as awkward attempts to turn formalism on its head by using formality to impose open-ended standards of conduct on the parties. This might be criticised on the basis that values of flexibility, co-operation and trust only be demonstrated through interaction between the parties, and that contracting for flexibility simply adds further layers of fiction and artificiality to the contract terms, or worse, empties co-operative behaviour of much of its value by interfering with its spontaneous development. If there is doubt about whether written contracts can capture or reflect all the understandings the parties have about their agreement, then there might be understandable scepticism concerning whether it is possible to *impose* obligations to be flexible and co-operative through contract terms. Campbell and Harris argue that a shift in attitude must come first and without this 'formal provision for flexibility is fruitless, for one cannot create a co-operative attitude by writing down that such an attitude will be taken to contingencies as they arise'.[95] This is a compelling point, and certainly one cannot imagine a situation more conducive to distrust than relative strangers signing an agreement containing obligations to be trustworthy and co-operative. The attempt to formalise flexible commitments certainly appears as an anomaly to the law of contract. Given the acontextual approach of the law, and where the documents stipulate an alternative and inherently separate reality, contract provisions for flexibility and co-operation appear as an attempt to conjure such commitments out of thin air and to impose them on a party. The answer to this is while it is true that a flexible or co-operative

[95] D Campbell and D Harris, 'Flexibility in Long Term Contractual Relationships: The Role of Cooperation' (1993) 20 *Journal of Law and Society* 166, 173.

relationship cannot be *created* by formulating a contract that contains such obligations, this argument overlooks that the parties will rarely begin an exchange relationship by attempting to negotiate contract terms and conditions which demand flexibility from contracting partners. The parties may agree a certain attitude is taken in performance, or more likely it simply arises naturally, and they may seek reassurance that this attitude will inform their dealings by including it in contract terms. The alternative argument relies on the idea that formalisation is associated with only adversarial or what are perceived to be likely antagonistic relationships. In any case, the sceptical view does not alter the fact that the parties often attempt to write flexible commitments into their agreements. Indeed it might be conjectured that it is precisely the contract law position of privileging the documents that has influenced the parties to act in this manner of attempting to formalise informality.

From a legal point of view the main difficulties posed by such obligations derive from their function of stipulating processes to deal with risks and uncertainties, rather than precise and fixed outcomes or risk allocations. Such flexible commitments may also appear out of step with the characteristics of commercial contractors assumed by classical contract law. These commitments may also pose difficulties of interpretation, since they require courts to assess the precise standard of behaviour necessary to meet these obligations in order to determine if breach has occurred and how it should be remedied. To a judge coming to such clauses with little evidence of context, they could be read in a variety of ways: they may appear as a compromise to reconcile opposing interests when absolute obligations could not be agreed and in that sense represent the best that could be achieved in a tense negotiating atmosphere; they could reflect genuine uncertainty concerning the future that militated against the stipulation of absolute obligations; they could signal that the relationship between the parties was broadly co-operative; or they could be regarded as a direct attempt to harness legal enforceability for the social norms that are expected to be relied upon later to deal with problems as they arise during performance.

The difficulties that the law may encounter with such clauses results largely from the legal understanding of the agreement, which is that a written contract creates obligations and is the ultimate reference point for all enquiries about the agreement. Some of these difficulties recede if the legal assumptions are reversed and the stipulation for flexible commitments is not considered as an attempt to create a flexible relationship and duties of co-operation where none existed before, but to achieve a greater level of fit between the documented agreement and the business relationship of which it is part. In essence, the point of such commitments may be to make the paper deal a more accurate reflection of the real deal, rather than an entirely separate entity fulfilling limited and discrete functions of risk allocation and legal planning.[96] While contracting for flexible obligations may appear counter-intuitive, the difficulties for the parties in formulating such obligations, and for the courts in seeking to enforce them, are arguably no worse than the problems raised for parties and courts by the legal preference for fully contingent contracts. Including flexible commitments in contracts shifts the burden to write complete contracts away from the parties and imposes on courts a requirement to develop interpretative techniques to deal with flexible obligations. One reason why the courts should have this burden is because while interpreting such obligations may be difficult for a court, achieving the legal ideal of fully contingent contracts may be impossible for the parties. It might also be argued that the attempt to formalise the more relational aspects of the agreement may be crucial if the parties are not to run the risk of complete legal unenforceability and have their relationship governed by only non-legal norms and sanctions.

The law sends decidedly mixed messages regarding the enforceability of such obligations. The lack of legal recognition of 'agreements to agree' provides an example of judicial intransigence.[97] If the parties have not reached agreement over some essential term, the courts will not enforce an agreement to settle the term in the future, since that leaves open the possibility that the parties may fail to agree at that future point. Such uncertainty leads to the result that there can be no contract. The addition of an obligation to undertake 'reasonable endeavours' to agree appears to make little difference to the legal understanding that such statements are ones of aspiration rather than obligation.[98] If the parties set out some mechanism or standard for determining the content of the obligation that may be enforceable.[99] In a similar fashion, if use of reasonable or best endeavours is linked to the achievement of some other outcome, event or end result stipulated in the contract, these clauses are more likely to be enforceable.[100] These distinctions may be relatively easy to draw in principle but applying them in practice is likely to prove challenging. While there has been some resiling

[96] Collins, above n 21, 149–51.

[97] *May and Butcher Ltd v The King* [1934] 2 KB 17.

[98] Eg, *Little v Courage Ltd* (1995) 70 P & CR 469.

[99] *Mamidoil-Jetoil Greek Petroleum Co SA v Okta Crude Oil Refinery AD* [2001] EWCA Civ 406; [2001] 2 All ER (Comm) 193, per Rix LJ [69]; *MRI Trading AG v Erdenet Mining Corp LLC* [2013] EWCA Civ 156.

[100] *Little v Courage*; *P & O Property Holdings v Norwich Union Life Insurance* (1994) 68 P & CR 261. See also *Phillips Petroleum Co UK Ltd v Enron Europe Ltd* [1997] CLC 329, where it was held that 'reasonable endeavours' can be framed and limited by the commercial considerations attaching to one party. There can be no argument that use of such a clause requires one party to disregard his own interests. See also *Yewbelle Ltd v London Green Developments* [2007] EWCA Civ 475, [2008] 1 P & CR 279. The Scottish case of *EDI Central v National Car Parks* [2010] CSOH 141, also held that there was no requirement in 'reasonable endeavours' to act against a party's own commercial interests.

from regarding such open-ended obligations as completely unenforceable, particularly when the parties have acted on any supposed agreement,[101] the problems the courts perceive is the lack of substantive content to the obligation, with consequent difficulties determining remedies for breach.

Similar problems surround contractual stipulations to act in good faith. It is well known that English law recognises no general duty to negotiate in good faith to reach an agreement. This applies to both a duty implied in law and an express duty imposed by the parties themselves through a contract.[102] The classic statement of the English law position comes from Lord Ackner, in *Walford v Miles*,[103] who stressed the 'repugnancy' of the idea of good faith duties to the adversarial and self-interested positions adopted by the parties during contract negotiations. The reasons for this attitude are varied, incorporating both principled and practical concerns. The practical reasons are the uncertainty surrounding the idea of good faith, which means it is difficult to tell what content the duty has, when it has been breached and what the measure of damages should be.[104] Given the strong individualist ethic underlying classical contract law, of which Ackner LJ's dictum is the classic modern statement, it is also difficult for the courts to draw a certain line between legitimate pursuit of one's self-interest in contract negotiation and illegitimate or unfair tactics. Policing this boundary could only become more complicated if the law was required to distinguish between situations where the pursuit of self-interest fitted within the contract scheme and when the parties have agreed that this should be curtailed for the advancement of a common endeavour or the contract purposes, although it is arguable that contracting context could do much of the work here. There may be scepticism amongst the judiciary about the extent to which such an attitude can be foisted on a party by contract terms, particularly when it cannot be said that the party has acted dishonestly.[105] Other concerns about good faith are more principled in nature. One view is that it is simply incompatible with the task of 'negotiating' to act in good faith, at least if good faith is understood as requiring some attenuation of the pursuit of one's self-interest. English contract law has simply set its face against the idea that a contracting party should be required to act with reference to the interests of the other party beyond the minimum level of

[101] *Foley v Classique Coaches Ltd* [1934] 2 KB 1; *Hillas v Arcos*, above n 84; *Sudbrook Trading Estate Ltd v Eggleton* [1983] AC 444.

[102] The problem with the latter is the lack of certainty in the scope of the duty. But see *obiter dictum* comment of Longmore LJ in *Petromec Inc v Petroleo Brasileiro SA Petrobas (No 3)* [2005] EWCA Civ 891; [2006] 1 Lloyd's Rep 121. He expressed doubts about the contention that express agreements to negotiate in good faith could never be enforceable, although the context in that case was a good faith obligation as part of an existing and enforceable agreement.

[103] *Walford v Miles*, above n 71, 138 (all the other Law Lords agreed).

[104] *Courtney and Fairbairn Ltd v Tolaini Bros (Hotels) Ltd* [1975] 1 All ER 716.

[105] Per Sedley LJ in *George Wimpey UK v V I Construction* [2005] EWCA Civ 77, [60].

co-operation necessary to achieve agreement. This is also bolstered by the argument that contracts and the legal norms of contract law are required precisely to allow interaction between strangers who have not built up a level of trust. Without that background co-operative context, it is perhaps easier to conclude that the parties' motivations for contracting (as opposed to utilising some other governance mechanism) are governed by self-interest rather than other-regarding interests.[106]

These arguments might be reckoned to have more force against a legally imposed duty of good faith than one written into the agreement by the parties themselves. While the law may have presently turned away from recognising free-standing obligations to negotiate or reach an agreement in good faith, good faith in performance of existing contractual duties when expressly created by the parties should prima facie be enforceable[107] and probably are in most contractual settings.[108] Difficulties may be encountered with identifying the precise content of the duty, but it is arguable that such difficulties only militate against enforceability if it is assumed that 'good faith' has a single meaning, rather than stipulating an inherently flexible and fluctuating set of requirements. Lord Bingham in the House of Lords decision in *Director General of Fair Trading v First National Bank plc* said that good faith as a concept 'looks to good standards of commercial morality and practice'.[109] This suggests a more context-dependent understanding of good faith, the precise content of which may vary with circumstances of 'commercial morality and practice'. Commercial standards operating in an industry, and the characteristics of the agreement, may be an important indicator of whether a party has acted in good faith.[110] It is likely that

[106] Compare the Draft Common Frame of Reference: 'A person who is engaged in negotiations has a duty to negotiate in accordance with good faith and fair dealing and not to break off negotiations contrary to good faith and fair dealing. This duty may not be excluded or limited by contract': DCFR Book II.—3:301 (2) and (3). A person breaching this duty is liable for the other's losses. Similarly, the UNIDROIT Principles of International Commercial Contracts, Art 2.1.15, provide that '(a) a party is free to negotiate and is not liable for failure to reach an agreement (b) however, a party who negotiates or breaks off negotiations in bad faith is liable to the loss caused to the other party'.

[107] Consider *United Group Rail Services v Rail Corp NSW* [2009] NSWCA 177: 'If business people are prepared in the exercise of their commercial judgment to constrain themselves by reference to express words that are broad and general, but which have sensible and ascribable meaning, the task of the court is to give effect to, and not to impede, such solemn express contractual provisions': [74].

[108] The construction industry is a case in point: see S Jackson, 'Good Faith in Construction—Will it Make a Difference and Is It Worth the Trouble?' [2007] *Construction Law Journal* 420, and J Mason, 'Contracting in Good Faith—Giving the Parties What They Want' [2007] *Construction Law Journal* 436.

[109] Per Lord Bingham, *Director General of Fair Trading v First National Bank plc* [2002] 1 AC 481, [17]. See also *Berkeley Community Villages Ltd v Pullen* [2007] EWHC 1330 (Ch), per Morgan J, [97] and *CPC Group Ltd v Qatari Diar Real Estate Investment Company Ltd* [2010] EWHC 1535, per Vos J, [246], echoing similar sentiments.

[110] See also *Jacobs UK Ltd v Skidmore Owings & Merrill LLP* [2012] EWHC 3293, per Coulson J, [20].

the courts will adopt a contextual approach to understanding good faith obligations, such that the meaning of the obligation 'takes its colour from the commercial nature of the contract'.[111] It may be that an agreement between two multinational banking corporations concerning a corporate debt restructuring with full legal support is likely to be performed in a semi-adversarial atmosphere with limited duties to the other party. In such a context the court may decide one party is *entitled* to act self-interestedly and that the other can protect themselves accordingly (although such a conclusion may not be mandated in all circumstances).[112] Good faith here may not extend much beyond a duty to act honestly. In other contexts, good faith requirements may translate into substantive duties of information sharing, co-operation and even loyalty between contracting parties, depending on the kind of parties involved and the nature of the agreement.[113]

While there are signs that English law is alive to the possibility of the parties stipulating good faith obligations between themselves, there are few grounds for optimism that this may lead to a wholesale change in judicial attitudes concerning the importance of co-operation in contract dealings, nor does it indicate that the default adversarial model of the contractor is weakening its grip. Allowing that express duties of good faith are acceptable in certain contracting contexts is a far cry from determining that all contractual relationships carry such a non-excludable obligation as a matter of law.[114] If anything, judicial recognition of express good faith obligations simply operates as an extension of the idea of freedom of contract. If judges operate in a framework where good faith duties are regarded as 'exceptional', such duties are at risk of being interpreted in an excessively stringent manner that substantially empties them of their potential to signal the parties' expectations of co-operative behaviour. This is a particular danger when the parties have set out well-defined contractual duties governing a project. These may be treated by courts as exhaustive of the obligations owed, leaving good faith duties with no sphere of operation. The ambivalent attitude of the courts towards good faith—embracing its potential on one hand, demonstrating the risk of it being interpreted out of existence on the other—is shown by two important recent decisions from the courts. More openness to the possibility of express duties of good faith

[111] Cranston J in *Compass Group UK and Ireland Ltd (t/a Medirest) v Mid Essex Hospital Services NHS Trust* [2012] EWHC 781, [32]. See also R Brownsword, 'Two Concepts of Good Faith' (1994) 7 *Journal of Contract Law* 197, 199 noting that good faith in performance 'is not to require good faith at large; the requirement can be related to the intentions or expectations of the particular contracting parties'.

[112] See, eg, *National Westminster Bank plc v Rabobank Nederland*, above n 42.

[113] *Yam Seng Pte v International Trade Corporation Ltd* [2013] EWHC 111 [142].

[114] Thus in the Proposal for a Common European Sales Law, good faith and fair dealing are defined as 'a standard of conduct characterised by honesty, openness and consideration for the interests of the other party to the transaction or relationship in question': Art 2(b). This follows the DCFR I—1:103(1).

providing the overriding normative framework for governing a long-term agreement appeared in the judgment of Cranston J in *Compass Group UK (t/a Medirest) v Mid Essex Hospital Services NHS Trust*.[115] Cranston J's determination that breach of an express obligation of good faith had occurred was overruled by the Court of Appeal, who drastically limited the duty by restricting its operation to the performance of certain other express obligations. More boldly, Leggatt J implied a duty of good faith in a distributorship agreement in *Yam Seng Pte Ltd v ITC Ltd*.[116]

Compass concerned a long-term facilities contract (anticipated to last seven years with provision for an extension for a further three years). The substance of the contract was the provision of catering services from Medirest to the Trust. Clause 3.5 imposed a duty to co-operate in good faith:

> The Trust and the Contractor will co-operate with each other in good faith and will take all reasonable action as is necessary for the efficient transmission of information and instructions as to enable the Trust or, as the case may be, any Beneficiary to derive the full benefit of the Contract.

'Service failures' under the contract, which were determined by the Trust, allowed the Trust to make deductions from contract payments. The performance of the contract hit trouble almost immediately, and there were failures on both sides which led Cranston J to conclude that both parties were entitled to terminate the agreement less than two years after commencement. Medirest were particularly aggrieved at the Trust's determination of 'service failures' with consequent deductions from payments. Some of these failures on the part of Medirest appeared very trivial (discovery of a box of out-of-date ketchup sachets attracted a deduction of £46,320). Medirest claimed the Trust had breached the good faith agreement. The Trust maintained that there was no breach since, first, none of the calculations was made in bad faith, the Trust was simply applying the contract according to its terms.[117] The judge rejected this, since for him good faith meant more than the absence of bad faith. The Trust's second main argument was that the clause imposed no general duty of good faith, but only a duty to co-operate in good faith for the explicit purposes mentioned in the clause. Relying on dicta from *Overlook v Foxtel*,[118] the Trust argued that the duty 'is not to prefer the interests of the other contracting party. It is, rather, a duty to recognise and have regard to the legitimate interests of both the parties in the enjoyment of the fruits of the contract as delineated

[115] *Compass Group UK and Ireland Ltd (t/a Medirest) v Mid Essex Hospital Services NHS Trust*, above n 111.
[116] *Yam Seng Pte v International Trade Corporation Ltd*, above n 113.
[117] *Compass Group UK and Ireland Ltd (t/a Medirest) v Mid Essex Hospital Services NHS Trust*, above n 111, [81].
[118] *Overlook v Foxtel* [2002] NSWSC 17.

by its terms'.[119] For the Trust, upholding good faith was connected to upholding contractual integrity—one can pursue one's own interests, and may be quite entitled to do so, provided one does not render the agreement empty or nugatory for the other party. 'Agreement' here refers simply to the express terms. On this basis, given the contract terms, the Trust argued Medirest could have no legitimate expectation that the Trust would surrender its contractual rights. The judge also rejected this argument, noting that performance would require 'continuous and detailed co-operation between the parties at a number of levels if it was to work smoothly'.[120] Given the context, it was not open to the Trust to interpret the clause in a self-interested manner as allowing for only narrow duties delineated by express terms.[121] The trial judge noted the 'objective character' of the clause, and the long-term, complex context of the contract, which involved the Trust in faithfulness to the common purpose of the contract with Medirest to the benefit of the public.[122] In adopting such an interpretation Cranston J recognised the good faith obligation as relevant to the management of the joint endeavour and contract purpose, and thus to be read within that wider contract context, not as a narrow obligation operating acontextually and independently of the overall project.

By complete contrast the Court of Appeal adopted a very formalistic interpretation of the good faith duty. In a reversal of the first-instance approach, the Court of Appeal regarded the term as having no effect on the overall conduct of the parties' relationship, since the parties were fully co-operating on performance of the agreement, patients were broadly satisfied with the services provided,[123] and the dispute only arose over the service failure points and deductions. This was kept separate from the delivery of the service.[124] The Court reckoned the Trust had acted mistakenly, but not dishonestly, in making the payment deductions. The Court reasoned that if the Trust had miscalculated the amount of the service failure payments then that would be a breach of contract entitling Medirest to take action (the Court found that these breaches had been cured by repayment). Lewison LJ also pointed out that the duty was 'to co-operate in good faith' and the imposition of service failure points and deductions did not require any co-operation between the parties.[125] The Court noted the decision in *Yam Seng*, but pointed out that duties of good faith would be implied only in

[119] This was quoting from *Overlook v Foxtel*, ibid [67]. At [68] it was said that the 'implied obligation of good faith is best regarded as an obligation to eschew bad faith'.

[120] *Compass Group UK and Ireland Ltd (t/a Medirest) v Mid Essex Hospital Services NHS Trust*, above n 111, [25].

[121] Ibid, [26].

[122] Ibid, [33].

[123] [2013] EWCA Civ 200, [48].

[124] Ibid, [118].

[125] Ibid, [146].

limited circumstances ('a duty of good faith is implied by law as an incident of certain categories of contract'[126]). The circumstances in which such an implication might be thought appropriate were not spelled out. The Court regarded the good faith stipulation as applying to the two immediately following provisions only: the efficient transmission of information and instructions; and enabling the Trust or any beneficiary to derive the full benefit of the contract.[127] The benefit of the contract was, according to Jackson LJ, 'that the catering and cleaning services should be delivered to the patients and the wards, for which the Trust is responsible'.[128] Good faith in this context meant that the 'parties will work together honestly, endeavouring to achieve the two stated purposes'.[129] Following the Court of Appeal's earlier logic concerning the deductions, one might say that if Medirest failed to provide the benefit of the contract (catering and cleaning services) to the Trust, then the Trust would have a claim for breach of contract. On such an interpretation, what does the good faith obligation add? The good faith obligation is emptied of any substantive content—one acts in good faith simply by performing the contract. The Court of Appeal approach illustrates the practical difficulty of expressly contracting for duties of good faith in complex agreements, particularly when the current understanding of English contract law is that 'contracting' is fundamentally a competitive and self-interested process that is dictated by terms. On the Court of Appeal's restrictive interpretation, it would be difficult to expressly contract for a broader principle of good faith as a behavioural stipulation governing how the parties will deal with one another over the entire project. Unless tied to particular express duties (where it risks being assimilated simply with performance of those duties) such a broad stipulation of good faith is likely to fail for uncertainty.

The judgment of Leggatt J in *Yam Seng* is perhaps of greater potential significance for its recognition that implied good faith obligations might be appropriate in some contract contexts, in that particular case, a distributorship agreement. The judge noted that many contractual contexts are informed by shared values and norms of behaviour, including trust and honesty.[130] He also understood the implicit nature of many of these understandings, referring to 'other standards of commercial dealing which are so generally accepted that the contracting parties would reasonably be understood to take them as read without explicitly stating them in their contractual document'.[131] Leggatt J in *Yam Seng* appreciates that certainly some

[126] Ibid, [105].
[127] Ibid, [106–07].
[128] Ibid, [108].
[129] Ibid, [112].
[130] *Yam Seng Pte v ITC Ltd*, above n 113, [134–35].
[131] Ibid, [138].

contractual contexts do not follow the model of contract as a competitive process, but involve a relationship more akin to 'partnership' where greater emphasis is placed on trust, co-operation, common goals, openness and information sharing. Now while the exact existence and content of the duty is determined by context, and predicting the contexts in which this duty may be operative is not an easy matter, the general recognition that good faith might operate as an underpinning principle for the contract scheme (related to the type of contract and purposes), rather than as an attachment to specific obligations in the contract, is to be welcomed. The Court of Appeal in *Compass* was not prepared to admit that an express good faith clause could signal a change to the paradigm of self-interested dealing, it could only qualify the contractual commitment to which it was attached. This still takes good faith as contingent on contract terms, rather than a fully independent duty owed by all contractors.[132] Even if parties contract for good faith duties, the restrictiveness of express terms, as opposed to the more expansive potential offered by implied terms, is unlikely to herald a change in the basic model of contract law from adversarial and competitive to co-operative or even other-regarding.[133]

The Court of Appeal's restrictive approach in *Compass* contrasts with instances where courts have shown willingness to accord some significance to flexible commitments as curtailing a contractor's capacity to refer only to his own self-interest, and even the possibility that such terms may require a party to act outside its own commercial interests. In *Jet2.com Ltd v Blackpool Airport Ltd*,[134] the parties entered into a letter agreement, drafted without significant legal assistance, intended to run for 15 years. The substance of the obligation was for Jet2 to operate low-cost flights out of the airport. One of the terms of the agreement was that 'Jet2.com and BAL will co-operate together and use their best endeavours to promote Jet2.com's low cost services from BA and BAL will use all reasonable endeavours to provide a low cost base that will facilitate Jet2.com's low cost pricing'. There was also a clause that said the parties would meet in good faith to review and agree a new 'charging scheme' just before the expiry of the 15-year period. There was nothing in the agreement concerning the hours during which BAL would accept aircraft movements. Flights ran outside the airport's normal opening hours, initially with BAL's support and co-operation. After a change in the parent company of the airport, BAL, who had never made a profit from the out-of-hours operation, said it would no longer accept flights outside its normal opening hours. BAL argued that reasonable endeavours only required them to act in a way consistent with their commercial interests, and it did not commit them to undertaking

[132] Brownsword, above n 111, 200.
[133] Ibid, 215–16.
[134] *Jet2.com Ltd v Blackpool Airport Ltd* [2012] EWCA Civ 417.

commercially unreasonable behaviour.[135] The trial judge thought that an endeavours clause would not fail for uncertainty provided there was a clear object to which the endeavours were directed. In this case this was the provision of low-cost air services.[136] The judge also noted that the parties had acted upon the agreement without difficulty for four years. From this it must have been relatively easy to conclude that BAL and Jet2 had the same expectations concerning the requirement to operate outside normal hours. The judge thought it could not be right that BAL could abandon the agreement when the venture became unprofitable, or had never been profitable. Thus commitment to 'all reasonable endeavours' meant BAL did not have complete freedom to consult its own commercial interests.

A majority in the Court of Appeal upheld the decision, although they were not prepared to lay down any general principles regarding a divergence between reasonable endeavours and commercial interests since this would depend on 'the nature and terms of the contract in question'.[137] Certainly just the fact of BAL being aware that they would be making a loss was insufficient, since operating outside normal hours was essential to Jet2's business and fundamental to the agreement, although there would come a point at which BAL would no longer be required to keep incurring losses in what was clearly a failing business.[138] It is arguable here that the majority of the Court of Appeal understands that creating obligations requires the binding of oneself in the future to act in ways that may turn out to be less optimum than thought. In other words, this is precisely what a *contract is for*. The problem with this is that BAL did not have an absolute obligation to allow Jet2 to operate outside normal working hours, only to use best endeavours to co-operate. This difficulty perhaps lay behind Lewison LJ's dissent. He argued it would be unusual for a business to agree to carry on making a loss, and clear words would be required before a contract could have this effect. This again appeals to a standard of commercial prudence.[139] Lewison pointed out that it was not a fiduciary relationship,[140] and he contrasted other cases which required a contractor under the duty to take defined steps in defined circumstances. He criticised the trial judge for creating a contract for the parties.[141] For Lewison LJ, the clause could have been attributed any number of meanings from the outset and therefore was too uncertain to be enforced. The majority, however, recognised the open-ended nature

[135] Ibid, [44].
[136] Ibid, [15].
[137] Ibid, [32–33].
[138] Per Moore-Bick LJ, ibid, [32].
[139] *Jet2.com Ltd v Blackpool Airport Ltd*, above n 134 [38].
[140] Ibid [39].
[141] Cf *Yewbelle Ltd v London Green Developments* [2007] EWCA Civ 475; [2008] 1 P & CR 279. 'Best endeavours' referred to technical practicality and did not require a contractor to sacrifice its own commercial interests.

of the term, but also that the obligation would be given content during the functioning business relationship.[142] Ultimately the difference in opinion between the majority and minority in the case is traceable back to what a contract is and the conditions for legal enforceability. For the majority, obligations can arise and be given substance through day-to-day performance, particularly when performance has extended over a period of years without significant problems. For Lewison J the obligations require to be stated certainly in advance in order to be legally enforceable. The latter approach assimilates the requirements for legal enforcement under the classical law with the sole conditions under which obligations can be said to exist. If one assumes that the express terms exist to serve legal processes and purposes only, it is easier to reach the conclusion that stipulated obligations that pose difficulties for the law, or that do not fit within the legal framework, are rendered substantially meaningless and hence unenforceable. This limits the contract to a device directed to protecting interests on breach, and does not recognise its potential to create or reflect a framework for the parties' understanding and conduct during performance. In some contexts it may be entirely appropriate to treat the documents as a statement of legal obligations relevant only to the breakdown of the business relationship. But in other contexts this will constitute an error.

CONCLUSION

From this examination of the discrepancies between the assumptions and requirements of contract law and the practices and expectations of the parties, a number of things become apparent. Chief among these is the rigidity of the rules of contract law and the association the law makes between 'the contract' and the documented agreement. These legal commitments cause problems since the law often requires a degree of certainty in stipulating obligations that may be beyond the capacity of the parties given their relationship or the nature of the project. Parties may attempt to get around this by using express terms as a repository for flexible obligations that stipulate contract processes and standards of conduct expected in a partner, rather than certain outcomes and risk allocations. The reasons why the parties may attempt to write such obligations into their agreements are not difficult to discern, although variable interpretations could be placed on such terms. They could be understood either as an attempt to articulate trusting obligations, or to reflect the trusting and co-operative commitments that underpin the relationship, or to reach a compromise when absolute obligations are impossible to formulate. Most likely the attempt to formalise duties of

[142] See Longmore LJ, *Jet2.com Ltd v Blackpool Airport Ltd*, above n 134, [70, 72].

flexibility represents a combination of all these factors, giving rise to doubts over whether the impetus towards contracting for flexibility has come from the parties, who are genuinely seeking to render these kinds of commitment legally enforceable, or whether the parties feel compelled to write such duties into contracts as a response to the law's preference for formalism.

Judicial attitudes towards the use of such flexible agreements are not uniform and much appears to turn on the attitude of the individual judge. There is some scope for optimism when judges recognise and enforce some kinds of flexible obligations, such as to use 'best' or 'reasonable' endeavours, or imply duties of good faith into particular agreements. While there might be scepticism as to how such a co-operative attitude can be created through contract terms, at the very least exposing the courts to express duties of good faith and so on could be the place to start a transformation of judicial attitudes. Some recent authorities suggest the courts are increasingly sensitive to the difficulties involved in advanced stipulation of obligations in situations of uncertainty, and may be more willing, in the context of an overall contract where performance has commenced, to allow that obligations would firm up as the project proceeded with the conclusion that such agreements are enforceable. Such a contract may give rise to uncertainty in the level of damages to be awarded, but such a contract is not thereby necessarily too uncertain to be *performed* by the parties. This recognises that obligations do not have to be transformed to fit the existing framework of legal rules, but that it is the legal framework that must be remoulded to reflect the reality of contractual performance. This would broadly be in keeping with a commercial-expectations approach. But these authorities are not uniform and the reassertion of classical contract norms to govern these flexible obligations—particularly strictness in interpretation—may substantially empty these obligations of any real content. They become simply a gloss on the performance obligations that already exist and are enforceable by the law of contract. Of course at the point of litigation when the relationship is over, the co-operative attitude the parties may have demonstrated towards one another when resolving the day-to-day problems thrown up by performance may appear irrelevant. But issues concerning the obligations the parties chose to impose on themselves should not be judged according to the separate context of the breakdown of the relationship and the ensuing litigation. This is always a danger during the litigation process, and suggests there is still some way to go before contract law achieves greater alignment with commercial expectations.

5

Commercial Expectations and Theories of Contract Law

THIS CHAPTER CONSIDERS whether there are any normative arguments that could be marshalled in support of the contention that contract law should be better aligned with commercial expectations and practices. The normative and prescriptive question is simply why the law should take commercial expectations or implicit dimensions into account in its legal reasoning processes. At its most abstract level there would appear to be two basic normative arguments that one might use to support the closer alignment between contract law and contract practice: a utilitarian, or efficiency-based argument, and a rights-based argument.[1] Support could be justified on either basis, although relationalists/contextualists and efficiency theorists are often opposed. This chapter considers whether either of these two foundations provide good support for the development of an incorporationist contract law that pays close attention to commercial practice and internal norms of the business relationship. In relation to rights-based approaches, non-instrumental promissory theories are considered as the main exemplar.[2] Neither of these accounts are without problems, and given the various debates that surround them it may not be fatal to a commercial-expectations argument that it does not neatly fit with the justifications offered by either theory. The point of this chapter is not to provide an exhaustive and comprehensive account of all the elements of both theories, nor to choose between them, but to see what insights they provide into this question of the relationship between contract law and commerce. Of course promissory and efficiency theories are not the only accounts that seek to explain and justify contract law. Other theories advance different concepts as central to understanding contractual obligations, such as reliance[3] or consent.[4] The account here might be regarded as under-inclusive. Nevertheless, rights-based and efficiency theories are the

[1] This account follows SA Smith, *Contract Theory* (Oxford, OUP, 2004) ch 4.

[2] Ibid, 142.

[3] PS Atiyah, 'Contracts, Promises and the Law of Obligations' in *Essays on Contract* (Oxford, OUP, 1988) 10.

[4] RE Barnett, 'A Consent Theory of Contract' (1996) 86 *Columbia Law Review* 269.

two dominant accounts of the underpinning justification for contract law. As such they are the most well-known and comprehensively developed normative accounts of contractual obligation.[5] If one of these theories provides a broad justification for contract law tracking commercial practice then there is no need to look any further. If neither of these can provide a good justification for why contract law should track commercial behaviour then other general theories are unlikely to fare any better.

While it is difficult to derive determinate answers concerning the role of diffuse commercial practices and expectations in the law from these broader accounts, if strong general normative grounds exist to support incorporation of these norms in at least some instances, then this accords the incorporation argument some additional weight against any countervailing practical considerations that may militate against it. The chapter makes little assessment of these two theories on their merits, but examines whether either provides some grounds for a closer alignment between contract law and commercial practices and expectations. To the extent to which it is possible to pin the expectations argument to one of these foundations, then some deeper justification for incorporation of business norms and behaviours may be provided that goes beyond an assertion that 'this is what contractors do' or that contract law should facilitate commerce. An alternative sort of account, the sociological theory of relationalism, in particular that version advanced by Ian Macneil, will be examined in the next chapter.

DISTINGUISHING RIGHTS-BASED AND EFFICIENCY ACCOUNTS OF PROMISING

Both efficiency analysis and rights-based promissory theories (or indeed any theory of contractual obligations) seek to address two questions whose answers are not always straightforwardly derived from the scheme of rules themselves:[6] (i) an analytical question concerning what are the essential features of a contractual obligation that distinguish it from obligations that might arise under other areas of law such as criminal law, torts, property

[5] Increasingly it has been sought to place the economic analysis of law on a surer normative footing and to explain its philosophical underpinnings to the extent that it can be regarded as the dominant account of the justification of contract law: see JS Kraus, 'Philosophy of Contract Law' in J Coleman and S Shapiro (eds), *The Oxford Handbook of Jurisprudence and Philosophy of Law* (Oxford, OUP, 2002) 687.

[6] See R Craswell, 'In That Case, What is the Question? Economics and the Demands of Contract Theory' (2003) 112 *Yale Law Journal* 903, 918. Internal, or interpretative accounts, such as those of Smith, above n 1, try to explain law's concepts in terms understandable to the legal community of judges, practitioners and so on. The premise of such accounts is that law can be understood in terms of the concepts and ideas in which it expresses itself. See also EJ Weinrib, *The Idea of Private Law* (Cambridge MA, Harvard University Press, 1995).

or unjust enrichment; (ii) a normative question concerning why the state is justified in enforcing and regulating these obligations by providing a scheme of general rules of contract law.[7] While these two theories are often regarded as offering entirely separate kinds of justification for contractual obligations,[8] there is also a degree of overlap between them.[9] It will be appreciated that law and economics scholars can defend the social utility of promising in instrumental terms:[10] 'Adherence to [the virtue of keeping promises] facilitates transactions (and so promotes trade and hence wealth) by reducing the costs of policing markets through self-protection, detailed contracts, litigation, etc'.[11] This sort of account of the normative value of promising differs from a rights-based one since under the economic approach the good in promising, and hence the justification for a system of contract law that enforces some promises, is instrumental upon whether observing the promise secures some other value thought beneficial, such as increases in wealth or social welfare. While both theories may rely on *moral* concepts, they differ on the detailed morality that is relied upon. In non-instrumental, rights-based accounts of promising it is usually the specific agreement between the promisor and promisee that is the focus of the enquiry and the source of the moral obligation. In instrumental accounts the justification for promise keeping may relate to specific agreements (is performing this promise efficient?), or to the general incentive effects that a system of reliable promise keeping creates amongst participants. The former has perhaps garnered less attention in the modern law and economics literature, being most closely associated with the troublesome notion of efficient breach. Stated simply, this expresses the idea that when the costs of performance to the promisor outweigh the value of performance to the promisee, the promisor has an incentive to breach which the law should not discourage. Some economists have argued that efficient breach has led to the misunderstanding that economic analysis dictates that only efficient individual agreements should be enforced, thus affording promise keeping only instrumental and contingent value. Craswell points out that no proponent of the economic analysis of law argues that non-performance of an inefficient contract should attract no remedy at all (unless non-performance is excused on some other ground, such as frustration).[12] For Craswell and

[7] Smith, above n 1, 42–50.

[8] Although Kraus notes the operation of the 'convergence' thesis whereby efficiency and autonomy theories are thought to provide both simultaneous and overlapping justification for contract law: above n 5, 688.

[9] Craswell, above n 6.

[10] See, eg, R Craswell, 'Two Economic Theories of Enforcing Promises' in P Benson (ed), *The Theory of Contract Law* (Cambridge, CUP, 2001) 19.

[11] RA Posner, 'Utilitarianism, Economics and Legal Theory' (1979) 8 *Journal of Legal Studies* 103, 123.

[12] Craswell, above n 10, 26–27.

other law and economics scholars the primary enquiry for economic analysis of law is not whether each individual contract is efficient, and calling for enforcement only for those contracts that pass the test, but whether the law creates incentives, through remedies and other devices, to promote efficient over inefficient behaviour when a promisor is faced with a decision whether to enter into an agreement and on what terms, or whether to perform a contract or breach, and so on.[13] 'Enforcement' here though refers to the totality of the law's response to breach, including awards of damages, not just positive enforcement by way of orders of specific performance. This incentive-effects strand of economic analysis may be more resistant to a charge of instrumentalism, since occasional defections from the individual promise on instrumental grounds may not detrimentally affect the institution of promise keeping, which remains intact and justifiable as a system which generally promotes efficiency through encouraging the wealth-creating exchange. However, any wrong that attaches to breaking a promise in this account is primarily done to a useful institution, since it potentially reduces the efficacy of promise making and promise keeping in facilitating the non-simultaneous exchange. It is not of primary significance that promise breaking is a wrong done to the individual promisee. To say otherwise would be to concentrate on the *ex post* effects of breach between the particular claimant and defendant, rather than the *ex ante* incentive effect the rules of contract law create for the general contracting community.

Non-instrumental accounts of promising differ from this instrumental account in two connected ways. The first is that it is a necessary part of the concept of promising that the promise creates obligations between individuals. The second is that the obligation to keep a promise by doing what was promised is necessarily built into what it means *to promise*, as opposed to doing something else. Thus by promising, one undertakes an obligation to another individual that *means* one must exclude from consideration countervailing preferences for not keeping the promise based on consequential or instrumental grounds.[14] In essence, promissory theories provide a particular answer to the question of why people contract. The reason is precisely to bind themselves to act or refrain from acting in certain ways, thus limiting their freedom of action and capacity for choice in the future.[15] Economists may regard these distinctions as quibbling over the semantics of 'promising', since one can show commitment to enforcing promises by awards of damages, not just by insisting that the promise is kept, and indeed

[13] Ibid, 30.

[14] J Rawls, 'Two Concepts of Rules' (1955) 64 *The Philosophical Review* 3, 6–17; J Raz, 'Promises and Obligations' in PMS Hacker and J Raz, *Law, Morality and Society* (Oxford, OUP, 1977) 210, 222. This need not imply there is an absolute obligation to perform the promise, just that it would rule certain considerations out of account *ab initio*.

[15] I Macneil, *The Relational Theory of Contract: Selected Works of Ian Macneil*, D Campbell (ed) (London, Sweet & Maxwell, 2001) 131.

for the law charged with the task of making certain kinds of agreement enforceable this may be the most realistic option.[16] For most supporters of non-instrumental accounts of promising, however, the primary obligation is to do the thing promised. This understanding has the added benefit of according with the participants' view of the practice of promising and how the law understands and explains itself.[17] Non-instrumental promissory accounts can also more readily distinguish the obligations of contract from those arising under other parts of the private law of obligations, such as non-voluntary, reliance-based obligations in tort, or the obligations imposed by unjust enrichment. For economic accounts, efficiency concerns play a large role in these other parts of law too.[18] These differences would not seem to address the main point of contention between the two accounts however, which is that ultimately the economic account places contingent rather than intrinsic value both on the performance of individual promises and the social practice of promising.[19] Under the rights-based account, a trial and judgment is primarily a matter of corrective justice and upholding pre-existing rights between the claimant and the defendant, not an instrumental process designed to add to the stock of rules (or interpretations of rules) for other prospective contracting parties or litigants.

PROMISSORY THEORIES

Main Features

Promissory theorists seek to answer both analytical and normative questions using the same concept. Thus a promissory theorist would hold that contracts are distinguishable from other obligations arising under the law since they are voluntarily assumed by the parties. An individual rights-based defence of promissory theories is usually rooted in ideas of individual autonomy.[20] However, even within autonomy justifications there are a wide range of positions taken on the issue of why promises should create obligations. An added complication is that some theorists may accept the normative arguments for why promises bind, but do not accept the analytical connection between contracts and promises.[21] In other words it may

[16] Craswell, above n 10, 26–27.
[17] Smith, above n 1, 132ff, 161.
[18] Kraus, above n 5, 699–700.
[19] Eg, C Goetz and RE Scott, 'Enforcing Promises: An Examination of the Basis of Contract' (1980) 89 *Yale Law Journal* 1265: 'Bargained for promises support value-enhancing exchanges. Such promises are thus seen as fully enforceable under the compensation rule in order to protect and encourage value-maximising resource allocation'. See also Kraus, above n 5, 689.
[20] Smith has constructed and defends such an account, above n 1, 74ff, 163.
[21] J Raz, 'Promises in Morality and Law' (1982) 95 *Harvard Law Review* 916, 921.

be accepted that promise keeping is intrinsically valuable, but denied that contracts are promises.[22] Alternatively, theorists may agree that a non-instrumental account of promising provides the normative and analytical foundation for contracts and contract law, but disagree over the precise grounds on which promises create binding obligations.[23] One particular difficulty here attaches to the seeming lack of harm that results to a promisee if a promise is broken (or contract breached) without more. Some theorists have sought to explain why the law is justified in enforcing agreements of this type.[24] Mindful of this difficulty, other theorists may offer accounts which, while not denying that contracts are a form of promise, do not rely on promising *alone* as sufficient to give rise to liability. In other words, the morality of promising and the importance to be attached to promise keeping, and by analogy the reason to enforce contracts, is not just because they are promises, but because the obligation to keep a promise, or perform a contract, ultimately collapses into some other species of moral wrong. For such accounts, the morality of promise keeping may be identified and defended only as part of a larger pattern of obligations and normative commitments. These wider commitments could be identified as the need to obviate the harm resulting from the likelihood of the promisee's reliance[25] or to prevent the moral wrong of raising and disappointing expectations and thus harming the value of assurance.[26] It is these 'other grounds' that give rise to the wrong of promise breaking. Thus in these accounts 'promising' as a social practice is not an essential component of the moral wrong. It is simply one mechanism, amongst others, by which these wrongs may be committed.[27] While these accounts may also be regarded as instrumental, they differ from economic accounts in that they seek to uphold some other value apart from efficiency in promise keeping. In these accounts, enforcing a promise is justified as a means to avoid the harm of an individual wrong

[22] D Kimel, *From Promise to Contract* (Oxford, Hart Publishing, 2005) 58.

[23] Consider the different accounts provided by, inter alia, C Fried—promising is a social convention which invokes trust and protects autonomy: *Contract as Promise* (Cambridge MA, Harvard University Press, 1981) 16; Smith—promising creates special relationships that allow us to lead valuable lives: above n 1, 143– 44 and SA Smith, 'Performance, Punishment and the Nature of Contractual Obligations' (1997) 60 *MLR* 360, 367. In R Craswell's terminology, under these accounts the value in promising is that it allows individuals to enjoy 'norm-creating power', which he contrasts with defences of promising based on the 'harm' caused by breaking a promise: 'Contract Law, Default Rules, and the Philosophy of Promising' (1989) 88 *Michigan Law Review* 489, 498.

[24] Eg, Smith, above n 1.

[25] PS Atiyah, above n 3; L Fuller and W Perdue, 'The Reliance Interest in Contract Damages' (1936) 46 *Yale Law Journal* 52, esp 52–65. For Raz the role of law, and contract law, is not to enforce promises, but to protect the practice of undertaking voluntarily assumed obligations, and those who rely on it, from the harm of erosion and abuse: above n 21, 933.

[26] TM Scanlon, 'Promises and Contracts' in P Benson (ed), *The Theory of Contract Law* (Cambridge, CUP, 2001) 86, 87.

[27] See in particular Scanlon, when discussing and criticising Fried's social convention theory: ibid, 87.

that demands redress from the defendant (although the precise 'harm' or wrong identified may not be the same across the different theories). Promise keeping is not an end in itself where enforcement is justified whether or not harm (loss) results from breaking the promise.[28]

Promissory Theories and Commercial Expectations

While it is not straightforward to move seamlessly from any of these accounts of the morality of promise keeping to an account of how contract law is to be designed or justified,[29] nevertheless it should be asked whether and on what basis rights-based promissory theories provide support for the idea that contract law should be informed by commercial practices, expectations and norms. To ask a more specific question, could an incorporationist argument be accommodated within non-instrumental accounts of promising? Rights-based accounts seek to provide general justification for contract law by elucidating why actions such as breaking promises are moral wrongs against individuals that the law may be justified in redressing. To the extent that such accounts place significance on party autonomy and choice in assuming contractual obligations then rights-based theories provide justification for upholding the agreed terms. One might find support for a commercial-expectations approach here, since there appears to be no reason why the contract could not include the norms and practices that constitute the implicit dimensions of the agreement, although to fit fully with promissory theory, this arguably requires at least some tacit knowledge and acceptance of these practices on the part of contractors. While it may be difficult to discern if the parties have this knowledge, this may be regarded as primarily a matter of evidence, and a more rigorous attention to context (for example, the pricing structures adopted in a particular industry) may provide some indication of the content of the agreement in this sense. Promissory theories do provide support for upholding the agreement, including all its identifiable elements. This may be more in keeping with a commercial expectations approach than according automatic primacy to the objective documentary version of the agreement, which may or may not be a faithful rendition of the parties' expectations. Some may take this as relying on a very broad understanding of what constitutes 'agreement', although much seems to turn here on whether 'agreement' is understood in objective or subjective terms and whether the social norms are used to understand and give content to the obligations or fill a gap in the agreement.

28 Raz, above n 21, 938.

29 W Lucy, *Philosophy of Private Law* (Oxford, OUP, 2007) 238, discussing the work of Scanlon.

Craswell has pointed out that it is difficult to build accounts of the design of contract gap-filling default rules from these very general accounts of promise keeping.[30] However, the concern here is not with the specific process of filling gaps in agreements but seeking to justify broadening the sources of obligations beyond the written document to which the parties can be taken to have given their agreement. While it might be difficult to regard justification for the legal recognition of commercial practices as securely rooted in the idea of upholding promises, the morality behind promise keeping may support in broad terms the idea that the law should uphold agreements as these are understood by the parties. One could regard the empirical finding that business people believe agreements should be performed as assimilable with the internal view of participants that promising entails that the promise should be kept.[31] It is an account that stresses the importance of the individual agreement and the obligations created under it rather than the effect that enforcement may have on the wider community. At the least, promissory theories could provide support for incorporation of expectations and understandings as interpretative criteria to increase the possibility of giving effect to the agreement created by the parties.[32]

Some support for this can be found in the promissory theory of Charles Fried. In defending the idea that contracts are promises Fried relied on the idea of a social convention of promising:

> The obligation to keep a promise is grounded not in arguments of utility but in respect for individual autonomy and in trust ... An individual is morally bound to keep his promises because he has invoked a convention whose function it is to give grounds—moral grounds—for another to expect the promised performance.[33]

Many have pointed out the weakness with this argument, chiefly that a wrong does not generally result simply from breaching a social convention alone but from the promisee's reliance, disappointed expectations and so on. In other words, the existence of a 'social practice' or norm on its own would be insufficient to ground an obligation to follow the practice. However, an account such as Fried's does provide some justification for regarding social or commercial conventions as incorporated into *an agreement*. Thus if the law seeks to uphold 'agreements' then this includes the social norms. Under Fried's account of contract as promise, social conventions play a part in giving content to promissory obligations, particularly through the process of interpretation, since background conventions can be

[30] Craswell, above n 23, 504. See also Kraus, above n 5, 690.

[31] S Macaulay 'Non-Contractual Relations in Business: A Preliminary Study' (1963) 28 *American Sociological Review* 55, 63. See also Smith, above n 1, 76.

[32] Scottish Law Commission, *Discussion Paper on Interpretation of Contract* (no 147) (Edinburgh, TSO, 2011) para 6.25: 'Business people place a high value on the formal contract giving effect to the agreements and bargains that they have struck'.

[33] Fried, above n 23, 16.

evidence of what a contractor has subjectively intended. These conventions play a part in defining the nature and scope of a contractual obligation since promises are necessarily made against an

> unexpressed background of shared purposes [and] experiences ... [t]here is always some deeper, more general level of shared experience and striving to which appeal can be made in order to make the particular project mutually intelligible. With mutual intelligibility the stage is set for an exchange of promises.[34]

In this way Fried's approach can give some justification for the decision in a case like *The Achilleas*.[35] For Lord Hoffmann in *The Achilleas* the extent of the charterer's liability was not a matter of the application of external legal standards. Instead the *Hadley v Baxendale* rule stated only the presumed intention of the parties. The relevant question was whether the charterers assumed responsibility for the risk of a loss which was unquantifiable when the contract was made. For Lord Hoffmann the answer to this was 'no' due to the tacit understandings prevalent within the industry. According to Lord Hoffmann, the industry understanding was that the charterer's liability was restricted to the difference between the market rate and the charter rate for the period of delay.[36] A contextual interpretative approach to the agreement permits incorporation of this broader conventional understanding. If it is the conventional understanding, it may matter little if the parties did not have the understanding in their mind when they entered into the contract. This conventional understanding may form part of their tacit intentions derived from the general background against which the parties reached their agreement, particularly if it was open to them to expressly contract for some other alternative set of obligations.[37] Such understandings are likely to form the basis of their internal acceptance over the *Hadley* default rule.

Accepting that these background standards and expectations exist does not mean that the standards must themselves incorporate normative criteria, although this may be a consideration for a court in making the decision whether to uphold the conventions or not.[38] But it does recognise that commercial contracting takes place against a normatively rich background (possibly a very long negotiating period, industry norms and customs,

[34] Ibid, 88. See also R Barnett, 'The Sound of Silence: Default Rules and Contractual Consent' (1982) 78 *Virginia Law Review* 821, arguing that when transaction costs are high, a court should formulate faults that reflect the social conventions of an industry or expectations of the community, since parties are more likely to consent to those: 866, 880.

[35] *Transfield Shipping Inc v Mercator Shipping Inc (The Achilleas)* [2008] UKHL 48; [2009] 1 AC 61.

[36] Ibid, [6]–[8]. See also Lord Hoffmann, 'The *Achilleas*: Custom and Practice or Foreseeability?' (2010) 14 *Edinburgh Law Review* 47, 48–49.

[37] For arguments along these lines see Barnett, above n 34, 826, 866; CA Riley, 'Designing Default Rules in Contract Law' (2000) 20 *OJLS* 367, 369ff; A Kramer, 'Implication in Fact as an Instance of Contractual Interpretation' (2004) 63 *CLJ* 384, 387ff. See also Kraus, above n 5, 690, 718ff.

[38] Fried, above n 23, 87.

previous dealings), which provides potentially relevant evidence of the parties' intentions and gives another layer of meaning to their agreement. So, for example, if we are to ask why in *The Achilleas* the 'tacit intention' of the parties is to incorporate the conventional understanding in the industry, rather than the *Hadley v Baxendale* default rule, it may be simply that if any intention must be attributed to the parties, it should be that derived from the conventional understandings, first, since parties are more likely to be aware of those and make their contract according to them[39] and, second, the substance of the convention (damages for period of delay only) was more certain than the *Hadley* rule, which required an evaluative judgment to be made about the likelihood of the loss. Promissory theories do support the idea that the contract is fundamentally created by the parties, and the courts' primary role is to uphold the agreements that the parties made rather than give primary consideration to the incentive effects of judgments on the commercial community as a whole.

One ground for scepticism concerning any link between commercial expectations and promissory theories is that the former argument appears rooted more in empiricism than morality. That is, the misalignment claim is concerned with making the law fit the reality of contracting behaviour. So, one source of evidence about misalignment is empirical studies of how commercial contracting is conducted. But there might be considerable doubt that empirical studies reveal anything important about the normative commitments that the law should display. The studies do not assist in justifying why the state enforces some varieties of voluntarily assumed obligations: what *is* done by contractors may provide no indication of what *ought* to be done, either by the contractors or the law. Thus if a strong rights-based justification can be advanced for why people should perform their contracts, then that argument is not defeated by an empirical revelation that most people breach. Whether these normative commitments accord with business expectations or practices is neither here nor there. Thus the claim that contract law should uphold commercial expectations could be rejected on the ground that contract law is not concerned (solely) with facilitating commerce by reflecting commercial norms and any connections between law and business practice are contingent at best. Under this view contract law is justified and can be reformed on grounds unrelated to the requirements of its users, and can therefore remain indifferent as to whether it supports the actions and norms of behaviour that commercial contractors may bring to bear on their business relationships.

It is difficult to draw any normative conclusions about contract law from empirical studies of contracting behaviour. Taken at face value, the studies tend to justify a pragmatic rather than value-laden or normative accounts

[39] See Barnett, above n 34, 829.

of contract law. The fact that such an approach may be castigated as normatively impoverished may not be too much of a concern. First, because the extent to which contract law manifests commitment to a single normative justification is itself subject to dispute. Second, because the expectations argument, at least as understood here, is precisely focused on *social practices*. While the empirical observation that people in a particular society did not generally keep promises may have no effect on an argument about the morality of promise keeping, it would surely impinge on the question of whether persons in such a society could have an empirically derived *reasonable expectation* that a promise to them would be kept. In any case, the normative and the empirical will not necessarily pull in opposite directions and indeed most empirical studies reveal that contractors believe it important that the other party will do what they said they would do. In addition, evidence from empirical studies might be obliquely relevant to the normative and analytical foundations of contract law in two related ways. First, by providing evidence concerning the internal point of view of the participants in the practice of commercial dealing and second, by raising questions concerning the congruence between the analytical boundaries of what constitutes a contract as drawn by the law and what participants may regard as a matter of contractual obligation. Thus law may give a particular answer to the question of what a contract is and how it is formed so as to guarantee legal enforceability, and this may be juxtaposed with the empirical evidence of what participants regard as binding obligations beyond the legal statement, or that show expected standards of conduct in commercial dealings.

The conclusions to be drawn from examination of rights-based promissory theories and upholding commercial expectations are not straightforward. Promissory theory might provide general support for upholding such expectations, if they can be linked to the parties' agreement or form part of the contract context. Certainly insofar as promissory theory regards upholding the individual agreement between the parties as its paramount concern, then this at least suggests attention to the 'real deal' should take priority over simply privileging the contract documents without any prior investigation into how far these constitute part of the real deal. Promissory theory does recognise that the development and communication of the rules and standards of commercial contract law through the litigation process, while important, are arguably secondary to effectuating the consent and autonomy of the parties by enforcing the actual agreement they made.[40] This 'agreement' is likely to incorporate both formal and relational elements. If contractual obligations are not being upheld due to failure to take

[40] See C Mitchell, 'Contract Interpretation: Pragmatism, Principle and the Prior Negotiations Rule' (2010) 26 *Journal of Contract Law* 134.

sufficient account of contractual context, then this demonstrates within the law a very attenuated commitment to the idea of upholding contracts and facilitating commercial agreements.

ECONOMIC ANALYSIS OF CONTRACT

Main Features

In broad strokes, economic analysis as applied to law is concerned with the incentive effects that legal rules and institutions may have on the behaviour of those to whom they are addressed. For Goodhart, 'the economist sees the law as a means of applying and maintaining appropriate incentive structures in society'.[41] These effects are examined by bringing a different set of methods and analytical tools to bear on the study of legal phenomena. The hallmark of the economic approach is that legal phenomena are not analysed in terms of whether the rules, institutions and outcomes reflect intrinsic values thought universally good, irrespective of their consequences, but rather in instrumental terms of whether efficiency (or, in older terms, utility) is promoted by their design and use. While efficiency is understood in different ways, in the economic analysis of law it is usually concerned with maximising wealth or social welfare. There is an important debate over this, but it will not be addressed here.[42] In relation to contract law, efficiency usually refers to allocative efficiency: 'When resources are being used where their value is highest, or equivalently when no reallocation would increase their value, we say they are being employed efficiently.'[43] At this point 'Pareto-optimality' may be achieved, where no further transfer will make one person better off without someone else becoming worse off.[44] Economic analysis therefore adopts a forward-looking approach to analysing legal phenomena. Justification according to the future states brought about by legal development is more important than attention to past facts.

While it may be disputed, it is relatively easy to demonstrate that some laws may be concerned with efficiency, in the sense that judges are often mindful of the costs imposed by their decisions in practical terms and the incentive effects the rules create in society. These outcomes appear derived

[41] CAE Goodhart, 'Economics and the Law: Too Much One Way Traffic' (1997) 60 *MLR* 1, 3.

[42] See, eg, R Dworkin, 'Is Wealth a Value?' (1980) 9 *Journal of Legal Studies* 191 and N Duxbury, *Patterns of American Jurisprudence* (Oxford, OUP, 1995) 397ff.

[43] RA Posner, *Economic Analysis of Law*, 6th edn (New York, Aspen, 2003) 10.

[44] A slightly lesser standard is expressed in Kaldor-Hicks efficiency, where losses imposed on some by a transfer can be tolerated, provided the gains from the transfer outweigh the losses: A Ogus, *Costs and Cautionary Tales* (Oxford, Hart Publishing, 2006) 27.

more from instinct, however, rather than a rigid application of economic methodology. Nevertheless, this would vindicate the claim of positive economic analysis that laws (and common law in particular) do tend towards efficiency.[45] Thus Richard Posner argued that the common law was not wholly justified in the terms presented on the surface of judgments but displayed a broad economic rationality. This does not entail that every common law doctrine is efficient, instead the claim is the rather less ambitious one that 'the common law is best (not perfectly) explained as a system for maximising the wealth of society'.[46] This is a controversial claim however, and the predictive and descriptive accuracy of efficiency analysis is difficult to determine. It is not clear whether any tendency towards efficiency in the common law is a product of judicial manipulation or sympathies, the vagaries of the litigation process and the kinds of disputes it generates, or the fluidity of economic analysis, such that it is possible to explain a range of outcomes using its methods.[47] These tools and methods have also been subject to criticism for abstracting individual actors from social institutions and contexts, regarding them as a collection of preferences and rational self-interested impulses leading to a formal/abstract and formal/doctrinal approach to both economics and law respectively.[48] If the descriptive claim is that the common law generally tends towards efficiency, the normative claim is that efficiency or wealth maximisation is a value that society should pursue. Even for those scholars who regard themselves as primarily engaged on a descriptive and explanatory undertaking, that efficiency is normatively desirable is usually the unstated assumption behind the exercise.[49] The details of this particular dispute will not be examined here.

Contracts and contract law are a natural subject for analysis for the economist. Since microeconomic theory encompasses the study of individuals and firms operating in markets then its insights seem particularly pertinent

[45] See AW Dnes, *The Economics of Law* (Mason OH, Southwestern, 2005) 9.

[46] Posner, above n 43, 25.

[47] PH Rubin has made the argument that the motivation for a tendency towards efficiency is litigants rather than judges, since firms are more likely to litigate inefficient rules and settle under efficient rules: 'Why is the Common Law Efficient?' (1977) 6 *Journal of Legal Studies* 51. See also GL Priest, 'The Common Law Process and the Selection of Efficient Rules' (1997) 6 *Journal of Legal Studies* 65. Litigation repeat players (or participants in industries where litigation is culturally acceptable) may also exercise a profound influence in this respect: M Galanter, 'Why the "Haves" Come Out Ahead: Speculations on the Limits of Legal Change' (1974) 9 *Law and Society Review* 95.

[48] RA Posner is usually regarded as the chief exponent of this kind of approach. See D Campbell and S Picciotto, 'Exploring the Interaction Between Law and Economics: The Limits of Formalism' (1998) 18 *Legal Studies* 249, who criticised the then law and economics movement as tending to 'reproduce the worst aspects of formalism in each discipline': 249.

[49] Kraus has argued that although many economic theorists engaged on 'explanatory work' do not seek to defend economic analysis explicitly on normative grounds, 'it is fair to assume [the theorist] finds the goal of efficiency a normatively plausible ground for the exercise of state coercion'. In other words the support for economic theory is often implicit in explanatory work: above n 5, 695.

to contracts and contract law, since contracting is a method of private ordering that allows satisfaction of preferences, and thereby is assumed to be a central institution facilitating the transfer of goods to their most valued use. A system of enforcing contracts provides security and a mechanism for the wealth-enhancing exchange to take place. This instrumental account of contract law fits with the instrumental nature of contracts themselves, since the point of exchanging between private actors is to create surplus.[50] Judges rarely undertake an enquiry into this aspect of contracts however, except insofar as necessary to determine the remedy for breach. Most transactions that are freely entered into between roughly equal contractors are assumed to be efficient as between the parties and contract law rarely concerns itself with whether such trades are actually efficient. Instead awareness of allocative efficiency may be manifest by contract law seeking to affect the incentives of those trading and thus the behaviour of economic actors. These efforts may be directed to reducing the costs of transacting—specifically by positing the ground rules according to which a transaction takes place (mandatory rules), encouraging private ordering and stipulating gap-filling defaults—or else by remedying various aspects of market failure (information asymmetry; opportunism) which impede the flow of resources to where they have most value.

Economic Analysis and Commercial Expectations

Economic analysis of contract law is a vast area of scholarship and even if the focus is limited to what it may reveal about the connection between commercial contract law and commercial practices, or the question whether economic analysis provides any justification for closer assimilation between law and commercial practice, or indeed the reverse, there are different aspects of the law and economics movement that could be harnessed to this endeavour. For example, transaction cost economics, as exemplified in the work of Ronald Coase and Oliver Williamson, concentrates on the costs involved in using various different contract governance regimes. Amongst other things it examines the conditions which prompt market transactions as opposed to internalising production processes within the firm. Such work takes as its subject matter the institutions upon which exchange and production are based rather than the individual decisions of a set of rational utility-maximising individuals operating within markets.[51] But

[50] D Campbell, 'What Do We Mean By the Non-Use of Contract?' in J Braucher, J Kidwell and WC Whitford (eds), *Revisiting the Contracts Scholarship of Stewart Macaulay* (Oxford, Hart Publishing, 2013) 159, 167.

[51] RH Coase, *The Firm, the Market and the Law* (Chicago, University of Chicago Press, 1988) 5; O Williamson, *The Economic Institutions of Capitalism* (New York, Free Press, 1985).

this branch also seeks to answer the question of when parties will resort to market transactions as embodied in contracts and when they may eschew contracts entirely in favour of some other method of regulating the productive relationship. As was seen in Chapter 2, Oliver Williamson's work suggests factors that may incline a transaction towards more relational and long-term forms of contracting, where internally generated norms of the business relationship, rather than contract law defaults, may be assumed to play a larger role. This sort of work may not produce any reforming agenda for contract law, since the design of the law may be treated as a given—it is the business relationships, characteristics of the trade, and the contracts themselves that are the material for analysis. This attention to law as it is may also be a feature of other forms of economic analysis. Goodhart notes that 'most economists tended to take the legal underpinnings of the economy for granted in most of our work'.[52] Economists may therefore be more concerned about explaining the current law than articulating robust proposals for its reform along efficiency lines. Nevertheless, whatever its ambition or lack of ambition for law, the insights revealed from transaction cost economics might be relevant to legal development since it identifies the broad circumstances in which contractors will use law or some other technique to govern their relationships. This knowledge of who uses contracts and contract law, and in what circumstances, may be relevant to the issue of whether any sort of reform is required and what its effects on the identified users may be. A different branch of the movement, behavioural economics, brings findings from human psychology to bear on the assumptions underlying neoclassical economic analysis.[53] This may be relevant in explaining why contractors do not write completely contingent contracts (bounded rationality), or why they may display a preference for the status quo in their contract dealings or in the law, or the behavioural limitations that operate on market actors. Despite the various branches within the discipline, most of the well-known economic analysis of contract law has remained rooted in neoclassical economics and rational choice theory.

While it is relatively straightforward to make a connection between contracting and maximising wealth, and the role of the law in facilitating this in general terms by providing a set of ground rules according to which contracting can take place, it is more challenging to make the connection between efficiency in neoclassical terms and a particular design of contract law rules. The question might be asked whether efficiency analysis supports an incorporationist and inclusive strategy with a contextual interpretative approach to legal reasoning. Answering this question in the abstract is difficult since it is dependent upon the phenomenon that is subject to

[52] Goodhart, above n 41, 2.
[53] See below, text accompanying n 59.

the efficiency analysis. Is the efficiency of contract law to be judged by how far it encourages or incentivises the wealth-maximising exchange and disincentivises the inefficient exchange amongst the general contracting community? Or how far the legal dispute resolution procedures are judged to be efficient? Or how far it encourages efficient contract design for the parties? These issues pull in different directions. Ultimately, the division is between whether law should be concerned with the efficiency or otherwise of individual decisions and outcomes reached in cases, or with the incentive effects created in society by judgments. Given that neoformalists are usually opposed to contextualists, this suggests that at least neoclassical economic analysis remains generally opposed to incorporation. Certainly many neoformalists in the US contract law literature would identify themselves with the law and economics movement, while those who call for a greater appreciation of contractual context view themselves as opposed to the approach of rational choice-based economic analysis. But this does not mean contextualists and relationalists necessarily reject efficiency as a social value that should be pursued by contract law.[54] Rather the source of disagreement lies not in the yardstick of efficiency, but the model of the contractor which underpins the judgments of efficiency. Classical and neoclassical economic analysis as expressed in rational choice theory has come under fire for basing itself on a one-dimensional view of the individual as a rational self-utility maximiser who acts always in his own self-interest to maximise his wealth and satisfy his preferences. Relationalists have pointed out that the determination of whether an outcome is 'efficient' is based on a model that ignores the social embeddedness of transactions. Nevertheless, while relationalist scholars may regard rational choice theory as deeply flawed, insofar as they consider the normative foundations of contract law (not all are concerned with this issue) they may accept, or at least be neutral towards, the pursuit of efficiency as a defensible social goal. They may further defend a claim that attention to relational norms would render the law more efficient.[55] Thus the debate between formalists and relationalists turns not on whether contract law development should be driven by efficiency concerns, but the assumptions upon which the determinations of efficiency should proceed: actual social conditions or on the basis of rational choice theory? The neoformalist usually rejects greater incorporation on the latter ground, regarding incorporation of business norms as inefficient for

[54] Thus A Schwartz argues that a reliance on internal norms of contractual relationships collapses into efficiency analysis in any case: 'Relational Contracts in the Courts: An Analysis of Incomplete Agreements and Judicial Strategies' (1992) 21 *Journal of Legal Studies* 271, 280. See also I Macneil, 'Reflections on Relational Contract Theory After a Neo-Classical Seminar' in D Campbell, H Collins and J Wightman (eds), *Implicit Dimensions of Contract* (Oxford, Hart Publishing, 2003) 207, 208.

[55] This is considered further in Ch 6, with particular reference to Ian Macneil's relational contract theory.

dispute resolution purposes since the possibility of judicial error is greater, legalising social norms will reduce their value, litigation will become more expensive and business or social norms are not necessarily efficient. But an incorporation strategy on the part of the law may also be superior in many respects as an incentive system since it may allow contractors greater flexibility in reaching different kinds of legally enforceable agreement. In any case, while it is readily understandable that the design of contracts and contractors themselves may be motivated by efficiency concerns, this does not entail that contract law must be. In what follows, selected issues on the efficiency considerations attaching to commercial norms and expectations are assessed in greater detail. This does not aim to be comprehensive, but addresses those matters that seem pertinent to the concerns lying at the centre of this work.

Characteristics of the Contracting Parties

Much of the well-known economic analysis of contract law is based on rational choice theory. Long-standing critiques have taken issue with the assumptions upon which this theory rests concerning the contracting parties and their motivations. The paradigm of the self-interested rational utility-maximiser is contrasted with the co-operative, flexible and conciliatory behaviour that many contractors display in their commercial relationships. It has been pointed out that actors' rationality is always bounded by the time and cost of seeking complete and accurate information about alternatives. Thus the real behaviour of actual contracting parties as evidenced from empirical studies or experimental methods casts doubt on whether the assumptions of the model of neoclassical law are a good starting point from which to construct rules of contract law. To the extent that classical law is built upon such a model it might be reckoned severely flawed, leading to legal rules that ignore the constraints that real contractors are under, forcing them into suboptimal patterns of behaviour in an attempt to meet the conditions of legal enforceability. So for example the law's undoubted preference for a degree of advance planning before performance may reflect its poor grasp of the conditions which militate against contractors achieving this and the efficiency concerns which may compel parties to other looser forms of contract arrangement. Courts may therefore lack sensitivity to the trade-offs parties must make between formation and enforcement costs in contract design. Contract law may be a blunt instrument in assuming the ideal of a fully contingent contract as the basis for its rules, as opposed to a more flexible conception that may take account of different contexts within which parties organise their productive behaviour.

Some flavour of this debate appears by considering Ian Macneil's criticism of simple efficient breach (that is, the thesis that a breach which can make one party better off without making the other worse off should not be discouraged by the legal rules). Macneil criticised this idea in forthright terms for ignoring the significant hidden costs involved in breaching a contract beyond the payment of compensation assessed on the expectation measure. These costs militate against any *certain* determination that a particular breach is efficient:

> [S]ome costs of initial planning in the *first* contract (including negotiations essential to the mutual planning required in contracting), costs of planning (again including negotiations) after the new opportunity comes along, costs of potential or actual litigation (including costs of delay), information costs, costs of inertia, costs of uncertainty, relational costs, such as damage to reputation and loss of future opportunities to deal, and undoubtedly others.[56]

The criticism here is that to achieve an accurate determination of whether breach is efficient, the rational choice model must take account of all these costs. But inaccuracy in calculating the real costs of breach is not really the thrust of Macneil's argument against the rational choice model. It is that the model is flawed as a description of social reality. The social embeddedness of transactions is a fact that cannot be ignored and, because this social context is so variable, it cannot be reduced to a limited set of abstract criteria according to which the analysis proceeds. Macneil does not deny that efficiency may be an overriding concern in legal analysis, but he would question whether the parties are likely to be concerned with the efficiency of the deal when formulating it. At the outset parties are more likely to be concerned with the project itself and its management, rather than the division of the spoils. He writes:

> At the time of decision about which governance structures to adopt, the parties will often have very limited information about the substantive effect of alternative structures on the future division of the pie to be produced by their efforts. For that reason, their individual interests are best served by presently paying little attention to how the pie will later be divided and a great deal to how it will be made.[57]

Such critiques are unlikely to make economic analysis entirely irrelevant. While rational choice theory supports formalism and anti-incorporation, there are other aspects of economic analysis that provide better support for incorporation. Relationalists share more common ground with transaction costs economists since, as Campbell and Piccioto have pointed out, transaction costs *are the social relations (relational factors)* that facilitate an

[56] See I Macneil, 'Efficient Breach, Circles in the Sky'(1982) 68 *Virginia Law Review* 947, 957–58, emphasis in original, footnotes in original omitted.

[57] I Macneil, 'Economic Analysis of Contractual Relations: Its Shortfalls and the Need for a Rich Classificatory Apparatus' (1981) 75 *Northwestern University Law Review* 1017, 1024–25.

agreement.[58] Alternatively, the economic model could incorporate changes that reflect the qualities of contracting parties as revealed by insights from psychology and social science. Thus ideas such as bounded rationality have made their way into the literature. This branch of law and economics scholarship notes that errors will be made, cognitive limitations abound and that contractors are likely to satisfice and rely on heuristics when making decisions rather than pursue their rational self-interest. This behavioural angle is reputed to make the predictions of economic analysis more accurate.[59] This work has yielded some findings that are particularly relevant for contract law such as the existence of the 'endowment effect', whereby individuals are shown to place a higher value on entitlements they possess than the same entitlements they are trying to acquire. In other words, the initial division of entitlements matters and 'losses are weighted more heavily than gains'.[60] These findings, usually evidenced by experimental methods, have placed some doubt on the predictive accuracy of the Coase theorem: that in a world without transaction costs, transactors will bargain to an efficient outcome irrespective of the initial allocation of entitlements. Other insights from behavioural economics such as the 'status quo bias' and 'default inertia' have also exerted some influence in contract theory.[61] Thus findings corroborating 'default inertia' are not only that parties may fail to contract around default rules but that express contract terms may effect the behaviour and attitudes of contractors, for example concerning the permissibility of breach when a contract contains liquidated damages clauses.[62] This branch of economic theory has been criticised for changing the methodology of rational choice to such an extent that it has moved beyond the boundaries of what can be meaningfully called economic theory. Other criticisms have included that its findings can be incorporated in rational choice theory,[63] that it repeats rather than remedies the errors of economic theory (chiefly ambiguity and indeterminacy) and that it replicates

[58] Campbell and Picciotto, above n 48, 253. Macneil, above n 57, 1022. Coase himself perfectly understood the nature of the real world, and the unlikelihood and undesirability of seeking to reduce transaction costs in all cases, see above n 51, 25–26.

[59] For a general account see C Jolls, CR Sunstein and RH Thaler, 'A Behavioral Approach to Law and Economics' (1998) 50 *Stanford Law Review* 1471.

[60] Ibid, 1484.

[61] On default inertia see I Ayres and R Gertner, 'Majoritarian vs Minoritarian Defaults' (1999) 51 *Stanford Law Review* 1591, 1598. See also R Korobkin, 'Behavioral Economics, Contract Formation and Contract Law' in CR Sunstein (ed), *Behavioral Law and Economics* (Cambridge, CUP, 2000) 116, 118–25 and 'The Status Quo Bias and Contract Default Rules' (1998) 83 *Cornell Law Review* 608.

[62] T Wilkinson-Ryan, 'Do Liquidated Damages Encourage Breach? A Psychological Experiment' (2010) 108 *Michigan Law Review* 633.

[63] RA Posner, 'Rational Choice, Behavioral Economics and the Law' (1998) 50 *Stanford Law Review* 1551, 1552.

certain interpretations of, and not facts about, human behaviour.[64] In this way behavioural theory is thought to provide just another understanding or outlook on legal phenomena, rather than a complete positive theory.

It has been argued that the economist need not show that the model relied upon in formulating the theory is descriptively accurate, and similarly that there are good reasons for law not to mimic real contracting behaviour. Real actors will seek to advance their own self-interest and will at least approximate to this model in some important respects. This is especially true for commercial contractors since many of these will be corporations motivated by profit. Businesses must at least follow *as far as possible* what appears to be the economically rational course if they are to flourish.[65] In addition, corporations act through agents who are usually precluded from acting against the employer's or principal's interests. The real difference between these two sides is that for economic analysis, hypothesising about what might be the optimal outcome under ideal conditions of economic rationality is worthwhile because it will bring to light pertinent considerations, if not determinate answers, that inform action. On this basis, even aspirational work undertaken on the basis of rational choice theory may therefore have value, however distant contractors may remain from such ideal conditions. Economic analysis thus does not, nor is intended to, operate as a description of how contractors behave in the real world. This argument may be applied to classical contract law itself. If it appears the law's assumptions are based on rational choice theory it can be discerned that, insofar as the law regards itself as setting standards it expects contractors to meet, it will naturally be some distance from real contracting behaviour. The law may be acutely aware that its ideals are unattainable, but it sets them for other reasons, such as stability, which lends predictability and certainty to the rules, or to try and reduce the costs of the contracting process for those that are happy with the rules, while allowing others that want something different to contract out.

However, it could be said that these 'other reasons' only acquire sense and force within a framework that assumes neoclassical economic reasoning is correct. For example, the idea of 'penalty defaults'[66] assumes a contractor will be aware of the legal default and will act rationally in responding to defaults it does not favour by expressly stipulating alternative obligations. A well-advised contractor may be in this position but others may not. That a penalty default will have the desired effect of leading to 'contracting around' cannot be assumed outside of the model. In terms of its application

64 M Kelman, 'Behavioral Economics as Part of a Rhetorical Duet: A Response to Jolls, Sunstein and Thaler' (1998) 50 *Stanford Law Review* 1577, 1579.

65 Duxbury, above n 42, 371.

66 I Ayres and R Gertner, 'Filling Gaps in Incomplete Contracts: An Economic Theory of Default Rules' (1989) 99 *Yale Law Journal* 87, 91.

to real behaviour, the issue becomes a difficult empirical one concerning the likelihood of parties contracting around the rules. The existence of 'default inertia' and the 'status quo bias'[67] amongst contracting parties suggests that the law should take some care over the design of its default rules, perhaps reflecting those the parties would choose, since they will often be adopted by the parties, even if only inadvertently. Of course any perceived commitment on the part of the law to penalty defaults designed along formalist lines could be an indication of the law's view of the primary audience for its rules. That is, contract law takes the view that the audience for its rules is large commercial contractors who are well advised on the legal position, can act appropriately to protect their own interests and should be encouraged to shoulder the costs of doing so. But if such contractors do display a self-conscious concern with contracting around the defaults, it may be a matter of indifference to these contractors what the legal rules are. If so, should the contract law defaults be tailored to their interests, in the sense of making such parties contract out (since they are likely to do so in any case)? For such contractors a contextual interpretative method may well represent the penalty default.

The issue for law then is whether it formulates its contract law rules for real contractors or ideal ones. In part this is related to whether litigation and its outcomes are backward looking to the parties and their agreement, or forward looking to other contracting parties and society. For a contextualist, greater incorporation of elements of the real deal may be sought in order to uphold the transactions that parties make, on the basis that these have been chosen relatively self-consciously by the parties. This is in keeping with the contractors' expectations, and these in turn are assumed to be efficient rather than proved to be so, since parties will act in their own interest to some degree, and even co-operative behaviour can be interpreted as motivated by taking a long-term rather than short-term view of one's self-interest.[68] Such an approach will seek to uphold the agreement as the parties understood it. As far as the law is concerned this debate about the assumed qualities of contractors can only matter insofar as law evinces a concern with efficiency and the model of the contractor is thought to affect this. However it is very difficult to reach conclusive answers about the abstract model on which the rules should rest. The question here is whether the development of law and judicial responses to commercial

[67] Ayres and Gertner, above n 61, 1598; Korobkin, above n 61.

[68] So, eg, Collins believes courts should adopt a contextual approach to the contractual relationship in order to better support market transactions. This entails courts taking greater account of the efficiency considerations that led to a certain contract design: *Regulating Contracts* (Oxford, OUP, 1999) 272. Similarly, the claim that judges should openly 'address the economic consequences of their decisions' has been made by AJ Duggan, 'Commercial Law and the Limits of the Black Letter Approach' in S Worthington (ed), *Commercial Law and Commercial Practice* (Oxford, Hart Publishing, 2003) 595, 598.

disputes should be influenced according to an economic ideal, or one that is more sensitive to the limitations and constraints that contractors operate under *in the pursuit of efficiency themselves*. Certainly the likely reality is that the parties' preferences are more nuanced, reflecting a requirement for both formalism and flexibility, but at different times and under different conditions. This may well require judges to consider more directly the economic consequences of their decisions, but what seems of greater importance is some sensitivity to the commercial concerns and constraints that led to a particular contract design, which might in some cases lead to a formalistic approach being taken to the agreement, and in other cases a contextual one.

The Efficiency of Social Norms

One debate within the law and economics scholarship concerns the question of whether commercial norms are efficient compared with rules. Eric Posner has argued that a set of rules is more efficient than a set of group norms, since the rules are designed to correct deficiencies of group norms.[69] These deficiencies arise because norms evolve over time, rather than being chosen by the group, thus the justification for adhering to them is more to do with habit and familiarity rather than their inherent suitability or worth. For Posner there are various causes of inefficient norms: information costs and lags; moulding by economically superior groups who may seek to align norms with economic interests or their own moral view; and possible deleterious effects on third parties who may be unaware of the operation of the norms. Norms may favour some groups, who therefore have an interest in the norm prevailing for as long as possible, and cultural tradition may lead to entrenchment of inappropriate norms. These problems are thought to raise significant difficulties for a judge attempting to identify and use business norms in dispute resolution, and also for the possibility of these inefficient norms (assuming these can be identified) to be litigated away. Similarly, if the law changes the norms it is difficult for those following a particular norm or practice to shed it in an instant.[70] One might argue that inefficient rules are subject to the same problems, particularly since litigation repeat players in discrete markets wield enormous influence over the

[69] EA Posner, 'Law Economics and Inefficient Norms' (1996) 144 *University of Pennsylvania Law Review* 1697, 1698; See also JS Kraus, 'Legal Design and the Evolution of Commercial Norms' (1997) 26 *Journal of Legal Studies* 377. Using a theory of cultural evolution, Kraus argues that adopting commercial practices may be cost-effective over seeking to design an alternative set of commercial norms from scratch, but the practices adopted are not likely in themselves to be efficient. Thus legal design may still have a role in selectively improving upon practices (383).

[70] Posner, above n 69, 1738.

development of the rules.[71] Longevity of the rule becomes a self-sustaining reason for it, irrespective of whether it is inherently efficient. In any case, as Posner himself has argued the relative efficiency or inefficiency of rules is difficult to determine absolutely since it depends on variables that are practically difficult to observe and measure,[72] such as 'uneconomic' factors concerning motivation and preference.[73]

A slightly different argument against the incorporation of social norms is taken by Schwartz, who argues that many issues arising out of contract contexts cannot be dealt with by legally enforceable terms and are 'non-contractible' in this sense.[74] This limits a judge's ability to adjudicate over such matters according to the parties' intentions and thus relationalism obliges a court to adopt an interventionist strategy and to complete the contract with a term/rule when a contract is silent.[75] The issue is how this should be done—by reference to an external standard of fairness, justice and so on, or internally, by reference to the norms derived from the parties' relationship. Schwartz argues the latter either collapses into the external approach or a law and economics approach, since many commercial relationships are too thin to generate a rich set of internal norms. Where such market conventions, or trade association norms, do exist and are used this has collapsed an internal approach into an external one, since these norms are imposed by a third party.[76] If courts use an 'expectations of the parties' test, and do what the parties would expect from one another, he argues that this collapses into efficiency analysis: parties will only do what is in their best interests to do and they will expect their contracting partners to do the same.[77] In other words, outwith the scope of what expectations may be gleaned from previous relationships or contracting practices and trade understandings, a contractor can only expect what the law dictates and that a contracting partner would act as a rational utility maximiser. This argument only suggests that there may still be a role for formal classical law rules in the resolution of disputes, which, as will be seen in the following chapter, a relationally constituted contract law would not deny. The thrust of Schwartz's point is that a contextual approach seeking to apply internal norms ultimately achieves justification for this on other normative grounds, but this is only to concede that contextualism is not a normative position, but a legal reasoning method that reflects the pragmatism of

[71] Galanter, above n 47.
[72] EA Posner, 'Economic Analysis of Contract Law After Three Decades: Success or Failure?' (2003) 112 *Yale Law Journal* 829, 830.
[73] D Charny, 'Illusions of Spontaneous Order: "Norms" in Contractual Relationships' (1996) 144 *University of Pennsylvania Law Review* 1842, 1858.
[74] Schwartz, above n 54, 280.
[75] Ibid, 275.
[76] Ibid, 276.
[77] Ibid, 276.

the contracting process itself. Judges rarely if ever adjudicate according to abstract principles of 'fairness' or 'wealth maximisation'. To be sure, these may be pursued more or less self-consciously in case determination, and the arguments appearing on the surface of judgments may eventually be traced down to one of these ultimate foundations, but there will be many layers to penetrate on the way. A contextual and relational approach will allow the identification of these various layers of context (or argument) with increased transparency. In any case, Schwartz's analysis seems to take a very limited view over what is a contractible interest. In keeping with economic analysis, a contractible interest for Schwartz is one when a term can be formulated to govern the contingency *ex ante*. Certainly there is an element of artificiality here since over the life of a relationship, parties will simply *deal with* those issues that appear non-contractible at the beginning of the relationship. In addition, the argument that there are certain issues that are 'non-contractible' seems to depend on a formal understanding of what a contract is, which is itself a position which contextualists would challenge.[78]

Cooter on the other hand is more supportive of the incorporation of business norms into legal reasoning. He refers to the enactment of custom as 'decentralized lawmaking'.[79] He argues that 'efficiency requires that as economies develop, the enforcement of custom in business communities becomes more important relative to the regulation of business'.[80] Such norms assist judges since they do not have to substitute their own view of what is commercially expedient for the parties' view as reflected in the norms, provided such norms are available. This argument is plausible when no default rule exists to cover a contingency that has arisen. It becomes problematic when there is both a legal default and a customary norm governing the same issue. It may be difficult to determine which standard the parties intended to govern, since this question may not have garnered much of the parties' attention *ex ante*, and *ex post* at the point of litigation the parties are likely to adopt opposed positions concerning this very issue, irrespective of whether it is the genuine focus of the dispute. Here the best outcome may be an assessment of the evidence as to the widespread nature of the practice and its level of acceptance (or knowledge of it) among the relevant commercial community. The issue to decide is whether such a community would ordinarily contract on the basis of the norm or the rule. Cooter admits the approach requires judges to decide on the efficiency of norms and that they may make errors,[81] but the efficiency of norms can be inferred rather than measured and proved.

[78] Eg, H Collins, 'Objectivity and Committed Contextualism in Interpretation' in Worthington (ed), above n 68, 193.

[79] R Cooter, 'Decentralized Law for a Complex Economy: The Structural Approach to Adjudicating the New Law Merchant' (1996) 144 *University of Pennsylvania Law Review* 1643, 1645.

[80] Ibid, 1646.

[81] Ibid, 1656.

If it is relatively easy or cheap for contractors to expressly contract out of the operation of the social norms of which they are aware, then their failure to do so could be taken as acceptance of the norms. Cooter points out that 'Specialized business is often organized so that efficient norms emerge from repeated transactions'.[82] Thus in *The Achilleas* if charterers always or usually contract according to the social norm (and adherence to the norm is widespread) then this suggests the norm is efficient, and should not be overturned simply when extreme circumstances arise. To fail to uphold the norm in these circumstances is to change the *ex ante* allocation of risks that the parties can be taken to have agreed. Cooter maintains that courts should resist opportunistic attempts to strategically undermine the norm when peculiarly large losses prompt a participant to privilege short-term gain over long-term co-operation.[83] On this basis the legal default rule—as with *Hadley v Baxendale*—is only relevant in situations where no implicit understandings or business norms can be shown to exist.

This question of the efficiency of incorporating social norms into agreements does not appear to have a determinate answer. Certainly it cannot be assumed that a general approach of incorporating norms is inefficient and thus that classical contract law default rules are superior on that basis. Part of the difficulty here is deciding how efficiency is judged and the precise phenomenon that is subject to the efficiency test. Incorporating elements of commercial practice rather than applying the established rule may appear the optimal outcome by the judge assessing the situation between the two contracting parties *ex post*, but the outcome may yield inefficiencies when applied *ex ante* across a range of economic actors whose behaviour could be influenced by the ruling. To the extent that economic analysis is concerned with judging general incentive effects it can be assumed that the latter consideration is more important than the former. Yet rigid rules assessed purely by incentive effects may force some parties into inefficient modes of behaviour in the attempt to achieve legal enforceability for their agreements according to those rules. This problem of indeterminacy also appears in other applications of economic analysis to contract rules, such as contract modification.

Contract Modification

The case of *Williams v Roffey*[84] provides an example of the indeterminacy of economic analysis. On the one hand the Court of Appeal broadly assesses

[82] Ibid, 1682–83.
[83] Ibid.
[84] *Williams v Roffey* [1991] 1 QB 1. Thus Dnes argues that while justified on the basis of the individual contractual relationship, as enforcing a freely agreed modification, the Court of Appeal decision did not take sufficient account of the incentive effects on other contractors:

the optimality of the modification between the two parties involved, the Court having ensured the modification was not procured through duress and yielded commercial benefits to the main contractor (the costs of the carpenter's breach of contract to the main contractor are minimised). On the other hand the decision seems to have paid insufficient attention to the *ex ante* perspective of the rest of the contracting community and in particular the problem of moral hazard, which occurs when the 'insurance' function of contracts is undermined.[85] The argument here is that the class of subcontractors as a whole will take less care in pricing contracts since they can rely on the law to uphold a later modification, and some may deliberately submit low tenders to secure contracts which can be renegotiated later.[86] This suggests that a no-modification rule (as a penalty default) should be the chosen strategy as it is more efficient—it keeps the contract enforcement system reliable in encouraging contractors to keep to their deals, avoids the costs of negotiating the modification and the costs of insuring against later opportunism at the point of contract formation.[87]

If the economic issue is taken to be whether the agreed modification should be enforceable, then economic analysis appears to pull in different directions dependent upon the point at which one applies the analysis and how widely one considers the incentive effects of the proposed ruling.[88] The main argument in favour of the decision, however, is that it reflects the practical reality of many contractual relationships where, in the particular contract context, renegotiation may be commonplace and expected, which in itself suggests the parties may care little for concerns of efficiency and more for maintaining a productive relationship and achieving the project outcomes. Social norms, such as a desire to protect reputation and secure repeat dealings, may also militate against the danger of subcontractors deliberately submitting low quotes to secure contracts, which is an oft-rehearsed criticism of the *Williams* decision. It may therefore be a commercial expectation, if not an economically based one, that in the absence of duress, such modifications will be enforceable. The efficiency of individual case outcomes is probably of least interest to the law and economics scholar and of most interest to the rights-based theorist for what it may reveal about the

AW Dnes, 'The Law and Economics of Contract Modifications: Williams v Roffey' (1995) 15 *International Review of Law and Economics* 225.

[85] Moral hazard is '[t]he tendency of an insured to relax his efforts to prevent the occurrence of the risk that he has insured against because he has shifted the risk to an insurance company': Posner, above n 43, 109.

[86] Dnes, above n 84, and *The Economics of Law*, above n 45, 83.

[87] VA Aivazian, MJ Trebilcock and M Penny, 'The Law of Contract Modifications; The Uncertain Quest for a Benchmark of Enforceability' (1984) 22 *Osgoode Hall Law Journal* 173, 211.

[88] MJ Trebilcock, *The Limits of Freedom of Contract* (Cambridge MA, Harvard University Press, 1993) 136–38.

doctrinal coherence and intrinsic values of the common law. Rhetoric apart, it might be doubted that judges are primarily concerned with assessing the incentive effects created by rulings, although the extent to which consideration of policy and consequences influence case outcomes differs between judges. This can also be seen by examining contract interpretation.

Contract Interpretation

Economic analysis usually supports more formalistic contract law interpretative regimes as superior to contextual ones.[89] From the *ex post* point of view of dispute resolution this makes sense. A contract law which pays close attention to formal contract terms, interprets them fairly stringently, adopts strict rules of evidence and all from a strong commitment to objectivity is cheaper to administer at the dispute resolution stage than a contextual law that attempts to reconstruct and enforce what the parties actually agreed (insofar as this differs from the statement of express terms). However such a scheme imposes *ex ante* costs on the parties in attempting to formulate a relatively complete, 'interpretation-proof' contract. Whether parties will incur these costs depends on a range of highly variable factors: the level of risk, the value of the agreement, the length of the relationship, the level of trust in a contracting partner, the availability of in-house legal advice or availability of a trade association to draft contracts, the level of uncertainty and likelihood of a dispute. Given this variability, it is difficult to formulate in advance the generalised and predictable rules that economic analysis favours. In adopting formalistic interpretation regimes a court may be motivated in part by the importance of maintaining the integrity of the written agreement by preventing its meaning being undermined by evidence of negotiations, context, social and business norms and so on. But this seems to overlook the fact that we should only care about upholding the integrity of the written contract *if it is an accurate recording of the actual agreement.* Judges themselves appear to accord no overriding importance to either *ex ante* or *ex post* perspectives. Their reasoning usually contains a mix of both forward- and backward-looking approaches. Lord Clarke in *RTS v Müller*, for example, begins his judgment by exhorting the commercial community to take care to plan contracts in advance while at the same time mounting a contractual rescue for the parties embroiled in the actual

[89] See, eg, RE Scott, 'The Case for Formalism in Relational Contract' (2000) 94 *Northwestern University Law Review* 847; RA Posner, 'The Law and Economics of Contract Interpretation' (2005) 83 *Texas Law Review* 1581; L Kaplow, 'Rules Versus Standards: An Economic Analysis' (1992) 42 *Duke Law Journal* 557; A Katz, 'The Economics of Form and Substance in Contract Interpretation' (2004) 104 *Columbia Law Review* 496.

dispute.[90] In efficiency terms it is not clear that *all* parties should be directed towards trying to draft 'complete', fully contingent and interpretation-proof contracts, bearing in mind the likely costs. Use of flexible standards, gaps in the agreement, beginning work and letting performance firm up the obligations may in fact be the most efficient way of managing the commercial relationship for many contractors. These contractors should probably not be encouraged to attempt to formulate 'complete' contracts. Here, the law should stipulate more precisely the circumstances in which the parties could be expected to write a relatively complete contract and be governed by it, and the circumstances in which the courts might be amenable to adopting a more interventionist and active approach.

Irrespective of the interpretation rules adopted by courts, interpretation difficulties will arise due to inadvertence, error, haste and so on, on the part of the contract drafters. The success of formalism as a legal strategy depends upon how far one believes parties strike their particular bargain (if they do so at all) with an eye to the rules of contract law. Thus Scott regards the hard rules of classical contract law (hard to incur contractual liability, but equally hard to escape it once assumed) as superior to broad standards (such as commercial reasonableness) as being more transparent and certain *ex ante*, whereas standards require an *ex post* specification of obligations and determination of liability that affects the certainty of the law for future contractors.[91] On the other hand, standards-based reasoning allows contractors to enter into a range of contractual arrangements that may suit them and their contracting circumstances, with awareness that the law may support them. In the end an incorporationist approach may or may not be efficient, depending on the context of an agreement. In this way it may not much matter if incorporating commercial expectations is inefficient if there are other good reasons to support such an approach. [92]

A VARIABLE APPROACH?

It is a very common criticism of economic analysis of contract law that it is indeterminate when directed to the issue of the optimum design of contract law rules. Trebilcock writes: 'appealing to efficiency or welfare considerations as external reference points … fails to yield a set of determinate

[90] *RTS Flexible Systems Ltd v Molkerei Alois Müller GmbH & Co KG (UK Productions)* [2010] UKSC 14; [2010] 1 WLR 753.

[91] RE Scott, 'The Death of Contract Law' (2004) 54 *University of Toronto Law Journal* 369, 374.

[92] Thus Smith argues that economic analysis denies meaning and plausibility to the principles that judges say they are using when determining case outcomes and doctrines, instead it requires us to believe judgments lack transparency and that judges act in bad faith: above n 1, 132–36. Kraus, above n 5, 698–99.

rules with clear implications for particular cases confronting the courts. It is not clear what other sets of external values are available that are likely to yield a more robust set of implications'.[93] Eric Posner has written that most modern economic analysis relies on variables that cannot realistically be observed or measured.[94] One retort is to say that all normative theories suffer from indeterminacy, and this does not necessarily prevent us from saying efficiency is worth pursuing, only that our subject matter is complex and that all theories have limitations.[95] Another is to say that the analysis does at least raise awareness of *some relevant effects* of the rules, and it illuminates the complexity of the subject matter under investigation, particularly for those scholars who defend efficiency as a normative goal.[96] The problem here is not *indeterminacy*, in the sense that efficiency provides no single answer, as *contingency*, in the sense that a range of answers may be supplied by economic analysis, depending on the circumstances and identification of the *object* of the judgment of efficiency (the individual contract in dispute, incentive effects on future contracting parties, the law of contract, the litigation process?). Assuming the rules should tend towards the efficient outcome, economic analysis rarely unequivocally favours one design of a rule over another as more or less likely to lead to increases or decreases in efficiency. Rather it presents a range of considerations that might materially incline the decision over the design of a rule or outcome, although ultimately the choice between the variables may depend upon where judicial sympathies lie and their own view about matters such as the relative importance of freedom of contract or the role of law in regulating commerce. Ultimately this then turns on whether consequential or principled decision making is the right way for courts to make decisions. It can at least be said with some confidence that efficiency arguments alone cannot rule out an incorporationist approach.

What this suggests then is that the complexity of commercial dealing requires a multifaceted legal approach, which, while not ignoring normative considerations, may demonstrate only attenuated commitment on the surface to any of these more specific and identifiable normative values. To the extent that contractors are motivated by wealth maximisation or efficiency in making certain kinds of contractual arrangements, and to the extent that the law following commercial expectations assists in this endeavour, economic analysis may provide the best justification for upholding

[93] Trebilcock, above n 88, 144.

[94] Posner, above n 72, 830, 834.

[95] Trebilcock, above n 88, 124, 126. Posner, above n 72, is a pessimistic piece along these lines. He points out that both the *Hadley v Baxendale* rule (limited compensation for consequential loss) and the reverse (full compensation) give a shipper an incentive to disclose private information, 837.

[96] Craswell, above n 6, argues that while the descriptive project of economic analysis has become uninteresting, the normative project is still worthwhile, 903, 909ff.

commercial expectations. To the extent that a commercial-expectations approach accords with upholding the agreement actually reached, rather than some ideal or written form of agreement, then promissory theories may provide the better fit. Other important values of the law of contract, and commercial contract in particular, give no clear steer regarding the underlying justification relied upon. One of the most oft-cited values underpinning commercial contract law, for example, is freedom of contract. Commitment to this value could be justified by appealing to non-instrumental promissory theories (stressing the importance of autonomy) or economic analysis (stressing the importance of free and voluntary exchange to the pursuit of allocative efficiency). If a commercial-expectations approach is equivocal between these two possible bases then it may be that these theories are just too general to be of use in yielding a specific design for contract law rules. In this way, neither may be wholly successful in explaining or justifying why contract law should uphold commercial expectations. If anything, either, or indeed both, may have a role in explaining the design of contract rules that will become necessary in the precise circumstances where commercial expectations are lacking.

If this is the case, the law may be better off seeking the 'right rules' within its own legal and normative framework rather than the 'cheap rules' allowing parties who want something different to shoulder the costs of doing this by letting their contract terms stipulate for an alternative. It may be regarded as setting the right rules if it chooses those that support, or coincide with, the internal point of view of the contractors themselves or that are openly based on moral grounds. Alternatively a more differentiating approach may be required. For certain classes of contractor and agreement the aim of contract law may be solely to pursue efficiency, although fairness and distributive concerns and deterrence may be relevant goals for the law in other kinds of agreement. Schwartz and Scott associate contract law with a specific form of regulation only operative in specific circumstances where a limited default rule set and textualist interpretation is appropriate.[97] In relation to such contracts Schwartz and Scott reject the idea that the state acts to encourage the autonomy of contractors or to protect the morality of promise keeping: 'The relevant question for a normative theory of commercial contract law is just when, if ever, the goal of welfare maximization requires legal enforcement of the contracts that business entities make'.[98] The difficulty with this approach is that the ideal conditions to which the analysis is most prescient are rarely found, and do not exhaust the range of contracting behaviours that the law must govern. To the extent that contract law is the *general law* relating to making and enforcing agreements it

[97] A Schwartz and RE Scott, 'Contract Theory and the Limits of Contract Law' (2003) 113 *Yale Law Journal* 541, 545.

[98] Ibid, 556.

needs to be flexible in approach. To the extent that contextualism allows parties to enter into more flexible arrangements that allow efficiency gains for them, it may not therefore disavow an economic form of reasoning, although it may run counter to the classical contract law and classical economic theory's view of the contract and the contracting parties.

CONCLUSION

Superficially, it seems support for a closer link between contract law and commercial expectations could be justified using either of these two foundations. Alternatively, a commercial-expectations approach might be relatively neutral between them, relying on a different sort of argument to make the case for incorporation. In addition, both accounts face problems. Assuming for the present that a contract law in line with commercial expectations and practices would routinely incorporate implicit understandings of the parties into contracts, or would use such dimensions in interpretation, a defender of efficiency theory might argue that recourse to implicit dimensions in this way when resolving disputes reduces the costs of the contracting process by obviating the need for the parties to write down all their obligations *ex ante*, including those that are difficult to formulate. The present legal demand for certainty could give way to the parties writing in flexible obligations which describe processes rather than outcomes and results. Such duties are easier to formulate in advance than hard obligations to bring about precise states of affairs. On the other hand, the saving in *ex ante* transaction costs may be offset by the increased *ex post* costs of proving those implicit dimensions or commercial expectations to the adjudicator if a dispute arises, including costs of judicial error and so on. How individual parties will make this trade-off depends upon a range of factors; the precise balance therefore will vary with each contractual relationship. In addition, whether courts should supply terms or harden up obligations in those circumstances depends upon the reason why parties fail to formulate these obligations in advance and for themselves. If this reflects a genuine difficulty, then the courts should be willing to supply terms; if it represents carelessness or opportunism, then they should not.[99] This is difficult to determine however, and will itself require attention to context. In relation to efficiency it might be noted that the reasons for entering into contracts may be wealth creating, but this does not necessitate that contract law should track *only* this value. To appropriate and recast Robert Scott's observation: *contracts* may be concerned with wealth creation and maximisation, but contract *law* may not.[100] While

[99] Ayres and Gertner, above n 66.
[100] Scott, above n 89, at 852.

contract law may provide a background security for enforcement that reduces the costs of the contracting process generally, it is clear that this is not its only aim. In addition, the efficiency argument is highly contingent. One suspects that efficiency theorists can justify contract law rules whether they are designed with a greater or lesser degree of formalism.[101] Efficiency arguments also lack fit with judges' understandings concerning the practice they are involved in.[102]

Given these difficulties, a rights-based argument may fare better in supporting a more incorporationist approach, particularly if one regards the prime function of the courts as adjudicating the dispute according to the terms, whether explicit or implicit, that the parties agreed and in providing a remedy to vindicate the claimant's rights in the event of the defendant's non-excused failure to perform. It is clear from empirical studies that contractors, even those acting as agents, place a premium on performance of obligations undertaken by a contracting partner, although they may judge these obligations as more extensive than those that appear as express contract terms.[103] For these contractors it is performance of obligations that is sought and that is an indicator of reputation, not ability to satisfy court judgments through the payment of damages. Insofar as the point of contract law is to enforce agreements made, then promissory theory provides a foundation that can accommodate both formal and informal (social conventions) commitments. The difficulty with promissory theory is its weakness on the detail of rules that could be reckoned to uphold this ideal, and provision of legal reasoning techniques that would achieve this. The support for a contextual approach to legal reasoning offered by promissory theories is thus very general. It will supply a justification for courts paying attention to such norms and interrogating the conditions under which they might be said to have been agreed, but lacks detail on how such a strategy might be pursued in legal reasoning. The other problem with promissory theory resides with the notion of consent to the incorporation. Contractors may not have any specific actual intention to incorporate certain expectations or practices, so there needs to be some further justification for why these should be incorporated when there is no express agreement to do so.

It is not straightforward then to make a direct link between either of the theories and the idea of incorporation, such that it can be said that one is better than the other at supporting the argument for greater alignment between contract law and commercial expectations. Rather, both provide different viewpoints from which the issues could be considered.

[101] For examples along these lines see Goodhart, above n 41; Posner, above n 72.

[102] See Smith, above n 1, 119ff, 132ff.

[103] B Burchell and F Wilkinson, 'Trust, Business Relationships and the Contractual Environment' (1997) 21 *Cambridge Journal of Economics* 217, 224.

Thus, the connections to be drawn, or the support that each theory offers, may be more opaque and indirect than clear and non-contingent. A third possibility is that neither of these two provide adequate support, since a commercial-expectations argument rests on a different type of theory to either efficiency- or rights-based justifications for contract law. The following chapter considers the possibility that relational contract theory supplies this alternative ground and the best justification for supporting commercial expectations in contract law.

6

The Relational Theory of Contract

THE PREVIOUS CHAPTER discussed the extent to which promissory theory and economic analysis provided support for greater alignment between contract law and commercial expectations and practices. Neither theory provided unequivocal support for incorporation of commercial norms into contract legal reasoning, although promissory theory could broadly support the idea that the agreement as understood by the parties should be upheld. Such theories seek to explain and justify legal phenomena according to a relatively limited set of values, and in neither theory do the experiences of contractors themselves carry much weight. A better supporting theory for the commercial-expectations approach would be one that places central importance on the idea that commercial contract law should, where appropriate, track the norms and behaviours of actual contracting parties. Such an alternative is presented by the relational theory of contract. It is this theory which arguably provides more robust support for the development of a commercially aligned contract law since it stresses the importance of the social embeddedness, or social context, of all exchange behaviour. Indeed the claim here is that a relationally constituted contract law would better meet commercial expectations. It is not the aim of this chapter to decide the extent to which the law already is relationally constituted, rather it is to examine the main features of relational theory and see how it might yield a theory about legal reasoning in commercial contracts that is more sensitive to commercial expectations. Relational contract theory is most closely associated with Ian Macneil and this chapter will explore Macneil's 'essential contract theory' as the exemplar of relational theories of contract. This is because Macneil's is the most influential, the most original and also the most fully worked-out of all relational theories of contract.

CHARACTERISTICS OF RELATIONAL ANALYSIS OF CONTRACTS

Macneil's relational theory regards both classical contract law and rational choice theory as fundamentally incomplete and potentially distorting of our understanding of the process of exchange. In abstracting from context and experience they fail to recognise or accord any significance to the social embeddedness of all forms of exchange and in particular the insight that exchange does not occur at all without some degree of co-operation between the parties to it.[1] For the relational scholar this attention to social embeddedness is important since it will influence the parties' understandings about their agreement. An initial point to grasp is that Macneil's focus is directed primarily towards contracts themselves, which he defines as 'the relations among parties to the process of projecting exchange into the future'[2], and not contract *law*. To understand contract, we need to think about 'exchange ... first, and law second'.[3] Macneil's theory is therefore rooted in an understanding of contract as essentially a social as opposed to an exclusively legal or economic phenomenon, although 'social' naturally incorporates these two perspectives. The theory does not seek to denigrate contract law or to relegate it to a sphere of irrelevance, since the law is an important social institution upon which the practice of contracting rests, but it does seek to reorient our understanding of law and legally enforceable contracts as just one part of the complex social fabric of exchange. Thus Macneil draws out the importance of the social foundations of exchange, such as the division of labour, the capacity for choice and human awareness of the future.[4] Of particular importance is his appreciation of the simultaneously social and selfish nature of human beings, which the possibility of co-operative exchange helps to bring into balance: in exchanging one has to give something up, but one also gets something in return.[5]

It can be surmised that Macneil's work is intended primarily to be descriptive of exchange behaviour, rather than evaluative or prescriptive. Having said that, he did develop his own 'essential contract theory' out of his descriptions, although he regarded this as just one version of relational contract theory out of many available. For Macneil, relational theories of contract, including his own, shared four key features or core propositions: (i) 'every transaction is embedded in complex relations';[6] (ii) understanding transactions involves understanding these relations; (iii) effective analysis of a transaction requires all essential enveloping relations that affect the transaction to be recognised and considered; (iv) 'contextual analysis of relations and transactions is more efficient and produces a more complete and sure final analytical product than does commencing with non-contextual

[1] I Macneil, *The Relational Theory of Contract: Selected Works of Ian Macneil*, D Campbell (ed) (London, Sweet and Maxwell, 2001), hereafter *Selected Works* (2001), 99.

[2] Ibid, 129; I Macneil 'Values in Contract: Internal and External' (1983) 78 *Northwestern University Law Review* 340, 341–42.

[3] *Selected Works* (2001) 130.

[4] Ibid, 127–29.

[5] Ibid, 153–54.

[6] I Macneil, 'Relational Contract Theory: Challenges and Queries' (2000) 94 *Northwestern University Law Review* 877, 881.

analysis of transactions'.[7] In short, an analysis of contracts must begin, and will usually end, with the social context, or the wider span of social relationships in which transactions take place. For Macneil, a weakness with classical contract law is its tendency to focus on disputes arising out of a transaction between two independent economic units[8] who are assumed, through the exercise of freedom of contract and consent, to have reached agreement on all matters material to the exchange at the moment in time when offer and acceptance coincide.[9] According to Macneil the classical model of contracts upon which the classical law rested had two particular features—presentiation: 'a rendering of past and particularly future events or structures influencing present allocative decisions as if they were present'[10] or bringing the future effectively into the present,[11] and discreteness: 'the separating of a transaction from all else between the participants at the same time and before and after'.[12] Macneil wrote:

> The structure of the principles of general contract law, instead of reflecting material relations as they actually exist, is based entirely on the non-existent discrete transaction ... This general contract structure omits vital aspects of real life material relations, and distorts the rest.[13]

Macneil's conceptualisation of contract as first and foremost a social relationship was in direct contrast to the classical contract law's conception of how and by whom contractual relationships were formed: atomistic, rational, self-interested individuals of roughly equal bargaining power who agree on contract terms and then commence performance. The law's focus on the transaction, as constructed according to the fictions and abstractions demanded by objective theory, emphasises the individualism and autonomy of the contracting parties, rather than their reliance on trust, co-operation and interdependence. Thus all living contracts, which will embody these latter qualities to a greater or lesser degree, can be contrasted with 'contracts-at-law'.[14] As far as the legal rules are concerned contract planning, formation and performance follow a particular pattern and chronology. These legal tendencies have the effect of treating particular transactions as isolated events and any investigation of the wider context may be kept to a minimum.

In the early stages of its development, relational theory was thought appropriate only to long-term agreements where obligations were difficult to formulate fully in advance, and may be left open or vague for future

[7] Ibid, 881. Efficiency here refers to productive efficiency, not rational choice theory.

[8] Ibid, 878.

[9] D Campbell, 'Ian Macneil and the Relational Theory of Contract' in *Selected Works* (2001) 5–6.

[10] Ibid, 39.

[11] Ibid, 182.

[12] Ibid, 154.

[13] Ibid, 126.

[14] Macneil, above n 6, 901.

negotiation or modification, matching the continuing and dynamic nature of the relationship.[15] Archetypes of such contracts were employment and franchising agreements.[16] For some, the anticipated length of the agreement was the crucial variable in identifying the relational contract.[17] On this understanding relational contracts were treated as a 'special category' of contracts more generally, and Macneil's position was thought to be that there existed a spectrum of contract types with discrete contracts occupying one end of the spectrum and relational contracts the other.[18] As far as the relationship between this model of relational theory and contract law was concerned, it was readily conceded that English law had no specific rules for dealing with the characteristics and problems of long-term arrangements. Some commentators believed that the flexibility of the common law meant that its established doctrines were sufficiently adaptable to account for the special requirements of long-term contracts, or that the parties could write the necessary terms governing their agreements into the long-term contract.[19] Thus it was thought the classical law could take on board insights from the relational account, without any fundamental alterations to the basic model. Relational contracts were simply exceptions to this model. However, one does not get to the heart of relational theory by recognising a new category of 'relational contracts' and admitting that these may require different treatment to discrete agreements. This idea is now deemed to be a significant misinterpretation of Macneil's relational account.[20] To the extent that all contracts are embedded in a complex web of relationships there is no relational subcategory of contracts.[21] For Macneil '*all* contracts are relational. Nevertheless, some contracts ... are far more relational than others'.[22]

While it might be recognised that all contracts are informed by general or specific contextual understandings or expectations,[23] even this insight is not Macneil's real contribution to contracts scholarship. He provides a set

[15] See RE Speidel, 'The Characteristics and Challenges of Relational Contracts' (2000) 94 *Northwestern University Law Review* 823, 823–24.

[16] Cf Leggatt J in *Yam Seng Pte Ltd v International Trade Corporation Ltd* [2013] EWHC 111 (QB), [142].

[17] H Collins, 'Competing Norms of Contractual Behaviour' in D Campbell and P Vincent-Jones (eds), *Contract and Economic Organisation: Socio-Legal Initiatives* (Aldershot, Dartmouth, 1996) 67, 71. See also *Total Gas Marketing v Arco British* [1998] 2 Lloyd's Rep 209, for recognition of the idea of relational contracts as long-term agreements.

[18] P Vincent-Jones, 'The Reception of Ian Macneil's Work on Contract in the UK' in *Selected Works* (2001) 67, 69–72; also *Selected Works* (2001) 5.

[19] E McKendrick, 'The Regulation of Long Term Contracts in English Law' in J Beatson and D Friedman (eds), *Good Faith and Fault in Contract Law* (Oxford, OUP, 1995) 305.

[20] Vincent-Jones, above n 18.

[21] See MA Eisenberg, 'Why There is No Law of Relational Contracts' (2000) 94 *Northwestern University Law Review* 805: 'There can be no special law of relational contracts, because relational contracts and contracts are virtually one and the same' 817.

[22] Macneil, above n 2, 341–42 (footnotes omitted, emphasis in original).

[23] Ibid, 344.

of tools—or common contract norms—for analysing and understanding exchange relationships of all kinds. Using these tools, the conclusions that might be drawn about individual contracts and exchange relationships are infinitely varied. In a relational approach, abstract generalisations about what may be discovered in a contractual relationship are not possible in advance—one can only generalise about how the analysis should be undertaken and what should be examined. An agreement displaying a high degree of reliance on relational norms may not necessarily be long term. A short-term agreement might be highly relational, a long-term agreement may display many discrete features. Admittedly, some of the contextual factors that impinge on the contractual relationship might be of a very general social and 'external' nature—a common language or a common currency for example, or social mores and public opinion, and contract law itself[24]—while others are generated *internally* and *specifically* to the parties' relationship through repeated dealings. Other expectations, emanating, for example, from membership of trade associations or manifested as particular understandings operating within industries (whether discrete or relational), seem to fall somewhere in between these two.[25] Internal norms that develop between the parties may be influenced by the external norms of society (payment conditions and methods, for example). The recognition of the relationality of all contract is of potential importance to contract law for reasons well expressed by Dori Kimel:

> The crux of the matter is that the relationship in question is such that it has the propensity to generate norms, define or inform parties' expectations, provide sources of reassurance, facilitate co-operation, create interdependence (and so on)—over and above, indeed potentially instead of, what can be gleaned from the express terms of the contract or contracts to which they are parties, and over and above what is provided by the bare legal norms and legal mechanisms that underlie or support these contracts in the relevant jurisdiction.[26]

One difficulty to be alert to when discussing Macneil's theory is the various ideas expressed in the word 'relational' and the phenomena to which it is applied. Thus there is 'relational theory', which is any theory of contract broadly adhering to the four core propositions set out above. There is also the 'relational contract', which is usually juxtaposed with the discrete contract or 'transaction', and to which the legal rules governing the discrete contract are usually regarded as inappropriate. In this sense a 'relational contract' is usually associated with long-term, flexible and open-ended

[24] Ibid, 343.

[25] Campbell, above n 9, 11–15.

[26] D Kimel, 'The Choice of Paradigm for Theory of Contract: Reflections on the Relational Model' (2007) 27 *OJLS* 233, 236. See also *Selected Works* (2001) 100–01: 'Over time, exchanges made with these long-range motivations produce norms to which the participants expect to adhere and to which they expect adherence from other participants'.

agreements that display a high degree of reliance on trust and ongoing co-operation in performance, rather than law. Contracts displaying these features may be regarded as inadequately governed by the classical law of contract due to the mismatch between the assumptions that law makes and the attitudes displayed by the parties engaged in such long-term or co-operative endeavours. There may also be reference to 'relational norms', which are those characteristics which relational contracts display and which are regarded as hallmarks of the relational contract, as opposed to discrete norms that identify and demarcate the discrete contract. The idea of 'relational norms and values' may also be used to refer to specific norms at work in a co-operative relationship, including flexibility, willingness to sacrifice one's own interests for the other contracting partners and the ongoing relationship, and so on.[27] These norms are often taken to the antithesis of the norms at work in discrete contracts, and constitute a contract's 'living norms'.[28] Finally, there are 'contractual relations'. This is the widest definition, incorporating an appreciation of all the contract norms that operate in an exchange relationship, discrete *and* relational. While all contracts involve *relations* and hence may be called 'relational contracts', they will vary considerably in the extent to which they display 'relational' as opposed to 'discrete' norms. The point to grasp is that discretism is a feature whereby a relationship outwardly displays commitment to discrete norms rather than relational ones, but this assessment of relative discreteness in any relationship can only reliably be made within a broadly relational approach which appreciates the operation of *all* the common contract norms.[29]

ESSENTIAL CONTRACT METHOD: MACNEIL'S COMMON CONTRACT NORMS

The four propositions outlined above form the core of any relational theory. In Macneil's hands those propositions provide the foundation for a more specific methodology that can be used to analyse exchanges of almost any kind. This methodology is expressed in a collection of norms which provide a set of analytical lenses through which one can examine the parties' exchange relationship. For Macneil, the common contract norms and behaviours identified are a superior way of satisfying the four core propo-

[27] See, eg, S Macaulay, who writes 'we should be content with almost any approach that leads to settlements that give expression, more or less, to relational norms and values': 'The Real and the Paper Deal: Empirical Pictures of Relationships, Complexity and the Urge for Transparent Simple Rules' in D Campbell, H Collins and J Wightman (eds), *Implicit Dimensions of Contract* (Oxford, Hart Publishing, 2003) 51, 53.

[28] 'Challenges and Queries', above n 6, 904.

[29] See Campbell, above n 9, 44–46.

sitions of relational contract theory. The norms are, in effect, a checklist for 'isolating all elements of the enveloping relations that might affect any transaction significantly', understanding them and analysing them.[30] While Macneil provides a set of tools with which to analyse exchange relationships, he does not engage in any sustained speculation or prediction about what might be revealed concerning the contractual relationships to which they are applied.[31] While all exchange relations will display the norms to some extent, certain of the norms will appear more pronounced in (as if) discrete relationships, others in relational contracts. The relational norms are: role integrity (consistency, conflict and complexity); reciprocity (mutuality); flexibility; contractual solidarity (society and preservation of the relationship, also 'a belief in being able to depend on another'[32]); restitution, reliance, and expectation interests (linking norms); creation and restraint of power (power norm); propriety of means (the way in which things get done, how the ends are legitimately achieved); harmonisation with the social matrix (that is, harmonisation with supracontract norms). In addition to these relational norms Macneil postulates the existence of the 'discrete norm', which is the product of two other norms: effectuation of consent (choice) and implementation of planning. Implementation of planning is 'the attempt closely to specify (and impose strict liability for) performance'.[33] Macneil occasionally stipulates relational norms (those most essential to ongoing contractual relations) as role integrity, preservation of the relation, harmonisation of relational conflict, propriety of means and 'supracontract norms'.[34] Supracontract norms are not contractual (under Macneil's theory) but encompass such values as distributive justice, liberty, human dignity, social equality and procedural justice, which might be taken to be the underpinnings of social institutions. These contract norms function both as descriptive criteria of contract behaviour and as expressions of the internal values of such behaviour. [35] Macneil asserts that the norms are present in all contractual relationships to varying degrees,[36] but their operation is not necessarily harmonious. Conflict between them is expected, as when the need for flexibility conflicts with planning and consent, although this is more likely to be problematic in relational agreements rather than in discrete transactions[37] where there may be a greater degree

[30] Macneil, above n 6, 893.
[31] 'Reflections on Relational Contract Theory after a Neo-classical Seminar' in Campbell, Collins and Wightman (eds), above n 27, 207, 215.
[32] Macneil, above n 2, 349.
[33] Campbell, above n 9, 21.
[34] Macneil, above n 2, 361.
[35] Ibid, 348. Speidel, above n 15, 827.
[36] Macneil, above n 2, 347.
[37] Ibid, 350.

of congruence between the formal contract framework and the expectations of the parties.

The scheme of the common contract norms has been criticised for being unduly complex and simpler alternatives have been offered by relational scholars.[38] The precise formulation of the norms does vary in Macneil's writings, although some (for example, the elements of the discrete norm) have remained static.[39] For the purposes of this work it is not necessary to examine all the elements of the common contract norms. The significance of the common contract norms is that ongoing contractual relations may be expected to display the norms in various combinations and to different degrees of strength across various kinds of relationship.[40] Although all these norms are present in all exchange relationships, some are more evident in discrete transactions, and some in relational agreements. It is therefore possible for contracts to be determined to be *more or less* relational, or *more or less* discrete depending on the operation and interaction of the common contract norms. Macneil writes: 'While all the contract norms operate in the behaviour and in the internal principles and rules of all kinds of contract, some assume special importance in discrete transactions and others assume special importance in contractual relations'.[41]

Within the scheme of the common contract norms, the idea of the discrete exchange is not irrelevant or a misconception. It only becomes a misconception if it is regarded as existing in isolation, rather than as part of contractual agreements and exchanges that are *always* relational. The discrete contract is a tool precisely designed to facilitate arm's-length dealing and in this sense it is an artificial construct.[42] For some scholars this constitutes a central point in our understanding of contracts. Thus Kimel argues against the notion that contract law either is or should be relationally constituted and that contract law should incorporate relational-style analysis, or relational norms, although he accepts that relational contracts exist. Rather 'the main function of contract law is to facilitate arm's-length transactions' and provide the standards and conditions for trading when the parties are not in a pre-existing relationship of trust.[43] For Macneil, though, there can

[38] R Austen-Baker, 'Comprehensive Contract Theory: A Four-Norm Model of Contractual Relations' (2009) 25 *Journal of Contract Law* 216, 221–22. Austen-Baker has argued that Macneil's system is overcomplicated and repetitious. He posits instead a four-norm model: (i) preservation of the relation (ii) harmonisation with the social matrix (iii) satisfying performance expectations (iv) substantial fairness.

[39] Thus P Vincent-Jones's list in *The New Public Contracting* (Oxford, Oxford University Press, 2006) differs slightly from that given here, including a further discrete norm of 'choice' and omitting the 'linking norms': 4–6.

[40] Macneil, above n 2, fn 30; *Selected Works* (2001) 153, 163.

[41] *Selected Works* (2001) 154.

[42] Kimel, above n 26, 237.

[43] Ibid, 242–43.

be no completely 'discrete contract' in reality. There may, however, be such a thing as an 'as-if-discrete' contract.[44] On this, Campbell comments:

> Given that even discrete contract rests on the common norms, the possibility of treating an exchange as discrete can 'properly arise only after a recognition ... that a decision is being made to treat the pertinent aspect of exchange relations as if it were discrete, although in fact it is not, in short to ignore the non-discrete aspect of the relation'.[45]

Macneil describes one of the as-if-discrete contract's characteristics in the following terms:

> [T]he closer the parties are to behaving and governing themselves in accordance with this discrete norm, the more they will choose planning that is completely binding (or as close to completely binding as they can get), thereby bringing the future into the present as much as is humanly possible.[46]

The discrete norm expresses a conservative value (it presupposes the status quo, including the power relations already manifest in the status quo).[47] The parties may therefore choose mechanisms that attempt to impose discreteness on the relationship, such as by specifying in advance as many of the obligations as possible, or embracing a preference for a formalistic interpretative approach to be taken to the agreement. In Macneil's view, this will be when the parties want precision and focus in their contractual dealings,[48] or when they want to be free of 'extraneous social baggage'.[49] But this decision to emphasise the discrete norm is not without sacrifice. The parties sacrifice the relational values that come from the relational norms such as 'preservation of the relation and harmonization of relational contract'.[50] In relation to the discrete transaction, Macneil writes:

> Flexibility is achieved, not within the discrete transaction, where all is rigid presentiation, but outside it, in the repeated use of numerous discrete transactions. Contractual solidarity is maintained only through external forces, such as the law of contract, implementing the presentiated discrete transaction.[51]

[44] Macneil, above n 6, 895–96.

[45] Campbell, above n 9, 23, quoting I Macneil, 'Relational Contract Theory as Sociology: A Reply to Professors Lindenberg and de Vos' (1987) 143 *Journal of Institutional and Theoretical Economics* 272, 277.

[46] *Selected Works* (2001) 154–55.

[47] Ibid, 160.

[48] Ibid, 158.

[49] I Macneil, 'Contracts: Adjustment of Long-Term Economic Relations Under Classical, Neoclassical and Relational Contract Law' (1978) 72 *Northwestern University Law Review* 854, 859.

[50] *Selected Works* (2001) 161.

[51] Ibid, 162.

Such parties may not be concerned with maintaining the relationship since substitute contracting partners may be freely available in the market.[52] But the loss that is involved here is well expressed by Charny:

> [N]egotiating a legally enforceable contract ... may create anxiety by making the parties conscious of the risks of breach. Negotiation may also create or intensify an adversarial atmosphere by raising the specter of litigation for transactors who wish to view themselves as friends or partners.[53]

Nevertheless, while allowing for the possibility of discrete agreements, these are understood as still relationally constituted: they are discrete because the parties have chosen to minimise the sphere of operation for relational norms. This is a different understanding of the discrete agreement to that found in the classical law where the discrete agreement represents the ideal-type for the operation of classical contract law, and the sum of its understanding and conception of what contracts are.[54]

SIGNIFICANCE FOR THE LAW OF CONTRACT

The primary focus for Macneil's relational theory is the practice of contracting or exchanging and its social dimensions. Macneil does not necessarily see himself as providing a normative theory of contracts or contract law. Indeed one can regard Macneil's work as countering such theories, or at least those championing promise or efficiency (as exemplified by rational choice theory) as a touchstone for explaining and justifying contract law. Fundamentally, Macneil disagrees with the methodology of seeking to explain complex phenomena by reference to a single value. Thus Macneil remarks on Fried's 'contract as promise' theory:

> What is important is that promise, and promise alone is *the* dogmatic base upon which Professor Fried analyzes contract. Everything else becomes something to be fed into that dogma ... [t]he most obvious values reflected by contract-as-promise are those of the discrete norm: precise focus, following through on planning and efficiency.[55]

Concentration on such a narrow set of considerations leads to the overlooking and sacrifice of relational values and norms. Other branches of contract theory criticise relational theory for its limitations in this respect, and this results in scepticism about the law's ability to take on board insights from relational theory. This sceptical branch includes scholars who might

[52] Ibid, 192–93.
[53] D Charny, 'Nonlegal Sanctions in Commercial Relationships' (1990) 104 *Harvard Law Review* 375, 407.
[54] Campbell, above n 9, 56–57.
[55] Macneil, above n 2, 390–91.

otherwise be sympathetic to the relational project. Thus Trebilcock has written that

> Macneil's approach, no matter how accurately it describes reality, does not yield determinate legal principles for governing the allocation of unassigned risks. It entails a highly amorphous sociological inquiry that seems well beyond the competence of courts in case-by-case adjudication and seems to exhibit all the vices of other particularistic approaches to designing default rules ... Moreover, it provides no normative criteria that allow us to move from the 'is' to the 'ought' and to disqualify some social norms (say, domination) as unworthy of recognition.[56]

It is certainly the case that Macneil's approach is not rooted in normative values, but in practice, experience and the expectations of the relevant 'contracting community'.[57] Given that it posits no overarching value (such as keeping promises or wealth maximisation) relational theory provides no *single* metric against which to calibrate legal effectiveness. There are only a set of diverse and often incompatible considerations. The price of this broad engagement with a range of social and contextual factors is indeterminacy and a certain degree of normative emptiness.[58] But relational theory embraces this as a natural consequence of the complexity of the phenomena under examination. The more factors to consider, the greater the degree of indeterminacy. Thus to concentrate on the legal relationship as being the sum of the 'contract' is to take a resolutely one-dimensional view. Insofar as Macneil identifies any normative issue raised by his relational theory, this is taken to be 'whether or not the failure of contract law to be coextensive with our more complex understanding of contract as an institution is a good idea or a bad idea'.[59]

One result of Macneil's methodological commitments is that while it is relatively straightforward to identify the operation of some of the contract norms in contract settings, and even in many contract law applications, it is more difficult to determine their implications for legal reasoning in contract disputes. The difficulty of working with broadly relational theory in a practical context is well expressed by Stewart Macaulay. He wrote, 'Macneil's relational approach and a law-and-society perspective do not offer elegant models of contracting behavior. You get a story and multiple factors to consider, but not a simple formula that produces results'.[60]

[56] MJ Trebilcock, *The Limits of Freedom of Contract* (Cambridge MA, Harvard University Press, 1993) 141–42.

[57] Ibid, 144.

[58] Macneil often noted this issue, but did not directly engage with it. See, eg, 'Values in Contract', above n 2, 343. He did discuss promise in *Selected Works* (2001) but only with respect to its role as an 'exchange projector', although it is not the only concept that has this function: 130.

[59] Macneil, above n 6, 902.

[60] S Macaulay, 'Relational Contracts Floating on a Sea of Custom? Thoughts About the Ideas of Ian Macneil and Lisa Bernstein' [2000] 94 *Northwestern University Law Review*, 775, 783.

Macneil himself never developed a comprehensive theory of relational contract legal reasoning, partly it seems because the project was not of most interest to him, but also because that was not a necessary feature of his sociological method or his overall enterprise. Macneil appeared sceptical of the role of contract law (legal enforcement or external enforcement) in other-than-discrete contracts, regarding it as having some role, but not an enhanced one in contractual relations, where the operation of law and formal contracts was likely to be ousted by internal norms created by the parties going beyond their strict legal entitlements.[61] This scepticism about the implications of relational theory for contract law appears rooted in doubts over whether the litigation process can uncover and utilise relational norms in dispute resolution. In a contract dispute a court inevitably must look back at the relationship 'to see what it once was'.[62] This examination can never be complete and will inevitably be distorted (litigation was once described by him as 'an autopsy on a corpse'[63]). For Macneil, while there is little that law can do in the case of a complete breakdown, relational contract theory may be more significant in cases of 'partial breakdown' where the living norms can be followed, such as those disputes that might be subject to arbitrations, mediations and so on.[64] Similarly, he considered generalist judges as deficient in their ability to use the living contract norms, as opposed to mediators and arbitrators.[65] However, Macneil's views on this may be more a reflection of his attitude towards existing contract law rather than constituting a complete denial of the possibility that the insights of relational theory could lead to any legal improvements or the development of an alternative kind of law.

That said, Macneil was not completely silent on this issue of legal reasoning, although his comments are not always helpful or easy to understand. While the question was not addressed in detail by Macneil, he thought that there were two possibilities for the legal approach to an agreement: 'One is the relational approach, and the other is to start at the transaction end and work from there into the remainder of the relations'.[66] The relational approach is characterised by three steps:

> (1) acquiring an overall grasp of the essential relations of which the transactions are an integral part; (2) working through the interaction of the pertinent transactions with the remainder of the relations until the limitations of transactional

[61] I Macneil, 'Economic Analysis of Contractual Relations: Its Shortfalls and the Need for a Rich Classificatory Apparatus' (1981) 75 *Northwestern University Law Review* 1017, 1033–34.

[62] I Macneil, 'A Primer of Contract Planning' (1975) 48 *Southern California Law Review* 627, 692.

[63] Ibid, 692.

[64] Macneil, above n 6, 905–06.

[65] Ibid, 906.

[66] Ibid, 888.

analysis are firmly established, and (3) engaging in whatever detailed discrete analysis is desired, subject to whatever constraints the first steps suggest.[67]

After such investigation one may find that the relations do or do not affect the transactions. For Macneil, transaction analysis usually proceeds on the basis of transaction cost analysis, but this starts at the wrong end as far as the relational approach is concerned.[68] He does point out some more direct link between his essential contract theory and legal reasoning:

> In essential contract theory there is a somewhat general assumption that typically the law will more or less track the common contract behavior and norms. This should not however be overread. There may often be good reasons why the law should not track the common contract behaviour and norms.[69]

He has also written 'that relational contract law should generally track the relational behavior and norms found in the relations to which it applies'.[70] And in a slightly different formulation, 'that contract law should generally track the behavior and norms found in any contract to which it applies'.[71]

Macneil did identify relational contract law as that 'which takes into significant account the fact that it is treating contracts towards the relational end of the relational/as-if-discrete spectrum. Since the world abounds with relational contract, the world necessarily abounds with relational contract law'.[72] The classification of a contract as relational or as-if-discrete follows from intensification of certain norms—planning and consent in the discrete contract for example, or reciprocity in the relational agreement. The implications of relational contract theory for the general law applicable to contracts is difficult to tease out. Certainly there are some contractual agreements that appear more relational than discrete in that they are heavily socially embedded in relations, and may be subject to their own bespoke forms of legal regulation operating outside of the classical law that take account of this, (employment contracts are probably the most obvious example here). How commercial contracts that display pronounced reliance on relational norms should be dealt with by contract law is not clear,

[67] Ibid, 888.

[68] Ibid, 889. Nevertheless for Macneil this seems partly an issue about how the methodology is described. Thus Macneil regards transaction cost economics, insofar as it is distanced from rational choice theory, as based on an unstated sociology and empiricism: see 'Challenges and Queries', 890, fnn 48 and 49. As J Wightman recognises, relational contract theory involves taking the internal norms of the business relationship and turning those back on the parties, rather than taking a set of wholly external norms (classical contract law) and applying those: 'Commentary on *Baird Textile Holdings v Marks & Spencer plc*' in R Hunter, C McGlynn and E Rackley (eds), *Feminist Judgments: From Theory to Practice* (Oxford, Hart Publishing, 2010) 184, 188.

[69] Macneil, above n 6, 893. This is a common assumption amongst other relational scholars.

[70] Ibid, 900, 903.

[71] Ibid, 84.

[72] Ibid, 897.

since Macneil, while seemingly accepting that relational contract law exists, did not offer much indication of what it should contain. However, there are some connections that can be made between relational principles and contract law, thus certain relational principles are identified by Macneil as being 'good faith' and 'reasonable expectations arising from the nature of the relationship'.[73] Macneil did attempt to clarify what the existence of relational contract law did *not* mean. It did not mean that

> relational contracts can never be dealt with by relatively discrete contract law. Indeed, the discrete elements in contractual relations tend to assure that they will be. It does mean, however, that discrete contract law can never be the beginning and the end of the law applicable to relational contracts. Nor does the observation [a great deal of relational contract law exists] mean that the applicable relational contract law should necessarily *always* track closely the behavior and norms of the exchange relations in question … [T]his observation does not mean that relational contract law should always aim to preserve relations, or even should have some presumption that such an aim is a starting point … Whether contractual relations continue or fall apart depends upon whether the common behavior and norms continue with sufficient strength. Where they do not, relational contract law may or may not appropriately step in.[74]

The most that might be said here is that relationalism is the starting point, but this can lead to a conclusion that the as-if-discrete contract should be governed by a discrete law, or even that a relational contract should be governed by a discrete law, if there is no need to preserve the relation. These determinations suggest that it is not just the nature of the parties' contract that should determine whether the application of relational norms is appropriate, but also the nature of the contract breakdown. It is difficult to be certain about this, however, since these articulations about relational legal reasoning lack clarity, and suggest that the legal status quo is not amenable to the necessary changes, but must largely be taken as a given. Ultimately, for Macneil, discrete contract law has a role, but only as part of a wider relationally constituted law: 'classical and neo-classical contract law can be seen as only a part—however important—of any overarching relational jurisprudence'.[75]

Relational Legal Reasoning: Initial Difficulties

Despite Macneil's own equivocation, is it possible to be more ambitious for the development of a relational contract law? If one wanted a simple exposition of what relational theory means for contract law one could probably

[73] Ibid, 904.
[74] Ibid, 898–99.
[75] Ibid, 907.

not do much better as a starting point than to say that context matters and that any legal determination of a contract problem without reference to contextual matters to justify the outcome is radically incomplete. If anything, relationalism seems to demand that a contract be regulated at least in part according to the internal norms as generated by the parties' interactions and complex web of relations that constitute their complete agreement, rather than an external set of rules that fail to appreciate and understand these various facets of the relationship. Insofar as it evinces normative concerns, relational theory simply demands attention to the social norms that reflect actual contextualised practice, whether self-interested and discrete or co-operative.[76] It is a case of affording significance and effect to relational values where they are shown to exist. There is nothing in this assessment to deny the possibility of discreteness. The fault with the law lies only in presenting and accepting discretism as a complete and independent concept around which to organise, explain and justify contracts and contracts law.[77] Macneil does not posit any of his common contract norms as inherently more valuable than others, he simply draws attention to their existence as descriptions and values of contracting (or exchange) behaviour. While 'relational' often refers to the use of co-operative norms, or is a synonym for just a contextual approach to agreements (which may turn out to be based on norms of self-interest as much as co-operation),[78] it will be appreciated that Macneil's identification of the contract norms does not mean that contract legal reasoning is required to impose relational norms of co-operation and flexibility on contractors, nor that the law must change the legal default to one where contract is regarded as a co-operative endeavour because this is more in keeping with the real behaviour of actual contractors (although this may be one appropriate strategy for the development of a more relationally constituted contract law).

To the extent that contract law may already take account of relational norms these are often articulated as exceptions to the classical law precepts. While such a law may recognise and occasionally accord significance to relational factors, this is not truly a relational law, but rather 'neoclassical'. Feinman has articulated the difference between these two as follows,

> Neoclassical contract ... emphasizes the autonomy of individuals and the limited liability that autonomy necessitates. It focusses therefore on the agreement process as an exercise of autonomy to create liability, and tries to construct the expectations of the parties from their agreement and the context that gives their agreement meaning. In contrast, relational contract emphasizes the interdependence of

[76] J Wightman, 'Beyond Custom: Contract, Contexts, and the Recognition of Implicit Understandings' in Campbell, Collins and Wightman (eds), above n 27, 143, 154–55. Also Macneil, above n 31, 207–08.

[77] See Macneil, above n 2, 383.

[78] Wightman, above n 76, 154, fn 29.

> individuals in social and economic relationships. Because its paradigmatic unit of inquiry is the extensive relationship rather than the discrete transaction, relational contract focusses on the necessity and desirability of trust, mutual responsibility, and connection.[79]

Beyond the stipulation that context matters and that neoclassical contract law is not relational contract law, determinate conclusions concerning the legal reasoning techniques required to effect relational theory are elusive. At present, and even in a neoclassical guise, situations where relational norms are on display are often regarded as anomalous within the scheme of contract law and largely irrelevant to its determinations.

There are evident difficulties in attempting to construct legal reasoning techniques from Macneil's theory. Assume for the moment that a relationally constituted contract law will have two connected features: first, the recognition that the paper deal generates only part of the normative framework that governs the parties' agreement, not the totality of it; and second, openness to the possibility that the 'real deal', including commercial practices, expectations and implicit dimensions, will determine how much weight should be placed on the paper deal, or may itself constitute an alternative normative framework for governing the agreement, and thus should be capable of giving rise to legally enforceable obligations. While Macneil's method draws attention to the existence and possible significance of the social norms operating in the particular context of an agreement, this of itself would provide no initial argument for legalisation of those norms as they appear in the relationship. It is evident that not all such norms can or should be legalised. Even in a commercial setting, legalisation will have an important transforming effect that may generate doubt that a relational legal reasoning method is possible, and that contractors wishing for such an approach should be directed towards alternative forms of dispute resolution. Macneil points out that

> [S]overeign imposition of norms on contract, in contrast to their generation within the contract, results in a transformation of the contract's values. That is, the values of imposing contract norms—whether common, discrete or relational—are not identical to the values reflected by their internal generation. Not only is an imposed norm theoretically different—respecting consent, for example—but it will be practically different as well.[80]

This is an important point, but it is directed to the legal resolution of the individual dispute, rather than the law itself. Where the material point under consideration is the design of contract *law*, and the general approach

[79] J Feinman, 'Relational Contract Theory in Context' (2000) 94 *Northwestern University Law Review* 737, 748. See also O Williamson, *The Economic Institutions of Capitalism* (New York, Free Press, 1985) 68–72.

[80] Macneil, above n 2, 370.

it takes to dealing with commercial agreements, not the resolution of a particular dispute, then the law's capacity and general acceptance of the need to reflect and recognise the internal norms of the business relationship is important to its own legitimacy in regulating commercial exchange. The point of contract law is not just to resolve the dispute, but to resolve it according to a set of standards and rules. The transforming effect that may be observed in a specific dispute is an inevitable consequence, but nevertheless engagement with contextual understandings is still an attempt on the part of the law to give meaning and effect to the norms generated *within* the relationship, rather than imposed externally. While the specific relationship being litigated may not be saved, it is possible that this increased legal sensitivity to the internally generated norms and expectations of the relationship would improve the law for other contracting parties. Nevertheless, that relational theory is not easily translated into a contract legal reasoning method must be conceded, and the difficulties are compounded by the renaissance of neoformalism in the US contracts literature.

Neoformalism

The neoformalist movement broadly supports a contract law understood in discretist terms.[81] The debate here relies in part on the distinction between contracts as social phenomena and as legal constructs. Thus, RE Scott has written that 'contracts are relational, complex and subjective. But contract law, whether we like it or not, is none of those things. Contract law is formal, simple, and … classical'.[82] Neo-formalism has been driven by two related concerns. The first is the doubts raised by scholars concerning the capacity of judges to access and use information about the wider context of a business agreement, and the increased possibility of error when judges attempt to utilise relational method within legal reasoning.[83] This concern is addressed more fully in the next chapter, but it could be said that the concern about error is a more specific manifestation of a second concern about the costs involved in a relational approach, particularly in contract enforcement and dispute resolution. That contracting parties might themselves *prefer* a more formal approach is supported by some empirical findings of how

[81] Thus Macneil associates law and economics scholars working within a methodology of rational choice theory as discretists, with Richard Posner being the chief exemplar: 'Challenges and Queries' above n 6, fn 78.

[82] RE Scott, 'The Case for Formalism in Relational Contract' (2000) 94 *Northwestern University Law Review* 847, 852.

[83] See J Gava and J Greene, 'Do We Need a Hybrid Law of Contract? Why Hugh Collins is Wrong and Why it Matters' (2004) 63 *CLJ* 605, 617. See also EA Posner, 'A Theory Of Contract Law Under Conditions Of Radical Judicial Error' (2000) 94 *Northwestern University Law Review* 749.

contractors resolve disputes, such as the work of Lisa Bernstein examined in Chapter 3. One of the conclusions drawn from Macneil's work by neoformalist scholars is that it is the precise point of *legal* regulation to act as a counter to the wider set of social norms, behaviours, expectations and so on that will play such a large part in how the relationship progresses. On this understanding, discreteness is the price that has to be paid for a set of relatively certain and predictable general laws that deal with various aspects of contract dysfunction within inevitably diverse business relationships.

The neoformalist argument is superficially attractive, but there is some warrant for regarding these relational/efficiency lines of scholarship as talking past each other because of their fundamentally incompatible methodological commitments. Ultimately, much of the neoformalist agenda makes perfect sense when formalism is assumed to be correct. It often appears that the neoformalist attempts to engage with relational theory by reference to the concerns presented by efficiency analysis or else to explain relational theory on the basis of the premises accepted by neoformalism and the classical law. Thus some efficiency theorists associated with the neoformalist movement regard relational contracts as simply incomplete agreements.[84] On this basis the legal issues that they raise concern how gaps should be filled. Should gap filling proceed according to internal or relational norms in order to achieve a tailored result for the parties, or with reference to the relevant default rules, or should courts simply refuse to interpret clear contracts or gap fill and let the loss lie where it falls?[85] The neoformalist usually supports one of the latter two positions.[86] Thus any attempt to fill a gap by reference to commercial norms, implicit dimensions or customs is treated as 'creative' interpretation or judicial activism, rather than an essential part of the judicial task.[87] This kind of understanding is replicated by other explanations, particularly prevalent in business literature, which contrast relational contracts with legal contracts: 'Relational contracting is characterized by the substitution of the legal system and its accompanying formal documents by informal agreements such as verbal promises, letters of intent, or 'gentlemen's agreements'.[88] Fundamentally this reveals the authors' understanding that a contract is something that replaces trust, it is not itself a symbol or gesture of trust. Trust can only be indicated through non-legally binding measures. Similarly Hviid regards relational contracts and long-term contracts as separate things. He writes, 'The literature on relational contracts assume that contract terms are *not*

[84] Scott, above n 82, 847.
[85] Ibid, 849–52.
[86] Ibid; Posner, above n 83.
[87] Scott, above n 82, 853.
[88] B Lyons and J Mehta, 'Private Sector Business Contracts: The Text Between the Lines' in S Deakin and J Michie (eds), *Contracts, Co-operation and Competition* (Oxford, OUP, 1997) 43, 51.

used and focus on how repeated interaction and social norms can ensure the obligations between parties can become self-enforceable'.[89] Relational contracts are again characterised here as lacking terms. This dovetails into another argument which is that there is a fundamental mismatch between the aims and scope of relational theory—the behaviour it attempts to identify and explain—and the problems that contract law is required to resolve and the circumstances it responds to. This objection recognises a practical point that contract law essentially deals with the situations where parties have not reached agreement rather than where they have. Contract law is concerned with providing defaults and plugging gaps, and many of its techniques—implied terms, interpretation and so on—are remedies for these sorts of problem.

The understanding of 'relational contracts' as a separate category of contracts identified by lack of legal trappings or concerns with legal enforceability rather than informal methods of self-enforcement bolsters the idea that the law of contract need have nothing to do with relational contracts. On a discretist or formalist model of contract law, such contracts are simply *defined* out of the scope of legal control,[90] or else are thought to raise concerns which are only remedied by economic analysis. Discreteness is still regarded as the hallmark of the legal approach and contract law is simply accepted as having a more limited sphere of operation than lawyers may previously have supposed.[91] Highly relational agreements may well operate largely outside legal control, but this question of legal enforceability is not so clear cut. The debate over the relevance of relational theory for contract law cannot be defined out of existence by maintaining that relational norms and expectations are not 'legal' criteria, and hence anything to which they are applied is not a contract. This is because relational scholars are precisely challenging contract law's determinations of relevant facts and rules for determining disputes and the content of the law. Indeed the design of many contracts militates against such a rigid approach to legality. Many legally enforceable contracts display relational features, as Macneil anticipates that they would, and contracts displaying a high level of reliance on relational norms and values may eventually end up before a court.

Contextualism and relationalism are therefore not appendages to be fixed onto a fundamentally formalist conception of contract law, rather they are a free-standing approach to the law, justified by a different set of considerations. Relational theory eschews the *unreflecting* application of

89 M Hviid, 'Long Term Contracts and Relational Contracts' in B Bouckaert and G De Geest (eds), *The Encyclopaedia of Law and Economics vol. III: The Regulation of Contracts*, (Cheltenham, Edward Elgar, 2000) 46, 47 (emphasis added).

90 *Baird Textile Holdings v Marks & Spencer plc* [2001] EWCA Civ 274 perhaps providing a good example of this phenomenon.

91 McKendrick, above n 19, 312.

contract express terms or contract doctrines to the parties' problem, and in this sense might be thought to involve illegitimate judicial investigations into commercial expectations, practices and contexts. Relationalism demands that the norms generated by the business relationship, context, power relations between the parties and so on, should form the greater part of the legal understanding of the relationship over express contract terms and contract law doctrines. This deeper understanding is the necessary precursor to any analysis of the terms and the resolution of the dispute. The problem with the current law for relational theorists is not that these elements of the business relationship are simply ignored—the law does not ignore contexts in all cases, and in any case it might be entirely right that such contexts are ignored—it is that the rules of contract law (and contract terms) are allowed to frame the contextual enquiry, determining the relevance of and weight to be attached to whatever is revealed by it. A relational approach requires a reverse of the particular reasoning dynamic that demands contextual or broader factual enquiries made by courts are directed towards satisfying the requirements for the operation (or not) of the rules of contract law.[92] So a relational approach may lead to a subset of particular rules or standards being applied—a subset that would be sensitive to the relational or 'as-if-discrete' elements of agreements. No particular outcome is mandated by these enquiries and 'gaps' may well be filled following the investigation or may not.

It is not clear, however, that a relational scholar *must always* support the proposition that gaps should be filled by internal norms of the relationship or commercial practice in every case. Rather, the real source of disagreement here is that relational method denies a view of contracts which assimilates them with the discrete express terms which can run out, rendering the agreement 'incomplete'. The idea that relational contracts are defined by 'incompleteness' in this sense is a finding derived from economic method that posits the possibility, theoretically at least, of a complete contract with explicit terms. Relational scholars simply do not perceive contracts and incompleteness in this way. To approach the express terms through the context of the agreement and (in Macneil's version) the common contract norms might make the 'incompleteness' disappear, or, to the extent that the contract is revealed after such a contextual enquiry to be 'as-if-discrete', make the default rule, or refusal to gap fill, the most appropriate course. On this basis the legal implications of relational theory do not relate just to gap filling in an incomplete contract, but to our entire understanding of what a contract is. It requires a social understanding of agreements which means any of the three approaches to incompleteness identified by Scott may be appropriate. Thus for relational scholars it appears that neoformalism is

[92] Macneil, above n 31, 210ff.

not understood as opposed to relational theory, but as an element of relational theory, appropriate for when the parties have imposed discreteness on their deal. Relationalism requires a richer analysis of background context than traditional economic approaches based on zero transaction costs and rational choice theory.[93]

Relational Legal Reasoning: Possible Processes

Some scholars argue that contract law already is relationally constituted to a great degree and that 'much of existing contract jurisprudence copes well with the reality of the contract relation, as seen through the lens of relational contract theory'.[94] On this basis law often reflects such norms and contains methods and techniques that can be tailored to account for their existence. For some scholars this is itself evidence that commercial contract law responds to the different legal/social elements of contracting by displaying a broad dualism that is sensitive to context and can differentiate between the situations in which the application of the classical law will be appropriate and where it will not.[95] Certainly the law already does evince concern with power relations,[96] the means by which contract ends are achieved and so on, as well as supracontract norms of justice (regulating various aspects of unfairness) and liberty (freedom of contract). Other scholars may be more circumspect about the law's capacity in this respect, including Macneil himself.

Relational theory requires great attention to the detail of the precise circumstances of the contracting parties.[97] In short 'relational analysis is

[93] R Craswell, while frustrated that many questions that appear central to the law and economics scholar appear beside the point to relationalists, believes no real debate between these two exists since they focus on different questions and have different methods: 'The Relational Move: Some Questions From Law and Economics' (1993) 3 *Southern Califormia Interdisciplinary Law Journal* 91.

[94] Austen-Baker, above n 38, 219.

[95] R Brownsword, *Contract Law: Themes for the Twenty-First Century*, 2nd edn (Oxford, OUP, 2006) 139ff. See also MA Eisenberg, 'The Emergence of Dynamic Contract Law' (2000) 88 *California Law Review* 1743, arguing that modern contract law has shifted from formal to substantive, objective to subjective, standardised to individualised and binary to multifaceted although not in all cases, 1749.

[96] Eg, in the Unfair Contract Terms Act 1977, Schedule 2, and in case decisions made under the Act, which require judges to assess the reasonableness of excluding and limiting terms.

[97] While not responding to Macneil directly, Collins also regards contract as occupying a smaller conceptual space than 'exchange': '[C]ontractual relations differ from other species of exchange, because they establish a discrete relation between people, an isolated exchange with its own point of reference', *Regulating Contracts* (Oxford, OUP, 1999) 15, and at 17: 'As a paradigm of types of human association, a contract resists or excludes claims for social solidarity. It favours instrumental relationships formed voluntarily by individuals containing precise undertakings'.

contextual with a vengeance'.[98] Thus what is required is an approach which self-consciously starts from the norms and context of the agreement. To be sure, not all that is revealed should be legally enforceable, but 'beginning analysis by recognizing [social norms and context] is likely to produce a broader set of obligations.'[99] The fully relational approach, then, starts with the agreement context, rather than with the express terms as something onto which context can be imposed. Context is of course a very wide category and it must be said that a great deal could be brought within its ambit. The main difficulty here relates to what is done with the information produced by these contextual enquiries and deciding what is relevant. For Feinman, this constitutes the main drawback of relational theory since 'it is not possible to immerse oneself in the facts of a situation and come to the correct solution that is immanent in those facts'.[100] For Feinman, the result is a 'policy analysis' approach to contracts that aims to achieve a result in a case, not the formulation of a rule.[101] This is likely to lead to increasing fragmentation of, and differentiation between, contracting situations and their differing expectations concerning how contractual relationships should be conducted (some broad categories, for example, might be construction, shipping, insurance, financial markets). Relational theory would arguably look first to context to decide what role the documents had in governing the relationship and what degree of emphasis should be placed on them—no particular information or form of information is privileged at the outset. This may form a kind of preliminary enquiry on the part of the judge to determine what set of norms is appropriate to resolve the dispute.[102] Macneil himself has remarked on the contextual nature of relational legal reasoning, such that one must approach terms through an appreciation of relational factors and not independently. This may lead to differences in the ways in which terms are interpreted across different contractual relationships, as well as requiring courts to be more forgiving of 'vague' clauses and the need to renegotiate and modify the agreement.

Although reference to 'contract context' might be regarded as unacceptably vague, Macneil does give some indication of what may be material to the legal analysis through the operation of the common contract norms. The articulation of the common contract norms is taken to a high level of abstraction to encompass the range of exchange behaviour that Macneil

[98] J Feinman, 'Relational Contract Theory in Context' (2000) 94 *Northwestern University Law Review* 737, 742.

[99] Ibid, 748. See also Williamson, above n 79, 68–72.

[100] Ibid.

[101] Ibid, 743.

[102] See R Brownsword on this idea of meta- or auxiliary agreements specifying 'the rules that are to govern the main contract dealings': 'Network Contracts Revisited' in M Amstutz and G Teubner (eds), *Networks: Legal Issues of Multilateral Co-operation* (Oxford, Hart Publishing, 2009) 31, 44.

wants to incorporate into his theory. The result of this abstraction is a certain lack of distinctness in articulating the norms with the result that some of the identified norms appear more useful to legal analysis than others. 'Role integrity', for example, captures the idea that contractors are invariably exchanging in some capacity and that, irrespective of the personal idiosyncrasies a contractor may bring to bear on an exchange, the role inhabited by an individual in the exchange itself raises expectations in others.[103] Roles are not just labels to be applied, but are constituted by certain forms of behaviour. Thus 'role integrity' explains and describes both Macaulay's finding that sales personnel would come into conflict with accountancy and legal personnel within the same firm because of their contrasting and often incompatible priorities,[104] and also Lord Goff's views concerning liquidators and the duties they have to perform in *Amalgamated Investment and Property Co Ltd v Texas Commerce International Bank*.[105] They are the attitudes that 'go with the territory' and they may be complex and internally conflicting. The law may already have regard to 'role integrity' as a differentiating aspect of its approach to commercial agreements, as when it is assumed that receivers of a bill of lading will pay attention to particular parts of it (and not the small print on the back) commensurate with their role,[106] or when it is assumed that a written document is addressed to lawyers rather than lay people, this conclusion then determining how the document should be interpreted.[107] Similarly, the power norm may be readily understood, and is often seen to be operating in contract contexts although its precise implications may not be fully drawn out. The requirement of reciprocity—'the principle of getting something back for something given'—is likewise discernible as a norm recognised by contract law.[108]

While it may be relatively straightforward to identify that some of these norms are recognised and accorded explanatory power in reaching outcomes in cases it is more difficult to say to what end this knowledge should lead. One tempting conclusion is to say that relational theory requires identification of a contract as liable to be treated as relational or discrete, and then to assess the relationship according to the particular framework suggested by that conclusion, whether it requires the operation of more formal

[103] R Austen-Baker, 'A Relational Law of Contract? (2004) 20 *Journal of Contract Law* 125, 126–27.

[104] S Macaulay, 'Non-Contractual Relations In Business: A Preliminary Study' (1963) 28 *American Sociological Review* 55, 66.

[105] *Amalgamated Investment and Property Co Ltd v Texas Commerce International Bank* [1982] QB 84.

[106] *Homburg Houtimport BV v Agrosin Private Ltd and others (The Starsin)* [2003] UKHL 12; [2004] 1 AC 715.

[107] *Investors Compensation Scheme v West Bromwich Building Society* [1998] 1 All ER 98. Lord Hoffmann seeks to justify his approach by reference to how lawyers would understand the documents, rather than the lay investor (at 115).

[108] Macneil, above n 2, 347.

rules or flexible standards. Macneil has posited a typology of factors that assist in distinguishing the relational from the discrete transaction, but this does not tell us what a law designed to address problems in the relational transaction would look like.[109] As Macneil wrote in an earlier article:

> In the neoclassical system, the reference point for ... questions about change tends to be the original agreement. In a truly relational approach the reference point is the entire relation as it had developed to the time of the change in question (and in many instances as it has developed since the change). This may or may not include an 'original agreement'; and if it does, may or may not result in great deference being given to it.[110]

The end behind this sort of contextual enquiry is to distinguish the situations in which the competitive norms of discrete contracting and the classical law (or broadly classical law) may be appropriate, from those where co-operative norms of relational contract are apposite. But the complexity of relationships that display elements of both competitive and co-operative behaviour means the possibility often presents itself that relationships and transactions do not fit comfortably and genuinely within either sort of framework.

Consider again *NatWest v Rabobank*.[111] While it is problematic to take evidence of the norms operating in the relationship from the case report, it will serve as an illustration. In *NatWest v Rabobank* the norms derived from the context (and the workout procedure) were operating as well as individualistic competitive norms as evidenced by the contractual scheme detailing the limited forms of duty owed by one contractor to the other. The relationship manifested elements of discreteness (reliance on contract) and relationalism (as demonstrated by the generally co-operative nature of the norms of the workout procedure). On the face of it this is a good example of 'Macneilian' conflict between co-operation and competition, with a choice to be made between the discrete normative framework of the express terms and the relational information-sharing norms of the workout procedure. What can be said is that Macneil's analysis would require consideration of factors left largely unexplored by the courts. Attention to role integrity, for example, might be manifest in an investigation of how the fact that the actors occupied roles of employees and agents of their respective banks impinged on the negotiating process and the expectations that were raised in each party about how the other would behave. Similarly, consideration of the norm of harmonisation with the social matrix might be taken to require that the norms of the workout procedure itself governed

[109] *Selected Works* (2001) 196–99.

[110] I Macneil, 'Contracts: Adjustments of Long-term Economic Relations Under Classical, Neoclassical and Relational Contract Law' (1978) 72 *Northwestern University Law Review* 854, 890.

[111] *NatWest v Rabobank* [2007] EWHC 1056 (QBD). See Ch 4 for the facts.

the parties' expectations—in effect that the workout was itself the relevant social matrix.

On the other hand, the NatWest–Rabobank relation could be analysed in transactional terms. Such an analysis might emphasise that this was not intended to be a productive relationship giving rise to mutual dependence and trust, but was an administrative, organisational and functional exchange of relatively short duration whose success to each side was to be measured primarily in financial terms (for example, did NatWest minimise the discount on its share of the debt taken out by Rabobank?). The parties were not producing anything which might have created a mutual interest in the success of a joint project and which would establish a strong motivation for co-operation and successful completion of the project. The parties' concerns were about transferring debt and liability. There was no ongoing relationship and probably no desire to preserve the relationship. To be sure, the parties might need to work together again but given the complexity of the organisations involved the likelihood was that this may involve different employees and different settings. The parties were separate entities brought together by the circumstance that both happened to be creditors of the same company, rather than choice, and the workout norms were imposed on them by social convention rather than growing organically and internally from the relationship between them. Both parties had legal advice and presumably were well aware of the risks involved. The parties acted through agents whose roles demanded, to an extent, loyalty to their own employer over the contract opposite number. In such a context, formalism may be the right approach and a decision focused on short-term self-interested economic rationalism, with only attenuated duties owed to a sophisticated and legally advised partner, appears as the appropriate strategy. The duties owed are simply those of not encroaching beyond the outer limits of censurable behaviour stipulated by the classical law. All these factors make it possible to conclude that the relationship was to be governed by the discrete norm and the dispute disposed of correctly according to the liabilities as set out in the planning documents: NatWest, provided not committing misrepresentation or fraud, was entitled to have primary regard to its own interests.

Certainly the examination of the operation of the common contract norms can build a more accurate picture of the relationship and its underpinning expectations. A more fully informed analysis of liability may proceed from this point. The reasons stipulated above are all plausible grounds upon which to assume discreteness is the applicable norm, with the natural corollary that the application of the classical law appears appropriate. However, relational analysis would also appreciate that it would be difficult to have complete confidence in this conclusion, since in the litigated case it is likely that the dispute is made to hinge strategically on a conflict between relational and discrete norms. Litigation creates a new context for understanding the relationship and it is part of *that context* to present arguments in a certain way that plays up conflict and plays down co-operation. In such a context Rabobank's argument appears distorted and dislocated next to the norms of the classical law. Choice of the legal framework perpetuates the legal understanding that it is irresponsible for commercial contractors to trust one another in a business environment.[112] One could regard the real insight of Macneil here is in revealing how 'conflict' between these two normative worlds of the legal contract and the workout procedure is more constructed than real, motivated by the adversarial and binary character of arguments made during the litigation process. Of course, a relational analysis may reach the same result as the legal outcome but with an important difference: the discrete agreement as represented by the documents is not the starting point and end point, but just a factor (possibly a very important one) in a holistic consideration of all the pertinent aspects of the relationship, including the extent to which the parties are self-consciously engaging with the 'legal' world. This may reveal that the seemingly different normative frameworks are not entirely separate, but that the formal and relational are essentially integrated phenomena.[113] For the operation of relational theory then, the material consideration in the case may well be whether the operative norms of the workout procedure influenced Rabobank's agreement to the express terms. But it is exactly this kind of enquiry that is precluded by the 'closed'[114] nature of the classical law and the tendency for relational theory to be regarded as a bolt-on to neoclassical law rather than an alternative to it. Dealing with exactly this point Macneil wrote:

> [Neoclassical law] will ... continue to rub in an unnecessarily abrasive manner against the realities of coexistence with relational needs for flexibility and change. Only when the parts of the contract law system implementing discreteness and presentiation are perceived, intellectually and otherwise, not as an independent system, but only as integral parts of much larger systems, will unnecessary abrasion disappear. By no means all the abrasion will disappear ... because real conflict exists between the need for reliability of planning and the need for flexibility in economic relations. What will disappear is the abrasion resulting from application of contract law founded on the assumption that all of a contractual relation is encompassed in some original assent to it, where that assumption is manifestly false.[115]

Although appearing radically indeterminate, at the stage of trying to *develop* a relationally constituted contract law, then arguably the first step is a better understanding of commercial relationships and the role of the legal

[112] 'Businessmen must be taken to be aware that, without specific contractual protection, their business may suffer in consequence': *Baird Textile Holdings v Marks & Spencer plc*, above n 90 [76].

[113] See Ch 4. Also Collins, above n 97, 141–43.

[114] Collins, above n 97, 37ff.

[115] Macneil, above n 110, 888.

norms within them. It matters that these considerations and conflicts in frameworks are first drawn out and their influence made apparent, so some attempt can be made to distinguish the norms that arise genuinely from the parties' relationship and those that flow from the assumptions and processes of the law. In terms of legal reasoning, relationalism may be regarded as too expansive and amorphous a theory to offer much reliable guidance to a judge charged with resolving a complex commercial dispute, and that it therefore leaves too much room for ill-advised judicial discretion. Nor will it always yield determinate conclusions. As was seen with *NatWest v Rabobank* the application of relational theory may often turn out to be inconclusive. To be sure, adopting a broadly relational course as advocated by Macneil's common contract norms may be too ambitious and expect far too much from the law and lawyers, but judges can at least approximate to the approach and take steps to incorporate *some* of its major insights. Indeed it is arguable that the law already adopts the contextual method required, as with contract interpretation for example, but not openly and with too little reliance on 'backstory'. By making a relatively minor change of appreciating the possibility that the formal and relational worlds are integrated phenomena then it may be that the conflicts between the discrete contract norms and relational norms would recede. Drawing such stark contrasts would no longer be encouraged by the legal framework. The considerations that compelled the parties to adopt the contractual forms that they did may be brought out into the open and the relationship between those forms and the internal business norms could be explored more fully, leading to better justified outcomes. This may eventually lead to commercial parties not feeling that they had to engage with a separate and remote legal world, and often failing in their attempts. It is perhaps awareness of these conflicts, and how they are encouraged and even created by the law, that is the legacy of Macneil's relational theory.

CONCLUSION

Macneil criticises neoclassical analysis for being based on the idea of discreteness, assuming 'moment in time' liability of a static character and 'zero relations' among the contracting parties.[116] The relatively simple account of neoclassical economics and contract law demands the law closes itself off from the social or relational aspects of an agreement. Law takes only a limited view of what is relevant to its investigations and thus may fail to pay regard to crucial factors that had an effect on the overall structure and workings of the contract. The legal commitment to the specifics of transactions

[116] Macneil, above n 61, 1039.

may produce distorted understandings concerning the basis upon which the parties entered into the agreement, while the legal imposition of bureaucratic processes on the contract may transform it into a different entity, remote from the concerns of the parties.[117] While Macneil may have been sceptical of the role of relational contract law in litigated disputes, it is nevertheless relational theory, with its eschewal of grand theorising along monist or single-value lines, that is best able to comprehend the multifaceted and complex realities of the commercial relationship, and thus may provide a suitable framework within which a contract law more aligned with commercial expectations could be developed.

The strength of relational theory is its flexible and pragmatic approach and its willingness to engage with a variety of contractual relationships on their own terms, rather than seeking to impose upon them some vision of the external values that contracting activity is thought to represent and uphold. It is perhaps not necessary for contract law to change radically to incorporate the findings of relational theory, but simply to become more aware of the wider social context of the commercial relationship, and indeed to understand and comprehend how that wider social context contributes to the very characterisation of a contractual relationship as discrete or relational. The potential to undertake this investigation using a specified framework is what relational theory offers. Recognition that all agreements are relational may go some way to heralding the change in attitude which is necessary for implementing any more specific legal adjustments or reforms. A relational conception of contract would replace freedom of contract with some other underlying values, such as some conception of contractual justice and the fundamentally co-operative underpinning of all contracting behaviour,[118] and may be taken to a higher level of 'trust' in some forms of exchange, especially, but not confined to, those involving long duration and uncertainty. Exceptions to such principles may have to be drawn to cover the situations where what is categorised as fundamentally self-interested dealing (within the specified legal limits) is deemed appropriate.

While relational theory is an expansive social theory requiring comprehensive analysis of all relevant parts of an exchange relationship that many would regard as beyond most judicial capacities, courts need not take on all the insights from it. One could point out that just as economic analysis or theories of contract as promise face problems of fit with the law as it is, and in yielding determinate propositions for reform, so does relational theory, but the problems are no worse for relational theory than any alternative theoretical account. This difficulty alone should not result in discounting the theory as having no implications for the law. Relational theory's impact

[117] Macneil, above n 6, 903–04.
[118] Campbell, above n 9, 11.

on contract law can be approximate and approximated. In many ways, with its appreciation of the different areas of law that might impact upon contracting (which the law has recognised—estoppel, restitution, tort) and its tendency to depart from discrete norms on occasion to embrace a more pragmatic or contextual approach, it could be argued that relational contract theory provides the best explanation for the current design of the law. The operation of the common contract norms can be revealed by a contextual analysis of the relationship and in this way the theory may help us to map out the considerations that may already operate in the determination of the commercial dispute but which are not specifically drawn out in current legal reasoning processes. It may not provide specific guidance concerning how contract law rules could be designed to achieve complete fit with relational theory. Macneil's relevance lies not in yielding concrete proposals for the reform of contract law, but in bringing to the fore, and making us confront directly, the elements of contracting behaviour that may remain resolutely obscured through the application of legal doctrine. Nevertheless the central insights of relational theory—that context is important, that indeterminacy in contract circumstances is rife, that classical law is manifestly unsuitable for some forms of contractual relationship—support the idea that commercial contract law should reflect commercial practice, since the theory demands that a range of considerations, not any single value, be factored into any analysis of exchange relationships. At the very least legal attention to the role of such norms in the business relationship may make the legal reasoning process more transparent and the outcomes from the process more robust. If contract law has any incentive effects, and doubtless this has some plausibility, this increased sensitivity to context and relational norms on the part of the law may at least free the parties from (unsuccessful) attempts to create discrete agreements. Macneil's insights bring into sharper focus the distinctive and precise role of law in commercial relationships, as well as bringing into relief its inherent limitations. Identification of these limitations must be the precursor to any meaningful reform, particularly when courts are required to deal with all manner of contracts, contract disputes and exchange behaviour.

7

Commercial Expectations and Legal Capacity

THE PREVIOUS CHAPTER explored some of the features of the relational theory of contract advanced by Ian Macneil. Since relational theory is driven in part by a concern that classical contract law is an incomplete account of contract phenomena it displays some overlap with the claim that contract law is misaligned with commercial expectations. There is therefore a plausible case for claiming that the development of a more relationally constituted contract law, that is, a law sensitive to the social embeddedness, complexity and normative richness of the parties' agreement, would go some way to alleviating the misalignment. For the purposes of the next two chapters, therefore, it is assumed that a law which is sensitive to commercial expectations will be one that is broadly relationally constituted. This only takes us so far however. It is one thing to identify relational theory as offering the foundation for greater legal attention to commercial norms and expectations, quite another to translate it into specific legal reasoning techniques that can be used by judges in resolving commercial contract disputes. Some of the problems involved in developing a relationally constituted contract law were explored in the previous chapter. These limitations largely resulted from difficulties with relational theory itself. Even a relatively unambitious effort to make contract law more relationally constituted faces significant difficulties, both practical and theoretical. While relational theory may face internal problems yielding a legal reasoning methodology, chiefly that it was not formulated with this function in mind and the legal system is not necessarily the main focus of its analysis, the law presents barriers of its own which may limit the extent to which a relational method can be pursued through common law processes. This chapter will consider the legal impediments to developing a contract law informed by commercial practices and norms. Barriers are presented by the rules of contract law themselves and their underlying commitments. There may also be limitations in the capacity of judges to understand and process all the relevant information about the business relationship that a contextual and relational approach will produce. A further objection is that it is illegitimate for judges to attempt to mould commercial contract law towards the needs and expectations of the business community. This chapter will also explore the obstacles presented by the 'litigation-centric' feature of contract law. Does the fact that contract law is forged out of disputes inevitably influence its design to the possible exclusion of other considerations concerning the co-operative, rather than adversarial, nature of most contractual relationships? The chapter considers whether these grounds present compelling arguments against the development of a relational contract law. The final chapter then considers what legal developments may be necessary to make contract law achieve potentially greater alignment with commercial expectations.

RELATIONALISM, CONTRACT LAW RULES AND COMMON LAW METHOD

Perhaps the most immediate difficulty with the development of a relational contract law is the mismatch between the need for generality in the application of contract rules and the individual approach to each business relationship required by relational theory. General rules usually require the reduction and often the reformulation of complex and specific facts into relatively discrete and predetermined categories of relevance that are provided by the rule structure. The external operation of the rules necessarily involve sacrificing some detail in their expression and also in their application, so that relevant facts can be isolated and decisions made under the rules relatively quickly. A fully contextualised approach to legal reasoning may appear to require the sacrifice of these benefits, since one starts from a wide-ranging examination of the facts and context of a commercial relationship to decide the obligations that have arisen, rather than the premises of a contract law rule. Any supposed conflict between the need for a set of contract law rules and a relational approach to legal reasoning does not stand up to sustained scrutiny however, and ultimately this is not a strong ground upon which to oppose the move to a more contextual and relational contract law. Certainly some importance must be attached to contract law as a system that displays values of certainty, consistency and some degree of stability. Lord Hoffmann recently identified that it was a 'sound practical intuition that the law of contract is an institution designed to enforce promises with a high degree of predictability'.[1] As Eisenberg points out, however, one must distinguish between the justification for a rule and the justification for following a rule.[2] Values of certainty and predictability do not provide rationales for the rules; since they are largely neutral over the content of the rules, they provide rationales for decision makers to follow the rules.

[1] *Chartbrook Ltd v Persimmon Homes Ltd* [2009] UKHL 38, [37].

[2] MA Eisenberg, 'The Emergence of Dynamic Contract Law' (2000) 88 *California Law Review* 1743, 1752.

The primary rationale for the rules of contract law is to enforce certain kinds of agreements. The primary questions for contract law therefore are (i) have the parties reached agreement? and (ii) what have they agreed? Relationalism does not require abandonment of the rules of contract law; it requires investigation of a wider range of factors and behaviours in determining the answer to those two questions. This investigation will determine what rules or principles of contract law will be applied and how.

In any case, it is difficult to hold to the line that the current law of contract is certain and predictable. The default status of many of the present rules and doctrines of contract law means that the rules may not always apply. While some rules of contract law are mandatory—for example those related to the requirements for a contract, the need for consideration and vitiating factors—many more are defaults that will only apply insofar as commercial parties do not stipulate for any alternative. The number of mandatory rules within contract law is reducing steadily. The formulation of a statutory exception to the privity rule provides one example,[3] the rule against recovery for non-pecuniary losses on breach provides another.[4] These developments have taken place precisely to make the law more effective in upholding the parties' expectations. In addition, parties may often use litigation to test the legal efficacy of contract tools and terms that they have developed. Contract disputes are not always concerned with seeking the application of an existing rule, but are attempting to influence the formation of new rules or make old rules subject to new considerations. Unlike other areas of law, the essence of contract lies not in a breach of some pre-existing duty imposed by law, as with tort or the criminal law, but in the actions of the parties. Contract law is not only about the limits on the exercise of rights that can be placed on rights holders, but gives mechanisms for creating such rights and making them legally enforceable. The law may set the limits of what contracting is and how legally enforceable agreements may be created, but the parties, and commercial parties in particular, undertake this activity as a means to achieve certain ends. Ultimately, given the existing complexity of the law, the range of commercial parties and the problems they raise, it is difficult to make a robust case against a more relational contract law by arguing that this interferes with the necessarily rule-bound approach of contract law, sacrificing its certainty and predictability. This is both because contract law does not display a fully rule-bound nature and because a relational approach does not deny the occasional need for the application of classical contract doctrines in dispute resolution. That said, there are other characteristics of law and legal processes that may

[3] Contracts (Rights of Third Parties) Act 1999.

[4] Questionably derived from *Addis v Gramophone Co Ltd* [1909] AC 488, see now *Farley v Skinner* [2001] UKHL 49; [2001] 3 WLR 899.

raise doubts about contract law's capacity to become more relationally constituted. These are examined in more detail below.

Relationalism, Judicial Legitimacy and Judicial Activism

One limitation on the law relates to the legitimacy of a judge adopting a relational approach to contract dispute resolution. John Gava has recently made the case for a legalistic account of judicial legitimacy that militates against adopting a more relational or commercial-contextual approach in contract law. He is opposed to what he perceives to be ill-conceived and ill-directed judicial activism and instrumentalism in the commercial sphere, particularly since this activism is often couched in opaque doctrinal terms with unclear justification. Instead he defends a form of pragmatic legalism—the idea of law as a relatively self-contained system of practice and justification—as a legitimate position for a judge to adopt.[5] Gava seeks to defend legalism as a judicial practice rather than a theoretical position. For him the practice of law is understood internally, but he does not seek to impose or find a coherent pattern of principles within the rules. Thus he accepts that the law is often incoherent and inconsistent, but it is nevertheless justified and supported by the institutional, constitutional and historical constraints which lend legitimacy to the common law.[6] The judge's duty is confined to applying the rules as justified through orthodox common law method characterised by interstitial development of the existing authorities and his acquired knowledge of the legal materials. This is as far as judicial legitimacy extends in constitutional terms. Judges can be creative, and indeed must be so, but within the boundaries of existing legal principle and without distortion that would result from an attempt 'to make the law commercially expedient and useful'.[7]

In another article with Janey Greene he regards greater contextualism in contract law as bound to fail because judges lack the relevant training and capacity to decide cases on the basis of business norms and expectations.[8] Gava presents the debate here as involving a stark choice between justified common law legalism and a common law of contract 'purely driven by

[5] J Gava, 'Dixonian Strict Legalism, *Wilson v Darling Island Stevedoring* and Contracting in the Real World' (2010) 30 *OJLS* 519.

[6] See also EJ Weinrib, *The Idea of Private Law* (Cambridge MA, Harvard University Press, 1995): 'Private law ... is more than the sum of its results. It also includes a set of concepts, a distinctive institutional setting, and a characteristic mode of reasoning', 4–5.

[7] Gava, above n 5, 535.

[8] J Gava and J Greene, 'Do We Need a Hybrid Law of Contract? Why Hugh Collins is Wrong and Why it Matters' (2004) 63 *CLJ* 605. See also RE Scott, who endorses a formal and literal contract interpretation strategy since this satisfies ex ante efficiency where the predictability of the rules is paramount: 'The Case for Formalism in Relational Contract' (2000) 94 *Northwestern University Law Review* 847.

an instrumentalist desire to make the law reflect the practices, needs and expectations of the business community'.[9] For Gava, such a transformation is illegitimate and would constitute crossing a 'fundamental constitutional barrier ... Instead of change and development in the law being driven by the legal reasoning of professional judges it would, instead, reflect the needs and desires of the market'.[10] Lord Grabiner has reiterated the same point, although his particular target is the attempt to undermine 'clear words of the agreement' by reference to 'commercial considerations': 'The court should not speculate on the commercial common sense behind those words and should not be tempted into constructing an abstract commercial purpose derived from the "factual matrix" in order to rewrite what is otherwise clear'.[11] For Gava, the connection between law and business is contingent, a result simply of the kind of cases that make it through to trial and judgment, particularly at the higher level of court proceedings.[12] It does not express any necessary truth about a more foundational connection between the form and functions of contract law and the needs of commerce or market transactors. Gava's argument does have explanatory power, since the facilitation of commerce is not the *sole* function of commercial contract law, nor *wholly* explanatory of legal change. But contract law does not simply take on the 'hue' of business, as he suggests, because of the cases it hears, although undoubtedly the cases litigated have considerable influence over the rules that result (this particular issue is discussed further below). It is clear that the common law of contract is primarily for business users, and changes in the law are often in response to perceived commercial needs. Gava's argument seems to be that contract law should not regard facilitating trade as forming any part of its role, and that its justification is, or should be, purely historical and constitutional, not market based.[13]

This position does not appear to accord with the views of judges themselves, who seem to regard their role as involving some attempt to balance *all* of these considerations. Commercial contract law, at least in England, has long regarded itself as a facilitator of commerce. This can, of course, be dismissed as empty rhetoric, but such a claim embraces the idea that our legal system allows, and may indeed require, a judge to consider the effect

[9] J Gava, 'How Should Judges Decide Commercial Cases?' (2013) 30 *Journal of Contract Law* 133, 150.

[10] Ibid.

[11] Lord Grabiner, 'The Iterative Process of Contract Interpretation' (2012) 128 *LQR* 41, 41. See also *Skanska Rashleigh Weatherfoil Ltd v Somerfield Stores Ltd* [2006] EWCA Civ 1732 [21–22] per Neuberger LJ.

[12] See GC Shaffer, 'How Business Shapes Law: A Socio-Legal Framework' (2009) 42 *Connecticut Law Review* 147, 157ff; M Galanter, 'Why the "Haves" Come Out Ahead: Speculations on the Limits of Legal Change' (1974) 9 *Law and Society Review* 95.

[13] J Gava, 'Can Contract Law Be Justified on Economic Grounds?' [2006] *University of Queensland Law Journal* 253, 265.

of his decisions on commercial contractors,[14] whether the mechanisms they employ to achieve commercial aims are legally permissible and how 'commercial' outcomes might be achieved through legal means. Disagreement between judges is usually over how law best facilitates contract making and performance, not over whether this is a legitimate aim of the legal practice. Must it be concluded that these 'professional judges' thoroughly misunderstand the practice that they are involved in? Or that they are engaged in some other project apart from legal reasoning? The latter might be a charge levied against a commercially 'activist judge'. One response here is to say that a relational or contextual approach to legal reasoning is not necessarily 'interventionist' or 'active'. Arguments against commercial activism do not necessarily have force against the relational project per se, since the relational approach does not necessarily call for judges to be more commercially active, simply to act with a better informed judgment about the parties and their exchange, including all relevant contextual factors. Nor is it clear that relationalism should be seen as mandating judges to undertake freestanding attempts to fill gaps in a contract when a determination is made that a contract is 'silent' concerning some contingency. To require judges to be more relationally aware or to incorporate insights from relational theory in their legal reasoning is not necessarily to require them to embrace judicial activism in the commercial sphere. In Macneil's version of relational theory, for example, this might be the right route only if it appeared appropriate after analysis of all the essential aspects of the context of the contract, including the internally generated norms of the business relationship. Relationalism does not require the application of some abstract, independent and static standard, expressed in the idea of 'commerciality', but rather recognition of the internal values of the agreement, whether or not this fits the prevailing classical legal paradigm. Given the thrust of the relational critique of the classical law, it may be more accurate to say the legal resolution of the dispute in terms of the announced rules constitutes the 'intervention' if it displays a marked departure from the parties' expectations derived from other parts of their relationship.

A further response is to say that 'activism' is a loaded word that suggests judges are behaving illegitimately whenever they stray beyond a consideration of the facts of the case, or the terms of a contract or the existing common law rules. On a simple level, one might respond that bringing a dispute before a judge is precisely asking the law to intervene where the parties were unable to resolve the problem between themselves. This is never without risk and with complete certainty about the result. There is usually some problem over the application of the existing rule set such that at least

14 See, eg, the legal reasoning approach advanced by N MacCormick in *Legal Reasoning and Legal Theory*, revised edn (Oxford, OUP, 1994), which accepts consequentialism as a legitimate factor in legal reasoning in 'hard cases'.

one of the parties will not want the usual rule applied. Gava's position relies on the availability of identifiable legal principles that exhaust the legitimate grounds for a decision and that allow a relatively clear boundary to be drawn between what count as 'legally valid reasons' for an outcome and what counts as instrumental and 'unprincipled' decision making. For Gava, the judicial remit extends no further than applying existing rules and principles that can demonstrate the right kind of legal pedigree. Thus he criticises the House of Lords in *The Eurymedon*[15] for taking Lord Reid's minority dictum in *Scruttons Ltd v Midland Silicones*,[16] suggesting how the problem of extending exclusions of liability to protect stevedores could be achieved, and elevating it to 'the status of binding legal authority'.[17] But even the theorist who disagrees with consequentialist legal reasoning must concede that legal reasoning and interpretation takes place on a wider plane than by reference solely to the extant legal materials. Lord Reid's dictum was not an isolated event, but was part of the general common law assault on the privity doctrine that took place throughout the twentieth century, much of which was motivated by a desire to make agreed commercial arrangements work as intended by the parties.[18] Legal reasoning may aim to resolve the dispute within a specified framework of rules, but it is not an exercise that is undertaken without a certain degree of ambition to improve upon what is already provided, either by reforming, explaining, justifying, clarifying, or distinguishing the law, or suggesting to counsel ways around a difficulty, certainly at the higher level of judicial proceedings. While it is politically appealing to believe that courts should be confined to working within a rule-bound framework, this seems to pay scant regard to the kinds of complex commercial disputes that courts are charged with hearing and resolving. In commercial cases, courts generally deal with incomplete agreements and interpretation problems, rather than fully formalised contracts which contain 'the answer' within the terms, or upon which some determinate legal rule exists. Gava's defence of 'pragmatic legalism' entails a very limited role for the courts in facilitating and policing commercial activity. While this might be desirable as a theoretical and political position, it is practically impossible. Complex cases will come before courts that demand answers to legal problems and those answers may not be found within existing law, or may only be obliquely derived from the legal materials following an extended process of generalising, abstracting, fact-finding/filtering and distinguishing

[15] *The Eurymedon* [1975] AC 154.

[16] *Scruttons Ltd v Midland Silicones Ltd* [1962] AC 446.

[17] Gava, above n 5, 536.

[18] Other common law exceptions to the privity rule were more doctrinally robust in that they can trace a lineage. For example, the exception to the privity rule developed in *Alfred McAlpine Construction Limited v Panatown Limited* [2001] 1 AC 518 and its reliance on *Albacruz v Owners of the ship or vessel Albazero (The Albazero)* [1977] AC 774 and *Dunlop v Lambert* (1839) 6 Cl & F 600.

on the part of the judge. Even this characterisation ignores the fact that, to begin with, counsel has likely exercised a good deal of control in the selection of 'relevant' precedents from a range of alternatives whose application might have yielded quite different outcomes. It is arguable that the real problem Gava identifies with 'commercial activism' on the part of judges is the lack of transparency in the judicial pursuit of commercial ends, and hence the impossibility of opening up the justifications publicly advanced to any meaningful sort of scrutiny. In articulating a range of criteria and tools for a judge to apply to any agreement, and which can be broadly specified in advance, relational contract theory arguably has the potential to be more transparent than some current judicial approaches, which tend to obscure their precise reasoning processes behind blanket references to 'commercial purposes', 'reasonableness' and the like, without fully articulating the relevant considerations.

Contract law, being largely produced out of commercial disputes, has always reflected the problems contractors encounter in operating in markets and, even in this limited sense, is concerned with market needs and expectations. 'Commercial activism', to the extent that it exists within such a system, is not free-standing and independent. Judges respond to social imperatives or pressures revealed through litigated cases as brought to them by the parties, they do not create these imperatives independently. If anything it is the common law's systemic tendencies themselves, coupled with the decline in similarity between fact patterns displayed by a non-homogeneous commercial contracting community, as well as changes in social norms, that embrace and demand 'activism'. As has been earlier demonstrated, judges deciding commercial contract disputes already display awareness of commercial contexts, pay some regard to commercial purposes, try to reach commercially acceptable decisions and make assessments of commercial consequences in deciding on contract liability issues. A departure from formal 'rules' will not necessarily give rise to unrestricted discretion and judicial freedom. A similar process can be detected when courts take an inherently flexible criterion and give it content through decision making. Judges frequently have shown that they are able to give substantive content to flexible standards imposed by the law. The Unfair Contract Terms Act 1977, for example, may require a judge to assess the 'reasonableness' of an attempted exclusion or limitation of liability in a commercial contract. Judges have developed a range of considerations to assess whether this 'reasonable' requirement is met, and in doing so have provided a workable set of criteria that are generally applied across a range of contracting circumstances.[19] Even this limited exercise of discretion

[19] See, eg, *Photo Production Ltd v Securicor Transport* [1980] AC 827; *Smith v Bush* [1990] 1 AC 831.

therefore still takes place within a general framework of contract law rules that sanction particular kinds of conduct and define, in general terms, the activity. There is no warrant for interpreting a relational approach as allowing that courts must provide a legal imprimatur of validity to every device that commerce develops, nor sanction whatever action a commercial party takes to be in their interests.

OBJECTIVITY

The next two possible barriers to an increased relationalism in the law are connected. If it is sought to express the crux of relational contract law in the language of the law itself, then it might be said that a relational approach to the contract would most likely require an agreement to be enforced according to the parties' common intentions as accessible from the evidence available, not limited to the contractual documents. This is very controversial in English contract law, however, and not a step that would readily be taken. Despite contract formation and interpretation being notionally a search for parties' intentions, traditionally courts have rejected evidence of what an agreement means to one of the parties, or what he thinks he has undertaken to do. Contract law rules are generally concerned with objectivity, both in relation to the operation of the rules and questions of evidence, and in terms of judging the effects rules may have on other sections of the commercial community. Judges are aware that their determinations reach beyond the parties in the dispute to the commercial community. The commitment to objectivity may thus be driven ultimately by policy and pragmatic considerations that appeal to the general commercial contracting audience for contract law rules. There may therefore be a clash between the expectations that individual contractors may have about their contractual obligations, the law and the resolution of the dispute, and other contractors that might be affected by a ruling. Thus the actual intentions of the parties concerning their agreement are not sought, but rather reasonable intentions are imputed to the parties.[20] In part this is due to the need to ensure that contractual agreements are broadly reliable, so that one party cannot escape liability on the basis of their lack of subjective consent if all the outward appearances of their behaviour indicated to the other party that agreement had been reached. The objective theory of agreement and interpretation recognises that there is no window into a person's mind to discover what they actually intended. Since this information is inaccessible to the other contracting party, they can only rely on outward manifestations of consent and agreement to terms, not any inner intentions. The law thus asks what

[20] See Lord Steyn, 'Contract Law: Fulfilling the Reasonable Expectations of Honest Men' (1997) 113 *LQR* 433, 433.

each party is entitled to conclude from the other's outward actions.[21] As Gava and Greene have written, 'formalism is designed to overcome the impossibility of anyone knowing what goes on in the minds of contracting parties'.[22] As well as these practical considerations, contract law, as part of the state apparatus of maintaining order and facilitating social and economic goals, tends towards generality and away from individualised justice that may take into account the weaknesses of particular contractors, concentrating instead on judging the conduct of the defendant.

The sense behind objectivity can be readily understood, but it is not clear why a standard applied to regulate the dealings between the parties *as individuals* should be applied to the parties understood as an entity engaged on a common project with a shared purpose. Even when actual intentions may be shared between the parties, so that both parties have the same intentions regarding their obligations and what their agreement is supposed to achieve, the law does not necessarily regard this as relevant to understanding what their contract means. Instead the law takes a depersonalised view of the parties' intentions and asks what a reasonable person in their position would have understood their words to mean.[23] Similarly in Lord Hoffmann's restatement of the principles of contract interpretation in *Investors*, the relevant consideration is what *the document* conveys to a reasonable person with the background knowledge of the parties. The traditional reference to the search for the parties' intentions as the object of the interpretation exercise has been dismissed by Lord Hoffmann as a mere matter of convention.[24]

Increased attention to the internal norms generated by the parties' relationship, expectations and practices might be criticised on the basis that it creates the danger of ousting the objective approach of English contract law, with attendant consequences for certainty in contractual dealings and the law itself. There is some potential for confusion here however. The idea that contract interpretation (and almost all other applications of contract law principle) does not turn on any party's subjective view of what they intended is accepted almost without question and no one seriously asserts the contrary. Instead, the debate centres on how far this injunction against subjective intent militates against the use of the parties' actual common or joint intention, where objective (that is, reliable) evidence of this exists, in deciding what the parties meant by their contract and what they are

21 Lord Reid in *McCutcheon v David MacBrayne Ltd* [1964] 1 WLR 125, 128.

22 Gava and Greene, above n 8, 617. See also D Charny, 'The New Formalism in Contract' (1999) 66 *University of Chicago Law Review* 842, 850.

23 Lord Grabiner, above n 11, 41.

24 *Attorney General of Belize v Belize Telecom Ltd* [2009] UKPC 10; [2009] Bus LR 1316, [16].

obligated to do.[25] Does 'subjective intent' mean only the unexpressed inner intention of one contracting party, or does it also include the parties' shared and communicated actual intentions?[26] It seems that English law is now in the position where contract meaning is entirely detached from the parties' intentions, in favour of what a reasonable person (the judge) thinks the parties meant by the contract language.[27] While the law's commitment to objectivity is understandable, it is not without cost and these costs affect the extent to which the law is able to take on board relational insights. Joseph Perillo argues that, in relation to interpretative approaches:

> A highly objective vantage point [e.g., a plain meaning rule] may be rather remote from the perspectives of the parties and may produce an interpretation that conforms to the intention of neither party ... This perspective subordinates the parties' intentions of the intrinsic meaning of words.[28]

When incontrovertible evidence exists of what the parties actually and jointly intended it is not clear why this should be excluded from consideration, although it often may be. The legitimacy of the search for actual intentions is connected to the ideas of self-regulation of commercial agreements and transparency. Atiyah points out that such an approach was important to Lord Mansfield, who

> stressed the importance of interpreting contracts in accordance with the intentions of the parties. In modern times, stress of this kind—insistence on looking for the actual intentions of the parties in the particular circumstances of the case, instead of reliance on fixed rules—is seen as a recipe for uncertainty in the law. But it was precisely the reverse to Mansfield, who assumed that if only contracts were interpreted in accordance with the intentions of businessmen, then businessmen would be able to perform their contracts and resolve their own disputes, whereas if contracts were subject to fixed and arbitrary rules of interpretation then only the court would ever be able to say what they meant.[29]

[25] One notable defender of the view that actual intent matters is Professor David McLauchlan. He attributes responsibility to OW Holmes for the assertion that the parties' shared, actual and objectively evidenced intention is of limited relevance to formation of agreement and contract interpretation: 'The Contract That Neither Party Intends' (2012) 29 *Journal of Contract Law* 26, 29.

[26] See ibid, 27–28.

[27] Lord Clarke in the Supreme Court decision in *Rainy Sky v Kookmin Bank* [2011] UKSC 50; [2011] 1 WLR 2900, [14]. In this respect it is well noted that English contract law is out of line with various international contract law instruments, eg, Article 8:101 DCFR. The DCFR puts common intention above reasonable meaning, while the English law position appears to be broadly the reverse: see *Attorney-General of Belize and others v Belize Telecom Ltd*, above n 24, [16]. More accepting of common intention was the Court of Appeal in *Svenska Petroleum Exploration AB v Government of the Republic of Lithuania and another* [2006] EWCA Civ 1529; [2007] 1 All ER (Comm) 909, [24].

[28] J Perillo, 'The Origins of the Objective Theory of Contract Formation and Interpretation' (2000) 68 *Fordham Law Review* 427, 431.

[29] PS Atiyah, *The Rise and Fall of Freedom of Contract* (Oxford, OUP, 1979) 190–91.

The downside of rigid objectivism and a reliance on fixed rules is excessive technicality on the matter of contract meaning. A case in point here is the law on contract interpretation, which is becoming increasingly filled with fine distinctions that are in danger of rendering it unintelligible and impenetrable to most contracting parties.[30] Moreover, there is an alternative argument that could be made here. Investigating the norms and expectations that operate in an industry, or a particular commercial community, is indicative of an objective approach that simply refers to a wider range of evidence of the business norms and expectations, beyond the contract documents, that would establish how a reasonable contractor would understand the contract and the extent of his obligations.[31] As with so much where the issues are presented as a conflict between two opposing positions, the degree of objectivity (good) or subjectivity (bad) required by any particular legal reasoning approach is a matter of degree. These two positions shade into each other at so many points in contracts legal analysis that it can be difficult to distinguish one approach fully from the other. Insofar as *these parties* are assumed to be reasonable contractors engaged on what was at least to some extent a joint enterprise, the search for an objective intent is a search for their common purposes.

LEGAL COMMITMENT TO THE WRITTEN AGREEMENT

The importance that English contract law places on the documented agreement was noted in Chapter 4. The commitment to form and objectivity is a formidable impediment to the development of a more relational contract law, since such a law would undoubtedly place less initial reliance on the contract documents as the sole repository of expectations and obligations about contractual performance. But it would be mistaken to regard a relational approach as stipulating that the documented version of the contract is thereby rendered irrelevant. It is not necessarily the case that formalism stands in stark opposition to relationalism. While relational *norms* are associated with values such as flexibility, co-operation and trust, in its widest sense relationalism requires that agreements are understood and examined within their social context. This does not mean that a relationally sensitive contract law must reject formalism out of hand. An examination of an agreement in context may suggest a fully formal and discrete approach to understanding an agreement is entirely appropriate. Of course it might be

[30] Consider, eg, the issue of when prior negotiations are admissible in evidence to assist with contract interpretation: *Chartbrook v Persimmon*, above n 1.

[31] See J Wightman, 'Contract in a Pre-Realist World: Professor Macaulay, Lord Hoffmann and the Rise of Context in the English Law of Contract' in J Braucher, J Kidwell and WC Whitford (eds), *Revisiting the Contracts Scholarship of Stewart Macaulay* (Oxford, Hart Publishing, 2013) 377, 398.

argued that the role of the law is not to comprehend, act upon or enforce all the elements of an agreement, but to resolve disputes according to the pre-announced rules. But since in contract law this usually requires a detailed investigation of the obligations undertaken, the agreement background and history, and social and industry contexts, may all provide information that is material to this enquiry.

Undoubtedly in some contracting contexts the documents will be important as the source of legal obligations, but in a relational approach it is also important to appreciate the range of motives and constraints that prompt detailed planning beyond purely attending to 'the legal'. While the law's undoubted preference for dealing with documents and for associating the contract with the text provides a powerful incentive for the parties to formalise their agreement, undoubtedly some parties would still undertake costly formalisation even if the law did not attach such significance to documents. It is clear that documents, whether they record watertight legal obligations or more flexible understandings, perform important functions even in broadly co-operative business relationships, although differing commercial contexts will alter how the written documents are perceived and understood, and thus the weight that should be placed on them in dispute resolution. Evidence from business organisations and management research shows the use of written contracts is fairly widespread, although they are used for a range of purposes beyond their potential legal significance. It is clear then that in many commercial relationships the documents perform a diffuse, and not always compatible, set of functions beyond being a record of what was agreed to satisfy legal formalities and that will only be referred to when a dispute breaks out. Roxenhall and Ghauri make an assessment of when formal contracts will be used in long-term business relationships. They identify three main reasons: for transmitting information (a communication tool) both within and between firms; to reduce uncertainty and increase certainty; and custom and symbolism.[32] Contractual documents and terms and conditions may serve important 'constitutional' and internal organisational objectives, such as controlling employees and managing the consequences of staff turnover, record keeping, accountability and planning as well as recording legal terms and obligations.[33] Evidently these functions will be useful even in long-term relationships where parties are confident that they can rely on trust and co-operation to manage most of their day-to-day affairs. Documents and formalisation may be important in a co-operative and trusting relationship, just as flexibility may be important in a discrete one. Given these multiple functions of contracts, Suchman argues

[32] T Roxenhall and P Ghauri, 'Use of the Written Contract in Long-Lasting Business Relationships' (2004) 33 *Industrial Marketing Management* 261, 267.

[33] P Vincent-Jones, 'Contractual Governance: Institutional and Organizational Analysis' (2000) 20 *OJLS* 317, 327–28.

persuasively that written contractual documents are themselves worthy of study as cultural and social artefacts, quite apart from whether contract is understood as either a relation or a doctrine: 'to capture their social relevance only a more interpretive approach will do'.[34] Suchman also remarks on the 'sometimes sizeable differences between describing a governance mechanism on paper and implementing a governance structure in practice ... At best contracts serve as blueprints and programs, not as actual governance mechanisms'.[35] The suggestion, therefore, is that courts should be mindful of the range of functions served by contractual documents during the course of an exchange relationship. In sum, contract documents may be drafted for a variety of purposes and for a variety of effects. For Suchman, contracts are, in effect, 'scripts' which provide 'reference points for stage managing complex multiplayer productions'.[36] They delineate the different 'roles' played by the parties and stipulate in advance the organisation of 'likely scenes'. The role of the documents is itself part of a contextual enquiry.

This expansive role for planning and documents does give rise to a difficulty for relational contract theory however. Macneil writes that 'Even meticulous performance of the most explicit planning transforms figments of the imagination, however precise, into a new, and therefore different, reality. A set of blueprints and specifications, however detailed, and a newly built house are simply not the same thing'.[37] Thus for relational theory, documents cannot capture important aspects of a contractual relationship. Nevertheless, a representation of something, even 'figments of imagination', can still be important and perform some genuine role (as do the blueprints and architectural drawings for a new house), despite the fact that it is not the tangible end-product of the project. The diffuse roles that may be performed by the documents suggests that the degree of *formalisation* of a relationship is not necessarily a reliable indicator of whether a commercial agreement should be characterised as discrete or relational. However, it could be said that all this means is that a judge or adjudicator should exercise some sensitivity over the range of functions that documents fulfil and should consider carefully the reasons for comprehensive planning documents and formalisation. It should not be assumed that a relationship is 'as-if-discrete' simply because documents exist.

The conclusions from this part are that the law's excessive reliance on documents is certainly problematic for a relational perspective since these do not constitute the contract as the discrete approach to contract law would

34 M Suchman, 'The Contract as Social Artifact' (2003) 37 *Law and Society Review* 91, 100.
35 Ibid, 107.
36 Ibid, 115.
37 I Macneil, 'A Primer of Contract Planning' (1975) 48 *Southern California Law Review* 627, 663.

suggest. Nevertheless, the law's continued reliance on documents need not completely preclude adoption of a relational approach. The role of express terms in moulding expectations may sometimes be significant. While the commitment to formalisation and objectivity appears as a current barrier to the development of a more relationally constituted contract law this is largely the result of how that commitment to formalisation is manifest within the law. It is not the commitment to writing per se that is the barrier, but the degree of certainty with which obligations are required to be expressed and outcomes formulated. The law is clearly right in many instances to accord significance to the documented agreement, but it should also recognise that the documents can be used for a variety of purposes beyond stipulating the legal framework, and that their capacity to record and plan for every contingency during the life of an agreement is limited. Unreflecting application of the express terms may certainly result in enforcing an agreement that is different to the one that exists in the minds of both parties. A step towards developing the right sort of attitude on the part of judges is for courts to acknowledge and render effective the parties' attempts to contract for flexible obligations and behavioural expectations to govern performance. While there is understandable scepticism over this use of documents to record expected attitudes towards performance, rather than milestones in the performance itself, judicial recognition in effecting such norms would at least mark a start in changing the requisite judicial mindset towards acceptance of the importance of flexible norms in contract performance.

THE LITIGATION PROCESS

The attempt to create a contract law more responsive to commercial norms, practices and the relational features of a contractual relationship runs up against a significant set of barriers arising from the fact that the common law rules of contract law are derived from the litigation process. The common law of contract is not the product of observations of real life contracting behaviour nor abstract theories about agreement making and performance derived from evidence of functioning commercial relationships. Criticisms that have been levelled at contract law over its lack of attention to the social norms underpinning the parties' business relationship have arguably failed sufficiently to acknowledge that the relative formality of contract law is the result of the kind of cases that reach trial rather than any lack of capacity of the law itself, or the capacity of judges to understand those different normative standards. As Macneil notes, 'contracts and contract litigation are not the same thing'.[38] Thus the law aims to design facilitative rules for

[38] I Macneil, *The Relational Theory of Contract: Selected Works of Ian Macneil*, D Campbell (ed) (London, Sweet and Maxwell, 2001) 6.

the commercial contracting community from a very small subset of litigated contract disputes, which itself forms a minute part of contracting activity.

That the common law rules of contract are derived from within a system of adversarial litigation impinges on contract law design in a number of ways, some of which may impede the development of a relational contract law. First, the type of commercial contractor that undertakes litigation, and the kinds of dispute they raise, can be reckoned to affect profoundly the rules that result. Second, the process of litigation itself may militate against accessing the more informal and social norms that have informed the conduct of the relationship and the parties' understandings about their deal. This is due to various factors: the litigation process signalling an irresolvable breakdown in a commercial relationship; that judges face significant limitations in identifying and assessing the significance of commercial norms during litigation; the lack of contract cases being litigated to trial and judgment. Third, offering dispute resolution services is a competitive business, and there is evidence that commercial contract law is regarded in some influential quarters as a product in a market, its distinctive feature being its relative degree of formality. The attraction of formality for some parties may be partly related to costs, but it may be reckoned more appropriate also for judges trained in the common law. Parties requiring a more contextual or investigative approach to their case can choose an alternative method of dispute resolution that is likely to display greater sensitivity to the relational aspects of their agreement. All these factors tend to emphasise the discrete nature of litigation process, which effectively constitutes an isolated context of its own with an accompanying set of considerations. The result is that the law's capacity for developing a relational contract law is being squeezed by various factors emanating from within the process under which most of the rules of contract law are created, applied and refined. Some of these factors are considered in greater detail below.

Litigating Parties

On the issue of what kind of contract disputes are litigated, some interesting evidence comes from the narrative parts of Hazel Genn's study of court-ordered alternative dispute resolution (ADR) in non-family civil disputes from 2002.[39] Following on from the Woolf reforms, judges are supposed to take a more active role in promoting settlement and encouraging the parties to explore ADR, but Genn recognised that this is often regarded as giving rise to conflicting priorities for the parties, their legal advisers and the law.

[39] H Genn, *Court-Based ADR Initiatives For Non-Family Civil Disputes: The Commercial Court And The Court Of Appeal* (Department for Constitutional Affairs, 2002) 60–61.

Although ADR has long been a feature of commercial contract dispute resolution, in her report Genn reproduced some comments from solicitors concerning the appropriateness of ADR in certain kinds of commercial dispute. These provide some insights into the kinds of cases that proceed to trial and judgment and from which the principles of commercial contract law spring:

> Everybody agreed it was a waste of time. It wasn't the sort of case where ADR was likely to solve things ... both fairly hard-headed people. It was a pure business dispute—not the sort of typical ADR case where there's hidden agendas and emotions coming into play. It was simply a fairly narrow point on the construction of a contract, and one side was right and one side was wrong.
>
> In a lot of cases the actual dispute matters, for instance if somebody is testing conditions of business. You get a lot of cases where people are trying to break conditions or limitation clauses, and it's those sorts of cases which we deal with day in and day out. And they can't really be settled by ADR because people are less likely to take a commercial view, despite economics, because they're arguments about conditions which would have an effect on the industry as a whole.[40]
>
> The disputes are about money, not emotional issues.[41]

Given the emphasis on encouraging ADR processes under a judge's case-management powers it might be surmised that those issues which proceed to trial and judgment are a specific type of dispute for which a formal law that ignores the relational elements of a parties' relationship might be wholly appropriate. Disputes that reach trial will almost by definition occur between adversarial and unco-operative parties. It might be expected that very few relationally constituted, or semi-relationally constituted, agreements will come before courts. In those litigated and reported cases where one party does raise an argument which juxtaposes an agreement's implicit dimensions against the certainty of formal contract provisions, then they are not likely to be successful, at least on the basis of the current law. Galanter's well-known thesis concerning the influence of litigation repeat players over 'one-shotters' also suggests a certain typology to the litigated commercial case. It will tend to be very individualised—the high-value, high risk, one-off deal that fails; a deal severely affected by unanticipated changes in circumstances; the relationship that has lost its value.[42] One of the well-known results of this is that the rules are predisposed to favour repeat litigating parties (or their legal advisers). Even as far as the profession is concerned, litigating parties may be regarded as a different species to compromising, settling and mediating parties. Given that litigation involving these sorts of parties is likely to involve a heavy strategic bias, it may

[40] Ibid, 41.
[41] Ibid, 64.
[42] Galanter, above n 12, 113–14.

not yield a close consideration of the genuine grounds for the dispute nor offer an opportunity to examine the internal norms that may have arisen during the course of the relationship. The court will investigate only the legal basis of the dispute and this can lead to a certain degree of advantage-taking among the parties if circumstances such as market movements alter the balance of advantage and risk of the deal away from that anticipated at the start. The fact that one party can often exploit an advantage that the law grants to him in opposition to what was probably intended at the time the agreement was made makes the legal distinction between legitimate pursuit of self-interest and dishonesty crucial, but difficult to determine in an adversarial setting.

Contract Law as a Product

One significant barrier to the development of a more relational commercial contract law is the view that domestic contract law is a product with a fairly limited market and that a more contextual or relational understanding of commercial expectations is neither wanted nor required by commercial contractors. Such a move may make the 'product' less attractive in the market for contract law and legal services.[43] Of course one consideration here is that the Commercial Court is itself a commercial entity, and the commercial law that it develops and applies could be regarded as a commodity. In an article appearing in the *Modern Law Review* in 1951, Lord Devlin wrote that:

> The knowledge that if a customer does not like your wares he may go elsewhere—to arbitration or to the courts of another country—is salutary ... the commercial law and commercial courts take a particular pride in attracting business and in dealing with it in a manner which is felt to be satisfactory.[44]

This is no less true today than it was 60 years ago. In part this relates back to an earlier argument provided by transaction cost economics concerning the characteristics of business people who are most likely to use contracts in managing their productive activity: impersonal market transactions involving non-asset specificity in conditions of relative certainty, where sources of likely dispute will be known in advance. The preferences of such a contractor are likely to be for speedy dispute resolution with reference to a relatively limited evidence set. To see this 'commodity' attitude at work, consider this comment by one-time Lord Chancellor, Lord Falconer,

[43] For the practitioner's view on this see A Berg, 'Thrashing Through the Undergrowth' (2006) 122 *LQR* 354; R Calnan, 'Construction of Commercial Contracts: A Practitioner's Perspective' in A Burrows and E Peel (eds), *Contract Terms*, (Oxford, OUP, 2007) 17.

[44] Lord Devlin, 'The Relation Between Commercial Law and Commercial Practice' (1951) 14 *MLR* 249, 250.

commenting on the possibility of increased EU harmonisation of contract law:

> [T]he English law of contract is the international law of choice over a wide range of areas, particularly in finance, shipping, and insurance. It contributes significantly to the earnings of the UK and thereby promotes the prosperity of the EU ... You could say, that the English common law of contract is now a worldwide commodity. It has become so because it is a system that people like. It provides predictability of outcome, legal certainty, and fairness. It is clear and built upon well-founded principles, such as the ability to require exact performance and the absence of any general duty of good faith ... This has made the common law without rival as the law of choice in commercial transactions. It is important for the UK, and important for the EU that it remains so.[45]

Leaving aside the question of whether English law does display 'predictability of outcome, legal certainty and fairness' it is clear that this view of English contract law (and commercial law generally) as a commodity exerts considerable influence over the courts. Forum selection and dispute resolution processes are a competitive business and there are many options available for the commercial contractor, particularly in the field of international commercial contracts. Commercial parties can readily opt into specific national and public rules of contract law and dispute resolution schemes that are perceived to best serve their interests, or other private systems of dispute resolution, whether provided intra-industry or by more general specialist organisations. Given this, it might be expected that litigation according to English contract law reflects a particular choice of the contracting parties who have certain expectations of how this litigation will be conducted, that 'it's not about doing justice and social duty and all that sort of thing. It's providing a service to the international market'.[46]

That litigation of a dispute reflects a choice of the parties (or more likely the stronger party) may be a driver in the design of contract law rules, since such parties are always likely to be sensitive to costs, which suggests a preference for speedy and cheap dispute resolution processes. This is turn may lead to a preference for formalism and pragmatic considerations taking precedence over principled ones. Thus English contract law is a distinctive commercial product that appeals to a certain class of contractor and so fills a gap in the market for law and legal services. In these respects there

[45] Lord Falconer, Opening speech for the European Contract Law Conference, 26 September 2005: www.ec.europa.eu/consumers/cons_int/safe_shop/fair_bus_pract/cont_law/conference092005/falconer2005.pdf (30 March 2013).

[46] Genn, above n 39, 65. The *Judiciary of England and Wales: Report and Recommendations of the Commercial Court Long Trials Working Party* commented that 50% of Commercial Court cases have parties all of whom are from outside the UK. 80% have at least one party from outside the UK: (Dec 2007), 15, fn 4. See also Lord Justice Jackson, *Review of Civil Litigation Costs: Preliminary Report Vol One* (London, TSO, 2009), chapter 10, paras 7.2, 7.3, 104.

may be a degree of satisfaction with the system as it exists.[47] This is not to suggest that the commodity approach has not escaped criticism. Lord Neuberger has criticised the idea that civil justice is a product in a market that is designed to appeal to a certain class of consumer.[48] Such concerns would focus on pragmatic and policy concerns of price and lowering costs at the expense of the development of legal principle.[49] Just such a concern was illustrated recently by Lord Hoffmann in the House of Lords case of *Chartbrook v Persimmon*, where policy considerations concerning the cost of litigation, and the certainty and predictability of the law, appeared more important than considering relevant evidence of what the parties objectively intended by their agreement.[50]

The product-like nature of the values ascribed to the operation of the Commercial Court, and commercial contract law generally, together with the character of litigators, all speak to a burgeoning process of commodification of contract law. Partly this can be regarded as a product of the importance of choice among the contracting parties, and the competition for clients among the profession. Arbitration systems (not to mention the arbitrators themselves) are also a product seeking a share of a competitive market.[51] Dingwall and Cloatre remark that the state is withdrawing in relation to English civil justice and is leaving civil justice to the market.[52] In such a system the courts may seek to achieve a difficult balance between developing the law according to principle and resolving the dispute as quickly and efficiently as possible to ensure English contract law retains some attractiveness in the market. The development of the law as a social and public good is relegated to just one of a number of competing considerations.

A common argument is that parties seeking a more relational approach to the breakdown of their agreement should choose an alternative dispute

[47] Thus the Jackson *Review of Civil Litigation Costs* found that, in relation to major commercial cases, the GC 100 Group (comprising the general counsel and company secretaries of FTSE 100 companies) 'believe that they receive good service from the courts. Court fees are modest. The UK is a good jurisdiction in which to litigate and the courts produce rational decisions ... This compares favourably with the experience of litigation in other jurisdictions': *Preliminary Report Vol One* ch 10, para 2.6, 100. See also Lord Justice Jackson, *Review of Civil Litigation Costs: Final Report* (London, TSO, 2009) ch 27, para 1.6, 274.

[48] Lord Neuberger, 'Has Mediation Had Its Day?' Gordon Slynn Memorial Lecture, 10 November 2010.

[49] Similar concerns were recently expressed by the New South Wales Court of Appeal in *Gordian Runoff Limited v Westport Insurance Corporation* [2010] NSWCA 57, 216.

[50] *Chartbrook Ltd v Persimmon Homes Ltd*, above n 1.

[51] See CR Drahozal, 'Contracting Out of National Law: An Empirical Look at the New Law Merchant' (2005) 80 *Notre Dame Law Review* 523, 549–51 (suggesting the number of commercial contractors contracting into arbitration schemes is quite low and prospective arbitrators 'talk up' the importance of arbitration to generate business).

[52] R Dingwall and E Cloatre, 'Vanishing Trials?: An English Perspective' (2006) *Journal of Dispute Resolution* 51, 70.

resolution method. But the push towards methods of alternative dispute resolution and mediation in particular, while conducive to settling individual disputes where it is important to preserve the operation of relational norms or where other significant relational features are apparent, is not conducive to developing a relational contract law. Genn points out that mediation is concerned with problem solving rather than upholding legal entitlements.[53] ADR has also been the subject of more general criticisms concerning its contribution to the stagnation of the law and unequal access to justice.[54] Genn has criticised the 'downgrading of the importance of civil justice ... and the diversion of civil cases to private dispute resolution, accompanied by an anti-litigation/anti-adjudication rhetoric that interprets these developments as socially positive'.[55] ADR processes do not yield any direct legal precedents (determinations may be binding between the parties, but they are not sources of law), and cannot be assessed for their contribution to the development of the law.[56] If anything, the encouragement of ADR processes may have the reverse effect of ensuring that the filtering nature of the litigation process undergoes even further refinement, such that it is only the most intractable of disputes between well-resourced parties that will reach the higher appeal courts. It might be doubted how far such cases are capable of heralding the development of a more relationally informed contract law.

The problem of an insufficient number of litigated cases is also apparent from a cursory glance at judicial statistics concerning trials. Although the precise figures fluctuate from year to year the general pattern post-Woolf reforms is one of decline.[57] In the Commercial Court approximately 70 per cent of all cases settle before the start of a trial.[58] The House of Lords and Supreme Court hear at most two to three contract cases a year.[59] For some relational theorists, a push towards settlement is the hallmark of the relational approach to contract dispute resolution. A substantially relational agreement ending up in court is an instance of failure. But, as with the development of ADR, the opposing argument is that the relative paucity of cases reaching trial and judgment, especially at the appeal level,

[53] H Genn, *Judging Civil Justice* (Cambridge, CUP, 2010) 116.

[54] Lord Neuberger, above n 48, para 8. C Knapp, 'Taking Contracts Private: The Quiet Revolution in Contract Law' (2002) 71 *Fordham Law Review* 761, 765.

[55] Genn, above n 53, 4 and 16ff.

[56] See L Mulcahy, 'The Collective Interest in Private Dispute Resolution' (2013) 33 *OJLS* 59, 60.

[57] See P Vincent-Jones, 'Contract Litigation in England and Wales 1975–1991: A Transformation in Business Disputing?' (1993) 12 *Civil Justice Quarterly* 337. Vincent-Jones noted that peaks in trial figures followed periods of economic recession.

[58] *Report and Recommendations of the Commercial Court Long Trials Working Party*, above n 46, para 25.

[59] Ministry of Justice, *Judicial and Court Statistics* (2011), ch 7, table 7.5: www.justice.gov.uk/statistics/courts-and-sentencing/judicial-annual-2011.

may raise concerns about the capacity of the law to respond to commercial concerns. As Genn writes, 'While the reality is that most cases settle, a flow of adjudicated cases is necessary to provide guidance on the law and, most importantly, to create the credible threat of litigation if settlement is not achieved'.[60] Without litigated cases, there is little opportunity to develop the law except by statute. Legislative intervention in the matters under discussion here is highly unlikely.

Litigation as a Self-contained Context

Scepticism about the relevance of implicit dimensions or commercial norms and expectations might result from the idea that a relatively closed and formal contract law already meets the needs of the *litigating* business community and this community (including lawyers) has no particular interest or desire to expose the legal machinery, on a regular enough basis, to the common problems that they face in making and performing agreements on a day-to-day basis. Given this lack of exposure, the law has limited opportunity to fashion legal tools to assist commercial contractors. This is compounded by the fact that litigation is a rarefied field of commercial activity and very often a specialised area within a law firm. The lawyers who may have been involved in planning the deal are not likely to be involved in litigating it if things go wrong, since that will be down to a separate department in the legal firm (possibly even a different firm). The conduct of the litigation is itself an independent project, bringing to bear a different set of personnel, with their own motivations, priorities, fields of expertise, limitations of role and so on, which are quite different to those anticipated by performance of the agreement. It involves a specific set of procedures, which constitutes a wholly new context and set of constraints. This new project, if complex, can easily escape the control of the commercial client in favour of in-house legal departments or independent lawyers.[61] In this way one can regard the litigation process, and the rules that result, as dealing with a specific, newly constructed entity, which bears little or no relation to the actual reality of planning and performance in which the parties were situated. Given that the process involves the input of lawyers and other third parties, the reliance placed on documentary evidence, rather than first-hand witness testimony, is likely to be significant, creating even greater disconnection between the dispute resolution procedures and the parties' experiences of the business relationship.

60 Genn, above n 53, 21.

61 *Report and Recommendations of the Commercial Court Long Trials Working Party*, above n 46, para 160, 57.

This dissonance is not just due to the litigation process however. It results also from the fact that litigation, particularly when pursued through to trial and judgment, often signals the end of the business relationship. Once the parties embark on litigation there is little a court can do to resurrect and apply relational norms: 'the contractual relationship ... has become simply a tool for securing or avoiding damages'.[62] The parties may not want commercial expectations to be taken into account at this stage and may prefer that the case is dealt with according to the norms of formal contract law and the formal terms as documented in the contract, where available. The application of classical contract law may appear to be entirely appropriate for resolving the dispute. This feature of contract law has led other scholars, even those otherwise sympathetic to the socio-legal project, to reconsider the role of law in the business relationship. Hugh Collins in *Regulating Contracts* hypothesises that

> litigation over contractual disputes should appear before the ordinary courts when either the transaction was discrete, that is, not embedded in any past or expected future dealings between the parties, or the plaintiff perceives that the business relations cannot be resuscitated. These instances should be rather unusual in an economy if our arguments about the importance of trust and long-term business relations in constituting markets are correct.[63]

Litigation, while thankfully rare, is an indicator of 'economic disintegration'[64] or when 'the business relation is perceived to have no future'.[65] Similarly, and when considering the relevance of her empirical findings for contract law, Lisa Bernstein drew upon the interrelationship of different types of norm operating at different points in a trading relationship. During the currency of a relationship the parties will be flexible and conciliatory in an attempt to keep the commercial relationship functioning effectively. The parties will employ relationship-preserving norms to this end. Once the relationship breaks down, or enters the 'endgame' stage (usually signalled by litigation), the parties may be more willing to insist upon their legal rights and go to court to solve disputes. During the 'endgame' maintaining a good relationship is no longer a priority.[66] This adds another layer to the normative complexity of contracts. Relational or implicit norms may not only govern aspects of the relationship, but also generate understandings concerning the interplay between formal and relational contract norms themselves, and the conditions under which appeals to one or other sort

[62] I Macneil, above n 37, 692.

[63] Collins, *Regulating Contracts* (Oxford, OUP, 1999) 326.

[64] Ibid, 322.

[65] Ibid, 324. Macneil, above n 37, 692.

[66] L Bernstein, 'Merchant Law in a Merchant Court: Rethinking the Code's Search for Immanent Business Norms' (1996) 144 *University of Pennsylvania Law Review* 1765, 1796ff.

of standard are appropriate.[67] As far as a court is concerned then, there may be little point in undertaking detailed enquiries into the context and background of the parties' relationship and deciding the case according to the flexible norms that the parties themselves may have used during the currency of their relationship. Recourse to courts of law is often interpreted as evidence of firms taking a hardnosed attitude towards suppliers, not a flexible, co-operative and conciliatory approach.[68]

These points concerning the influence exerted by the litigation process are salient. The process acts as a filtering and transforming device ensuring that only particular problems from certain kinds of parties are heard and judgment delivered upon them.[69] In the litigated dispute it may be difficult to discern both the role played by expectations and informal norms in the business relationship and their relevance, particularly when the existence and significance of these norms is disputed by the parties or where the norms appear inconsistent with a set of formal contractual documents. Even if the law is presented with evidence of extra-contractual norms, expectations and dimensions, litigation may present limited opportunities for contract law to change the approach it takes to commercial disputes through the trial process. At the stage of litigation, the parties are likely to be using the formal contract and contract law in order to achieve some end, such as forcing renegotiations of terms, or seeking to escape from what has become an unprofitable bargain. Similarly the features of litigation will encourage the parties and their lawyers to present their dispute and arguments in certain ways (for example, as an issue about implied terms, or interpretation of the formal documents) which may be quite remote from the actual source of the original dispute. Thus the law may remain insufficiently exposed to the everyday problems faced by business people and it remains stuck in a relatively formalistic cycle of seemingly limited relevance to co-operative commercial relationships. It is therefore unsurprising that it finds broadly co-operative relationships difficult to accommodate with the tools and processes available to it.

In response to the above, one could point out that while the litigation process is bound to influence the rules that result, this does not alter the fact that contract law is the *generally applicable law* on contractual agreements. To regard it as a product with a limited market comprising of a certain species

[67] J Wightman, 'Beyond Custom: Contract, Contexts, and the Recognition of Implicit Understandings' in D Campbell, H Collins and J Wightman (eds), *Implicit Dimensions of Contract* (Oxford, Hart Publishing, 2003) 143, 157.

[68] B Lyons and J Mehta, 'Private Sector Business Contracts: The Text Between the Lines' in S Deakin and J Michie (eds), *Contracts, Co-operation and Competition* (Oxford, OUP, 1997) 43, 62.

[69] 'Legal actors are not merely transposing the facts of their client's problem into legal terminology but actively manipulating the situation and the rules to seek advantages': S Wheeler, *Reservation of Title Clauses* (Oxford, OUP, 1991) 2.

of commercial contractor—those with good resources, access to legal advice, involved in arm's-length transacting in an industry where litigation is regarded as the local sport and where everyone who plays knows the rules—is to take a very limited view of its reach. Litigating parties may have these features, but the law that results from the litigation process supposedly facilitates contractual dealings for the *general* commercial contracting community. This community is not a homogeneous group sharing a complete identity of interest over the design of the rules of commercial contract law. Empirical studies show this quite clearly, as do examples of cases coming before courts. Law must therefore be capable of regulating and facilitating all manner of commercial agreements, not limited to any specific type nor limited to the range of problems presented by litigation repeat-players. To the extent that relationalism does not pursue a single value, but allows for a multitude of considerations in the determination of the dispute and the development of the law, it would appear to be the superior strategy for dealing with the variety of problems presented to courts by commercial contractors. In any case it might be doubted that commercial contracting parties require only a dispute resolution process that is quick and cheap. Some parties may be motivated by such concerns, but not all will.

While the factors explored above raise doubts concerning the capacity for contract law to consider the wider contractual context and apply relational norms to resolve the dispute, it could be argued that the fact that the parties are now in dispute about what the provisions of the contract mean should not blind the court to the possibility that at one point they may well have been in agreement, and that this agreement continued up to and beyond entering into the formal contract. To suggest otherwise puts the 'dispute resolution' function of the courts above the 'standard setting' function and makes the development of a coherent contract law, based on the value of upholding the intentions of the parties, appear of minimal concern.[70] The internal norms and implicit dimensions of the business relationship will still be relevant to dispute resolution. The point about the implicit dimensions/relational critique is to bring to the fore that the parties' expectations about their relationship, agreement and obligations are not wholly derived from the statement of express terms. Insofar as those norms and expectations feed into the parties' understandings about their obligations, then this must be relevant to determining their legal entitlements. Determining these entitlements is usually the object of litigating. It is therefore appropriate to resolve the dispute with due reference to these norms as they appear relevant, not least for the development of the law. Nevertheless, it cannot

[70] See discussion in D McLauchlan, 'Contract Interpretation: What is it About?' (2009) 31 *Sydney Law Review* 5, 25–29.

be doubted that the litigation process may prevent the easy reception and consideration of these norms into legal reasoning processes.

TRANSFORMATION AND LEGALISATION OF NORMS

To the extent to which a relational approach to legal reasoning involves recognition that norms of behaviour and expectations may be generated internally between the parties, one problem is that the law cannot readily assimilate and apply these norms. One way to deal with this problem is to ignore such norms altogether. Another strategy is to transform and adapt the norms in order to make them more easily absorbed within the legal framework and its recognised forms. The difficulty here is that norms of behaviour that carry certain meanings or are indicative of certain attitudes in one context are taken and applied in an alternative context where they may be given a different, possibly erroneous, interpretation in the process of reaching legal conclusions. Where this occurs the law has not truly incorporated these norms into its own discourse and manner of reasoning, but has adapted them in order to fit with the legal conditions of relevance and significance, altering their character as relational norms in the process. In a contract context, this occurs quite often when some element of the parties' conduct during the business relationship or performance is interpreted to yield conclusions concerning legal rights and obligations which may not have been intended.

Hugh Collins has considered this particular problem. He urges contract law to develop techniques of 'hybrid reasoning' which incorporate the normative standards generated by other frameworks of the parties' relationship, specifically the long-term business relation and the economic deal, rather than exclusive reliance on the formal documented agreement. He criticises courts' investigations of the economic and other motivations behind adopting a particular contract structures (such as penalty clauses or limitations of liability) as superficial. In Collins's view the legal analysis should proceed in the manner of institutional economists and courts should undertake a more thorough enquiry of the 'efficiency considerations that led to the creation of [the] particular contractual structure'.[71] Collins recognises that while its tendency towards isolation, 'self-reference' and 'closure' causes law to overlook, or regard as irrelevant, material that is relevant to understanding the contract, it also distorts the insights that law does take on board from other parts of the business relationship.[72] Collins is alert to the argument that judging efficiency considerations might be beyond the capacity of legal

[71] Collins, above n 63, 272.
[72] Ibid, 54.

institutions, or else will compromise their legitimacy.[73] He concedes that judges may make mistakes in attempting to analyse the optimality or otherwise of the deal, and that techniques such as economic analysis will be distorted and corrupted when filtered through legal reasoning. Problems of norm dislocation would be stark if the courts require commercial practices and behaviours to achieve some coherent fit with the existing legal context. Such behaviour as did not achieve this fit may be ignored or misinterpreted. The legal tendency to remould the facts, actions, motivations and disputes of the parties into legally ordered categories can have the effect of obscuring the real source of the dispute, and treating as irrelevant any behaviour between the parties that cannot be explained in legal terms.

This transformation from the social to the legal is never straightforward, but involves a degree of manipulation and strategic promotion (or undermining) of the agreement. A good illustration is the decision in *Total Gas Marketing v Arco British*.[74] The decision involved a gas supply agreement. The dispute between the parties was cast in classical legal terms concerning Total's right to terminate the agreement for failure to fulfil a condition precedent, namely that the seller, Arco, was to enter into a second contract—an allocation agreement—by the agreed first delivery date for the gas. The speeches in the House of Lords are given over to the facts of the case and a close analysis of the contract terms. Very little attention is given in the judgments to the reasons for seeking the termination, the motivations for including the contentious term, or the relevant conventions concerning 'the first delivery date' that operated in the industry. Litigation then has the effect of recontextualising the dispute within the specific framework of the law and court proceedings. Within this framework, the parties' understandings as derived from the contract context are a secondary consideration next to the correct classification of the term and consideration of its legal ramifications. The wider operation of the term within the parties' relationship or context of the agreement is not explored. The term is treated as an abstracted entity whose meaning is entirely legally derived. Of course, it could be that it is also an understanding in the industry, shared by the participants in the agreement, that Total is fully able (independently of its legal right to do so) to terminate the agreement and seek to renegotiate the terms. It is possible that a breakdown in those negotiations led to the litigation, but this is not deemed relevant nor addressed by the court. The court assumes, perhaps entirely correctly, that sophisticated commercial parties intend to use terms in their technical legal sense, and act with complete awareness when they do so. But bearing in mind other elements of the contract, such as that this was anticipated to be a 14-year deal in a volatile market and

[73] Ibid, 271–74.

[74] *Total Gas Marketing v Arco British* [1998] 2 Lloyd's Rep 209. The case is discussed more fully in Ch 8.

that the contract involved substantial investment by Arco necessitating protection by a long-term supply agreement, such a straightforward conclusion over termination rights appears simplistic.[75]

Given all these constraints and difficulties it is clear why the ideas and insights of relational theory and the implicit dimensions of agreement have not really taken hold in the practice of contract law. Does this mean relational-sympathetic scholars should be pessimistic about the law's capacity to take on board relational insights? Not necessarily. There are two reasons for this. First, since the initial step in any reform is to recognise that a problem exists, a relational approach not only renders more visible the fact that there are different normative systems at work in contractual relationships, it also fully appreciates the problems of normative dislocation to which the reception of such norms into law gives rise. In some respects, as with other areas of the relational project, if there is even some halting recognition that relational norms exist then there is potential for a change in judicial attitudes, however slowly this might advance. While there are clearly difficulties here, imposed by the structural constraints of the process of litigation, the need to keep costs down and the concerns of practitioners, even the most cursory examination of cases that do reach trial and judgment demonstrate some engagement by judges with relational norms, at least in the guise of 'matrix of fact', background or context. It is true that complaints on increased costs have been made, but this may be overstated in some respects.[76]

Second, problems like those of transformation and legalisation occur in part because of the way in which the frameworks for understanding the exchange are sharply differentiated, and the very closure of the legal system to which Collins refers. This of itself may lead to inconsistency between the various frameworks. As has been argued already, many of the supposed limitations of the law are premised on the basis that the legal regulation of contracts will remain fundamentally unaltered even with an appreciation of the relational elements of an agreement, and that relational reasoning merely operates as an addition to existing contract doctrine, leaving the doctrine largely intact. The issue here is one of cause and effect. It is probably the case that the factors explored in this section and the previous one are largely self-reinforcing. In other words, the institution of contract law, including its rules, procedures and institutions, encourages certain

[75] See especially the doubts expressed by Lord Hope in the case at 223. For support for the decision see B Davenport, 'Thanks to the House of Lords' (1999) 115 *LQR* 11.

[76] JE Bayley, 'Prior Negotiations and Subsequent Conduct in Contract Interpretation: Principles and Practical Concerns' (2011–12) 28 *Journal of Contract Law* 179. Bayley argues that the exclusionary rules appear to have little effect on lawyers' advice or disclosure: 185. Neither do they appear to have an effect on litigation (since prior negotiations are considered in a claim for rectification) thus the costs ground appears neutral, both in relation to the costs of giving advice and litigation costs, ibid, 186.

contracting parties displaying certain characteristics (chiefly reliance on lawyers) to litigate certain limited forms of contract dispute, which reinforces the existing rule structures. Thus these litigation 'barriers' may be unconnected to any intrinsic and immutable values of contract law, but reflect instead a path dependency that emanates from both lawyers and the law. If so, it may be that this could be expected to break down (or at least law could be set on a different path) if the approach of the law changes to adopt a more relational method. A relational approach, in taking a holistic view of the exchange relationship, may therefore render this differentiation between the different frameworks for analysis less sharp, giving rise to the potential to interpret relational behaviour in ways that achieve a measure of consistency between the different frameworks. Of course, this may be to harbour too much ambition for relational theory. Nevertheless, a relational approach may not render all these considerations reconcilable, but it will at least bring them to the fore, where the difficulties they pose can be confronted directly.

JUDICIAL EXPERTISE AND ERROR

A common strand of criticism of the greater incorporation of commercial norms questions the capacity of judges to identify, understand and act upon the norms generated by the business relationship, resulting in an increased likelihood of errors. Sunstein writes:

> In the law of contract, an error can be defined as an outcome different from what the parties would have chosen if they had made explicit provision on the point ... Courts that do not care about what the parties would have done, and that look instead to the objective meaning of contractual terms, should be taken to be saying that this method of interpretation is most likely to minimize decision costs and error costs.[77]

Error, then, might be found in producing outcomes at the litigation stage which the parties would not have agreed to if they had been asked at the formation stage. This might occur if the courts enforced some extra-contractual statement the parties did not want enforced, or interpreted the contract in a way that was counter to the parties' intentions.[78] This problem

[77] C Sunstein, 'Must Formalism be Defended Empirically?' (1999) 66 *University of Chicago Law Review* 636, 648. See also EA Posner, 'The Parol Evidence Rule, the Plain Meaning Rule and the Principles of Contractual Interpretation' (1998) 146 *University of Pennsylvania Law Review* 533, 542–43; EA Posner, 'A Theory of Contract Law under Conditions of Radical Judicial Error' (2000) 94 *Northwestern University Law Review* 749; A Schwartz and RE Scott, 'Contract Theory and the Limits of Contract Law' (2003) 113 *Yale Law Journal* 541, 587.

[78] J Kraus and S Walt, 'In Defense of The Incorporation Strategy' in J Kraus and S Walt (eds), *The Jurisprudential Foundations of Corporate and Commercial Law* (Cambridge, CUP, 2000) 193, 193.

about judicial incapacity and error is closely related to the above points concerning the processes by which these conflicts about norms come before the courts and through which the rules are derived. It has been noted that John Gava and Janey Greene have expressed doubts that judges working within the common law tradition, given their background, training and the limitations of their role, can comprehend and apply relational norms error-free.[79] Similarly it is doubted that generalist judges have the professional expertise to replicate the kind of decision-making process one might find in specialist arbitration.[80]

Whether formalist or non-formalist judges will produce more errors depends on empirical evidence. Some care needs to be taken with the points about error, since the reality is that a court may have to make a decision on matters that the parties had not considered and over which they had no intentions. This makes it difficult to assess whether an error has in fact occurred. Nevertheless, there are some general points to be made. The contextual approach arguably increases the chances for error by increasing the amount of information deemed relevant to the interpretation exercise. Judges may have to deal with a significant amount of contextual material, some of it connected to particular frameworks of analysis whose conventions will be unfamiliar to them. They may easily become 'bewildered by a large set of conflicting evidence'.[81] In the competition law case of *Crehan v Inntrepreneur Pub Company*, for example, expert evidence of context was provided by economists, accountants, valuers, surveyors and investment analysts.[82] It must be acknowledged that the courts could err in dealing with this sort of evidence.[83] There is no guarantee that contextualism will produce error-free decision making. Of course the reverse is also true, and formalism will produce errors, but it has been argued that this kind of error may be easier for the parties to predict and take steps to avoid, particularly if they know the interpretation rules the courts will generally apply.[84]

The argument about error is related to the particular characteristics of law and, in particular, private law reasoning. The distinctive concepts of 'institutional setting' and 'mode of reasoning' of private law[85] undoubtedly give rise to limitations in judging the context of commercial contractual agreements, particularly where that context is informed by distinctly non-legal

[79] Gava and Greene, above n 8. See also JD Heydon, 'How the Courts Develop Commercial Law by Looking Outside the Trial Record into the External World' [2012] *LMCLQ* 30, 57.

[80] D Charny, above n 22, 848.

[81] A Vermeule, 'Three Strategies of Interpretation' (2005) 42 *San Diego Law Review* 607, 614.

[82] *Crehan v Inntrepreneur Pub Company* [2004] EWCA 637, [53].

[83] Posner, 'A Theory of Contract Law under Conditions of Radical Judicial Error', above n 77, 753; Gava and Greene, above n 8, 616–20.

[84] Posner, 'A Theory of Contract Law under Conditions of Radical Judicial Error', above n 77, 752; Bernstein, above n 66, 1790, 1795; Sunstein, above n 77, 647.

[85] Weinrib, above n 6, 4–5.

subject matter, such as economics.[86] A court's conclusions on the social context of a commercial agreement may be impressionistic at best, despite hearing testimony of witnesses and experts. One reason for drafting comprehensive documents is to provide a more reliable source of evidence than witnesses, who are more likely to give evidence of their states of mind and subjective intent, along with the 'context'. There is also the danger that witness evidence is self-serving and unreliable. Some judges are clearly ambivalent about the usefulness of witness evidence, preferring to rely on the documents.[87] Reliance on documents simplifies the interpretative task since the court is better able to place itself in the position of a reasonable recipient of the document than it is of a participant in oral negotiations and so on. Such discussions are difficult to accurately recall *ex post* within a very different context (the dispute) to that in which they were made.

With regard to these problems about judicial incapacity and error, various responses can be made. One is to say that the law does, however imperfectly, incorporate elements of 'commercial expectation' either directly or indirectly into agreements, and in this sense judges are already engaging with relational aspects of commercial agreements. The conclusions generally reached by judges in commercial disputes are not reached or justified independently by them but will have been *argued for* by one of the parties in circumstances where the parties have failed to resolve the dispute themselves. In a simplistic way it could be said that the outcome of this process is likely to accord with the expectations of at least one of the parties. Any kind of legal reasoning process is likely to produce errors. A non-contextualised formalism will not operate error-free, and may indeed be more likely to produce errors, since this kind of formalism will exclude relevant information that might allow a court to avoid an erroneous result. As Charny writes:

> Of course, it is possible that the courts are so likely to 'get it wrong', and at elaborate expense, that the parties would prefer a highly formalistic system, but it is equally possible that the parties would prefer an occasionally erroneous effort to apply their norms over legal rules that made no attempt at all to make sense of their commercial practice.[88]

In addition, what counts as a 'judicial error' depends entirely on the legal reasoning approach your system demands and your criteria for a 'correct decision'. Is the criterion for correctness some higher normative principle, or

[86] Gava and Greene, above n 8, 609, on the distinction between economics, sociology and law as academic disciplines. For judicial appreciation of the limitations of judges in this respect, see comments of Peter Gibson LJ in *Crehan v Inntrepreneur*, above n 82, [76].

[87] See *Emcor, Drake & Scull v McAlpine* [2004] EWCA Civ 1733, [6].

[88] D Charny, 'Illusions of Spontaneous Order: "Norms" in Contractual Relationships' (1996) 144 *University of Pennsylvania Law Review* 1841, 1855. Contra see F Schauer, *Playing by the Rules* (Oxford, OUP, 1991) 214.

the single right answer that could be discerned from the previous precedents by the ideal judge, or one of a range of answers that could be derived from those legal materials by a skilful judge, or one that accords with the intentions of the parties, or that captures the broad consensus of the commercial contracting community? In contract a right answer might be taken to be one that accords with the common intentions of the parties when they made their agreement. In *Chartbrook v Persimmon*,[89] for example, the application of formal norms of interpretation would almost certainly have led to the wrong interpretation being placed on the contract, assuming here that the correct interpretation is that intended by the parties, clearly and objectively discernible from all the other evidence. But even here it is not clear whether 'correctness' in contract is a function of the application of the relevant formal rules, or an independent criterion such as upholding the agreement the parties intended even if this differs from the formal statement. The more contextual evidence that is heard, the more reliable the court's determination is likely to be concerning what was intended and what the parties agreed. It is possible that a greater expertise among the judiciary could emerge by confining them to commercial cases only. Use of specialist judges and a docketing system would also have benefits in allowing consolidation and development of commercial expertise. Thus in the Mercantile Courts the same judge will manage a case during its life and will conduct the trial if there is no settlement.[90] The Litigators' Forum recommended docketing as an answer to issues about judicial expertise, so an increasingly specialised judiciary could emerge.[91] Judges, however, were reluctant, favouring the variety of experience gained by going on circuit.[92]

The concern about judicial error therefore appears overstated. A single judge rarely gives the last word on the operation of a rule or principle, and judgments are subject to overrulings, questioning, revision and confinement by later courts.[93] To be sure, this may not be a quick process, but the advantage of the common law is that a skilful judge is very often able to depart from a precedent whose application may be thought to lead to an unwelcome result, however this is determined. Error is often determined on efficiency grounds. A particular outcome or ruling may be judged inefficient

[89] See above n 1.

[90] See Lord Justice Jackson, *Final Report*, above n 47, para 3.1, 260.

[91] Lord Justice Jackson, *Preliminary Report Vol One*, above n 46, ch 10, para 11.11, 118. See also *Final Report,* ibid, chapter 27, para 2.15–2.17, 279, and ch 39, para 4.1ff, 391. Some practitioners regard the requirement to go on circuit as a disincentive to apply to the High Court Bench: *Final Report*, above n 47, ch 27, para 2.17, 279. See also *Report and Recommendations of the Commercial Court Long Trials Working Party*, above n 46, paras 165–66, 59.

[92] *Report and Recommendations of the Commercial Court Long Trials Working Party*, above n 46.

[93] T Rakoff, 'The Law and Sociology of Boilerplate' in O Ben-Shahar (ed), *Boilerplate: The Foundation of Market Contracts* (Cambridge, CUP, 2007) 200, 209.

in leading to sub-optimal incentives, or other decreases in wealth or welfare, or deleterious effects on freedom of contract. But these outcomes are very difficult to judge and likely themselves to be fiercely contested. If there is little confidence that a judge following an efficiency methodology will reach the right result then this must be largely true of all methods of resolving cases that involve *judgment* rather than random allocation. There can therefore be no certainty that a judge has reached the correct decision in any case. This is so even with common law method, where a pertinent precedent may go unconsidered, be misinterpreted or be incorrectly applied. What is required from our judges is not perfection—such an expectation hardly sits well with common law method—but an improved general understanding of business behaviour and refinements to the classical model that at present appears to represent a rather poor fit with many elements of commercial dealing.

PATH DEPENDENCY AND THE CHARACTERISTICS OF LEGAL REGULATION

One conclusion that can be drawn from the issues considered above concerning who litigates and when is that 'courts try cases and hear arguments that are directly shaped by the courts' prior decisions'.[94] This is the problem of path dependency. Path dependency acknowledges the power of the status quo, and the difficulties likely to be encountered in trying to effect any significant transformation.[95] It encapsulates the idea that history exerts a strong influence over institutions, locking in patterns of behaviour and making them resistant to change.[96] Of course in relation to the common law, changing patterns of behaviour is not straightforward, since 'path dependency', or following history, is an important means of justifying and legitimising common law method. What may be interpreted by some as an unwelcome legal inertia may be a consequence of law's stability and commitment to certain moral values that have remained relatively constant over time.[97] While some may regard this as a virtue, path dependency does have the more insidious feature of obscuring the need for legal changes that may be beneficial. If courts adopt a stark anti-flexibility stance, they are much less likely to hear cases brought by parties who relied substantially on

[94] OA Hathaway, 'Path Dependence in the Law: The Course and Pattern of Legal Change in a Common Law System' (2001) 86 *Iowa Law Review* 601, 629.

[95] Ibid. Lord Hoffmann in *Chartbrook Ltd v Persimmon Homes Ltd* is also an example of this. Whatever the benefits of abolishing the exclusionary rule and however incoherent the rule has become, it has one very powerful argument in its favour—it represents the status quo.

[96] R Korobkin, 'The Status Quo Bias and Contract Default Rules' (1998) 83 *Cornell Law Review* 608.

[97] Gava, above n 13, 264; Hathaway, above n 94, 640.

flexible or co-operative norms during the life of their relationship. Litigating such cases presents a big risk for the parties concerned. Following the *Baird v Marks and Spencer* decision, for example, it is likely that parties in a significantly similar situation will be deterred from attempting to persuade courts to accord legal recognition to the kind of diffuse and open-ended obligations that may be characteristic of many long-term business relationships. Parties may instead attempt to commit those obligations to paper as best they can, which may be time consuming, costly and ultimately unachievable.

A particular difficulty is that path dependency obscures the reasons why certain ways of doing things, or certain designs of rules, endure. This may lead to misunderstandings concerning the causes of stability in rules. So, rule systems may remain stable not because they are efficient but because of the influence of path dependency.[98] In efficiency terms it will almost always be more costly to change course than to continue in the same direction, but that in itself provides no argument for refusing to institute necessary change. Individuals often pursue a less beneficial course simply because they have already invested heavily in it, and for that reason they prefer it, notwithstanding the appearance of better alternatives. Path dependency can make some arguments in favour of keeping to the status quo appear more compelling, but in reality these arguments are supportive of the status quo simply because it is the status quo. An example of this argument at work in law is the predictable and familiar string of complaints, usually emanating from lawyers, when any changes to commercial contract law rules are proposed: that change will make the law uncertain, too costly and so on. This argument concerning the deleterious effects of legal change is almost always taken to be persuasive (amongst judges at any rate) despite the lack of sophistication in the reasoning and the dearth of evidence provided to substantiate the claims. Concerns about costs are usually not verified except anecdotally by judges complaining about the amount of paperwork generated in modern trials. It has been doubted that allowing prior negotiations into the process of contract interpretation will materially increase costs of providing legal advice or litigation.[99] Similarly, one only need look at the range of different and dissenting judgments on issues of interpretation to see that the certainty attributed to commercial contract law is in many respects illusory. The arguments behind these appeals then is not that the rules should be kept because they work (although they might, but the evidence for this is rarely presented), but because we are used to them and they are generally accepted. In short, the accepted ways of doing things appeal because they have become a habit, or represent a cultural preference

[98] Hathaway, above n 94, 637–38.
[99] See Bayley, above n 76.

for stability.[100] The lure of the familiar is understandably quite strong, even amongst lawyers. For example, it might be thought that creation of a statutory exception to the privity rule would be welcomed by lawyers. But it seems that use of the provisions of the Contract (Rights of Third Parties) Act 1999 to create third-party rights in contract is negligible, and while it is difficult to find reliable evidence, anecdotally it is suggested that the operation of the Act is often excluded altogether.[101] If the argument about path dependency is accepted, it suggests that the stability of the law of contract (and the practitioner preference for stability) may not necessarily be such a virtue after all.

Path dependency may pose a barrier to the development of the common law of contract, but it is one that can be overcome. While the common law is dependent upon 'initial conditions'[102] which are sought to be identified in subsequent cases before a particular rule or principle will be applied, it is not static. Although the application of the legal principles is repeated, those initial conditions are never (or at least very rarely) repeated precisely, but will present different facts and circumstances in each case. The sheer number of available precedents and the possibility of distinguishing gives rise to a certain leeway in judgments, including opportunities for creating an upset and for setting the law on a new path,[103] particularly as new social norms emerge which require new rules to be developed.[104] Cunningham recognises a tension between 'doctrinal stability' and 'social congruence', that is the harmonisation of legal rules with social norms. He attributes judicial breaks with the past to when the recognised rule is under pressure because of declining 'self-similarity' between fact situations. Legal change becomes necessary when social congruence is deemed more important than doctrinal stability.[105] Of course the process of remaking the past is frequently displayed within the common law of contract, and there are grounds for thinking that 'new social norms' are emerging (if not already emerged) in commercial contracting activity and in the legal response to it. To the extent that the law can and does respond to changes in social norms there is perhaps room for optimism about the development of a relational contract law. *Williams v Roffey*[106] provides a micro-example, where an older conception of consideration, as appearing in the precedent of *Stilk v*

[100] LA Cunningham, 'The Common Law as an Iterative Process: A Preliminary Enquiry' (2006) 81 *Notre Dame Law Review* 748, 773.

[101] H Beale, 'A Review of the Contracts (Rights of Third Parties) Act 1999' in A Burrows and E Peel (eds), *Contract Formation and Parties* (Oxford, OUP, 2010) 225. Beale describes the Act as 'underused', 250.

[102] Cunningham, above n 100, 749.

[103] See, eg, Lord Denning in *Central London Property Trust Ltd v High Trees House Ltd* [1947] KB 130.

[104] Cunningham, above n 100, 762.

[105] Ibid, 774.

[106] *Williams v Roffey* [1991] 1 QB 1.

Myrick,[107] appeared inappropriate to apply in an entirely different fact situation where other social norms pertained. An example of this occurring on a macro-scale is consumer law which, after many years of trying to incorporate developments within the common law, rendered the common law of contract unstable, and was therefore hived off into a separate sphere of regulation. This allowed the rules of commercial contract law to regain stability, and the rules of consumer law to gain stability within their own separate system.

CONCLUSION

The above suggests that English contract law does lack some capacity for becoming more relationally constituted. This is not because of any inherent limitations in the rules, but rather difficulties related to the processes by which the rules are developed. Considering the kinds of cases that reach trial and judgment it is difficult to discern how *generally* applicable facilitative rules of contract law, based on contract as a co-operative, rather than a competitive endeavour, could emerge from such a process. Those parties seeking to uphold uncertain agreements or informal understandings through litigation face an uphill struggle, with the result that many agreements characterised by high reliance on relational or informal norms are allowed to fall outwith the scope of legal regulation. This leads to a cycle of path dependency in contracting disputes and contract law. The project of trying to break this cycle faces many objections, but these only establish that teasing out the relationship between contract law and commercial expectations is complex, and that some care needs to be exercised in seeking a fuller understanding of the implications of incorporating commercial expectations into legal reasoning. They do not establish that the law need not consider how well it accords with commercial expectations, nor that such expectations and practices are simply irrelevant. This chapter raises questions concerning whether an adversarial dispute resolution process, beset by criticism relating to time and costs, can ever be a suitable forum within which to discover, let alone implement, the parties' (non-contractual) commercial expectations. It appears that the development of contract law is being squeezed on either side by incompatible considerations relating to the social constitution of agreements and the litigation and trial process. Relational norms may be regarded as belonging to a different sphere of the parties' agreement and the fact of the dispute will render such norms even more distant from the 'here and now' in which the parties find themselves. One might take the view that litigating contracting parties are a

[107] *Stilk v Myrick* (1809) 2 Camp 317; [1809] EWHC KB J58.

self-selecting group with a preference for a formal law, formally applied. A relationally constituted contract law is an irrelevance for such a group—the court should apply their agreement as written, literally interpreted, and if the conditions for legal enforceability of the agreement are not met then the agreement cannot be enforced. These kinds of arguments suggest a relational contract law is not necessary, or is even positively unhelpful to supporting contractual relationships.

Such arguments should not carry the day however. Given that the law is not charged with the role of simply upholding commercial interests or pandering to the requirements of the litigating business community, but has more general application as a facilitative institution, any perceived incapacity on the part of law to become more relationally constituted should be a cause for concern. There is, however, some scope for optimism. While the limitations and context of the litigation process provide some barriers to the development of a contract law more aligned with commercial expectations, this does at least suggest that it is litigation processes and case management that prevents development of a relationally constituted contract law, not anything internally related to the law of contract itself. Lower courts undertake often expansive enquiries into factual background, context and so on, including consideration of other norms that affect the dispute. Cases in the lower courts show how courts are constantly made aware of the relational aspects to the agreement. If the agreement as made includes these relational norms, there is little justification for leaving them out of consideration. Judges will not simply be able to forget such evidence when they have heard it. It may be that they are already familiar with the day-to-day workings of the contractual agreement, even if it has a negligible impact on case determination. There is thus considerable scope for a substantial shift to a more relationally constituted contract law. The following chapter considers further some techniques for effecting this.

8

Conclusion: Aligning Contract Law and Commercial Expectations

THERE ARE MANY potential strategies available to address the misalignment between contract law and commercial practice and expectation. Precise choice of strategy will likely be connected to what is identified as the main source of the misalignment. The broad critique emanating from within relational theory, for example, is that the classical law of contract is inadequate because it is based upon faulty foundational assumptions that render it inappropriate to most exchanges falling outside the discrete model. The inadequacy identified here may therefore be addressed by seeking to effect some change in the model of the commercial contractor and contracting process to embrace a default position of co-operation as opposed to competition, and contextualist legal reasoning as opposed to formalism.[1] Alternatively, inadequacy may be detected in the law's closure to alternative frameworks for analysing commercial exchange, for example the wider business relationship and the specific economic imperatives underlying a particular deal. Here the reform required may involve opening up the legal analysis to information derived from these alternative frameworks.[2] This may involve some very specific reforms, such as relaxing the rules that prevent the courts from examining certain kinds of evidence, such as preliminary negotiations.[3] In keeping with the traditions of contract law, Brownsword, building on earlier work distinguishing the contract ideologies of dynamic market individualism and its static counterpart,[4] has suggested that the parties must first demonstrate assent

[1] R Brownsword, 'From Co-operative Contracting to a Contract of Co-operation' in D Campbell and P Vincent-Jones (eds), *Contract and Economic Organisation* (Aldershot, Dartmouth, 1996) 14.

[2] Collins, *Regulating Contracts* (Oxford, OUP, 1999) 143–48.

[3] The rule against admission of prior negotiations was recently reasserted quite forcefully by Lord Hoffmann in *Chartbrook Ltd v Persimmon Homes Ltd* [2009] 1 AC 1101; [2009] UKHL 38.

[4] R Brownsword, *Contract Law: Themes for the Twenty-First Century*, 2nd edn (Oxford, OUP, 2006) 139ff.

to the application of particular 'transactional ground rules',[5] as well as any contract agreed under those ground rules. For Brownsword this underlying consent to the ground rules could be based on two alternative foundations: the consent of the parties or the fairness of the rules according to whatever moral criterion is fixed upon. This latter justification for enforcement is that these are the best rules whether one agrees with them or not.[6]

Insofar as a commercial-expectations approach to legal reasoning is identified with the findings of relational theory then the difficulties are apparent. Chief among the difficulties is that it may appear that the wrong questions are being asked of relational theory. Relational theory provides a set of tools to analyse exchange relationships. It provides guidance as to the norms and values that may be detectable in any contract, but it does not say where this information should lead once it is uncovered. Thus while relational theory has implications for contract law, it sets no clear reforming agenda for it. Rather, relational theory reveals new subjects and objects for the application of already existing legal tools, discernible from the wider elements of the exchange relationship. Nevertheless, it now needs to be considered along what familiar legal pathways such contextual enquiries could be conducted, and what should be done with the information revealed.

This chapter considers what legal-reasoning techniques and strategies might be available to assist in the endeavour of developing a more relationally constituted contract law. It is apparent that the broad hallmark of a commercial-expectations approach to contract legal reasoning is a form of contextualism, that is, perceiving the (legal) contractual relationship as a part of a wider social and commercial network of understandings, together with a degree of openness to the possibility that this wider context, and the norms generated by and within it, are relevant to how the contractual relationship should be understood, obligations derived and interpreted, and disputes resolved. In terms of specific legal development, context sensitivity demands less attention to the pursuit and refining of doctrine as an end in itself, and increased appreciation of the diverse ways in which commercial contractors will seek to organise their productive relationships, including the motivations and constraints that impel the parties towards particular methods and mechanisms to govern their exchange activity. This translates into the need for some flexibility in legal approaches in order to recognise and comprehend that commercial contractual relationships will not only be heterogeneous, but that within themselves they will display pluralistic techniques and tendencies. This may be perceived as weakening the hold of some deep-rooted principles of contract law, such as objectivity and commitment to the documented agreement as the main source of evidence

[5] R Brownsword, 'Network Contracts Revisited' in M Amstutz and G Teubner (eds), *Networks: Legal Issues of Multilateral Co-operation* (Oxford, Hart Publishing, 2009) 31, 34.
[6] Ibid, 34.

concerning obligations. Certainly some shift in the focus of contract law is demanded. It must be sensitive to the specific norms of behaviour that may arise between the parties (internally generated norms), or from the industries or other commercial contexts in which they find themselves (externally generated norms).[7] This is not just a matter of contract law following commercial practices, but rather making these practices effective within a legal framework. Ultimately an expectations-based contract law requires the abandonment of a one-size-fits-all model of contractual agreements in favour of a more dynamic and responsive system.

Greater alignment between contract law and commercial expectations could be effected through a method with which contract law is already very familiar—contextual interpretation. The move to contextual interpretation of contract terms requires greater attention to be paid to the factual background of the parties' agreement, including anything relevant which could have affected the meaning of the terms. This gives courts some leeway in considering a range of contextual factors in the interpretation exercise. In undertaking the interpretative task, courts have considered, amongst other things, the conventions operating in the industry or market,[8] power relations between the parties,[9] and understandings generated by previous dealings.[10] Contextual understandings of some sort are usually in play in case determination, even when courts impose a strict interpretation of the parties' contractual rights.[11] However, to truly embrace a relational approach the object of the interpretation exercise should not be the contractual documents, but the entire business relationship. This chapter considers this interpretative technique in more detail, and suggests some of the material factors concerning contractual relationships which will affect the way in which the interpretative process is carried out. The expansive nature of interpretation means it is arguably the best technique to understand and operationalise the range of considerations that compete for attention on the contextual-formal legal-reasoning continuum that exists under the umbrella of relational theory. The strategy discussed in this chapter is by no means comprehensive, but it marks an attempt to identify the broad features of the technique by which a clearer link between contract law and commercial expectations could be forged. The chapter first considers the division between formalism and contextualism in legal reasoning, and the idea that legal reasoning must commit to one of these, and why this is an unhelpful

[7] I Macneil, *The Relational Theory of Contract: Selected Works of Ian Macneil*, D Campbell (ed) (London, Sweet and Maxwell, 2001) 14–15.

[8] *Transfield Shipping Inc v Mercator Shipping Inc (The Achilleas)* [2008] UKHL 48; [2009] 1 AC 61.

[9] *St Albans City and District Council v International Computers Ltd* [1996] 4 All ER 481.

[10] *McCutcheon v David MacBrayne Ltd* [1964] 1 WLR 125.

[11] *Union Eagle Ltd v Golden Achievement Ltd* [1997] AC 514; *British Crane Hire Corp v Ipswich Plant Hire Ltd* [1975] QB 303.

way of conceptualising the debate about the misalignment between contract law and commercial expectations. It considers scholarly work already done to develop a relational legal-reasoning method, including the material factors that might incline legal reasoning towards different approaches. It then sketches the features of the interpretative approach, using case examples to illustrate and draw out the material considerations that might incline contract legal reasoning in more substantive or formal directions.

THE BINARY DIVIDE OF FORMALISM AND CONTEXTUALISM

There is a tendency both in doctrinal and theoretical legal scholarship to conceive of legal reasoning processes in binary and exclusive terms. While one might use the findings from empirical studies to build an argument for formalism as exclusively the correct approach, this empirical evidence is indeterminate and equivocal as to whether contractors themselves would prefer a more formal or a more contextual contract law regime.[12] Similarly, it is unlikely that the necessary changes in the substance of the rules and judicial attitude can be effected by adjusting the emphasis of contract law away from bright-line rules towards more flexible standards. It is arguable that a choice between 'this or that' type of rule design, and complete commitment to that choice, is not a matter for abstract determination remote from the actual contractual relationships to which the rules are applied. A method is required which includes a set of criteria that articulates and distinguishes the material considerations behind the different legal-reasoning techniques applied to each agreement, and isolates the features of commercial relationships that should prompt a particular legal-reasoning approach, whether inclining towards more formal or more substantive methods. Each agreement has its own unique context, and of course there is nothing here to suggest that such a context would not demonstrate a preference for a rigorously formal and individualistic approach on the part of the contractors.[13] There is undoubted difficulty here in attempting to isolate a set of general considerations from the great mass of contracting circumstances. Yet there seems no compelling reason why factors that might prompt different legal treatment for different types of contractor and contracting context cannot be broadly articulated.

[12] WJ Woodward, 'Neoformalism in a Real World of Forms' (2001) *Wisconsin Law Review* 971, 984. Woodward rejects the call for more formalistic interpretation in the Uniform Commercial Code, 1004.

[13] D Campbell, 'Ian Macneil and the Relational Theory of Contract' in Macneil, above n 7, identifies share dealing as one such possibility, 24–25: 'The normative permission of narrowly selfish behaviour is ... integral to the working of a stock exchange. But this is (or should be seen to be) normatively constituted behaviour which has clear limits'.

In seeking to draw together the foundational elements of relational theory (which provides the strongest underpinning justification and methodology for a commercial-expectations approach), contextual contract interpretation (the legal technique) and commercial expectations (the substantive social practices), an initial stage is to relinquish the idea that a straight choice must be made between formalism or contextualism in contract legal reasoning, along with the accompanying idea that acceptance of one technique means the rejection of the other. While this dichotomy expresses and simplifies the basic positions in the argument in familiar legal terms, it is misleading to assume that this division reflects some underlying reality about how business relationships will be organised. If anything, conceptualising the debate in this way simply replicates and endorses the adversarial character of legal argument where one finds the issues are often displayed as a choice between two opposing alternatives that are thought to exhaust the possible legal-reasoning routes for resolving the dispute. As has been seen, contracting parties may often display a simultaneous reliance on flexible and formal norms in their contractual relationships, but without demonstrating unequivocal allegiance to either as representing the overarching governance regime. Or else this commitment is manifest only in a somewhat superficial adherence (or attempt to adhere) to a scheme of express terms. In such circumstances, the legal commitment to and imposition of one of these values over another appears perverse. What is required is an appreciation of how context and motivation shape the use of contract formalities, and affect how those formalities should be understood and interpreted. Relational theory demands exactly this kind of broader enquiry in contract disputes, and it can be effected broadly through a contextual interpretative method.

The issue here is not that the tensions apparent in commercial dealing remain largely invisible to the law. It is easy to detect within case law how the contradictory commercial pressures of 'formalist' or 'not-formalist' are reflected in commercial contract disputes coming before the courts.[14] Rather the legal engagement with these tensions, both in terms of scholarly contributions and case law determinations, suggests a simple dichotomy that obscures what may be a much more nuanced relationship between the normative frameworks that occur in a relationship. The idea that there is a real and a paper deal, for example, while fully understandable as a shorthand way of articulating the basic problem, tends to accentuate this divide. This distinction quickly runs into problems if pressed too far. The main difficulty is that it assumes the real and paper deal are easily severable and that *conflict necessarily exists* between these two. This perceived separation

[14] For a recent Supreme Court example, see *Lloyds TSB Foundation for Scotland v Lloyds Banking Group plc* [2013] UKSC 3.

plays into the hands of adversarial legal reasoning in two related ways. First, it raises the possibility of the strategic reliance on the paper deal to achieve ends at variance with the understandings of the parties, for example by seeking to enforce a literal interpretation of an agreement because such a course has become attractive due to market movements. The courts may well uphold this literal interpretation.[15] Second, contract terms are frequently regarded as having a specified, self-contained and free-standing role, and they are not given meaning or substance by trade practices or business norms. As it stands, if the terms are clear, any custom or practice which might suggest either how the terms were expected to work, or that an alternative meaning could be placed upon them is unlikely to sway a court. A court may often be presented with a stark choice between the documents and other normative frameworks. But exhorting courts to take into account informal norms will not solve the problem, since the presentation of the issues in this way is already loaded in favour of the legal framework. This is amply demonstrated in *Tekdata v Amphenol*[16] where the battle-of-the-forms rules were allowed to dictate the terms of the agreement as against the actions and understandings of the parties. In reality the existence of a sharp division between the real and paper deal is likely to be overstated, and is produced, to an extent, by the rules themselves.[17] Nevertheless, while there is clearly a connection between commercial expectations and immanent business norms, care should be taken that these norms are not equated entirely with commercial expectation, leaving no space for the operation of a relatively formal set of rules when it appears appropriate. The 'real deal' may well be expressed in the written terms, and assimilating the 'real deal' with only a norms-based outcome may obscure the possibility of combining the real and paper deal into a unified scheme. This is not to deny that there may be situations where either trusting and social norms or a discrete contract, appear more appropriate. The advantage of relational method and contextual interpretation is that they are able to subsume all these different considerations and possible approaches.[18]

[15] *Total v Arco* [1998] 2 Lloyd's Rep 209.

[16] *Tekdata v Amphenol* [2009] EWCA Civ 1209; [2010] 1 Lloyd's Rep 357.

[17] D Campbell argues that gaps in a contract only exist because of the classical law's preference for presentiation, rather than the law learning to live with uncertainty and indefiniteness in contractual obligations: 'The Incompleteness of Our Understanding of the Law and Economics of Relational Contract' (2004) *Wisconsin Law Review* 645, 654.

[18] H Collins, 'Objectivity and Committed Contextualism in Interpretation' in S Worthington (ed), *Commercial Law and Commercial Practice* (Oxford, Hart Publishing, 2003) 189, 193. Collins argues here that contextualism in interpretation subsumes formalism and literalism.

METHODS OF EFFECTING A RELATIONALLY CONSTITUTED CONTRACT LAW

While we can say that relationalism subsumes both contextualism and formalism, developing contract law in this direction is without doubt the most challenging aspect of the relational enterprise. Relational theory is not likely to yield a set of substantive rules to rival classical or neoclassical contract law. If relational theory wants to have an impact in the courts (and it must be admitted that, at least with some of its proponents, it is not always clear that it does), its supporters must address the question of how it can yield a set of legal or regulatory tools that judges can use. As Eisenberg has written:

> [C]onstructing a body of relational contract law requires more than rejecting the approaches and assumptions of classical contract law. It also requires the formulation of a new body of legal rules based on approaches and assumptions that are justified by morality, policy, and experience.[19]

Theorists have responded in various ways to this challenge. Some have argued that the trade-off between form and substance in contractual dealings (which might be regarded as a more specific concern of relational theory) is a matter that is best left to the parties to decide upon, rather than public lawmakers, who should concentrate their efforts on facilitating contract making by developing appropriate defaults.[20] Others may argue that relational legal reasoning should become more like policy analysis.[21]

When thinking about the implications of relational theory for contract law, is it possible to move beyond the necessarily true, but undoubtedly trite, statement that context matters? Some socio-legal scholars, while not associating themselves with relational theory, have engaged with this issue. Hugh Collins argues that a contextual approach to contractual disputes, not sole reliance on the closed system of legal rules, could be articulated in the language of reasonable expectations and good faith.[22] He writes that reasonable expectation is a 'broader, open-textured standard' that can be utilised to 'expand the range of information that will describe the standards governing the contractual arrangement'.[23] Along with greater differentiation between contract types, this will have the effect of recontextualising the agreement in the light of the wider business relationship and market

[19] MA Eisenberg, 'Why There is No Law of Relational Contracts' (2000) 94 *Northwestern University Law Review* 805, 813.
[20] AW Katz, 'The Economics of Form and Substance in Contract Interpretation' (2004) 104 *Columbia Law Review* 496.
[21] J Feinman, 'Relational Contract Theory in Context' (2000) 94 *Northwestern University Law Review* 737, 743.
[22] Collins, above n 2, 146–48.
[23] Ibid, 146.

conventions.[24] For Collins, this greater attention to the expectations of parties is necessary to ensure the law's effectiveness in supporting contracts and markets. Thus one direction to a court is to examine all terms of an agreement, not just single terms in isolation, and ask what advantage may have been gained from agreeing to exclusion clauses, or penalties, which on the face of it may appear unfair. Collins's approach is undoubtedly correct in suggesting that contract law could set itself on the right path by a more direct and open commitment to standards and values such as good faith and commercial reasonableness in contract legal reasoning. Courts already appear to have started down this path by demonstrating a greater willingness to accord enforceability to flexible obligations and imply duties of good faith in some commercial agreements,[25] although consistency in approach is lacking. However, while these standards might do useful work in articulating in broad terms the moral framework that underlies the law, exactly what behaviour is required to uphold these standards may be disputed. In addition, such broad criteria appear as labels imparting a veneer of coherence to the multi-value and often difficult-to-formulate set of considerations applied to an agreement. This renders them less useful except as general and abstract modes of *expression* for the change in approach. This is not to say that they are inherently meaningless—it is often sought to ascribe them quite precise meanings—just that they are open to a variety of interpretations such that appeals made to them, without a careful consideration of what they are taken to signify, may serve to obscure as much as illuminate. They gain meaning through application in particular settings so it must always be important to consider the conditions under which such obligations (to act in good faith) or the application of such standards (commercial reasonableness) may be triggered.

If articulating these broad standards is not the end of the story, then what else is required? What may be important is not to identify the substance of a free-standing independent rule set, but to identify distinguishing features of different types of contracting parties and processes, including a set of criteria to apply to contractual relationships that allow courts to negotiate between the different strategies the parties might adopt during the course of performance and which might indicate whether a more formal or more contextual approach is appropriate when dealing with the dispute. Scholars have already done some important work examining this issue, although it must be said that they have not had judges in mind as possible users of their work. Katz has developed a taxonomy of considerations that would influence the choice of more formal or more substantive interpretative regimes, but he has argued that it is a matter for private parties to choose

[24] Ibid, 143–48, 356–60.

[25] *Yam Seng Pte Ltd v International Trade Corporation Ltd* [2013] EWHC 111; *Jet2.com Ltd v Blackpool Airport Ltd* [2012] EWCA Civ 417.

interpretative regimes *ex ante*, rather than public authorities *ex post*. Thus his taxonomy is directed towards contracting parties and their lawyers, rather than courts and legislators.[26] Nevertheless, his framework makes sensible suggestions concerning what kind of contracting parties will prefer what kind of contracting regime, with implications for how disputes are resolved:

> [S]mall and infrequent traders will tend to benefit from a more substantive interpretative regime for a variety of reasons: they are relatively less well-placed to undertake the fixed cost of detailed ex ante negotiation; they have relatively poor access to reputational networks ex post; they are likely to do their own contract negotiating but to contract out when acquiring legal services; they are less likely to be able to recover specific investments in other exchanges; and they are possibly less likely to face bias in ex post judicial tribunals. Conversely, large and experienced mercantile traders should prefer their contracts to be governed by relatively formalistic rules of interpretation—and this prediction is consonant with the observation that, in general, it is such traders whom we observe contracting into relatively formal enforcement regimes through devices such as arbitration, choice of law, and forum selection clauses.[27]

Such an approach does not deny that contract terms could be important, but their level of importance in governing the contractual relationship is determined by contextual factors (such as whether contracting parties are 'large and experienced mercantile traders'). These contextual factors may suggest reasons why formalism is the appropriate strategy for the parties and the courts. For certain classes of contractor and agreement—contracts between sophisticated economic actors organised in corporate form, less likely to be affected by 'cognitive error'—the aim of contract law may be to pursue efficiency through formalism.[28] Earlier it was seen that there is a line of scholarship on the circumstances which will influence the choice of contracting governance regime.[29] Williamson's work on the factors motivating 'buy or make' decisions with corresponding 'market or hierarchy' governance mechanisms also suggests in broad terms the material factors that determine choice of contract governance. Three specific relevant factors in the decision are asset specificity, uncertainty and frequency.[30] Issues concerning frequency of transacting, asset specificity, and level of uncertainty are all

[26] Katz, above n 20, 500. See also RE Scott, 'The Promise and the Peril of Relational Contract Theory' in J Braucher, J Kidwell and WC Whitford (eds), *Revisiting the Contracts Scholarship of Stewart Macaulay* (Oxford, Hart Publishing, 2013) 105, arguing a court should 'follow the parties' instructions' over the choice of a contextual or textual contract interpretative method: 127.

[27] Ibid, 537.

[28] A Schwartz and RE Scott, 'Contract Theory and the Limits of Contract Law' (2003) 113 *Yale Law Journal* 541, 545.

[29] O Williamson, *The Economic Institutions of Capitalism* (New York, Free Press, 1985) 68–72.

[30] Ibid, 72.

contextual enquiries that a court can undertake in its investigation of the agreement and in its choice of applicable norms. The courts must be placed in the situation of the parties who make these decisions and trade-offs, rather than confining themselves to an examination of the relationship from an outside viewpoint and applying a set of external norms justified by a set of assumed criteria concerning the parties and their relationship. However, separating out all the conditions of transactors, contracting circumstances, market conditions, level of uncertainty and so on is not straightforward. While it may be relatively easy to state a set of characteristics that may be regarded as indicating a degree of 'relationality' or 'discreteness' on a scale, and even to hypothesise about the kinds of agreement, market conditions, project type, and relationships which might display these characteristics, it is more difficult to trace a connection between commercial contractual relationships and the legal-reasoning techniques that should be applied to such relationships. Nevertheless since the court will be examining the relationship/contract in full knowledge of what has occurred, it will have access to evidence and can exercise considerable judgment over where it thinks an agreement lies on the relational continuum.

Creating a loose taxonomy of the factors that might influence the parties in their choice of contract regime would be important.[31] It would be a difficult task to sketch out all the possible variables here, but some general points can be made. Parties contracting in similar industries with active trade associations, strong intra-industry networks, patterns of repeat trading and heightened awareness of accepted division of risks could be expected to contract on the standard form terms and conditions. Even on the occasions where the parties omit to use the formal terms that are available to them, they may still be expected to agree on the basis of those terms.[32] They might also expect the terms to be interpreted relatively literally. Nevertheless, dependence on internal norms, either generated from within the industry or between the parties, should not be ruled out here either, if material, since these may well affect the interpretation to be placed on the terms. Parties engaged in more complex, longer-term trading with high levels of uncertainty, or where conditions militate against long-term planning, and where there are relationship-specific investments, may demand a more individualistic approach. Similarly if the relationship displays a high level of interdependence between the parties, a high level of flexibility, whether within the day-to-day running of the relationship or the contract terms themselves, and project planning (to the extent it occurs

[31] See Macneil, above n 7, 196–99; J Hagedoorn and G Hesen, 'Contract Law and the Governance of Inter-firm Technology Partnerships—An Analysis of Different Modes of Partnering and their Contractual Implications' (2007) 44 *Journal of Management Studies* 342, 357; Katz, above n 20.

[32] *British Crane Hire Corp v Ipswich Plant Hire Ltd*, above n 11.

at all) is on the basis of processes, rather than substance of what is traded or transferred, this suggests dispute resolution according to standards and internal norms, rather than rules, may be appropriate. In some of these latter situations, matters such as the circumstances of the project or industry conditions may militate against comprehensive advanced planning, yet a set of well-developed internal norms may not be available either. Such relationships may display greater reliance (or attempted reliance) on contracts and legal enforcement, but the precepts of the classical law of contract appear manifestly unsuitable to regulate the agreement. Parties may try to negotiate the difficult path between form, substance and process through the use of flexible terms, but on the basis of the current state of English contract law it cannot be assumed that such commitments will be legally enforceable. In this respect, increased exposure on the part of courts to the commercial constraints that direct the parties towards these forms of commitment may of itself trigger some increased sensitivity to commercial expectations.

These general considerations would be a starting point in helping to explain and bring to the fore the factors and reasons that might have prevented the parties formulating a complete agreement, the extent to which they relied and had to rely on each other, the extent of power and control exercised over each other and the extent of interdependence between the parties. Similarly it could be expected that judges would develop some sense of norms operating in particular industries[33] and the contexts in which a more formalist approach might be expected. There should also be some important generalised understandings—that certain and formal documents that set out precise obligations are not capable of governing the life of an agreement which is expected to endure over a period of time.[34] Nevertheless such general considerations could be starting points only, and routes into a more specific and contextualised inquiry as to what the parties expected from their agreement and each other.

CONTEXTUAL INTERPRETATION

To give contract law doctrine its due, a contextual approach to interpretation as advocated by Lord Hoffmann in *Investors Compensation Scheme v West Bromwich Building Society* could be a route to accessing implicit norms and expectations since the background against which interpretation takes place includes 'absolutely anything [relevant] which would have

[33] As they already demonstrate with shipping cases for example: *The Achilleas* [2008] UKHL 48; [2009] 1 AC 61 and *The Scaptrade* [1983] 1 QB 529; [1983] 2 All ER 763.

[34] Recognised in *Multi-link Leisure Developments Ltd v North Lanarkshire Council* [2010] UKSC 47; [2011] 1 All ER 175 and *Lloyds TSB Foundation for Scotland v Lloyds Banking Group plc* [2013] UKSC 3.

affected the way in which the language of the document would have been understood by a reasonable man'.[35] If it is understood by the law that contract interpretation cannot be a wholly formal or literal exercise in uncovering the meaning of words, it is not apparent why this insight cannot be applied to illuminate the role of the 'contract' within the commercial relationship. However, contract interpretation is presently regarded primarily as a process applied to the documents and the transaction, rather than the wider business relationship. If contextual interpretation is to provide a means to access and give effect to the internal norms of the agreement it must be grasped that the subject matter for interpretation is the entire commercial relationship, of which the text may be an important but not exclusive and conclusive part. The neoclassical approach to contract interpretation still takes the express terms as the object to be interpreted whereas a relationally constituted approach would examine more closely the precise role of the documents in the relationship.[36]

Understood as a technique which is not confined to ascribing meaning to words and phrases in formal contractual texts, contextual interpretation has implications for contract law rules and doctrines. Lord Hoffmann's judgment in *The Achilleas*[37] illustrates this wider effect of interpretation and its potential scope for incorporating a broader set of contextual considerations into the parties' agreement. The issue in this case concerned the extent of a charterer's liability following the late return of a ship to the owners, with the consequence that the owner was obliged to renegotiate the hire on the following fixture and accept a lower rate. Was the charterer liable for the loss of profit on the entire following fixture, or just for the period of the delay? One possibility is that the case should be determined by applying an external legal standard, that is to say, the remoteness rule in *Hadley v Baxendale*.[38] Lord Hoffmann preferred the view that the extent of the charterer's liability was not a matter of the application of external legal standards, but a question of contract interpretation (broadly understood).[39] An interpretative approach allowed Lord Hoffmann to take account of the

[35] *Investors Compensation Scheme v West Bromwich Building Society* [1998] 1 WLR 896, 912–13, as amended by *Bank of Credit and Commerce International SA (in liquidation) v Ali* [2001] UKHL 8; [2001] 2 WLR 735. See generally J Wightman, 'Contract in a Pre-Realist World: Professor Macaulay, Lord Hoffmann and the Rise of Context in the English Law of Contract' in Braucher, Kidwell and Whitford (eds), above n 26, 377.

[36] H Collins, 'Objectivity and Committed Contextualism in Interpretation' in Worthington (ed), above n 18, 189, 191–93.

[37] Above n 33.

[38] *Hadley v Baxendale* (1854) 9 Exch 341.

[39] Above n 33, [11]. Lord Hope was largely in agreement, but Lord Rodger and Baroness Hale preferred the narrower ground that preserved the operation of *Hadley v Baxendale*: since the loss on the following fixture was the result of an extremely volatile market it was not within the charterer's contemplation and was not recoverable. Lord Walker agreed with elements of both approaches.

industry understanding that the charterer's liability was restricted to the difference between the market rate and the charter rate for the period of delay. For Lord Hoffmann the starting point for assessing liability is not *Hadley v Baxendale*, but the agreement between the parties, which includes the tacit understandings prevalent within the industry (including shipping lawyers). Such practices provide an important marker against which the 'fit' of various competing interpretations offered by the parties can be judged. *Hadley v Baxendale* would still apply where such norms and industry understandings did not exist. One can take Lord Hoffmann's judgment in *The Achilleas* as a far-reaching, but inevitable, consequence of his contextual interpretative approach to contractual relationships. The case demonstrates the possibility of unifying the law and the parties' understandings into an integrated scheme that attempts to do some justice to both the law's role as background regulator of economic exchange and the complexity of agreements and relationships that contracting parties create. Responding to market volatility and uncertainty (social pressures) required the abandonment of the classic default rule on remoteness of damage, lest the defendants be saddled with disproportionate liability. The decision provides a further illustration of the capacity of the common law of contract to break with the past and set the law off on a new path.

The key to the approach is to understand that, as Macneil has it, the terms are approached through the wider social context of the agreement. This will often give insight into the reliability of the documents as a record of the parties' obligations, or will influence the interpretation that could be placed on the express terms, or provide a window into contract design that explains why parties may have stipulated for flexible obligations or may have failed to execute a formal agreement at all. Chiefly, courts should recognise that the documents may serve a variety of purposes depending on such variables as the quality of the parties' relationship, the nature of the project at the centre of the agreement, and any wider regulatory context that imposes its own set of demands. It seems likely that the documents perform a more perfunctory role in short-term, one-shot deals (for example, a basic record of specification, quantity, price, delivery arrangements and so on) than in agreements expected to endure over a longer period. In 'as-if-discrete', or broadly non-trusting relationships, the formal contract may be a protective and security measure, specifying monitoring and enforcement procedures that safeguard the parties from opportunism. In trusting relationships or long-term relationships the contract may be used for more benign purposes of project co-ordination, record keeping and reassurance.[40] Similarly, contract design may vary between different kinds of relationship.

[40] RK Woolthuis, B Hillebrand and B Nooteboom, 'Trust, Contract and Relationship Development' (2005) 26 *Organization Studies* 813–40, 834–35.

This would explain why parties often impose standards of co-operation and flexibility through express terms. Courts have been hostile towards parties' attempts to impose duties of good faith, information sharing and performance standards (using 'reasonable' or 'best endeavours' and so on) through contract terms, but there seems to be no strong argument of principle for this hostility.[41] Industry context and the nature of the project may provide important information to a court about the standard of precision that can be expected in a written contract and about the participants' attitudes towards legal enforcement. Similarly, the law should take account of industry understandings about why specific terms are included in formal documents. Such enquiries may lead a judge to conclude the parties placed little reliance on express terms. Alternatively, other enquiries concerning risk, uncertainty and bargaining power between the parties may lead a judge to conclude that the parties did enter into an 'as-if-discrete' contract and to implement an interpretative strategy that supports that approach. It also demands an agreement- and relationship-centred as opposed to doctrine-centred approach to the contractual relationship.

Case examples will be helpful here to illustrate in broad terms the kinds of methods that might be adopted to combine relational theory with commercial practices and contextual interpretative method. Models and organising criteria will never achieve perfect fit with the factual circumstances they are applied to—that is a general feature of law.[42] This is not a new difficulty, however, since the classical law also presents such limitations. Nevertheless, it might be appropriate to consider how a contextual interpretative method attuned with relational theory might yield a different approach to dealing with complex commercial agreements. The examples illustrate different ways of managing the contracting process and business relationship. While illustrating complexity, they are also broadly illustrative of the circumstances in which contract law may be called upon to determine the extent of legal rights and obligations. The examples show how factors such as lack of homogeneity, relationship-specific investments, length of agreement, high uncertainty and a challenging economic environment, may combine to render fully contingent long-term agreements problematic. These are likely to be relationships where formal contractual and informal social norms intersect. In what follows the focus will be on examples which amply demonstrate the complexity of modern commercial contractual arrangements, and how the current, relatively formal, legal tools appear ill equipped to deal with this complexity. There will also be an attempt to demonstrate how relational legal reasoning might be employed to achieve

[41] See comments of Longmore LJ in *Petromec Inc v Petroleo Brasileiro SA Petrobas (No 3)* [2005] EWCA Civ 891; [2006] 1 Lloyd's Rep 121.

[42] T Rakoff, 'The Law and Sociology of Boilerplate' in O Ben-Shahar (ed), *Boilerplate: The Foundation of Market Contracts* (Cambridge, CUP, 2007) 200, 202.

either an alternative result, or a better justification for the actual result reached.

Case Examples

(i) Conflict between Formal and Informal Norms: RTS Flexible Systems Ltd v Molkerei Alois Müller GmbH & Co KG (UK Productions)[43]

This Supreme Court decision arose out of an agreement between RTS and Müller for RTS to design, manufacture, install and test automated machinery on a packaging line in one of Müller's factories that produced yogurts. The parties had been in negotiations for a number of years before RTS were informed that they were the preferred bidder to provide the machinery. Work proceeded according to the terms of a letter of intent dated February 2005, which set out the basics of the project and the total price. The letter of intent also stipulated that the formal contract terms would be finalised, agreed and executed within four weeks of the letter of intent. The proposed formal agreement was to be based on Müller's standard terms with certain amendments agreed by the parties. One of these terms, Clause 48, stipulated that 'This contract may be executed in any number of counterparts provided that it shall not become effective until each party has executed a counterpart and exchanged it with the other'. Despite negotiations over the terms, and substantial agreement being reached, the contract documents were never formally executed. Performance nevertheless continued with the letter of intent being extended to May 2005. In August 2005 there was an agreed 'variation' of the delivery plan and testing procedure for the machinery in order to meet an important order for Müller's products from the Tesco supermarket chain. By this time work on the formal contract documents had largely ceased while the parties concentrated on delivering the project so Müller could meet its obligations to Tesco. This was crucial if Müller was to avoid temporary blacklisting by the supermarket. The case report remains curiously silent as to what precipitated the final dispute in November 2005, except that it was only at this time that 'points were taken as to whether there was a contract'.[44]

That three courts reached entirely different conclusions concerning whether a legally enforceable agreement was reached, and on what terms, illustrates the difficulties presented to the law by these facts. Yet these facts are by no means unusual in commercial agreements. The decision also

[43] *RTS Flexible Systems Ltd v Molkerei Alois Müller GmbH & Co KG (UK Productions)* [2010] UKSC 14; [2010] 1 WLR 753.

[44] Ibid, [61].

shows that claims to certainty made on behalf of commercial contract law are somewhat spurious. The trial judge's view was that a contract existed for the work at the price agreed, initially on the basis of the letter of intent. Evidently the judge faced a difficulty when the letter expired but the parties continued with performance.[45] The judge concluded an agreement had been entered into on the basis of some schedules to the formal agreement, although not the formal agreement itself since Clause 48 precluded its coming into effect.[46] The Court of Appeal took a completely different approach, arguing that a formal contract never came into existence and the parties were thrown back on to the law of restitution to enforce payment provisions. To their credit, the Supreme Court recognised that the Court of Appeal approach of 'no contract' was untenable in an agreement of this kind. They concluded that the parties had reached agreement on Müller's standard terms, as 'varied' in August 2005, and that the parties had waived operation of Clause 48. The Supreme Court recognised that the best remedy for vagueness and uncertainty in agreements was *performance* and that the parties' desire to put the relationship on a solid formal footing was overtaken by events.

Taken as an example of the contradictory pressures of formalism/not-formalism in the contracting process *RTS v Müller* is instructive. First, it shows the way in which obligations evolve and change between the parties as the commercial relationship progresses, particularly when responding to external pressures. The parties do not exist in momentary worlds of 'no liability' and 'liability', as classical contract law assumes and as formalism demands. The parties instead drift into contractual obligations by agreement and performance. Second, negotiating and drafting a formal contract serves not only legal purposes, but also performance-planning purposes. While these functions of the paperwork are not easily severable, performance inevitably takes precedence over *planning* the performance, particularly when the project is expected to extend over a period of time. Third, the case is a good example of how the parties choose both formal legal mechanisms (letters of intent) and relational norms (agreed amendments to the planning and substantial co-operation over fulfilling the Tesco contract) during the life of their agreement. Fourth, it illustrates the biggest weakness with the legal approach. For the law, the formalities, or lack of them, provide the overarching framework within which the parties' behaviour and motivations are examined, described and justified. The context of the agreement is not taken to shape the interpretation that should be placed on the documents, nor is it taken to expose the inherent limitations in the documents. Instead, the documents are taken as a free-standing explanatory

[45] Ibid, [65].
[46] Ibid, [72].

framework according to which the actions and motivations of the parties are measured and judged, and conclusions drawn about the extent of their obligations. This sort of reasoning can lead to some surprising and counter-intuitive legal conclusions about the facts, such as that when the letter of intent expired 'the agreement would come to an end'.[47] Of course this outcome makes sense within the rigid legal framework that concludes that when the period of time or job covered by a letter of intent finishes, there is no further obligation between the parties, even though this appears contrary to the context and the parties' behaviour.[48] Such a conclusion flies in the face of the extent of relationship-specific investments undertaken by the parties and their continuing reliance on one another. The parties' view of their obligations as continuing is entirely opposed to the legal conclusion that follows from these facts. Similarly the importance of the Tesco contract to Müller is not accorded the weight it undoubtedly had with the parties. The Tesco deal is treated as a background fact, not the crucial economic motivation that it clearly would be, nor an important 'implicit dimension' that explains the shifting priorities of the parties and an important consideration both for why they failed to reach a formal agreement but also why they continued to co-operate to realise the project. This legalisation of experience, which demands that the parties frame their relationship in a formal way if they want the court's attention, leads one to the conclusion that the law is concerned with fictions and constructions of reality, rather than the reality that is experienced by the parties. The result of this, well illustrated in the case, is that the law has unrealistic expectations of what can be achieved in the paper deal, even by parties who seemingly manifest a clear intention to go down the formal route. The law thus struggles to give effect to their intentions through the existing contract doctrines.

Disputes like *RTS v Müller* are illustrative of the precise problems the law of contract is increasingly required to resolve and they throw into relief the inadequacy of the legal tools in dealing with such agreements. Positing only two alternatives of 'contract' or 'no contract' is too blunt for dealing with relationships of this kind, particularly since it creates a risk that the parties may fail to effect the legal protection that they have expended considerable cost in striving to achieve. Ultimately, the Supreme Court managed to avoid this risk in *RTS v Müller* by recognising that the parties' preference for formality was probably justified in the circumstances, but that the circumstances also militated against achieving it. The Court was thus willing to bestow legal enforceability onto the formal contract, despite its never being executed. In doing this the Court gives tacit recognition to the point

[47] First instance decision [2008] EWHC 1087, [39].

[48] See, eg, *Emcor Drake & Scull Ltd v Robert McAlpine Ltd* [2004] EWCA 1733 and *Merit Process Engineering Ltd v Balfour Beatty Engineering Services (HY) Ltd* [2012] EWCA 1376.

that, as relational theory anticipates, contracting parties' commitment to formality is always dependent upon wider contextual factors surrounding the commercial relationship and the project—it is contingent and not absolute. However, the legal recognition of this is not open and explicit, it is only achieved through filtering the parties' actions and motivations through obscure legal rules—variation, waiver—and presenting the outcome as a conclusion reached through the application of those external doctrines. One of the important effects of this is that factors and considerations leading to this conclusion, which would be central to the relational approach to contract, are not drawn out, but remain hidden. A relational approach to the *RTS* case, for example, would demand an investigation of the wider considerations that prompted a preference for a 'discrete' contract to govern the parties' relationship and whether this evinced a genuine commitment in the light of the context of the transaction, or reflected other imperatives, such as the stronger party's preferred way of doing business. The law tends to take the preference for discreteness at face value, as a conclusion that follows naturally from the existence of the documents themselves, or from the fact that the parties chose to engage in litigation when the dispute arose. In a fully relational approach these are not natural conclusions that can be drawn from such premises. This is because relationalism recognises that formalism, and classical contract law itself, is simply one strategy for managing the exchange process. Understood as just one strategy, it can be appreciated that the parties' preference for formalism results from a set of motivations and considerations that operate separately from what 'formalism' or 'discreteness' themselves entail. These considerations provide a kind of test for discovering whether a more formal and less contextual approach (or the reverse), is required when resolving any dispute.

In many ways relationalism provides a better justification for the outcome reached than the classical or even neoclassical law, since it is clear that the Supreme Court appreciated the parties' wider relationship and degree of interdependence, even if that consideration forms no part of the stated reasons for the decision. In *RTS v Müller* the combination of uncertainty, infrequency of the exchange (which meant there was no rich normative structure developed internally to the parties' relationship to rely on) and high asset specificity provides some explanation for both the parties' attempted formalisation of the agreement and the difficulties they encountered in this attempt. The Supreme Court's decision to enforce the formal planning documents reflects what was probably the best conclusion that could be reached in the circumstances. The point to grasp is that this outcome can be better justified within the framework of relational theory, rather than the existing rules and precepts of the classical law of contract expressed in a set of concepts that mean little to the parties themselves. It is clear from cases like *RTS v Müller* that courts will increasingly be called upon to adjudicate disputes in agreements that raise difficult issues concerning certainty, intention to create legal obligations, and the remedial consequences following breach of flexible obligations. Undertaking contextual enquiries to reach answers in these matters is not beyond their capacity however, as will be seen below.

(ii) Interpreting the Agreement as a Unified Scheme: Total Gas Marketing v Arco British[49]

The second case example illustrates the possibility of taking a combined approach to understanding the real and paper deal. In *Total v Arco*, a seemingly important but overlooked point of context was that the contract condition upon which the gas buyer, Total, was able to rely on escaping from the agreement was one usually inserted into the agreement for the protection of the gas seller, Arco. This case concerned a complicated contract for the supply of gas to Total by Arco and other licensees of the Trent gas field in the North Sea. It was anticipated that the agreement would last for the life of the field, about 14 years. A stated 'condition' of the contract was that Arco would enter into an 'allocation agreement' which determined mathematically how much gas transported to the terminal was to be regarded as derived from the Trent field. The date by which Arco had to enter into this agreement was not fixed by the contract. However, the contract specified various options as to the 'first delivery date' when Total would receive its first supply of gas. At the nominated first delivery date (31 October 1996) Arco had not entered into an allocation agreement. It did so a few days later and the gas flow commenced shortly thereafter. Although entry into an allocation agreement was essential for the supply of gas, evidence suggested that it was a common occurrence in the industry that allocation agreements were completed only just before the first delivery, that this was rarely regarded as a serious breach and that the contract provisions concerning the allocation agreement were inserted into the contract to give the seller (Arco) some flexibility and protection from having to accept onerous conditions or make excessive payments in entering into the allocation agreement. Given all this relevant context, it was therefore unlikely that Total would believe the deal was off simply because the allocation agreement had not been entered into by the first delivery date. Nevertheless, Total sought to terminate the contract on the grounds of non-fulfilment of the condition. Their real motive in seeking to terminate was the downturn in the price of gas. The House of Lords decided that failure to enter into the allocation agreement by 31 October entitled Total to terminate the contract. The Court's view was that the relationship was governed by the contractual documents. Arco's argument that some flexibility over the start date was necessary was

[49] [1998] 2 Lloyd's Law Rep 209.

judged not to give 'sufficient emphasis to the importance of the first delivery date in the scheme agreed to by the parties'.[50] Some of their Lordships were evidently unhappy with this result. Lord Hope clearly felt unable to depart from the language of the contract despite his appreciation of the wider social context that could have provided justification for such a departure.[51] The result would have been in keeping with the objective intentions of the parties—this was a provision to protect the seller—rather than the subjective intentions of Total. The practices and understandings in the industry were central to a full and accurate understanding of how the express condition about the first delivery date in the contract should be enforced, and in whose interests the term was expected to work. This implicit understanding was ignored, however, and the terms interpreted as being a free-standing statement of the parties' obligations. The possibility that the understanding affected the way in which Arco acted in agreeing to the 'condition' is ignored. The disposal of the *Total* case appears precisely to rely upon a juxtaposition between the social and the legal; between the real world and the legal world; between 'documents' and 'understandings', completely overlooking that there was a way to make these two 'worlds' consistent. This separation of the market practice and the terms is unfortunate. To the extent that the parties were attempting to build a formal framework for their agreement, the Court arguably did not uphold it but subverted it by an act of literalism.

(iii) Avoiding a Doctrine-driven Approach: Durham Tees Valley Airport Ltd v BMIBaby Ltd[52]

A doctrine-driven outcome allows that the legal rules provide the essential framework for understanding and analysing the parties' relationship. For example, in *The Achilleas* an outcome based on the application of *Hadley v Baxendale* is a doctrine-centred approach. Such an approach is often unavoidable, as when the parties fail to stipulate expressly or impliedly what is to happen upon some contingency. But it can also occur when courts let the available remedies drive the recognition of legal obligations. *DTVA v BMIBaby* is an example of where this outcome was narrowly avoided. The owners of DTVA entered into a 10-year contract with BMIBaby (the budget-airline subsidiary of British Midland Ltd) under which the airline agreed to base two aircraft and operate flights out of the airport. BMIBaby were not able to make a profit from the operation and the airline withdrew from DTVA with eight years of the agreement left to run. The first-instance judge agreed that a contractual obligation had arisen, and breach

[50] Per Lord Slynn, ibid, 216.
[51] Ibid, 223.
[52] *Durham Tees Valley Airport Ltd v BMIBaby Ltd* [2010] EWCA Civ 485 (CA).

had occurred, but he found the obligations stipulated under the agreement were too vague and open ended to allow recovery of substantial damages. Questions as to how many flights BMIBaby were expected to operate and the number of passengers they were obliged to carry did not have any objectively ascertainable answers.[53] The agreement was therefore too uncertain to be enforced. What weighed with the judge in the case was his inability to formulate specific terms that could yield a quantifiable damages award for breach. Within the backward-looking legal context of litigation, this concern is understandable, but to regard it as determinative of the issue of liability fails to interpret the agreement in its industry context, since it did not take account of industry conditions that militated against specifying formal obligations as to flying programmes with any degree of certainty or any expectation of permanence. A further problem with this approach is that it conflates the issue of whether there is a contractual obligation to do 'x' with the issue of what are the remedies for breach of the obligation to do 'x'. The trial judge retrospectively seeks to impose the constraints demanded by the legal rule framework onto the parties' 'living' agreement with the predictable result that the agreement fails to meet the conditions for legal enforceability.

The Court of Appeal, on the other hand, accepted that the contract did not fail for uncertainty since performance would give its vague provisions content.[54] For the Court of Appeal it was an error, although an understandable one, to filter the determination of the obligations arising through the remedial scheme for breach of contract and allow the difficulty of formulating a remedy to determine the entire issue of enforceability. The Court held that once the judge had determined that liability for breach had arisen on the basis of interpreting the contract, he was left simply with the task of assessing damages. While this would be difficult, it was not impossible, and did not prevent the contract being enforceable. A remedy could be fashioned without the Court having to decide the detailed obligations (passenger numbers and so on) that performance required—the Court did not have to complete the contract because it already was complete. Deciding on matters such as passenger numbers, flight schedules and so on might be necessary to assessing damages (although experts could be called upon to assist with this), but not to whether obligations along these lines existed. The Court of Appeal's reasoning is to be welcomed as allowing for an agreement-centred rather than doctrine-centred approach to the contract framework. It should also be noted that in terms of practical effect the Court also enforces, at least in an oblique way, an obligation to be co-operative. The Court of Appeal appeared willing to concede that such an open-ended

[53] [2009] EWHC 852 (Ch).

[54] Above n 52, [55].

contract, in the context of a long-term relationship, is enforceable between the parties *as if it had been performed* without issue. Content could not be given to the obligations in advance, only by the parties working together to achieve the desired outcomes throughout the duration of the agreement. Even if legal enforcement is imperfect in the sense that damages are hard to assess and may appear ad hoc—this feature would hardly be unusual in the law of contract damages—determining that a party was not free to renege on such an obligation, despite its open-ended nature, recognises the significance and importance of collaboration and interdependence between the parties. Such an approach also resists one party's strategic attempts to undermine the relational underpinning of the contract scheme by superimposing inappropriate formalistic norms on the agreement. One implication of the change in approach to regarding interpretation as a technique to be applied to the business relationship is that judgments concerning the contract governance structure the parties adopted can only be decided by examining a much greater range of material than presently considered. This investigation will be with a view to establishing 'what degree of competitive or co-operative negotiation will produce the optimum outcome in that case'[55] or alternatively, 'what degree of market or state governance provides the best outcome'.[56]

Contextual interpretation then could be a strategy to achieve consistency with the history, purposes and norms of the business relationship. In other words, it may be possible in some circumstances that the documents, business expectations, market conventions and so on can be regarded, as far as possible, as a unified scheme, not involving separate and dissonant frameworks of analysis. Undoubtedly one might express scepticism that this unification exercise is a strategy that can be pursued through an adversarial litigation process. This process compounds dissonance between law and expectations since it encourages the sides in the dispute to organise their disagreement around what are perceived as 'legal' and 'non-legal' norms (or alternatively, the 'established' formal position and the 'exceptional' counter-norm alternative). But it is arguable that the more courts engage head-on with the difficulties that real contracting parties present, and use context to arrive at more accurate determinations of the parties' obligations, the more this strategic juxtaposing of informal norms and express terms might be expected to recede, simply because there is little benefit to be gained by presenting disputes in ways that stress conflict between contextual and legal norms. This is not to suggest that this confrontation can never be a genuine reflection of the dispute, nor that in some circumstances the legal-reasoning process must make a choice to apply formalist or contextualist modes of

[55] D Campbell, 'The Relational Constitution of the Discrete Contract' in D Campbell and P Vincent-Jones (eds), *Contract and Economic Organisation* (Aldershot, Dartmouth, 1996) 47.

[56] Ibid 59.

reasoning to an agreement, but this choice in itself can only be driven by a contextual understanding of the parties' relationship and the place of the express terms within it.

Changing Mindset

Many of the perceived problems with developing a relationally constituted contract law are based on the assumption that if the law changed, contracting and party behaviour would remain static. But this conclusion is not necessarily warranted. Many contractors will assume the law does not just state *a position* from among the many possible, or a neutral position, but the *correct* position and that the rules (whatever their content) set standards for behaviour. They may therefore adjust their behaviour accordingly. Korobkin has argued that parties' and lawyers' preferences generally tend towards the status quo, whatever that happens to be. If the status quo changes, lawyers will eventually adjust their behaviour accordingly to any new status quo announced by courts. While this is a factor, it overlooks that lawyers do not just respond to change, but play a vital part in instigating legal change.[57] Practitioners can change attitudes and 'mindset' by developing new arguments to put before the courts based on evolving and changing social norms and in exposing courts to evidence about business behaviour, including the reality of how agreements are created and performed and the difficulties of meeting criteria for full enforceability under the classical law. By exposing judges to experiences of contracting parties, rather than adhering to the script presented by the application of legal doctrines and contract terms, lawyers may aim to subvert some hardened point of view on a phenomenon. This may operate as a relatively conservative way of instigating legal change.[58] Thus while lawyers may replicate structures of legal argument and its particular binary patterns, they are also responsible for challenging a court's perceptions. Thus we have allusions to the real social world and the artificial legal world of contract made by counsel in *Balmoral Group Ltd v Borealis (UK) Ltd.*[59] The constant telling and retelling of these ruptures to the 'common law script', or breaks with expectations, eventually makes those ruptures themselves appear ordinary and more readily integrated into, and representative of, our experience. Thus increasing exposure of the courts to contractor experiences is a method of

[57] See C Mitchell, 'Narrativising Contract Law' (2009) 29 *Legal Studies* 19.

[58] G Binder and Robert Weisberg, *Literary Criticisms of Law* (Princeton, Princeton University Press, 2000) 205.

[59] *Balmoral Group Ltd v Borealis (UK) Ltd* [2006] EWHC 1900, [339].

taking legal reasoning in a new direction.[60] The lawyer's vital role in this process is concisely described by Winter:

> [T]he advocates slowly expose the courts to ever greater accretions of experience that do not fit the reigning legal paradigm until, ultimately, the courts are led to reformulate the available models to fit the experiences they had previously ignored. Here we have crossed the divide from the persuasive to the transformative.[61]

Atiyah also recognised the importance of lawyers to the growth of ideas of commercial freedom and freedom of contract that grew towards the end of the eighteenth century, arguing that lawyers, barristers in particular, were receptive to these ideas before society at large since the values of individual merit, freedom, enterprise and competition were championed within their own profession.[62] Nevertheless, litigating parties face the problem of reluctance to deviate from the judicially accepted norms. It may be that parties and litigators would rather remain with what is familiar until a critical mass of contractors makes the transition to an alternative.[63] However, while litigation and contract law outcomes from courts seem to demonstrate the 'self-reinforcing expectation effect',[64] litigation is also the key to legal change and development. To be sure, significant costs may be incurred by a party seeking to overturn or reduce the influence of a precedent and thereby bring about a change in the law. But for such parties, litigation operates as a kind of investment. There is a risk involved, but also the possibility of authoritative and general legal backing for one's preferred outcome.[65] For some this will make the possible pay-off outweigh the risk: 'Where there is a knowable and feasible improvement to be gained from moving onto a better path, those who will benefit from the improvement, and who know it, will be willing to pay to bring the improvement about'.[66] As has been seen, there are recent decisions emanating from English courts that illustrate that arguments made along 'non-traditional' or 'non-doctrinal' lines can be successful in higher courts, although it must be admitted that this movement is not all one way. If these arguments can be successful in litigation then it also suggests the

[60] AG Amsterdam and J Bruner, *Minding the Law* (Cambridge MA, Harvard University Press, 2002) 140. DM Patterson, 'Law's Pragmatism: Law as Practice and Narrative' (1990) 76 *Virginia Law Review* 937, 988.

[61] SL Winter, 'The Cognitive Dimension of the *Agon* Between Legal Power and Narrative Meaning' (1989) 87 *Michigan Law Review* 2225, 2275.

[62] PS Atiyah, *The Rise and Fall of Freedom of Contract* (Oxford, OUP, 1979) 113.

[63] CP Gillette, 'Lock-In Effects in Law and Norms' (1998) 78 *Boston University Law Review* 813, 819.

[64] OA Hathaway, 'Path Dependence in the Law: The Course and Pattern of Legal Change in a Common Law System' (2001) 86 *Iowa Law Review* 601, 612.

[65] Gillette, above n 63, 824.

[66] SJ Liebowitz and SE Margolis, 'Path Dependence, Lock-In, and History' (1995) 11 *Journal of Law Economics and Organization* 205, 224.

change in practice leading to the new and accepted legal argument can also find a foothold amongst other contractors as an *acceptable commercial practice* and not just a litigation strategy. An example might be the increasing recognition that open-ended obligations, which may have been thought previously to be too uncertain to enforce, and provision of express flexible obligations, can give rise to contractual liability,[67] and also that in some circumstances such obligations should be implied.[68] If this is observed by others, then other commercial contractors may make use of the judgment to regulate their own contract governance schemes, perhaps by making their contractual arrangements more reflective of the reality of their relationship and the project they are engaged in.

CONTRACTING IN OR CONTRACTING OUT OF CONTEXTUALISM?

It might be argued that increasing the receptiveness of contract law to the relational elements of the parties' deal can be accommodated within the broadly classical and formalistic model of contract law since it is open to the parties to contract around formalist defaults by communicating to the courts that their agreement should be interpreted contextually, or that their dispute should be resolved by reference to substantive standards such as reasonableness and good faith. This raises the issue of whether the law should be relatively formal and allow the parties to contract out, or should adopt contextualist reasoning as a starting point, embracing a co-operative model of the contracting process, and allow parties that require a stricter regime to contract around this default.[69] For scholars working within an efficiency framework the choice between these two strategies usually comes down to a matter of costs. Assuming parties are aware of the relevant defaults and act self-consciously in bargaining around them to an optimum outcome, then if more contractors would bargain around a default than adopt it into their agreement, this suggests the default should reflect the majority preference, thereby saving the costs of writing specific terms for most contractors. On the other hand, penalty defaults might be used to encourage the parties to expressly contract for their preferences.[70] However, there is the possibility that parties do not respond in this way to defaults, but instead display status

[67] *Jet2.com Ltd v Blackpool Airport Ltd*, above n 25; *Durham Tees Valley Airport Ltd v BMI Baby Ltd*, above n 52.

[68] *Yam Seng Pte Ltd v International Trade Corporation Ltd*, above n 25.

[69] Brownsword, above n 1, 37.

[70] See I Ayres and R Gertner, 'Filling Gaps in Incomplete Contracts: An Economic Theory of Default Rules' (1989) 99 *Yale Law Journal* 87. They argue that penalty defaults might be appropriate if the failure to contract around the default is due to strategic withholding of information rather than the costs of contracting around the default.

quo bias or default inertia.[71] If parties do not generally contract around the rules supplied by the law, then arguably contract law should adopt either defaults that the majority of parties would favour or defaults that are justified on other grounds thought to be important, such as, for example, upholding the parties' intentions at the time they made their agreement, as far as these can be discerned. Since identifying majoritarian defaults relies on empirical evidence of contractors' general preferences, which is difficult to obtain or unavailable,[72] the latter might be the better approach for the law to follow, particularly since there are few parties that are likely to support a position whereby the law does not attempt to discover and enforce what they agreed at the outset. Contextualism would most likely be the better default strategy, with the possibility for the parties to indicate a preference for formalism, if this is indeed the aim, or one of the aims, of a system of contract law. This may become apparent by briefly examining the case for a formalist default position.

Morgan argues that contract law should adopt a formalist default, at least in contract interpretation, because it is easier to direct the courts to show a deference for contextual norms against a formalist backdrop than the reverse. In other words it is easier for the parties to contract out of formalism than contextualism.[73] He argues it is more difficult for the parties to 'opt in' to formalism from a contextualist starting point, since the underpinning commitment of the law to contextualism may make the genuineness of the desire for formality difficult to impress on a judge, who will have recourse to the contract context to determine if the parties intended their agreement and dispute to be dealt with formally, thus immediately defeating the point of opting in to formalism. Of course one could say the same about the reverse position of contracting into contextualism within a broadly formalist system. The parties may risk a finding of complete unenforceability by failing to adhere to formalist norms in their attempts to signal to a court their preference for a contextualist interpretative method. One need only examine the case law to see the difficulties presented to parties attempting to contract into contextualism as their preferred legal reasoning strategy within a system that manifests a preference for formalism.[74] Use of flexible terms such as good faith provisions and 'endeavours' clauses could be one strategy to signal a commitment to contextualism and relational values. But a judge in a formalist default contract law system may

[71] R Korobkin, 'The Status Quo Bias and Contract Default Rules' (1998) 83 *Cornell Law Review* 608.

[72] See EA Posner, 'Economic Analysis of Contract Law After Three Decades: Success or Failure?' (2003) 112 *Yale Law Journal* 829.

[73] J Morgan, *Contract Law: Great Debates* (Basingstoke, Palgrave Macmillan, 2012) 74. See also Scott, above n 26, arguing 'parties can embed within the formal contract directions for the context within which the contract should be interpreted': 127.

[74] See in particular Ch 4.

struggle to make such clauses effective and give them meaningful content. Complex paperwork with detailed specification of duties, monitoring and so on may be necessary for project purposes, rather than as an indicator of strict legal entitlements. But that very commitment to a set of comprehensive written terms (irrespective of their content) may be taken by the judge to indicate a preference for formalist interpretation which proceeds upon the narrow basis of a close reading of the contract text. Contracting for a contextualist interpretation method within a formalist system risks being misunderstood or distorted by formalism. The Court of Appeal decision in *Compass Medical Group* is an ample demonstration of how narrowly 'good faith' clauses can be interpreted when they appear in detailed formal documents. Such clauses are treated as having meaning only in relation to the other express terms, with the result that such clauses are emptied of much of their substantive value in communicating the need for loyalty, co-operation, and so on, as well as their capacity to signal the parties' commitment to a standards-based understanding of their obligations and the resolution of their dispute. Entreating the parties to draft their commitments with greater caution is unlikely to solve this problem, since the more carefully such terms are drafted the more restrictively they are likely to be interpreted. Thus the parties have to tread a difficult path between sufficient certainty in such clauses, which demands a degree of specification in the good faith duty, with enough generality to enable a judge to accord such duties the requisite degree of significance in the contract scheme. In a contextualist system, however, the judge's attention to context, rather than poring over syntax and language, may be the best objective evidence of what the parties intended by such a clause. Even a relatively brief investigation of the contract purposes, the wider project of which it is part, length of anticipated relationship, degree of co-operation necessary to bring about project purposes, and so on may give a judge a clear steer in interpreting the clause. Contracting out of formalism may therefore be difficult to achieve and places an increased burden on the parties to write into their agreements with some care (and in an interpretation-proof manner) the diffuse obligations that govern their relationship. Certainly some parties—those well-resourced parties with access to legal advice—may be predisposed towards formalism, but such parties are also better positioned to contract around the defaults that do not suit their purposes. It may matter little to those parties that prefer formalism what the defaults are, provided there are ways for them to communicate their preferences concerning dispute resolution to a court. It is probably much easier for the parties to signal formalism both within the terms and when the contextual factors (nature of the trade, availability of trade associations and lawyer-drafted terms) readily support the formalist interpretation, particularly since courts will doubtless be aware that formalism will be the preference for some, even most, sophisticated contracting parties.

CONCLUSION

Relational contract theory is individualised and dynamic,[75] and a contract law that takes on board some of its insights is likely to reflect this individualism and dynamism. Such a law can be castigated as unpredictable and ad hoc, but to the extent that its hallmark is close attention to context, its method is entirely predictable and from this starting point outcomes may be broadly predictable also. The indeterminacy simply reflects the complexity of the phenomenon that is subject to the legal controls. The main benefit of a relational and commercial-expectations approach to contract law is that it seeks to draw out and apply the internally generated norms of the business relationship to questions concerning the scope of contractual obligations or dispute resolution. This is preferable to an approach which champions a set of external standards whose assumptions and expectations are a poor fit with the actual practice that the law is supposed to regulate and facilitate. In this respect the contextual factors that may be examined as part of the legal reasoning process will be familiar to the parties because they constitute and inform the environment in which they make and perform their agreement. Stability in the system is achieved by courts routinely upholding the provisions agreed between the parties, and fashioning remedies for breach that mesh consistently with the context of the parties' agreement, its aims and purposes. While this may be the broad thrust of the approach, the matters discussed above are all very tentative suggestions as to how relational factors and commercial expectations might be operationalised within contract legal reasoning processes. In truth there are a variety of possible strategies available to further the development of a relational contract law, but the overall point is that such an approach may offer better support for the parties' commercial expectations than alternatives.

To an extent, such a discriminating and individualistic approach is nothing new in contract law. The law already demonstrates considerable capacity to take an individualistic approach to contract dispute resolution. Commercial courts pride themselves, rightly or wrongly, on being able to reach outcomes which either reflect specific commercial practices, or are motivated by business common sense. In relation to the operation of doctrine, investigation of the wider context of an agreement may bring to light shared understandings that were not made express. Once uncovered, there are legal techniques which allow courts to incorporate the parties' implicit understandings into agreements—implied terms and collateral contracts are two examples—as well as doctrines which allow them to enforce an agreement where the strict contractual requirements might be lacking,

[75] MA Eisenberg, above n 19, 812–13.

such as estoppel.[76] In addition, courts have on occasion shown willingness to decide cases based on parties' reasonable expectations arising from the business relationship or to show a flexible approach towards contract modification.[77] Nevertheless, these developments take place within a system that still regards contracting as primarily an adversarial and competitive process, and that evinces a preference for the contract text as the main source of evidence about obligations.

The argument for relationalism and contextualism can easily be hijacked by semantics, since one may regard 'informal' norms and implicit dimensions as precisely falling outwith the scope of the legal. But the precise assimilation of legality with formalism is exactly what relationalism denies. While lawyers may content themselves that agreements displaying a high degree of relationality are unlikely to be litigated, this seems an inadequate response for the general law to give, and raises the danger of the law remaining stuck in a relatively formalistic cycle. While it must undoubtedly be the case that the law cannot and should not interfere in all aspects of commercial relationships, there are limits as to how far this argument should be taken. Formalism may be an effective strategy for some parties, especially those with access to reliable legal advice, or strong trade associations that can incur the costs of formalisation by drafting a set of well-tailored terms that are known and used throughout the industry. But these sorts of contracting party should not be taken as representative of contractors as whole, nor should the preferences amongst such parties be taken as justifying formalism as the template against which all contractual agreements should be judged. Agreements that are neither entirely relationally constituted, where recourse to law may be unnecessary, nor fully arm's length, where there might be more confidence that *caveat emptor* was the relevant default, would be allowed to fall through a regulatory net in such a system. Without change the law will continue to find it difficult to accommodate these agreements within its scheme of rules. If commercial contract law is to remain responsive to commercial practice and expectation it must be capable of governing an extensive range of contracting circumstances and contexts. In substantially disregarding implicit norms as irrelevant the court effectively abdicates its role as 'standard-setter' in commercial agreements.[78] The point of a relational contract law is to achieve some overall sense of how *the parties* understood their agreement. There is nothing in

[76] For a discussion of how courts are frequently required to factor contractors' implicit understandings into agreements through doctrinal means, see D Campbell and H Collins, 'Discovering the Implicit Dimensions of Contract' in Campbell, Collins and Wightman (eds) *Implicit Dimensions of Contract* (Oxford, Hart Publishing, 2003) 28–49.

[77] Illustrated respectively in *Blackpool and Fylde Aero Club v Blackpool Borough Council* [1990] 3 All ER 25 and *Williams v Roffey* [1991] 1 QB 1.

[78] H Collins, 'Competing Norms of Contractual Behaviour' in D Campbell and P Vincent-Jones (eds), above n 55, 67, 93.

that idea that suggests that the conclusion must always be that the parties intended the relationship to be co-operative—this must depend upon what the parties say about their agreement and the adjudicator's assessment of the evidence. The problem is that the courts rarely approach the issues by first considering how the parties wanted their agreement to be governed. Courts commence with a particular conception of the law of contract and this starting point largely determines their conclusions. What relational theory demands is sensitivity to a range of contracting circumstances and a denial of the traditional binary lines along which debates are often drawn. Pragmatism, context and flexibility are the hallmarks of a relational approach to contractual agreements. There will be costs involved in developing a relational contract law, but the institutional costs in not developing it, particularly in terms of our confidence in contract law's capacity to facilitate commercial dealing and commercial expectations in all their forms, are likely to be greater.

Bibliography

Aivazian, VA, Trebilcock, MJ and Penny, M, 'The Law of Contract Modifications: The Uncertain Quest for a Benchmark of Enforceability' (1984) 22 *Osgoode Hall Law Journal* 173

Amsterdam, AG and Bruner, J, *Minding the Law* (Cambridge MA, Harvard University Press, 2002)

Amstutz, M and Teubner, G (eds), *Networks: Legal Issues of Multilateral Co-operation* (Oxford, Hart Publishing, 2009)

Amstutz, M, Karavas, V and Teubner, G, 'Preface: What is Legal Analysis of Contractual Networks?' in M Amstutz and G Teubner (eds), *Networks: Legal Issues of Multilateral Co-operation* (Oxford, Hart Publishing, 2009) vii–xviii

Armour, J and Deakin, S, 'Norms in Private Insolvency: The "London Approach" to the Resolution of Financial Distress' (2001) 1 *Journal of Corporate Law Studies* 21

Arrighetti, A, Bachmann, R and Deakin, S, 'Contract Law, Social Norms and Inter-firm Co-operation' (1997) 21 *Cambridge Journal of Economics* 171

Arvind, TT, 'Contract Transactions and Equity' in LA DiMatteo, Q Zhou, S Saintier and K Rowley (eds), *Commercial Contract Law: Transatlantic Perspectives* (Cambridge, CUP, 2013) 146–77

Atiyah, PS, *The Rise and Fall of Freedom of Contract* (Oxford, OUP, 1979)

Atiyah, PS, *Essays on Contract* (Oxford, OUP, 1988)

Atiyah, PS, 'Contracts, Promises and the Law of Obligations' in *Essays on Contract* (Oxford, OUP, 1988) 10–56

Austen-Baker, R, 'A Relational Law of Contract?' (2004) 20 *Journal of Contract Law* 125

Austen-Baker, R, 'Comprehensive Contract Theory: A Four-norm Model of Contract Relations' (2009) 25 *Journal of Contract Law* 216

Ayres, I, 'Valuing Modern Contract Scholarship' (2003) 112 *Yale Law Journal* 881

Ayres, I and Gertner, R, 'Filling Gaps in Incomplete Contracts: An Economic Theory of Default Rules' (1989) 99 *Yale Law Journal* 87

Ayres, I and Gertner, R, 'Majoritarian vs Minoritarian Defaults' (1999) 51 *Stanford Law Review* 1591

Bachmann, R and Inkpen, AC, 'Understanding Institutional-based Trust Building Processes in Inter-organizational Relationships' (2011) 32 *Organization Studies* 281

Badawi, AB, 'Interpretative Preferences and the Limits of the New Formalism' (2009) 6 *Berkeley Business Law Journal* 1

Baker, JH, 'From Sanctity of Contract to Reasonable Expectation' (1979) 32 *Current Legal Problems* 17

Baker, JH, 'The Law Merchant and the Common Law before 1700' (1979) 38 *CLJ* 295

Barnes, R, 'Commerciality and the Construction of Commercial Contracts: Some Observations on the Use of Legal Reasoning' in C Twigg-Flesner and G Villalta Puig (eds), *Boundaries of Commercial and Trade Law* (Munich, Sellier, 2011) 179–204

Barnett, RE, 'The Sound of Silence: Default Rules and Contractual Consent' (1992) 78 *Virginia Law Review* 821

Barnett, RE, 'A Consent Theory of Contract' (1996) 86 *Columbia Law Review* 269

Bayley, JE, 'Prior Negotiations and Subsequent Conduct in Contract Interpretation: Principles and Practical Concerns' (2011–12) 28 *Journal of Contract Law* 179

Beale, H, 'A Review of the Contracts (Rights of Third Parties) Act 1999' in A Burrows and E Peel (eds), *Contract Formation and Parties* (Oxford, OUP, 2010) 225–50

Beale, H, 'The Impact of the Decisions of the European Courts on English Contract Law: The Limits of Voluntary Harmonization' (2010) 3 *European Review of Private Law* 501

Beale, H and Dugdale, T, 'Contracts Between Businessmen: Planning and the Use of Contractual Remedies' (1975) 2 *British Journal of Law and Society* 45

Ben-Shahar, O, 'The Tentative Case Against Flexibility in Commercial Law' (1999) 66 *University of Chicago Law Review* 781

Ben-Shahar, O (ed), *Boilerplate: The Foundation of Market Contracts* (Cambridge, CUP, 2007)

Benson, BL, 'The Spontaneous Evolution of Commercial Law' (1989) 55 *Southern Economic Journal* 644

Benson, P (ed), *The Theory of Contract Law* (Cambridge, CUP, 2001)

Berg, A, 'Thrashing Through the Undergrowth' (2006) 122 *LQR* 354

Bernstein, L, 'Opting Out of the Legal System: Extralegal Contractual Relations in the Diamond Industry' (1992) 21 *Journal of Legal Studies* 115

Bernstein, L, 'Merchant Law in a Merchant Court: Rethinking the Code's Search for Immanent Business Norms' (1996) 144 *University of Pennsylvania Law Review* 1765

Bernstein, L, 'The Questionable Empirical Basis of Article 2's Incorporation Strategy: A Preliminary Study' (1999) 66 *University of Chicago Law Review* 710

Bernstein, L, 'Private Commercial Law in the Cotton Industry: Creating Co-operation Through Rules, Norms and Institutions' (2001) 99 *Michigan Law Review* 1724

Binder, G and Weisberg, R, *Literary Criticisms of Law* (Princeton, Princeton University Press, 2000)

Blois, K, 'B2B "Relationships"—A Social Construction of Reality?' (2003) 3 *Marketing Theory* 79

Blois, K, 'Is it Commercially Irresponsible to Trust?' (2003) 45 *Journal of Business Ethics* 183

Bradgate, R, 'Contracts, Contract Law and Reasonable Expectations' in S Worthington (ed), *Commercial Law and Commercial Practice* (Oxford, Hart Publishing, 2003) 651–90

Braucher, J, Kidwell, J and Whitford, WC (eds), *Revisiting the Contracts Scholarship of Stewart Macaulay* (Oxford, Hart Publishing, 2013)

Bridge, M, 'Documents and Contractual Congruence in International Trade' in S Worthington (ed), *Commercial Law and Commercial Practice* (Oxford, Hart Publishing, 2003) 213–40

Bridgeman, C, 'Contracts as Plans' (2009) *University of Illinois Law Review* 341

Brownsword, R, 'Two Concepts of Good Faith' (1994) 7 *Journal of Contract Law* 197

Brownsword, R, 'From Co-operative Contracting to a Contract of Co-operation' in D Campbell and P Vincent-Jones (eds), *Contract and Economic Organisation* (Aldershot, Dartmouth, 1996) 14–39

Brownsword, R, 'After *Investors*: Interpretation, Expectation and the Implicit Dimension of the "New Contextualism"' in D Campbell, H Collins and J Wightman (eds), *Implicit Dimensions of Contract* (Oxford, Hart Publishing, 2003) 103–41

Brownsword, R, *Contract Law: Themes for the 21st Century*, 2nd edn (Oxford, OUP, 2006)

Brownsword, R, 'Network Contracts Revisited' in M Amstutz and G Teubner (eds), *Networks: Legal Issues of Multilateral Co-operation* (Oxford, Hart Publishing, 2009) 31–52

Burchell, B and Wilkinson, F, 'Trust, Business Relationships and the Contractual Environment' (1997) 21 *Cambridge Journal of Economics* 217

Burrows, A and Peel, E (eds), *Contract Terms* (Oxford, OUP, 2007)

Burrows, A and Peel, E (eds), *Contract Formation and Parties* (Oxford, OUP, 2010)

Buxbaum, RM, 'Is "Network" a Legal Concept?' (1993) 149 *Journal of Institutional and Theoretical Economics* 698

Calnan, R, 'Construction of Commercial Contracts: A Practitioner's Perspective' in A Burrows and E Peel (eds), *Contract Terms* (Oxford, OUP, 2007) 17–24

Campbell, D, 'The Relational Constitution of the Discrete Contract' in D Campbell and P Vincent-Jones (eds), *Contract and Economic Organisation* (Aldershot, Dartmouth, 1996) 40–66

Campbell, D, 'Reflexivity and Welfarism in the Modern Law of Contract' (2000) 20 *OJLS* 477

Campbell, D, 'Ian Macneil and the Relational Theory of Contract' in I Macneil, *The Relational Theory of Contract: Selected Works of Ian Macneil*, D Campbell (ed) (London, Sweet & Maxwell, 2001) 3–58

Campbell, D, 'The Incompleteness of Our Understanding of the Law and Economics of Relational Contract' (2004) *Wisconsin Law Review* 645

Campbell, D, 'What Do We Mean By the Non-Use of Contract?' in J Braucher, J Kidwell and WC Whitford (eds), *Revisiting the Contracts Scholarship of Stewart Macaulay* (Oxford, Hart Publishing, 2013) 159–90

Campbell, D and Collins, H, 'Discovering the Implicit Dimensions of Contract' in D Campbell, H Collins and J Wightman (eds), *Implicit Dimensions of Contract* (Oxford, Hart Publishing, 2003) 25–49

Campbell, D, Collins, H and Wightman, J (eds), *Implicit Dimensions of Contract* (Oxford, Hart Publishing, 2003)

Campbell, D and Harris, D, 'Flexibility in Long Term Contractual Relationships: The Role of Cooperation' (1993) 20 *Journal of Law and Society* 166

Campbell, D and Picciotto, S, 'Exploring the Interaction Between Law and Economics: The Limits of Formalism' (1998) 18 *Legal Studies* 249

Campbell, D and Vincent-Jones, P (eds), *Contract and Economic Organisation* (Aldershot, Dartmouth, 1996)

Canavan, R, 'English Commercial Law and Private Legal Systems' in C Twigg-Flesner and G Villalta Puig (eds), *Boundaries of Commercial and Trade Law* (Munich, Sellier, 2011) 153–78

Cane, P and Kritzer, HM (eds), *The Oxford Handbook of Empirical Research in Law* (Oxford, OUP, 2010)

Charny, D, 'Nonlegal Sanctions in Commercial Relationships' (1990) 104 *Harvard Law Review* 375

Charny, D, 'Illusions of Spontaneous Order: "Norms" in Contractual Relationships' (1996) 144 *University of Pennsylvania Law Review* 1841
Charny, D, 'The New Formalism in Contract' (1999) 66 *University of Chicago Law Review* 842
Chen-Wishart, M, *Contract Law*, 3rd edn (Oxford, OUP, 2010)
Coase, RH, *The Firm, the Market and the Law* (Chicago, University of Chicago Press, 1988)
Coleman, J and Shapiro, S (eds), *The Oxford Handbook of Jurisprudence and Philosophy of Law* (Oxford, OUP, 2002)
Collins, H, 'Competing Norms of Contractual Behaviour' in D Campbell and P Vincent-Jones (eds), *Contract and Economic Organisation* (Aldershot, Dartmouth, 1996) 67–94
Collins, H, *Regulating Contracts* (Oxford, OUP, 1999)
Collins, H, *The Law of Contract*, 4th edn (London, Lexis-Nexis Butterworths, 2003)
Collins, H, 'Objectivity and Committed Contextualism in Interpretation' in S Worthington (ed), *Commercial Law and Commercial Practice* (Oxford, Hart Publishing, 2003) 189–209
Collins, H, 'Lord Hoffmann and the Common Law of Contract' (2009) 5 *European Review of Contract Law* 474
Collins, H, 'Introduction to Networks as Connected Contracts' in G Teubner, *Networks as Connected Contracts* (H Collins, ed) (trans M Everson) (Oxford, Hart Publishing, 2011) 1–72
Cooter, R, 'Decentralised Law for a Complex Economy: The Structural Approach to Adjudicating the New Law Merchant' (1996) 144 *University of Pennsylvania Law Review* 1643
Cranston, R, 'What Do Courts Do?' (1986) 5 *Civil Justice Quarterly* 123
Craswell, R, 'Contract Law, Default Rules, and the Philosophy of Promising' (1989) 88 *Michigan Law Review* 489
Craswell, R, 'The Relational Move: Some Questions From Law and Economics' (1993) 3 *Southern Califormia Interdisciplinary Law Journal* 91
Craswell, R, 'Do Trade Customs Exist?' in JS Kraus and SD Walt (eds), *The Jurisprudential Foundations of Corporate and Commercial Law* (Cambridge, CUP, 2000) 118–48
Craswell, R, 'Two Economic Theories of Enforcing Promises' in P Benson (ed), *The Theory of Contract Law* (Cambridge, CUP, 2001) 19–44
Craswell, R, 'In That Case, What is the Question? Economics and the Demands of Contract Theory' (2003) 112 *Yale Law Journal* 903
Cross, FB, 'Law and Trust' (2005) 93 *Georgetown Law Journal* 1457
Cunningham, LA, 'Toward A Prudential and Credibility-Centered Parol Evidence Rule' (2000) 68 *University of Cincinnati Law Review* 269
Cunningham, LA, 'The Common Law as an Iterative Process: A Preliminary Enquiry' (2006) 81 *Notre Dame Law Review* 748
Davenport, BJ, 'Thanks to the House of Lords' (1999) 115 *LQR* 11
Deakin, S and Michie, J (eds), *Contracts, Co-operation and Competition* (Oxford, OUP, 1997)
Deakin, S and Wilkinson, F, 'Contracts, Co-operation and Trust: The Role of the Institutional Framework' in D Campbell and P Vincent-Jones (eds), *Contract and Economic Organisation* (Aldershot, Dartmouth, 1996) 95–115

Lord Devlin, 'The Relation Between Commercial Law and Commercial Practice' (1951) 14 *MLR* 249
DiMatteo, LA, Zhou, Q, Saintier, S and Rowley, K (eds), *Commercial Contract Law: Transatlantic Perspectives* (Cambridge, CUP, 2013)
Dingwall, R and Cloatre, E, 'Vanishing Trials?: An English Perspective' (2006) *Journal of Dispute Resolution* 51
Dnes, AW, 'The Law and Economics of Contract Modifications: Williams v Roffey' (1995) 15 *International Review of Law and Economics* 225
Dnes, AW, *The Economics of Law* (Mason OH, Southwestern, 2005)
Drahozel, CR, 'Commercial Norms, Commercial Codes and International Commercial Arbitration' (2000) 33 *Vanderbilt Journal of Transnational Law* 79
Drahozal, CR, 'Contracting Out of National Law: An Empirical Look at the New Law Merchant' (2005) 80 *Notre Dame Law Review* 523
Duggan, AJ, 'Commercial Law and the Limits of the Black Letter Approach' in S Worthington (ed), *Commercial Law and Commercial Practice* (Oxford, Hart Publishing, 2003) 595–614
Duxbury, N, *Patterns of American Jurisprudence* (Oxford, OUP, 1995)
Dworkin, R, 'Is Wealth a Value?' (1980) 9 *Journal of Legal Studies* 191
Eisenberg, MA, 'The Emergence of Dynamic Contract Law' (2000) 88 *California Law Review* 1743
Eisenberg, MA, 'Why There is No Law of Relational Contracts' (2000) 94 *Northwestern University Law Review* 805
Epstein, RA, 'Confusion about Custom: Disentangling Informal Customs from Standard Contractual Provisions' (1999) 66 *University of Chicago Law Review* 821
Epstein, RA, 'Reflections on the Historical Origins of the Law Merchant' (2004) 5 *Chicago Journal of International Law* 1
Esser, JP, 'Institutionalizing Industry: The Changing Forms of Contract' (1996) 21 *Law and Social Enquiry* 593
Lord Falconer, *Opening Speech for European Contract Law Conference*, Mansion House Walbrook, London, 26 September 2005 www.ec.europa.eu/consumers/cons_int/safe_shop/fair_bus_pract/cont_law/conference092005/falconer2005.pdf
Feinman, J, 'Relational Contract Theory in Context' (2000) 94 *Northwestern University Law Review* 737
Flanagan, PM, 'Dymythologising the Law Merchant: The Impropriety of the Lex Mercatoria as a Choice of Law' (2004) 15 *International Company and Commercial Law Review* 297
Fried, C, *Contract as Promise* (Cambridge MA, Harvard University Press, 1981)
Fuller, L, 'Consideration and Form' (1941) *Columbia Law Review* 799
Fuller, L and Perdue, W, 'The Reliance Interest in Contract Damages' (1936) 46 *Yale Law Journal* 52
Furmston, M and Tolhurst, GJ, *Contract Formation: Law and Practice* (Oxford, OUP, 2010)
Galanter, M, 'Why the "Haves" Come Out Ahead: Speculations on the Limits of Legal Change' (1974) 9 *Law and Society Review* 95
Gambetta, D (ed), *Trust: Making and Breaking Cooperative Relations* (Oxford, Basil Blackwell, 1988)
Gava, J, 'False Lessons from the Real Deal: Campbell, Collins and Wightman on Implicit Dimensions of Contract—Discrete, Relational, and Network Contracts?' (2005) 21 *Journal of Contract Law* 182

Gava, J, 'Can Contract Law Be Justified on Economic Grounds?' [2006] *University of Queensland Law Journal* 253

Gava, J, 'Dixonian Strict Legalism: *Wilson v Darling Island Stevedoring* and Contracting in the Real World' (2010) 30 *OJLS* 519

Gava, J, 'How Should Judges Decide Commercial Contract Cases?' (2013) 30 *Journal of Contract Law* 133

Gava, J and Greene, J, 'Do We Need a Hybrid Law of Contract? Why Hugh Collins is Wrong and Why it Matters' (2004) 63 *CLJ* 605

Genn, H, *Court-Based ADR Initiatives For Non-Family Civil Disputes: The Commercial Court And The Court Of Appeal* (Lord Chancellor's Department, 2002)

Genn, H, *Judging Civil Justice* (Cambridge, CUP, 2010)

Gessner V (ed), *Contractual Certainty in International Trade* (Oxford, Hart Publishing, 2009)

Gibbons, K, 'A Conversation with Lord Hoffmann' (2010) 4 *Law and Financial Markets Review* 242

Gillette, CP, 'Lock-In Effects in Law and Norms' (1998) 78 *Boston University Law Review* 813

Gilson, RJ, Sabel, CF and Scott, RE, 'Braiding: The Interaction of Formal and Informal Contracting in Theory, Practice and Doctrine' (2010) 110 *Columbia Law Review* 1377

Gneezy, U and Rustichini, A, 'A Fine is a Price' (2000) 29 *Journal of Legal Studies* 1

Goetz, C and Scott, RE, 'Enforcing Promises: An Examination of the Basis of Contract' (1980) 89 *Yale Law Journal* 1265

Lord Goff, 'Commercial Contracts and the Commercial Court' [1984] *Lloyd's Maritime and Commercial Law Quarterly* 382

Goode, R, 'The Codification of Commercial Law' (1988) 14 *Monash University Law Review* 135

Goode, R, 'Usage and its Reception in Transnational Commercial Law' (1997) 46 *ICLQ* 1

Goode, R, *Commercial Law in the Next Millennium* (Hamlyn Lecture Series, London, Sweet & Maxwell, 1998)

Goodhart, CAE, 'Economics and the Law: Too Much One Way Traffic' (1997) 60 *MLR* 1

Lord Grabiner, 'The Iterative Process of Contract Interpretation' (2012) 128 *LQR* 41

Hacker, PMS and Raz, J, *Law, Morality and Society* (Oxford, OUP, 1977)

Hagedoorn, J and Hesen, G, 'Contract Law and the Governance of Inter-firm Technology Partnerships—An Analysis of Different Modes of Partnering and their Contractual Implications' (2007) 44 *Journal of Management Studies* 342

Hart, HLA, *The Concept of Law*, 2nd edn (Oxford, OUP, 1994)

Hathaway, OA, 'Path Dependence in the Law: The Course and Pattern of Legal Change in a Common Law System' (2001) 86 *Iowa Law Review* 601

Hayek, FA, *Law, Legislation and Liberty* (London, Routledge and Kegan Paul, 1982)

Heydon, JD, 'How the Courts Develop Commercial Law by Looking Outside the Trial Record into the External World' [2012] *LMCLQ* 30

Lord Hoffmann, 'The Intolerable Wrestle with Words and Meanings' (1997) 114 *South African Law Journal* 656

Lord Hoffmann, 'The *Achilleas*: Custom and Practice or Foreseeability?' (2010) 14 *Edinburgh Law Review* 47

Hogg, M, 'Fundamental Issues for the Reform of the Law of Contractual Interpretation' (2011) 15 *Edinburgh Law Review* 406

Hunter, H, 'The Growing Uncertainty about Good Faith in American Contract Law' (2002) 20 *Journal of Contract Law* 31

Hunter, R, McGlynn, C and Rackley, E (eds), *Feminist Judgments: From Theory to Practice* (Oxford, Hart Publishing, 2010)

Hviid, M, 'Long Term Contracts and Relational Contracts' in B Bouckaert and G De Geest (eds), *The Encyclopaedia of Law and Economics vol. III: The Regulation of Contracts* (Cheltenham, Edward Elgar, 2000) 46–72

Lord Irvine, 'The Law: An Engine for Trade' (2001) 64 *MLR* 333

Lord Justice Jackson, *Review of Litigation Costs: Preliminary Report Volume One* (London, TSO, 2009)

Lord Justice Jackson, *Review of Litigation Costs: Preliminary Report Volume Two* (London, TSO, 2009)

Lord Justice Jackson, *Review of Litigation Costs: Final Report* (London, TSO, 2010)

Jackson, S, 'Good Faith in Construction—Will It Make a Difference and Is It Worth the Trouble?' [2007] *Construction Law Journal* 420

Johnstone, JS, 'Should the Law Ignore Commercial Norms? A Comment on the Bernstein Conjecture and its Relevance for Contract Law Theory and Reform' (2001) 99 *Michigan Law Review* 1791

Jolls, C, Sunstein, CR and Thaler, RH, 'A Behavioral Approach to Law and Economics' (1998) 50 *Stanford Law Review* 1471

Joskow, PL, 'Contract Duration and Relationship-Specific Investment: Empirical Evidence from Coal Markets' (1987) 77 *The American Economic Review* 168

Judiciary of England and Wales, *Report and Recommendations of the Commercial Court Long Trials Working Party* (December 2007)

Kalnins, A and Mayer, K, 'Relationships and Hybrid Contracts: An Analysis of Contract Choice in Information Technology' (2004) 20 *Journal of Law, Economics and Organization* 207

Kaplow, L, 'Rules versus Standards: An Economic Analysis' (1992) 42 *Duke Law Journal* 557

Katz, AW, 'The Economics of Form and Substance in Contract Interpretation' (2004) 104 *Columbia Law Review* 496

Katz, AW, 'The Relative Costs of Incorporating Trade Usage into Domestic versus International Sales Contracts' (2004) 5 *Chicago Journal of International Law* 181

Keating, D, 'Measuring Sales Law Against Sales Practice: A Reality Check' (1997) 17 *Journal of Law and Commerce* 99

Keating, D, 'Exploring the Battle of the Forms in Action' (2000) 98 *Michigan Law Review* 2678

Kelman, M, 'Behavioral Economics as Part of a Rhetorical Duet: A Response to Jolls, Sunstein and Thaler' (1998) 50 *Stanford Law Review* 1577

Kimel, D, *From Promise to Contract* (Oxford, Hart Publishing, 2005)

Kimel, D, 'The Choice of Paradigm for Theory of Contract: Reflections on the Relational Model' (2007) 27 *OJLS* 233

Knapp, C, 'Taking Contracts Private: The Quiet Revolution in Contract Law' (2002) 71 *Fordham Law Review* 761

Konradi, W, 'The Role of *Lex Mercatoria* in Supporting Globalized Transactions: An Empirical Insight into the Governance Structure of the Timber Industry' in V Gessner (ed), *Contractual Certainty in International Trade* (Oxford, Hart Publishing, 2009) 49–86

Korobkin, R, 'The Status Quo Bias and Contract Default Rules' (1998) 83 *Cornell Law Review* 608

Korobkin, R, 'Behavioral Economics, Contract Formation and Contract Law' in CR Sunstein (ed), *Behavioral Law and Economics* (Cambridge, CUP, 2000) 116–43

Korobkin, R, 'Empirical Scholarship in Contract Law: Possibilities and Pitfalls' (2002) *University of Illinois Law Review* 1033

Kramer, A, 'Implication in Fact as an Instance of Contractual Interpretation' (2004) 63 *CLJ* 384

Kraus, JS, 'Legal Design and the Evolution of Commercial Norms' (1997) 26 *Journal of Legal Studies* 377

Kraus, JS, 'Philosophy of Contract Law' in J Coleman and S Shapiro (eds), *The Oxford Handbook of Jurisprudence and Philosophy of Law* (Oxford, OUP, 2002) 687–751

Kraus, JS and Walt, SD, 'In Defense of The Incorporation Strategy' in JS Kraus and SD Walt (eds), *The Jurisprudential Foundations of Corporate and Commercial Law* (Cambridge, CUP, 2000) 193–237

Kraus, JS and Walt, SD (eds), *The Jurisprudential Foundations of Corporate and Commercial Law* (Cambridge, CUP, 2000)

Lane, C and Bachmann, R, 'The Social Constitution of Trust: Supplier Relations in Britain and Germany' (1996) 17 *Organization Studies* 365

Law Commission, *Law of Contract: The Parol Evidence Rule* (No 154) (London, HMSO, 1986)

Law Commission, *Privity of Contract: Contracts for the Benefit of Third Parties* (Law Com No 242, Cm 3329) (London, HMSO, 1996)

Law Commission, *Unfair Terms in Contracts,* (Law Com No 292, Cm 6464) (London, TSO, 2005)

Law Commission and Scottish Law Commission, *Unfair Terms in Consumer Contracts: A New Approach? Issues Paper* (2012) http://lawcommission.justice.gov.uk/docs/unfair_terms_in_consumer_contracts_issues.pdf

Lawton, D, 'Four Building Blocks of Efficient Capital Markets', address at the Practising Law Institute on 1 February 2013: www.fsa.gov.uk/library/communication/speeches/2013/0201-dl

Lazzarini, SG, Miller, GJ and Zenger, TR, 'Order with Some Law: Complementarity versus Substitution of Formal and Informal Arrangements' (2004) 20 *Journal of Law, Economics and Organization* 261

Lewis, L, 'Contracts Between Businessmen: Reform of the Law of Firm Offers and an Empirical Study of Tendering Practices in the Building Industry' (1982) 9 *Journal of Law and Society* 153

Liebowitz, SJ and Margolis, SE, 'Path Dependence, Lock-In, and History' (1995) 11 *Journal of Law, Economics and Organization* 205

Linzer, P, 'The Comfort of Certainty: Plain Meaning and the Parol Evidence Rule' (2002) 71 *Fordham Law Review* 799

Lorenz, EH, 'Neither Friends Nor Strangers: Informal Networks of Subcontracting in French Industry' in D Gambetta (ed), *Trust: Making and Breaking Cooperative Relations* (Oxford, Basil Blackwell, 1988) 194–210

Lucy, W, *Philosophy of Private Law* (Oxford, OUP, 2007)
Lyons, B and Mehta, J, 'Contracts, Opportunism and Trust: Self-interest and Social Orientation' (1997) 21 *Cambridge Journal of Economics* 239
Lyons, B and Mehta, J, 'Private Sector Business Contracts: The Text Between the Lines' in S Deakin and J Michie (eds), *Contracts, Co-operation and Competition* (Oxford, OUP, 1997) 43–66
Macaulay, S, 'Non-Contractual Relations in Business: A Preliminary Study' (1963) 28 *American Sociological Review* 55
Macaulay, S, 'Relational Contracts Floating on a Sea of Custom? Thoughts about the Ideas of Ian Macneil and Lisa Bernstein' (2000) 94 *Northwestern University Law Review* 775
Macaulay, S, 'The Real and the Paper Deal: Empirical Pictures of Relationships, Complexity and the Urge for Transparent Simple Rules' in D Campbell, H Collins and J Wightman (eds), *Implicit Dimensions of Contracts* (Oxford, Hart Publishing, 2003) 51–102
Macaulay, S, 'Contracts, New Legal Realism, and Improving the Navigation of the Yellow Submarine' (2006) 80 *Tulane Law Review* 1161
MacCormick, N, *Legal Reasoning and Legal Theory*, rev'd edn (Oxford, OUP, 1994)
Macneil, I, 'A Primer of Contract Planning' (1975) 48 *Southern California Law Review* 627
Macneil, I, 'Contracts: Adjustment of Long-Term Economic Relations under Classical, Neoclassical and Relational Contract Law' (1978) 72 *Northwestern University Law Review* 854
Macneil, I, 'Economic Analysis of Contractual Relations: Its Shortfalls and the Need for a Rich Classificatory Apparatus' (1981) 75 *Northwestern University Law Review* 1017
Macneil, I, 'Efficient Breach, Circles in the Sky'(1982) 68 *Virginia Law Review* 947
Macneil, I, 'Values in Contract: Internal and External' (1983) 78 *Northwestern University Law Review* 340
Macneil, I, 'Relational Contract Theory as Sociology: A Reply to Professors Lindenberg and de Vos' (1987) 143 *Journal of Institutional and Theoretical Economics* 272
Macneil, I, 'Relational Contract Theory: Challenges and Queries' (2000) 94 *Northwestern University Law Review* 877
Macneil, I, *The Relational Theory of Contract: Selected Works of Ian Macneil*, D Campbell (ed) (London, Sweet & Maxwell, 2001)
Macneil, I, 'Reflections on Relational Contract Theory after a Neo-Classical Seminar' in D Campbell, H Collins and J Wightman (eds), *Implicit Dimensions of Contracts* (Oxford, Hart Publishing, 2003) 207–17
Mason, J, 'Contracting in Good Faith—Giving the Parties What They Want' [2007] *Construction Law Journal* 436
McKendrick, E, 'The Regulation of Long Term Contracts in English Law' in J Beatson and D Friedman (eds), *Good Faith and Fault in Contract Law* (Oxford, OUP, 1995) 305–33
McKendrick, E, 'English Contract Law: A Rich Past, an Uncertain Future?' (1997) 50 *Current Legal Problems* 25
McKendrick, E, 'The Interpretation of Contracts: Lord Hoffmann's Restatement' in S Worthington (ed), *Commercial Law and Commercial Practice* (Oxford, Hart Publishing, 2003) 139–62

McKendrick, E, *Contract Law: Text, Cases and Materials*, 2nd edn (Oxford, OUP, 2005)
McKendrick, E, *Goode on Commercial Law*, 4th edn (London, Penguin, 2010)
McLauchlan, D, 'Contract Interpretation: What is it About?' (2009) 31 *Sydney Law Review* 5
McLauchlan, D, 'The Contract That Neither Party Intends' (2012) 29 *Journal of Contract Law* 26
Mescher, B, 'Business Ethics and the Law of Contract' (2009) 8 *Journal of Law and Financial Management* 8
Millett, PJ, 'Equity's Place in the Law of Commerce' (1998) 114 *LQR* 214
Ministry of Justice, *Judicial and Court Statistics* (2011), www.justice.gov.uk/statistics/courts-and-sentencing/judicial-annual-2011
Mitchell, C, 'Contract: There's Still Life in the Classical Law' [2003] *CLJ* 26
Mitchell, C, 'Leading a Life of its Own? The Roles of Reasonable Expectation in Contract Law' (2003) 23 *OJLS* 639
Mitchell, C, 'Entire Agreement Clauses: Contracting Out of Contextualism' (2006) 22 *Journal of Contract Law* 222
Mitchell, C, 'Contracts and Contract Law: Challenging the Distinction between the "Real" and "Paper" Deal' (2009) 29 *OJLS* 675
Mitchell, C, 'Narrativising Contract Law' (2009) 29 *Legal Studies* 19
Mitchell, C, 'Contract Interpretation: Pragmatism, Principle and the Prior Negotiations Rule' (2010) 26 *Journal of Contract Law* 134
Morgan, J, *Contract Law: Great Debates* (Basingstoke, Palgrave Macmillan, 2012)
Mouzas, S and Ford, D, 'Managing Relationships in Showery Weather: The Role of Umbrella Agreements' (2006) 59 *Journal of Business Research* 1248
Mouzas, S and Furmston, M, 'From Contract to Umbrella Agreement' (2008) 67 *CLJ* 37
Mouzas, S, Henneberg, S and Naudé, P, 'Trust and Reliance in Business Relationships' (2007) 41 *European Journal of Marketing* 1016
Mulcahy, L, 'The Collective Interest in Private Dispute Resolution' (2013) 33 *OJLS* 59
Mulcahy, L and Andrews, C, 'Judgment: Baird Textile Holdings v Marks and Spencer' in R Hunter, C McGlynn and E Rackley (eds), *Feminist Judgments: From Theory to Practice* (Oxford, Hart Publishing, 2010) 189–202
Mummery, Sir J, 'Commercial Notions and Equitable Potions' in S Worthington (ed), *Commercial Law and Commercial Practice* (Oxford, Hart Publishing, 2003) 29–50
Murray, J, 'Contract Theories and the Rise of Neoformalism' (2002) 71 *Fordham Law Review* 869
Narayandas, D and Rangan, VK, 'Building and Sustaining Buyer-Seller Relationships in Mature Industrial Markets' (2004) 68 *Journal of Marketing* 63
Lord Neuberger, 'Has Mediation Had Its Day?' (Gordon Slynn Memorial Lecture, 10 November 2010) www.judiciary.gov.uk/Resources/JCO/Documents/Speeches/moj-speech-mediation-lectureA.pdf
Lord Nicholls, 'My Kingdom for a Horse: The Meaning of Words' (2005) 1 *LQR* 577
Ogus, A, *Costs and Cautionary Tales* (Oxford, Hart Publishing, 2006)
Palay, TM, 'Comparative Institutional Economics: The Governance of Rail Freight Contracting' (1984) 13 *Journal of Legal Studies* 265

Patterson, DM, 'Law's Pragmatism: Law as Practice and Narrative' (1990) 76 *Virginia Law Review* 937

Perillo, J, 'The Origins of the Objective Theory of Contract Formation and Interpretation' (2000) 68 *Fordham Law Review* 427

Poppo, L and Zenger, TR, 'Do Formal Contracts and Relational Governance Function as Substitutes or Complements?' (2002) 23 *Strategic Management Journal* 707

Porat, A, 'Enforcing Contracts in Dysfunctional Legal Systems: The Close Relationship Between Public and Private Orders: A Reply to McMillan and Woodruff' (2000) 98 *Michigan Law Review* 2459

Posner, EA, 'Law Economics and Inefficient Norms' (1996) 144 *University of Pennsylvania Law Review* 1697

Posner, EA, 'The Parol Evidence Rule, the Plain Meaning Rule and the Principles of Contractual Interpretation' (1998) 146 *University of Pennsylvania Law Review* 533

Posner, EA, 'A Theory Of Contract Law Under Conditions of Radical Judicial Error' (2000) 94 *Northwestern University Law Review* 749

Posner, EA, 'Economic Analysis of Contract Law After Three Decades: Success or Failure?' (2003) 112 *Yale Law Journal* 829

Posner, RA, 'Utilitarianism, Economics and Legal Theory' (1979) 8 *Journal of Legal Studies* 103

Posner, RA, *Law and Literature*, rev'd edn (Cambridge MA, Harvard University Press, 1998)

Posner, RA, 'Rational Choice, Behavioral Economics and the Law' (1998) 50 *Stanford Law Review* 1551

Posner, RA, *Economic Analysis of Law*, 6th edn (New York, Aspen, 2003)

Posner, RA, 'The Law and Economics of Contract Interpretation' (2005) 83 *Texas Law Review* 1581

Powell, WW, 'Neither Market Nor Hierarchy: Network Forms of Organisation' (1990) 12 *Research in Organizational Behaviour* 295

Priest, GL, 'The Common Law Process and the Selection of Efficient Rules' (1997) 6 *Journal of Legal Studies* 65

Radin, MJ, 'Boilerplate Today: The Rise of Modularity and the Waning of Consent' in O Ben-Shahar (ed), *Boilerplate: The Foundation of Market Contracts* (Cambridge, CUP, 2007) 189–99

Rakoff, T, 'The Law and Sociology of Boilerplate' in O Ben-Shahar (ed), *Boilerplate: The Foundation of Market Contracts* (Cambridge, CUP, 2007) 200–10

Rawls, J, 'Two Concepts of Rules' (1955) 64 *The Philosophical Review* 3

Raz, J, 'Promises and Obligations' in PMS Hacker and J Raz, *Law, Morality and Society* (Oxford, OUP, 1977) 210–28

Raz, J, 'Promises in Morality and Law' (1982) 95 *Harvard Law Review* 916

Richman, BD, 'Ethnic Networks, Extra-legal Certainty and Globalisation: Peering into the Diamond Industry' in V Gessner (ed), *Contractual Certainty in International Trade* (Oxford, Hart Publishing, 2009) 31–47

Riley, CA, 'Designing Default Rules in Contract Law' (2000) 20 *OJLS* 367

Rock, EB and Wachter, ML, 'Islands of Conscious Power: Law, Norms, and the Self-Governing Corporation' (2001) 149 *University of Pennsylvania Law Review* 1619

Rogers, JS, *The Early History of the Law of Bills and Notes* (Cambridge, CUP, 1995)
Roxenhall, T and Ghauri, P, 'Use of the Written Contract in Long-Lasting Business Relationships' (2004) 33 *Industrial Marketing Management* 261
Rubin, PH, 'Why is the Common Law Efficient?' (1977) 6 *Journal of Legal Studies* 51
Scanlon, TM, 'Promises and Contracts' in P Benson (ed), *The Theory of Contract Law* (Cambridge, CUP, 2001) 86–117
Schauer, F, 'Formalism' (1988) 97 *Yale Law Journal* 509
Schauer, F, *Playing by the Rules* (Oxford, OUP, 1991)
Schwartz, A, 'Relational Contracts in the Courts: An Analysis of Incomplete Agreements and Judicial Strategies' (1992) 21 *Journal of Legal Studies* 271
Schwartz, A and Scott, RE, 'Contract Theory and the Limits of Contract Law' (2003) 113 *Yale Law Journal* 541
Scott, RE, 'The Case for Formalism in Relational Contract' (2000) 94 *Northwestern University Law Review* 847
Scott, RE, 'The Death of Contract Law' (2004) 54 *University of Toronto Law Journal* 369
Scott, RE, 'The Promise and the Peril of Relational Contract Theory' in J Braucher, J Kidwell and WC Whitford (eds), *Revisiting the Contracts Scholarship of Stewart Macaulay* (Oxford, Hart Publishing, 2013) 105–39
Scottish Law Commission, *Discussion Paper on Interpretation of Contract* (no 147) (Edinburgh, TSO, 2011)
Seal, W and Vincent-Jones, P, 'Accounting and Trust in the Enabling of Long-Term Relations' (1997) 10 *Accounting, Auditing & Accountability Journal* 406
Shaffer, GC, 'How Business Shapes Law: A Socio-Legal Framework' (2009) 42 *Connecticut Law Review* 147
Sheinman, H, 'Contractual Liability and Voluntary Undertakings' (2000) 20 *OJLS* 205
Sims, V, 'Good Faith in Contract Law: Of Triggers and Concentric Circles' (2005) 16 *Kings College Law Journal* 293
Sitkin, S and Bies, R (eds), *The Legalistic Organization* (Thousand Oaks, Sage, 1994)
Smith, SA, 'Performance, Punishment and the Nature of Contractual Obligations' (1997) 60 *MLR* 360
Smith, SA, *Contract Theory* (Oxford, OUP, 2004)
Smith, SA, 'The Normativity of Private Law' (2011) 31 *OJLS* 215
Smitka, MJ, 'Contracting without Contracts: How the Japanese Manage Organizational Transactions' in S Sitkin and R Bies (eds), *The Legalistic Organization* (Thousand Oaks, Sage, 1994) 91–108
Speidel, RE, 'The Characteristics and Challenges of Relational Theory' (2000) 94 *Northwestern University Law Review* 823
Lord Steyn, 'Does Legal Formalism Hold Sway in England?' (1996) 49 *Current Legal Problems* 43
Lord Steyn, 'Contract Law: Fulfilling the Reasonable Expectations of Honest Men' (1997) 113 *LQR* 433
Suchman, M, 'The Contract as Social Artifact' (2003) 37 *Law and Society Review* 91
Summers, R, '"Good Faith" in General Contract Law and the Sales Provisions of the Uniform Commercial Code' (1968) 54 *Virginia Law Review* 195
Sunstein, CR, 'Must Formalism be Defended Empirically?' (1999) 66 *University of Chicago Law Review* 636

Sunstein, CR (ed), *Behavioral Law and Economics* (Cambridge, CUP, 2000) 13–58

Sunstein, CR and Vermeule, A, 'Interpretation and Institutions' (2003) 101 *Michigan Law Review* 885

Teubner, G, 'Coincidentia Oppositorum: Hybrid Networks Beyond Contract and Organisation' in M Amstutz and G Teubner (eds), *Networks: Legal Issues of Multilateral Co-operation* (Oxford, Hart Publishing, 2009) 3–30

Teubner, G, *Networks as Connected Contracts* (H Collins, ed) (trans M Everson) (Oxford, Hart Publishing, 2011)

Lord Justice Thomas, 'The Financial Crisis: The Role of Law and Regulation' The University of Glamorgan, 5 March 2009, http://www.judiciary.gov.uk/Resources/JCO/Documents/Speeches/ljt-speech-lord-merlyn-rees-lecture-2009.pdf

Trebilcock, MJ, *The Limits of Freedom of Contract* (Cambridge MA, Harvard University Press, 1993)

Twigg-Flesner, C and Villalta Puig, G (eds), *Boundaries of Commercial and Trade Law* (Munich, Sellier, 2011)

Twigg-Flesner, C and Villalta Puig, G, 'Introduction: The Boundaries of Commercial Law' in C Twigg-Flesner and G Villalta Puig (eds), *Boundaries of Commercial and Trade Law* (Munich, Sellier, 2011) 1–20

Ulph, J, 'The UCP 600: Documentary Credits in the 21st Century' [2007] *Journal of Business Law* 355

Vermeule, A, 'Three Strategies of Interpretation' (2005) 42 *San Diego Law Review* 607

Villalta Puig, G, 'The Misalignment of Commercial Law and Commercial Practice' [2012] *LMCLQ* 317

Vincent-Jones, P, 'Contract Litigation in England and Wales 1975–1991: A Transformation in Business Disputing?' (1993) 12 *Civil Justice Quarterly* 337

Vincent-Jones, P, 'Contractual Governance: Institutional and Organizational Analysis' (2000) 20 *OJLS* 317

Vincent-Jones, P, 'The Reception of Ian Macneil's Work on Contract in the UK' in I Macneil, *The Relational Theory of Contract: Selected Works of Ian Macneil*, D Campbell (ed) (London, Sweet & Maxwell, 2001)

Vincent-Jones, P, *The New Public Contracting* (Oxford, OUP, 2006)

Vlaar, P, Van Den Bosch, F and Volberda, H, 'Towards a Dialectic Perspective on Formalization in Interorganizational Relationships' (2007) 28 *Organization Studies* 437

Vogenauer, S and Weatherill, S, 'The European Community's Competence to Pursue the Harmonisation of Contract Law—An Empirical Contribution to the Debate' in S Vogenauer and S Weatherill (eds), *The Harmonisation of European Contract Law* (Oxford, Hart Publishing, 2006) 105–48

Vogenauer, S and Weatherill, S (eds), *The Harmonisation of European Contract* Law (Oxford, Hart Publishing, 2006)

Weinrib, E, *The Idea of Private Law* (Cambridge MA, Harvard University Press, 1995)

Weintraub, R, 'A Survey of Contract Practice and Policy' (1992) *Wisconsin Law Review* 1

Wheeler, S, *Reservation of Title Clauses* (Oxford, OUP, 1991)

Wheeler, S, 'Contracts and Corporations' in P Cane and HM Kritzer (eds), *The Oxford Handbook of Empirical Research in Law* (Oxford, OUP, 2010) 125–50

Whitford, WC, 'Relational Contracts and the New Formalism' (2004) *Wisconsin Law Review* 631

Wightman, J, 'Beyond Custom: Contract, Contexts, and the Recognition of Implicit Understandings' in D Campbell, H Collins and J Wightman (eds), *Implicit Dimensions of Contract* (Oxford, Hart Publishing, 2003) 143–86

Wightman, J, 'Commentary on *Baird Textile Holdings v Marks & Spencer plc*' in R Hunter, C McGlynn and E Rackley (eds), *Feminist Judgments: From Theory to Practice* (Oxford, Hart Publishing, 2010) 184–88

Wightman, J, 'Contract in a Pre-Realist World: Professor Macaulay, Lord Hoffmann and the Rise of Context in the English Law of Contract' in J Braucher, J Kidwell and WC Whitford (eds), *Revisiting the Contracts Scholarship of Stewart Macaulay* (Oxford, Hart Publishing, 2013) 377–401

Wilkinson-Ryan, T, 'Do Liquidated Damages Encourage Breach? A Psychological Experiment' (2010) 108 *Michigan Law Review* 633

Williamson, O, *The Economic Institutions of Capitalism* (New York, Free Press, 1985)

Williamson, O, 'Calculativeness, Trust and Economic Organization' (1993) 36 *Journal of Law and Economics* 453

Winter, SL, 'The Cognitive Dimension of the *Agon* Between Legal Power and Narrative Meaning' (1989) 87 *Michigan Law Review* 2225

Woodward, WJ, 'Neoformalism in a Real World of Forms' (2001) *Wisconsin Law Review* 971

Woolthuis, RK, Hillebrand, B and Nooteboom, B, 'Trust, Contract and Relationship Development' (2005) 26 *Organization Studies* 813

Worthington, S (ed), *Commercial Law and Commercial Practice* (Oxford, Hart Publishing, 2003)

Yates, D, *Exclusion Clauses in Contracts*, 2nd edn (London, Sweet & Maxwell, 1982)

Zheng, J, Roehrich, JK and Lewis, MA, 'The Dynamics of Contractual and Relational Governance: Evidence from Long-term Public-Private Procurement Arrangements' (2008) 14 *Journal of Purchasing and Supply Management* 43

Index